ILLUSIVE MATERIALISMS

Illusive Materialisms

THE PLEASURES OF FEMININITY IN
EIGHTEENTH-CENTURY FRANCE

Natania Meeker

Fordham University Press gratefully acknowledges financial assistance and support provided for the publication of this book by the University of Southern California.

Copyright © 2026 Fordham University Press

All rights reserved. No part of this publication may be reproduced, stored in a retrieval system, or transmitted in any form or by any means—electronic, mechanical, photocopy, recording, or any other—except for brief quotations in printed reviews, without the prior permission of the publisher.

Fordham University Press has no responsibility for the persistence or accuracy of URLs for external or third-party Internet websites referred to in this publication and does not guarantee that any content on such websites is, or will remain, accurate or appropriate.

Fordham University Press also publishes its books in a variety of electronic formats. Some content that appears in print may not be available in electronic books.

Visit us online at www.fordhampress.com.

For EU safety / GPSR concerns: Mare Nostrum Group B.V., Mauritskade 21D, 1091 GC Amsterdam, The Netherlands, gpsr@mare-nostrum.co.uk

Library of Congress Cataloging-in-Publication Data available online at https://catalog.loc.gov.

Printed in the United States of America

28 27 26   5 4 3 2 1

First edition

Contents

PREFACE   vii

Introduction: The Materialist Pleasures of Femininity   1

1 Feminine Fictions of Radical Materialism: Diderot, La Mettrie, Helvétius   31

2 *Volupté* in a Ruined World: Puisieux's Libertine Images   67

3 Illusions Without Error: Du Châtelet Loves Enough for Two   105

4 "I am, I live, I exist": Graffigny's Pleasure of Being   141

Postscriptum: Olympe de Gouges chez Ninon   179

ACKNOWLEDGMENTS   187

NOTES   191

BIBLIOGRAPHY   225

INDEX   239

Preface

Materialist philosophy since its origins in antiquity has sought out ways to make or take pleasure in times of oppression, despair, war, illness, and suffering—which is to say, all times—to conjugate the vulnerable malleability of animate bodies with the hope for a lasting satisfaction. What does it mean to seek delight in the midst of pain, whether real or imagined, or real because imagined? What authorizes this search, and for whom? The answers to these questions have morphed over time and according to the persons posing them. Eighteenth-century materialisms often linger gorgeously at the point where the seemingly opaque, sometimes unwilled endurance of bodies meets the endless frittering of matter—the wearing out and through of stuff. Denis Diderot (1713–1784) writes movingly of the ways in which the perceptual elements that constitute experience recur within the mind and body, acquiring perdurance even when memory wains. In the *Éléments de physiologie*, a compendium of reflections that Diderot worked on up until his death, he deftly renders a whole ecology of sensation, which is both susceptible to the vicissitudes of time and strangely impervious to destruction. Contemplating the work of memory, he writes:

> I am inclined to believe that everything that we have seen, known, perceived, heard; down to the trees of a long forest, which is to say, to the arrangement of the branches, to the shape of the leaves, and to the variety of colors, of greens and of lights; down to the appearance of the grains of sand on the shore of the sea, to the disparities in the surface of the waves either agitated by a gentle breeze, or foamy and stirred up by the tempestuous winds, down to the multitude of human voices,

of animal cries, and of physical noises, to the melody and harmony of all the airs, of all the pieces of music, of all the concerts, that we have heard; all of this exists in us without our knowing it.[1]

In Diderot's account, the colors of the forest—the play of light and shadow—and the movement of ocean waves intermingle with the sound of human voices, of animals, of music once heard and forgotten. All of these instances of perception are themselves ever-shifting, variegated, impossible to pin or to fix, yet at the same time they live on and within the body that receives and registers them. Diderot goes on to write of the brain as a mass of living wax, impressionable and labile—or, in yet another plangent metaphor, as a book that reads itself. "If the writing weakens, we forget it. If the writing is erased, it is forgotten. If the writing comes back to life, we remember it," he affirms.[2] This tension between the persistent and the evanescent—a tension that is expressed not just in the substance of the body but in the patterns that experience acquires—enduringly marks the relationship of the perceiving mind to the world of which it is a part. If the latter is always changing form in the patterns and colors it assumes, the former is holding these forms in abeyance, waiting to be excavated. Yet at the moment of contact between the two, a shift takes place in the substance that generates consciousness. In Diderot's image, the mind as book becomes a figure for both the power and the tenuousness of memory. But the comparison also suggests the intensity with which the act of writing may, in both the best and worst of circumstances, animate and reanimate sensation. The ephemeral endures in the changes that it works.

The material flexibility of the mind or brain—its openness to impression—is definitively a source of pleasures, whether lost or recovered, but it is also a genuine vulnerability to harm. Contingency and malleability collude to generate pain as well as enjoyment. In her moral work *Réflexions et avis sur les défauts et ridicules à la mode,* published in 1761, the author Madeleine d'Arsant de Puisieux (1720–1798) writes, possibly in an observation drawn from experience: "There is neither small feeling nor weak gratitude for a philosophical and sensitive soul: everything strikes a blow; everything is endearing or revolting; in the end everything inspires in it either pleasure or revulsion. These souls, moved ceaselessly by pain or pleasure, are often the victims of their attachments."[3] Puisieux's moralist writings and fiction frequently stress the extent to which the ability to receive and respond to material stimuli, whether aesthetic, erotic, or ethical, is also the capacity to be wounded. Unlike Diderot, however, Puisieux is reluctant to identify herself as a philosopher. In her work, when perceptions, like images, strike and seize unsuspecting subjects and reactivate unwanted attachments and memories, neither pleasure nor autonomy are guaranteed. She is exquisitely aware of the extent to which she is beholden, as a writer and a thinker, to her context; she presents herself as slipping across and through propositions or assertions yet held fast in many instances by certain encounters, pictures, forms. Yet the fragility and receptivity of consciousness are never, for Puisieux, abstract quantities. The capacity of the sensitive body for enjoyment, even in memory, especially in desire, is always tightly linked to the precise situation in which this body is made legible to itself, to the constraints that render palpable its compulsions.

Diderot and Puisieux knew one another well, and their shared emphasis on the ceaseless movements of sensation is the mark of a certain reciprocity of influence. Diderot, attentive like no other to the work of matter in the labor of thought, occupies a prestigious place in a long history of materialist writing that stretches from antiquity, beginning with the philosophy of Epicurus and Lucretius, passing through Michel de Montaigne (1533–1592) and the *libertins érudits* of the seventeenth century, and into the so-called radical materialisms of his own day. The formal flexibility of his style, the diversity of his philosophical and aesthetic instances, the originality of his search for pleasure in the unending changeability of memory and thought—they all position him as an authority within a tradition of materialist philosophical experimentation that has long been vaunted precisely for its resistance to authoritative pronouncements, celebrated for its willingness to explore the contradictions inherent in the attempt to "fix" a matter always on the move. Puisieux, for her part, writes aslant this ambivalent legacy, unwilling to assert herself as an adherent of any school or even any precise position. At stake, for her, in the affirmation of the flexibility of matter is the prejudice that materialist philosopher Paul Thiry d'Holbach (1723–1789) expresses succinctly in his *Théologie portative ou dictionnaire abrégé de la religion chrétienne*. Under the heading *Novateurs* (or "innovators"), d'Holbach writes of these personages that they "make as need be dogmas *à la mode*, for the use of women, who as we know delight in change, especially in the matter of Doctrine."[4] Puisieux, in asserting the powerful malleability of sensation as the latter is recalled to mind, in attending to the reflexivity of relational perspectives, is not so much bucking as exemplifying a stereotype, precisely by virtue of her closeness to the matter at hand. In following a materialist insight, she appears—but only appears—to succumb to a material reality.

This book is an attempt to reckon with tensions internal to the embrace of a materialist ethic of pleasure by persons, both feminine and masculine, who inhabit distinct subject positions even as they together seek to make a case for the flexibility of material embodiment as a mode of responsiveness to stimuli and to desire. It is also an effort to mobilize for a feminist and queer purpose the willingness of materialist thought to productively disavow itself or to alter its form, to be as invested in its effects as in its doctrine. Gerard Passannante, in *Catastrophizing: Materialism and the Making of Disaster*, describes how, "for some early moderns . . . the experience of materialism did not involve the deliberate adoption of a philosophical paradigm or an intellectual commitment but was instead a reflexive habit or style of thought." Passannante is interested in the way in which "the making of images" might itself become a "form of argument."[5] The feminine persons whom I study here adeptly deploy the power of the textual image to make a certain kind of materialist case, but the way in which they do so varies in accordance with their voluntary and involuntary attachments to the situation of femininity itself. Their discretion becomes an index not so much of the intensity of their materialist conviction as of their proximity to a materialist condition—namely, that of the feminine person, who stands as an icon of matter's inherent pliability. The three women whose work I consider in detail in later chapters thus expose femininity not as a materialist object but as a materialist practice. For them, an ethic of pleasure becomes a question of delicate craft and care; in this way, they reveal in their own distinct fashion the kinship between materialism and artifice, between the construction of an idea and the consumption of an image. They also demonstrate the limits of a politics of reflexivity—so lovingly elaborated by Diderot— that seeks to blur the boundaries between subject and object, knower and known, thought and thing, but does so often in the name of a feminine ontology that those persons identified as women can only ambivalently inhabit.

Finally, this book contains an effort to explore, in part through my reflections on the process of its production, the workings of vicissitude in my own thought and writing, and to do so from a feminine subject position that is perhaps still all too tightly linked, at least within the history of philosophy, to ambivalence and ambiguity of mind. I take inspiration from materialist thought that offers *both* a set of truth claims—about the nature of matter in movement—*and* a method for generating delight that takes into account the fragile, pliable status of pleasure. In so doing, I articulate the ways in which certain materialist intuitions already prioritize femininity as a kind of work—both pleasurable and painful—that does not so much generate a legacy as produce a series of effects. The women authors I discuss were for various reasons reluctant to lay claim to a materialist identification for their own work and practice. Yet in this work and practice, they articulate materialist commitments, recuperate and revise materialist precepts, and read materialist texts. I see my own engagement with their writing as a small entry in a long and ever-changing series of encounters, textual and actual, that potentially activate femininity as a privileged relation to pleasure-giving materialist technique. My hope is that *Illusive Materialisms* might allow the work of the eighteenth-century women I study to resonate however elusively or elliptically with instances of contemporary feminist and queer creative and intellectual production, including new work in trans studies by Grace Lavery and Luce deLire, the art of Jane Benson and Jessica Rath, and the poetry and essays of Lisa Robertson.[6] Together, these artists and thinkers cultivate modes of expression that stress the power and fragility of pleasures that are made rather than taken, generated in communities real or imagined rather than alone.

ILLUSIVE MATERIALISMS

Introduction
The Materialist Pleasures of Femininity

For some years during the last decade of her short life, the scientist and philosopher Émilie Du Châtelet (1706–1749) worked on an essay on happiness. The *Discours sur le bonheur*, which circulated in manuscript copy before her death but was not published until 1779, is in certain respects a text typical of its era. Many men wrote similar treatises, including the philosophers Bernard Le Bovier de Fontenelle (1657–1757) and Julien Offray de La Mettrie (1709–1751), Du Châtelet's friend Claude-Adrien Helvétius (1715–1771), and her lover Voltaire (1694–1778). But in other ways the work stands out. It is not only a reflection on the happy life that specifically prioritizes pleasure; it is also an acknowledgment of the need to find joy where it can be cobbled together from within the desires, limitations, and particular investments of a feminine body inclined to age and infirmity as well as to passion. Du Châtelet writes:

> Finally, I say that to be happy one must be susceptible to illusion, and this scarcely needs to be proved; but, you will object, you have said that error is always harmful: is illusion not an error? No: although it is true, that illusion does not make us see objects entirely as they must be in order for them to give us agreeable feelings, it only adjusts them to our nature.[1]

At this moment in the discourse Du Châtelet embraces a practice rather than a principle. For her, the pursuit of illusion without error—a technique in which humans actively cultivate the enjoyment that they may derive from within the contingent exercise of perception—is not so much the key that unlocks a persistent happiness as a means of sustaining pleasure where it haphazardly or momentarily occurs. In other words, hers is a materialist ethic that "focuses on what works," as Grace Lavery describes the pleasure-giving capacities of realism in *Pleasure and Efficacy: Of Pen Names, Cover Versions, and Other Trans Techniques*.[2] And it is consonant with a rejection of error or untruth even as it is not the same as enlightenment, conventionally understood.

In the *Discours* and elsewhere in her writings on science, Du Châtelet maintains a subtle and sometimes deceptively oblique relationship to a materialist corpus that includes the scientific epic of the ancient Roman philosopher Lucretius (first century BCE), the writings of Anglo-Dutch social theorist Bernard Mandeville (1670–1733), and the neo-Epicurean materialism of La Mettrie. She valorizes and foregrounds the work of writing and reading as a source of enjoyment and meaning, but she also attends to specific practices of image-making, including theater and puppetry. Together with Madeleine de Puisieux (1720–1798) and Françoise de Graffigny (1695–1758), she is one of three women authors whom this book will identify as "illusive materialists," and this for two reasons. First, while their thought is in dialogue with materialist currents that cut across premodernity and reach back to antiquity, they never identify themselves directly with materialism as a doctrine. Indeed, they are in certain respects averse to any dogmatic logic, seeking instead to concoct or draw out pleasure where they may, and often with a recognition of the vulnerability of their own situations in doing so. Second, they all take seriously—albeit from different vantages—the work of what Du Châtelet calls "illusion" as part of a materialist practice of pleasure-seeking. While on the one hand their materialism might be called *elusive*, in that it is difficult if not impossible to excavate a systematic adherence to materialist dogma from within their explicit commitments and interests, in the end it is their investment in the material effects of illusion-making that most crucially defines their ambiguous appropriation of materialist texts and traditions. And it is in this attachment to an illusive materialism that they at once privilege their own situations as feminine subjects and underscore the work of femininity as a pleasure-giving deception from which a life may nonetheless be made. They thus inhabit a moment that is doubly a threshold. On the one hand they participate in a transitional moment within materialist philosophy when an ethic of pleasure is becoming explicitly identified with a new mode of feminine subjectivity. Yet on the other hand they rework this tight association between femininity and matter to create a heterodox variant of feminine belonging, one that responds to materialist injunctions by stressing the delight-enhancing work accomplished by a particular craftiness in practice (if not always in theory) open to all bodies.

While women contribute massively to *ancien régime* literary culture,[3] they rarely participate overtly in the elaboration of a libertine materialism that occurs in both literary and philosophical contexts in eighteenth-century France. The reason for this may seem obvious: In an environment where expectations of decorum weigh more heavily on women than on men, it is difficult if not impossible for the former to embrace hedonism as either a philosophical position or a code of conduct. Women are almost entirely absent from the development of both libertine fiction and materialist philosophical argument, with certain remarkable exceptions such as the seventeenth-century critic and courtesan Ninon de Lenclos (1620–1705) and, reaching further back, the philosopher Leontion (~300–250 BCE), known for her Epicureanism, and to whom Ninon de Lenclos was often compared. It isn't until the beginning of the nineteenth century that the first libertine fictions by women authors appear in French contexts, including Suzanne Giroust de Morency's 1799 *Illyrine, ou l'écueil de l'inexpérience* and the somewhat better-known two-volume *Julie, ou j'ai sauvé ma rose*, published in 1808 and commonly attributed to Félicité de Choiseul-Meuse.[4] Women authors are also more or less excluded from the history of materialist philosophy up until the emergence of socialist feminism in the mid- to late nineteenth century, not just despite the radical politics that have been associated with this tradition but because of them.[5]

In the eighteenth century, even elite women faced severe difficulties in acquiring a philosophical education; it was the rare aristocratic girl who was taught to read both Greek and Latin, although Du Châtelet herself was one exception to this rule. But the challenge of articulating a materialist argument was not only one of access, although the latter posed a significant problem on its own. The figure of the woman philosopher as an arbiter of critical thought and potentially emancipatory politics flies in the face of ideals of feminine modesty and decorum. As Florence Lotterie demonstrates with care in *Le Genre des Lumières: Femme et philosophe au XVIIIe siècle*, the emergence of the *femme philosophe* as a fictional character marks the literature of the eighteenth century as a scene of struggle and debate around ideas of gender, sexual difference, and sociability. Even for elite, educated women, including women authors, efforts to defy or revise these ideas came at a high price. As Lotterie points out, "The majority of socially visible cultivated women are careful about publishing and inscribe themselves in the paradigm of feminine modesty, inherited from *préciosité*. Showing that one wants to depart from this paradigm invokes an immediate sanction."[6] These tensions and challenges are all heightened in the context of materialist philosophy and its endorsement of a libertine ethic of pleasure—a domain in which men too faced serious repercussions for departures from convention, including imprisonment and exile. It thus should come as no surprise that recognized contributions of women to this field are not just limited but practically nonexistent.[7] Recent significant efforts to draw women back into the history of materialist thought and literature, including Jessie Hock's *The Erotics of Materialism: Lucretius and Early Modern Poetics* and Kristin M. Girten's *Sensitive Witnesses: Feminist Materialism in the British Enlightenment* have focused mainly on Anglophone examples, included prominently among them Lucy Hutchinson and Margaret Cavendish.[8] Hock's excellent study of materialist poetics ends in the seventeenth century. While Girten excavates a tradition of what she calls "sensitive witnessing" within women's writing of the British Enlightenment, her focus is on an "entanglement . . . with the material world" that she reads as anticipating in many respects the concerns of new materialism.[9] A libertine focus on pleasure as *summum bonum* is necessarily secondary, in her analysis, to the construction of an ecological sensitivity undergirded by a critique of the human/nonhuman binary.

Illusive Materialisms recenters pleasure as a materialist value with feminist and queer potential in order to explore a specific turning point in French Enlightenment debates around matter and gender. This book situates itself at a moment toward the end of the 1740s when the philosopher La Mettrie may have become the first to embrace the descriptor "matérialiste," intervening decisively but mischievously in a long history of deploying the term as an epithet. During this period, Rococo art and design provided ample opportunities for contemplating and investigating the role of femininity in generating aesthetic, erotic, and sensual pleasures. And the literary culture of the French Enlightenment often highlighted women's voices, in the work of Diderot, Pierre de Marivaux (1688–1763), and Jean-Jacques Rousseau (1712–1788) among many others, as a way of experimenting with new theories of subjectivity. *Illusive Materialisms* is thus an entry in a discussion in which femininity is simultaneously at the center—as a form of being that so often makes pleasure possible for masculine and feminine bodies alike—and at the margins—as a situation structured around a particular set of social and cultural norms. Of course, as Lotterie and other feminist critics have rightly insisted, it is impossible to separate femininity as an orientation toward the world on the one hand—an expression of a particular position—from femininity as an experience of the world on the other—a perception of a particular condition. Clearly, the manner in which women and feminine persons are depicted shapes the way in which femininity itself is lived; the choice of femininity as a style of self-presentation cannot be detached from the assignment of femininity as the "truth" of certain bodies. At the same time, the absence of eighteenth-century women authors—subjects who often understand their gender as a condition to which they are at first relegated involuntarily—from the endorsement of what

James Steintrager has called the "autonomy of pleasure" matters in various ways to the means by which pleasure is itself understood, recognized, valued, and felt.[10] This absence (and its effects) become acute in the domain of libertine and materialist critique, both of which participate actively in framing and designing the desiring subjects of what will become liberal modernity. This is the case as much during the eighteenth century proper—when philosophical authors were often inclined see themselves as participants in the making of a new social order—as it is today—when the capacity to experience, recognize, and account for one's pleasures is still sometimes taken as an index of what it means to be modern, "free," and enlightened.

Eighteenth-century materialist philosophy couples a particular valorization of feminine bodies and persons, indeed positing femininity as the condition toward which *all* bodies might tend, with a special resistance to the investment of women authors in the very ethic of pleasure to which this valorization is linked. By making this point, I am not claiming that women's experience is necessarily or essentially distinct in itself or that women as a group should be understood to form a special class. In Chapters 2, 3, and 4 of this book, I explore the work of Puisieux, Du Châtelet, and Graffigny not in order to petition for their solidarity in exclusion but to show the ways in which they are also engaged with a materialist legacy that both influences and effaces their contributions. This engagement often emerges as a set of tactics rather than as a series of principles, techniques that might be reanimated or revisited by future readers. In this focus on pleasure as pragmatics, these three authors remain true to a certain Epicurean message—namely, the idea that the goal of philosophical inquiry is just as much the cultivation of satisfaction as it is the quest for truth. They form a distinct grouping not by virtue of shared precepts but thanks to a certain continuity of practice that emerges in their writing and their thought as it is lived. At the same time, their views are clearly shaped by varying degrees of privilege, which they often wholeheartedly embrace as forms of distinction that matter to them and others in both visible and invisible ways. They nonetheless all take up the question of pleasure—its constraints and possibilities, its potentially liberatory and damaging effects—from within social situations that differ from those of their masculine counterparts, with whom they were consistently in conversation and debate. What would it mean to consider their contributions as a doubly hidden or deceptive variant of materialist thought or philosophy—one that may have the potential to reorient in certain key respects the way in which an enlightened ethic of pleasure is received and remembered? How does the obligation to evade or eschew certain positions illuminate the manner in which pleasure might be lived? The analyses worked through here, accompanied by accounts of my own shifting relationships to the texts and authors I discuss, attempt to provide some preliminary and contingent answers to these questions.

This study owes a great deal to the work of feminist literary critics who have labored tirelessly to excavate, collect, and analyze the writing of eighteenth-century women as a fundamental part of the French Enlightenment. Indeed, it could not exist without this work, which is both abundant and illuminating.[11] In the chapters that follow, I attempt on the one hand to expand on this conversation by picking out and tracing some of the materialist moments in a feminine corpus that of necessity cannot explicitly stress its own materialist convictions. On the other hand, I argue on behalf of enlarging a certain canon of Enlightenment materialism in this oblique and illusive way in order to consider what happens to this canon when women and feminine persons interact with it. In both instances, I strive to put two disparate bodies of work in contact with one another—studies of women's writing on the one hand and analyses of materialist thought on the other. Debates by feminist critics over women's participation in the Enlightenment have often understandably focused on the prominence of women's particular contributions to more normative or legitimized genres and themes. Historians of materialism, for their part, have had little reason to explore a feminine corpus of writing that did not explicitly intersect with the traditions and concepts that define their field. Yet these three eighteenth-century women authors do recuperate and rework materialist themes in order to craft distinctive modes of critique. In their literary writing, their philosophy, their science, and their correspondence, they too are invested in the manifold pleasures to be derived from nature and the diverse capacities for sensory and sensual enjoyment that may be shared across different kinds of bodies. If the proper incitement of pleasure is crucial to the larger interests and aims of eighteenth-century philosophy, Puisieux, Du Châtelet, and Graffigny find in their various particular efforts to reframe and reenvision their situations—in the practice of science, in the production of works of art, and in the cultivation of modes of sociability—the potential for a transformation of feminine experience in and with the world. The activation of this potential does not necessarily anticipate modern feminisms, especially since each of these authors is skeptical in her own way of gendered solidarities, but it does communicate a set of tactics for the careful and deliberate cultivation of a feminine position that aims toward pleasure. And it opens a speculative portal toward a future in which this artful variant of materialist femininity might be reworked and revised across other bodies and in other forms.

In *Illusive Materialisms*, I first consider the invocation of feminine tropes and figures as a central rather than a marginal aspect of eighteenth-century materialist philosophy—a unifying motif that stretches across different approaches to the problem of what it means to be a body made of matter. Next, I look to the work of Puisieux, Du Châtelet, and Graffigny in order to understand how this feminized and feminine materialism might be received, understood, and ultimately, lived by persons whose feminine investments are not just theoretical but of necessity practical and pragmatic. I argue that these women do more than elaborate a *savoir faire* or *savoir vivre* that could and did resonate with materialist values, as historians beginning with Edmond and Jules de Goncourt in the nineteenth century have long asserted.[12] I suggest instead that these women authors, who all circulated in the same *milieux* as the materialist men whose names make regular appearances in the histories of enlightened thought, make substantive interventions in a materialist interrogation of pleasure as a value, even when these same women are reluctant to identify themselves with this interrogation, or even to lay claim to the status of philosopher at all. In the context of a field that has rightly given an important place to clandestine and transgressive texts, I strive to make the case for a different kind of clandestine writing and thought—one that is in one sense hiding in plain sight and in another twice concealed.[13] To do this, I study Puisieux, Du Châtelet, and Graffigny with an eye to the way in which their work comments on the materialist conversations that were taking place around them (and in certain cases, thanks to them). I attempt to uncover in their writings an investment in an illusive (and often elusive) materialism at the same time as I insist on the patent significance of femininity for a very different kind of materialist philosophy—one elaborated almost exclusively and entirely by men.[14]

What is distinct about the kinds of materialist arguments or ideas that these three women are willing to entertain, whether in their published or unpublished writings? First, I want to stress that they often disagree with one another, in certain cases directly and explicitly. The points of commonality that cut across their writing do not add up to a unified theory. Indeed all three of these women are hesitant to articulate their materialist ethical commitments as a form of position-taking predetermined by the pleasures that they seek. In this way, they depart from the tendency, visible in the work of their masculine peers and collaborators, to find in the sweet, yielding, and feminine subject of enjoyment a necessary and natural starting point for the interrogation of pleasure's sense. At key moments, Puisieux, Du Châtelet, and Graffigny all avoid or evade the universalizing ascription of femininity to soft and unformed bodies that marks better-known materialist criticism. Instead, they are all attentive (sometimes to a fault) to the specific constraints and possibilities that both generate and shape the production of thought where feminine persons are concerned. They open up access to femininity not as a preexistent nature—a degree zero of embodiment—but as a practice in which illusion-making and pleasure-seeking may be delicately conjoined in the work of living through.

This practice may ideally be accessible to all, but it is inevitable for no one. It also takes place in diverse genres and forms, including those that are not historically associated with the production of philosophy or the labor of thought, including for instance theater, dance, lyric poetry, portrait-painting, embroidery and needlework, puppetry, fashion, and love letters. These various modes of interacting with the world, both passing and sustained, function as zones where acts of consumption and production come together in the sometimes idiosyncratic search for pleasures that may outlast the experiences that generate them. The reluctant materialisms that they engender value illusion as a resource in a ruined world. For Puisieux, for instance, the engagement with a materialist ethic occurs not just in the zone of the conduct book—inherently anti-philosophical in the sense that its emphasis is necessarily pragmatic—but in poetry or allegorical narrative. In her novels, short stories, and poems, literary figures and rhetorical devices seize hold of and engage the feminine body, so that it is in a kind of image-work that desire might be both held at bay and guaranteed. At the same time, in her moral writing, Puisieux articulates the challenges of finding pleasure-giving techniques that operate successfully for the feminine persons who are presumed to be pleasure's very sign. Du Châtelet, for her part, suggests that what appears to be a universal human orientation toward pleasure-seeking is both fragile and, to a certain extent, artificial. In her scientific work and in her amorous correspondence, grappling with the material conditions of her existence entails the crafting of illusions to which she might enduringly remain attached even as she seeks to dispel error in her transmission of scientific truth. Finally, in her most famous novel, Graffigny deploys the lures of sentiment with an obliquely Epicurean intention: To imagine a space in which the feminine pleasure of being overcomes and overwhelms the marriage plot, and in which the text itself exists as a kind of self-perpetuating machine for enjoyment's recovery. But she exposes, in doing so, the way in which ethnic identity still functions as a proxy for a kind of difference that gender fails to mark.

For each of these women, pleasure is an animating and stimulating force that defines and guarantees their humanity: In this way they take up the gauntlet of their period's libertine affinities. But they rarely write about this force as inherently or fundamentally emancipatory, thus countering an enduring strain of libertine critique, which stretches from the seventeenth century into our contemporary moment. Instead, their emphasis is most often on forms of constraint—not as an interruption of pleasure's effects, but as a condition of pleasure's emergence. Where the libertine novel delights in unveiling the hypocrisy of men (and women) who turn out to be in pursuit of pleasure all along, despite the conventions by which they only appear to abide, Puisieux, Du Châtelet, and Graffigny all take an interest in convention as pleasure's enabling condition. They are collectively skeptical of the idea that voluptuous delight comes from outside of the historical or social situations in which bodies circulate. Their affinity with materialism appears not just in their shared willingness to invoke pleasure as an ideal or as a *telos* of their work, but in their commitment to an examination of the material circumstances of pleasure's production, an examination that refuses to view the propensity for enjoyment as extra- or transhistorical. They rework the association between femininity and the Epicurean ideal of *voluptas* to reveal how the latter is never guaranteed. Nonetheless, it is in the making and remaking of a feminine-coded subjectivity that pleasure becomes in practice available to many.

It follows that none of these women could be usefully described as protofeminist in the sense of addressing other women or feminine persons as a political group or class. They are clear-eyed about the disadvantages that inform their situations, but they are just as often explicit about their strong attachments to the privileges that their status affords them. They regularly resist what we might now refer to as feminine solidarity, sometimes casting themselves as exceptions to a dispiriting rule of women's general inferiority, sometimes embracing aristocratic hierarchies and values, sometimes deploying racial stereotypes or reifying ethnic differences. They do not represent a purer or more ideologically rarified variant of the kind of materialist critique that interests their masculine counterparts and companions. But it is in part for these very reasons that it is important to include their writings in a broader consideration of what the French Enlightenment might contribute to a contemporary understanding of both matter and gender. Collectively, these women reveal the dangers of assuming that pleasure appears as an intrinsic compulsion or drive of the body that culture only shapes and molds. Instead, as Émilie Du Châtelet puts it, "So it is desirable to be susceptible to the passions, and let me say it again: passions do not come for the asking."[15] Each of these women launches a critique of materialism from within, limning the risks of libertine naturalism for women in particular. But they nonetheless retain an attachment to a materialist ethic of pleasure that might be carried out from the positions that in fact they are obliged to inhabit. They thereby display both the limitations and potential of a materialist critique that seeks to remake the connection between life and thought.

Why have I chosen to focus on the work—and to a certain extent, lives—of these three women in particular? First, they all are active during a key moment in the history of French materialisms—namely, the span of years around 1750 that, as Peter Reill has argued, marked a transition from older mechanistic explanations of matter into a newly vitalist mode.[16] Franck Salaün describes the 1740s generally as a kind of turning point (or *tournant*) in not just the orientation but the status of French materialisms, thanks to an intensification of public and private interest (both positive and negative) in materialist debates. As Charles Wolfe has recently discussed, while the term itself (*matérialiste*) had long been deployed as a pejorative by opponents of the doctrine, only around mid-century does it begin to be used with a positive valence.[17] The women I study here were all publishing during this same time period, and were all in one way or another interlocutors for some of the most important participants in materialist discussions, without themselves laying explicit or consistent claim to materialist philosophical positions. Moreover, while they are all writing at a transitional moment for Enlightenment materialisms more generally, Puisieux, Du Châtelet, and Graffigny are also all active at a turning point in the history of women's writing. The 1740s represent a shift in the visibility of women's public contributions to cultural debate, as Karen Green discusses in *A History of Women's Political Thought in Europe*.[18] These three authors each benefit in certain ways from an acceptance of women's writing—and elite women's intervention in social critique—even as each of them also negotiates in her own fashion the difficulty, if not impossibility, of operating as a philosopher in a context where the work of philosophy remains at odds with ideas of feminine modesty and propriety. At the same time, they all emerge from and comment on a cultural situation in which femininity often operates as an aesthetic ideal and even a social norm, much to the dismay of some of their contemporaries. In both textual and visual culture, the Rococo feminine subject is an iconic object of desire, invested at this moment with intense erotic and emotional power. These three women remobilize the artifice of this still-dominant vision of femininity at the same time as they reanimate the pleasure-seeking drive of an increasingly visible materialist ethos.

Certainly, there are other women authors and public figures who were intimately connected to the philosophical debates around materialism even as they contributed in important ways to the representation of feminine subjectivity and women's status. Notable among them are Julie Jeanne Éléonore de Lespinasse (1732–1776) and Marie Jeanne Riccoboni (1713–1792). Lespinasse was not only an astonishing and illuminating letter writer, she was also a literary host and a memorable (fictional) interlocutor in Diderot's key materialist dialogue, *Le Rêve de d'Alembert*, written in 1769 but not published as a freestanding text until 1830. Riccoboni was an actress and a novelist whose correspondence reveals her close ties to a transnational network of Enlightenment figures including Pierre Choderlos de Laclos (author of the *Les Liaisons dangereuses*, published in 1782, as well as an essay on women's education) and David Hume, among many others. These women are fascinating and worthy interlocutors in discussions of what it means to live, write, think, read, and enjoy from a feminine position. Yet they intervene either at a different moment, in the case of Lespinasse, or from an entirely different vantage point, in the case of Riccoboni, than the three women who form the focus of this book. *Illusive Materialisms* posits the 1740s and early 1750s as both a formative and a transitional period—a decade or so when a culture of feminine artifice intersects in a powerful but also enigmatic way with a newly vibrant materialist philosophy. Puisieux, Du Châtelet, and Graffigny each articulate in their own way a moment of possibility and peril, when the pursuit of an ethic of pleasure seems to hold potential for the feminine persons that they understand themselves to be but is nonetheless withheld from them.

These three women do not hold equal status in the reevaluations of Enlightenment culture and thought that have marked the twentieth and twenty-first centuries. While Du Châtelet and Graffigny have benefited from the ongoing efforts of feminist scholars to demonstrate the importance of women to the Enlightenment, Madeleine de Puisieux remains best known not for her moral writings—or for her contributions to the novel and the short story—but for her role as Denis Diderot's lover. An examination of her corpus, however, reveals her ongoing yet idiosyncratic investment in libertine themes and motifs, and her attachment to a view of pleasure as the motivating instance of all action. Émilie Du Châtelet is perhaps the most renowned of the three authors studied here and certainly the most directly affiliated with the discipline of philosophy, which she exercised to both acclaim and derision throughout the 1730s until her death in childbirth from puerperal fever. While her theory of matter is a metaphysical one (indebted to Leibniz, Locke, and Descartes), her ethical (and personal) writings reveal a strong Epicurean bent and a significant engagement with the work not only of philosopher Bernard Mandeville but of La Mettrie himself. Like Puisieux, but in an entirely different genre, Du Châtelet's participation in the intellectual debates of her time can seem idiosyncratic—certainly difficult to square with a "progressive" reading of the Enlightenment as moving ineluctably toward an increasingly radical materialist position. Her corpus demonstrates how difficult it is for feminine persons in particular to embody a philosophical or intellectual norm. Yet she also reveals gorgeously and persuasively the many ways in which the practice of philosophy can itself be sustained as a pleasure-giving technique, even in the absence of dogmatic materialist attachments. Françoise de Graffigny was for a time friendly with Du Châtelet, and the two women traveled in some of the same social circles. As the author of perhaps the most celebrated sentimental novel of the period, the *Lettres d'une Péruvienne* (first published in 1747 and substantially revised in 1752), Graffigny (like Du Châtelet) is absent from histories of materialism and libertinism.[19] Yet she too is invested in an ethic that foregrounds pleasure as a defining and necessary feature of feminine happiness, and in her salon and elsewhere sustained lasting relationships with at least one of the most prominent materialist philosophers of the age, Claude-Adrien Helvétius. All three women write and think in proximity to materialism without ever fully participating in materialist conversations. And all three are interested in pleasure as an ethical imperative closely tied to feminine experience. The fact that they are not understood as having actively contributed to these conversations is not just a function of the genres in which they write, it is also a function of their gender, which works upon them as a constraint but is also reworked by them as a zone of intellectual, aesthetic, and erotic potential.

My goal here is not necessarily to advocate for an inclusion of these women in the conventional scene of materialist philosophy, and not just because it is highly unlikely that any of them would aspire to such a repositioning. Instead, I argue first for a consideration of their engagement with materialist ethical commitments, and second, for an understanding of their work as reactivating the connection between materialism and femininity with a distinct emphasis on illusion (whether perspectival, poetic, theatrical, or amorous) as an instrument of materialist transformation and feminine delight in which diverse bodies might participate. They expose the absence of women's voices from the long history of materialist philosophy even as they invoke the important work done by femininity in forms of materialist thought and practice that might include art, spectacle, dance, and literature as well as philosophical debate. All of them, in different ways, take up the theme of pleasure in its connection to a long history of ethical discussion, and each of them endorses something close to an Epicurean position on delight or voluptuousness as a goal sufficient unto itself. While their thought does not resemble the kind of libertine naturalism that is most obviously associated with the neo-Epicurean materialism of the period, their rejection of libertinism is not a refusal of the pleasures of sexuality, desire, or the body, all of which they acknowledge and in various ways endorse. Graffigny comes closest to a form of political critique that aims for a wholesale revision of French society (and sociability) and establishes a transcultural ideal of feminine virtue. But she finds her vision of feminine solidarity not within French society—which is riven by class divisions—but outside of it, in the formation of an Indigenous feminine subject who travels across time to craft a message of the pleasure in being. Du Châtelet and Puisieux, for their part, are even less inclined than Graffigny to engage with a strong political critique of French society; yet they each reactivate a materialist ethos in order to think about the ways in which women may navigate the situations in which they find and remake themselves.

In their idiosyncrasies, in their failure or inability to conform to a masculine template for what it means to do philosophy, in their unwillingness to lay claim to a materialist position even while endorsing an ethic of materialist pleasure, these women expose what it means to pose certain philosophical questions—about the nature of being, the ethics of enjoyment, the role of gender in society—not from a position of strength, but from one of vulnerability. They approach the question of pleasure's effects as emerging not in the move to free up or liberate the feminine body from its constraints, but in the recognition of constraint itself as the mechanism that makes femininity legible to begin with. They are looking for pleasure, then, not in the triumphant exit from immaturity, as Kant would have it, but in the ruins of hope and in the embrace of illusion as a technique for navigating a profoundly imperfect, often disappointing world. For these reasons, they look not only toward the future but just as often into the past, taking up and reworking motifs from seventeenth-century debates around women's social role in order to articulate them with a newly modern emphasis on feminine pleasure. If they write at a turning point, they also often explore the vicissitudes of history itself—its divagations but also the legacies time leaves—as a way of thinking about how to sustain pleasure in a feminine life. In other words, Puisieux, Du Châtelet, and Graffigny all retain a certain connection to earlier modes of materialist thought—often but not always by means of glancing or cryptic references to Epicurus or Lucretius—even as they traffic in explicitly feminine themes. They are invested in femininity as a scene of embodiment—as a way of perceiving, acting, writing, and enjoying that is both willed and unchosen—even as they view what we moderns might call gender orientation as a means of engaging with and intervening in matter, that delicious artificer. Femininity becomes a materialist practice in their works and in their life. They labor in the profound acknowledgment of an imperfect world that nonetheless provides openings for pleasure to generate new connections. On occasion, they seem to ratify transformations that they cannot themselves directly envision.

In the fabrications that they sustain, Puisieux, Du Châtelet, and Graffigny each carve out a space for specific kinds of feminine pleasure to be had, and each one imagines a public that might conceivably receive or perpetuate these pleasures in lasting and satisfying ways. Yet this public is often explicitly a speculative one—whether in the form of a posterity that does not yet exist or in the mode of an exceptional feminine person (a woman who is neither a libertine nor a prude, as Puisieux puts it) who is hardly ever to be found. In certain instances, these three authors call on the performative power of artifice or imagination to bring the reception they imagine into being, but they are just as often skeptical about the success of this project. Their collective interest in the power of matter to trick as well as to console stems from a recognition of the vulnerability of feminine subjects to particular kinds of deception often practiced in the service of seduction. But it also suggests the ability of acts of creation, whether poetic or otherwise, to foster and preserve "mistakes" that may be beneficial to those who make them. Their relation to artifice thus comes close to what Marian Hobson discusses in *The Object of Art: The Theory of Illusion in Eighteenth-Century France* as the Rococo ideal of *papillotage*—which Hobson describes as "a flickering of illusion and awareness."[20] Hobson writes of *papillotage* as "express[ing] both the gaze, the acceptance of the object seen, and the blink which cuts off the eye from contact with the world and, in so doing, brings the self back to self."[21] Illusion here indicates a willingness to be momentarily deceived, to collaborate in the flexibility induced by the work of art. The illusive materialists of this book all suggest that this condition of oscillation or flickering—in which agency is at once lent and suspended—is both a state in which women exist and a capacity at which they potentially excel: The cultivation of illusion in this mode allows for remnants of delight to persist, and possibly to develop, in a world that refuses to endorse feminine pleasure in its attachment to feminine persons.

If, as these authors claim, constraint is necessary to bring pleasure into being in the first place, this limits delight's deployment as a radical tool of social change. It also suggests the necessity of understanding where to embrace and where to refuse the artifice that makes feminine subjects come to be. At the same time, it illuminates pleasure's function as an instrument of getting by and making do. In a world that neither respects nor indulges feminine persons in their sensitivities, not to mention their aspirations, Puisieux, Du Châtelet, and Graffigny encourage their readers to be complicit with certain perceptual tricks but not to indulge in conceptual or cognitive falsehoods. The illusive materialisms that these women endorse, never quite explicitly, might be understood as secretive, but not in the sense that they are developed behind closed doors, or within an elite circle that cannot reveal its commitments to the world for fear of what would follow. They are difficult to track because they are nondogmatic, but also because they depend on a pragmatic transmission of technique. Puisieux, Du Châtelet, and Graffigny engage in a crafty cultivation of an ethic of pleasure that is both expressed and concealed in the pages of their writing—whether in the prose of conduct books that seek to harden readers against disappointment and thereby to preserve a private space for a certain receptiveness of mind or heart; or in the conscious memorialization of the pleasures of love in full awareness of the pain they will bring; or in the construction of fictions that both remember and forget the pleasure of being that it might be possible for certain women to indulge. Each of these scenarios invokes and imagines a different kind of reader, but they all have in common an attachment to the potential of the suffering or even debased feminine body to reconstitute itself, momentarily, for joy.

Pleasure and Its Feminine Vicissitudes

Puisieux, Du Châtelet, and Graffigny write at a moment when the pleasures of femininity are a matter of great public interest and concern. The eighteenth century is still known as a moment when "pleasure came into its own," as Roy Porter has put it.[22] Thomas Kavanagh, in his book *Enlightened Pleasures: Eighteenth-Century France and the New Epicureanism*, refers to the era's pursuit of pleasure as not just a source of private or personal delight but "the foundation of a new social contract."[23] "Eighteenth-century France," Kavanagh writes, "was a century of Pleasure."[24] In Kavanagh's reading of the period, the "new Epicureanism" of the eighteenth century gives rise to an enthusiasm for pleasures of all kinds—from the erotics of *volupté* to the economics of *luxe*—as the special province of a modern humanity. Michel Delon, in *Le Principe de délicatesse: Libertinage et mélancolie au XVIIIe siècle*, similarly asserts that "The hunt for pleasure overtakes all of society." For Delon, this quest for pleasure cuts across disparate social groups and strata, so that the difference between the libertine novel, set in the context of "polite" society and elliptical in its depictions of sexual activity, and the obscene text, frank in its descriptions of both sex and social norms, is one of form rather than content. "Aristocratic good manners and popular vulgarity do not share the same vocabulary," Delon writes, "but the reality of the sexual impulse stays the same."[25]

As Delon, Kavanagh, and Porter all compellingly show, this epochal turn to pleasure is visible in disparate genres, modes, experiences, and social and political shifts. New sites of social exchange, including the cafe and the theater, new forms of commercial culture, including the increasing globalization of luxury trade, and new styles of representation and aesthetic production, such as the Rococo, collectively seem to collude in the fantasy of pleasure's rise. Historians of pleasure in the Enlightenment have rightly acknowledged the objectification of women that cuts across these different economies. Yet this objectification works in tandem with the positioning of femininity as a form that all bodies (including those of men) may and can take—a mode of receptivity that inherently drives pleasure-seeking. The treatment of pleasure as a drive unmarked by gender threatens to ignore the extent to which a yielding but impassioned feminine figure so often emblematizes, for the men and women of the Enlightenment and even today, what it means to receive and experience delight. To take one example of this tendency, Delon ends his short chapter entitled "Variations" with a description of the philosophical Thérèse, the eponymous heroine of the 1748 pornographic novel often attributed to the marquis d'Argens. For Delon, Thérèse is a figure who conjugates the philosophical emphasis of an older, more erudite libertinage with the open, unrestricted sensuality of an obscene tradition that both addresses and invokes a more popular audience (albeit through the clandestine circulation of texts). She takes responsibility for her own pleasures and recognizes her own desires. She is on the one hand an exemplar of the century's embrace of pleasure for its own sake, but she is on the other hand a sign of the apparent capacity of pleasure to reconcile social distinctions and divisions, including both gender- and class-related divides. If, for Delon, pleasure can take on many shapes, as he eloquently shows across his prolific corpus, its reality as he renders it ultimately transcends these formal constraints, including those of style as a technique of representation and embodiment, a way of both holding and "having" a body. Thérèse thus appears to invite men and women alike to identify with her philosophical education without regard to gender, even though the particular path she takes is marked and shaped by her femininity. She serves as an exemplary harbinger of a modernity that invites everyone into its emancipatory delights—or at least those who are enlightened enough to read and receive the message that she is transmitting. Does the nature of her invitation change if we take seriously the fact that her philosophical injunctions are issued in the voice, shape, and form of a woman? In fact, as I hope to demonstrate, her femininity is not a contingent but necessary element of her exemplary pleasure-inducing force.

Indeed, in the eighteenth century, the association between pleasure and femininity makes up a kind of leitmotif that reunites materialists and their detractors, enlightened critics and dogmatic theologians, radicals and reactionaries. The age of pleasure becomes, when viewed with this association in mind, an era when men are persistently turning into women even as they turn to them to ratify their desires. A preoccupation with the contagious effects of femininity cuts across visual and textual culture, philosophical debate, and social critique—and in fact remains a prominent feature of the way the eighteenth century continues to be represented today, as a moment of aristocratic decadence and excessive pleasures, where handsome but supercilious gentlemen overdo it daily on the *maquillage*. If we take for granted a "two-sex" model of gender difference,[26] it is hard to see a fear of feminization as anything but symptomatic of attempts to regularize and delimit a bifurcated "sex," and thus to shore up masculinity. But the claim that pleasure persistently makes men into women might also suggest that masculinity is an especially enfeebled and unappealing norm, embattled because wantonly susceptible. And the kind of transformation that worries and excites many eighteenth-century authors is much more than a superficial one: It is a process of becoming that implicates bodies and minds, and, crucially, bodies *in* minds.

Charles-Louis de Secondat, baron de Montesquieu (1689–1755), provides a paradigmatic expression of his era's concern with the creeping effects of femininity. He does so in a form that is both distilled and ambiguous, both brief and excessive. Starting in the 1720s, probably sometime after the publication of the *Lettres persanes* in 1721, and continuing until his death, Montesquieu worked with the help of secretaries to compile a collection of notes (his *pensées*, or thoughts) that would eventually fill three bound volumes. Often edited, annotated, and on occasion scratched out, the notes recount experiences, encounters, memories, reflections intellectual and personal, and readings. They are in some sense a monument to an exceedingly powerful and ever-active mind, but they are far from monumental in their form. Piled one upon the other, shifting in meaning and expression, corrected and recorrected, they reveal the difficulty and labor of thought in process—its infinite susceptibility to revision as well as its force. Montesquieu writes in one of the *pensées*, perhaps around 1737, which I render here with the edits and revisions included:

> I was asked why no one had a taste for the works of Corneille Racine etc. any longer I replied that ~~there was no more taste for can no longer put up with those things for which wit is necessary since it had become ridiculous and everyone was so inclined to that way of thinking that there was no taste for anything any longer it is proven that~~ everything for which wit was necessary had become ridiculous ~~and everyone~~ the evil is more general no one can bear ~~things~~ anything that has a defined goal, men of war cannot stand war men of politics cannot stand the ministry [*three words scratched out and indecipherable*] thus of all else we know only generalities ~~which~~ and in practice all this is reduced to nothing it is traffic with women that has led us to this because ~~their wit and~~ their character is to be attached to nothing permanent ~~thus we have become like them~~ there is only one sex any longer and ~~and if one~~ we are all women in mind and if one night we changed faces no one would perceive anything different even if women were to take up all the roles that society offers and men ~~in~~ were deprived of all those that society could take away ~~from a sex other than their own~~: neither sex would be burdened.[27]

In this moment, Montesquieu laments the effects of interactions with women on masculine thought and sociability. More broadly, he comments on the changing tastes of his era, which signal for him a general turn away from both intellectual focus and practical commitment.[28] Everything that requires thought has become ridiculous, he asserts, and everything that requires determination has become impossible. It is traffic in women [*le comerce des femmes*] that is to blame.

Montesquieu situates his commentary in his present day, but in diagnosing a society-wide decline as an inclination toward femininity, he is building on a much older idea, returning to and expanding a mode of cultural critique that extends back at least to the seventeenth century, when modernity and the *goût moderne* associated with it first became linked to the public exercise of feminine judgment.[29] For Montesquieu, women's distractedness—their inability to concentrate on any given thing—has come to infect all of modern culture. Detachment from specific goals or objects—whether in the realm of thought or action—has resulted in a world in which neither war nor politics can reach its aims. Knowledge is impeded by a flood of generalities that fail to gain purchase on either reality or the imagination. The very style in which the passage is rendered suggests the challenge of deriving reasoned argument from an overflow of images and ideas. The authority of the patriarchal voice is here shown to be the result of a process of extraction whereby the deluge of words and *ratures* must be worked over to yield, eventually, a singular concept. But in this instance the concept in question—that the impermanence of women has destroyed taste—appears only as an effect of this very destruction, semi-emergent among the erasures, hesitations, and crossings out that determine it.

Femininity pervades everything: It is vexing precisely because it is inescapable. It infects and inflects the terms of its own depiction. But the evil [*le mal*] that Montesquieu describes involves more than a mode of thought or apprehension. In fact, Montesquieu describes the feminization of his social world in more literal terms: We have all become like women, he asserts at one point, before crossing this formulation out in favor of a more complete and totalizing affirmation. "There is only one sex any longer," he insists instead. Were men one morning to wake up with women's faces, their insides would simply match their outsides. Life would be no different than before. And at this point in the *pensée* he projects a scene in which the social status and occupations of the genders are reversed, with men inhabiting women's roles and vice versa. No one would be bothered, he suggests, so far-reaching has women's influence on society—and indeed on subjectivity itself—become. Everyone is a woman now, because no one is immune to the creeping effects of femininity on society at large. Moreover, femininity, in its very preoccupation with superficiality, functions as a totalizing force—overcoming the split between appearance and essence precisely by insisting so powerfully on the interest and pleasures of the former. The one thing that women are attached to with any persistence is change, and the delight they take in it.

Montesquieu's musings might seem unmoored from the reality of eighteenth-century social life, but they are not eccentric. They occur as entries in a much larger set of contemporaneous conversations around women's place in eighteenth-century culture—a discursive field that has been extensively analyzed and documented by feminist historians and literary critics.[30] They also build on Montesquieu's earlier reflections in the *Lettres persanes* on women's cryptic but mighty political influence within the absolutist French state. In the latter half of the novel, the Persian traveler Rica observes that, in *ancien régime* France, elite women form their own kind of shadow republic—"a sort of government," he writes, "a new state within a state."[31] In this context, as Rica explains, someone who only studied the men active in governmental roles, without attention to the women influencing them, would be in the same position as someone else attempting to explain the structure of a machine at work [*une machine qui joue*],[32] without an understanding of the springs that drive the mechanism. In both cases, the spectacle at hand is animated by an underlying set of energies that are powerful but invisible to casual observers. As women's secret puppets, men become similar to automata: machines that are unable to act or move for themselves, whose agency is a mere appearance. The recurrence of mechanist metaphors here is not a coincidence, for while women's power is cryptic and illusive, it is also effective. Femininity is a practice that *works*.

While for Montesquieu feminine authority (however secretively exercised) is characteristic of French society in particular—where women appear freer to express their own interests and desires than in Persia—the image of a society of men totally enthralled by femininity is also stereotypically associated with Persian culture, where elite men live surrounded by women in the harem. The *Lettres persanes* plays on this stereotype both to insist on the difference between France and Persia and to subvert this same distinction. The French court, ostensibly an emblem of Western power, turns out to have in common with the Persian seraglio the covert exercise of feminine influence, even if women in France lead public and private lives unlike those of their Persian counterparts.[33] In both cases, women's desire is mobilizing (and emasculating). Men are turning to (and into) women everywhere. At issue here is not just the nature of gender difference, but the extent to which gender relations affect and structure political life at the same time as they are produced within and by particular political institutions. The clandestine power of women cuts across ethnic differences but also makes these differences legible, since its deployment is culturally variable. The epidemic force of femininity suggests a theory of globalization.

Montesquieu's *pensée* from the late 1730s thus doubles down and expands on his formulation of feminine influence in the 1720s. If in the *Lettres persanes* women have reshaped men's interests according to their own, in his later reflections the influence of women appears to have extended beyond the domain of government, into the very nature of perception itself. Women are not only secretly pulling the puppet strings of power, they have succeeded in rendering men in their likeness—"there is only one sex any longer." This startling affirmation moves out of the domain of politics and into the sphere of daily experience: Women are not just exercising authority, they are changing the way in which social roles are organized, distributed, valued, and lived. Even more impressively—or absurdly—their preferences have reoriented the capacity for discernment and desire, depleting masculine focus and capability and shaping the way in which men experience and inhabit social spaces. The menace here is cultural, but it is also ontological—threatening to destabilize political functioning but also vitiating masculinity from within. Disposition wins out over mind: The feminine character ascribed to women takes its revenge on masculine habits of thought, transforming them in its image, making serious work impossible, putting at risk the distinctiveness of national bodies.

Montesquieu is not alone in his fears. Another twenty years or so after the author of *L'Esprit des lois* formulated his *pensée*, Jean-Jacques Rousseau would make a similar set of connections—between feminine agency and masculine constraint, French women's authority and orientalist figures of male depletion, desire, and discipline. In the *Lettre à d'Alembert* (1758), Rousseau condemns metropolitan French culture for having utterly succumbed to feminine influence. The most natural state of society, for him, involves keeping men and women separate from one another, precisely because men have the tendency to become womanly as a result of too much contact with feminine manners and behaviors: "for this weaker sex, not in the position to take on our way of life, which is too hard for it, forces us to take on its way, too soft for us; and, no longer wishing to tolerate separation, unable to make themselves into men, the women make us into women," he writes.[34] Rousseau revisits the specter of emasculation that haunts Montesquieu's portrayal of robotic men who do women's bidding without knowing it, at the same time as he insists on the link between feminization and decadence. In Rousseau's framing, the elite Parisian woman's salon resembles a queer seraglio,[35] where women rule over men who are in fact women themselves: "every woman at Paris gathers in her apartment a harem of men more womanish than she," he asserts.[36] The artifices of femininity overtake men and women alike in their epidemic and epidermic vitality. They constitute on the one hand a cultural style—ways of acting and of thinking that express a certain relation to the world.[37] At the same time, the transformation of men into women is not just a function of how bodies or cultural texts are positioned. It is also a matter of matter itself. The feminization of the male body is linked not only to specific modes of self-presentation, as in Rousseau's description, where men move distractedly about the salon, unable to sit still but equally unable to leave, but also to a quasi-mechanical drive for sensual satisfaction that leaves men in particular overwhelmed and powerless. They become incapable, Rousseau argues, of republican modes of virtue. The pleasures of femininity are intimately connected to the feminizing force of pleasure.

Rousseau, in his portrayal of a seraglio of men, suggests that the denizens of the salon are present there to dally not only in discursive exchange but in sex. He makes this point explicit by asserting that the men in question "know how to render all sorts of homage to beauty except that of the heart, which is her due."[38] Part of the purpose of the *Lettre à d'Alembert* is thus to endorse a different mode of satisfaction—a lasting happiness over the "vain pleasures" that are valorized and cultivated in Parisian society.[39] These pleasures have distinct physical effects: The passivity and weakness of the participants in the salon are a direct result of their frenetic sexual activity. For Montesquieu, in his *pensée*, it is also an excessive contact with women that is to blame for the social shifts that he, like Rousseau, deplores. Traffic in women: Intellectual, commercial, and sexual encounters collapse together in this heavily freighted formulation.[40] *Com[m]erce*, the term used by Montesquieu, implies a zone of communication—and can suggest in French an ease and facility in social relations generally—just as it references a scene of economic exchange. Simultaneously, the word evokes the sexual act. While Montesquieu and Rousseau take different sides in the extended eighteenth-century debate around luxury and consumption, they both connect the exercise of women's power (whether in the *cabinet* or in the *salon*) to the circulation of women's bodies in erotic scenarios. They underscore not just the increasing participation of women in cultural and political life, but the enhanced visibility and acceptability of pleasure (and sexual pleasure in particular) in both public and semiprivate venues. To be modern is to enjoy like a woman, and, as a result, to become one.

The decadently[41] feminine modernity that they decry in different terms thus involves not only the emergence of new forms of sociability, in which women participate alongside men, but the assertion of pleasure as a value that brings men and women together in varied yet specific configurations.

With their descriptions of French Enlightenment society as the scene of an erasure of gender difference—where "one sex" effaces the other—both Montesquieu and Rousseau are reacting, albeit in distinct ways, not just to what they perceive as the triumph of women as cultural authorities but to the rise of sensual pleasure as a sensation affirmed and celebrated by enlightened society. The pursuit of erotic satisfaction not only puts men in proximity to women, but grants them the possibility of being (like) them. Women are a cipher for pleasure, but pleasure also functions as a cipher for femininity. The "autonomy of pleasure," to use James Steintrager's formulation, is inseparable from a fascination with femininity as a sovereign force that both feminizes and standardizes, even when women themselves are denied any substantial or direct political power. Unsurprisingly, then, the image of an inescapable feminine influence, which shapes and governs social life, is a recurrent trope not only in cultural critique but in literary texts that both play on the attraction of a culture of pleasure and analyze its effects. In Crébillon fils's *Les Égarements du cœur et de l'esprit* (1735–1738), for instance, the libertine Versac describes the means by which a young man may achieve renown in Parisian society: "The simplest and at the same time most pleasant way to succeed, is to appear to only think of women in everything that one does, to believe that only that which seduces them is appealing, and that the sort of wit that pleases them, whatever it is, is in fact the only one that should please at all."[42] The use of the word *appear* is important here, since the ability to feign submission to women's interests and wishes is for Versac a means to an end; in pleasing women, he seeks to dominate them. But at the same time, the admission of women to positions of cultural visibility—and the need to act *as if* in accordance with women's preferences—accompanies a turn toward pleasure as a social fact: In Crébillon's text as in the work of Rousseau and Montesquieu, it is both cause and symptom of this turn.[43] It is this nexus—where the cultivation of enjoyment intersects with a contagious femininity, stimulated by new opportunities for social exchange—that creates an opportunity for certain philosophers to rethink the function of materialism itself in its own long-standing relation to pleasure as an inherently feminine *effect*.

Embracing Emasculation

Crébillon, Montesquieu, and Rousseau, for all their differences, share an ambivalence about the ways in which an elite culture bent on sensual satisfaction, as they understand it, prioritizes feminine pleasures and demands. They conjure the specter of emasculation as a symptom of a feminine cultural authority that derives from and encourages pleasure's rise. This authority is at least partly (if not wholly) imaginary—and the fear of becoming (like) a woman is at least partly (if not wholly) a result of misogynist and racist ideas that link sensual receptivity to vulnerability and weakness. But the connection between femininity and pleasure—in which to feel and pursue delight is in some sense to think, act, and perceive like a woman—persists and even intensifies in contexts where this culture of pleasure is embraced rather than deplored. One crucial scene of this embrace is an increasingly dynamic materialism, where the leveling force of pleasure is celebrated as a source of social, political, and ethical potential. In works that admire (rather than excoriate) the responsiveness of the body to the many desires that move it, femininity is the privileged expression of a newly and productively tractable materiality. Still, this connection is not unique to the eighteenth century. The conversion to materialism is closely linked to the initiatory power of femininity already in Lucretius's *De rerum natura* (first century BCE), with the invocation of Venus as an engine of voluptuous animation.[44] Sometime after the reemergence of the Lucretian epic onto the European cultural scene in the fifteenth century, this ancient association takes on new life. The generative encounter between the pleasure-seeking body, as outlined in various Epicurean source texts, and feminine tropes or figures recurs across multiple strands of libertine philosophy in the seventeenth and eighteenth centuries but is already visible in the works of Michel de Montaigne (1533–1592), who on occasion endorses women's freedom to desire but also to consent.[45]

Nearly one hundred years later, the investment of materialist philosophy in femininity takes on a particularly innovative form in Cyrano de Bergerac's lunar travel narrative, *Les États et Empires de la Lune* (written in the 1640s), in which the hero Dyrcona (an anagram of the author's name) journeys to the moon, is mistaken for a female pet by the inhabitants he encounters, and is finally placed in a cage with a male partner (whom he may in fact have had sex with—the text is not entirely clear on this point). The narrator's introduction to both libertine critique and materialist argument takes place while he is obliged to assume a woman's position, which he does without complaint or even much concern. One of the earliest entries in the tradition of the libertine materialist novel thus already experiments with the speculative feminization of its hero, in a way that condones rather than abhors the new sensations that might arise from this playful inversion of roles. In the century and a half that follows, this kind of endorsement will continue to knit together novelistic explorations of feminine subjectivity and scientific investigations of matter's nature. In materialisms both literary and philosophical, femininity is ratified as the necessary form that bodies take—the means by which pleasure becomes visible and legible as such and the scene, paradoxically, of a radical universalism, rather than a marker of inherent difference.

This point is made particularly explicit in Diderot's *Les Bijoux indiscrets* (1748), a text that Michel Foucault famously cites as inaugurating the transition to a modern *scientia sexualis*.[46] In this orientalist libertine novel, which Diderot at first abjured as a youthful bagatelle yet returned to for revision much later in his career, femininity characterizes both the objects and subjects of enlightened pleasure. The talking vaginas that give the text its title are meant to speak the truth of women's sexuality, although they often do so reluctantly or inaudibly.[47] The protagonist, the sultan Mangogul, receives a magic ring from the genie Cucufa that allows him to force women's *bijoux* to talk, thereby (presumably) revealing their secrets and providing a loosely organized structure to the narrative, which proceeds from one *bijou* to the next in the manner of Mangogul himself. Yet it is not only the putative objects of narrative interest—namely, the vaginas—that are explicitly feminine. Diderot also dedicates the novel to an imaginary feminine reader—Zima, a young woman particularly curious about the secrets of sex and already well versed in libertine literature—and sets the intrigue in a voluptuously exotic court (meant to invoke that of Louis XV) in which women figure as arbiters of political, cultural, and social power. As in the *Lettres persanes*, it is the contagion of femininity that serves as the bawdy link across cultures—both the sign of an orientalist difference and the condition that overcomes *all* difference. But this femininity is not just distilled in the image of the vagina, it is also used to characterize a particularly sensitive and responsive disposition. In the development of the character of Mirzoza—Mangogul's lover, and a woman of cultivation and discernment—Diderot presents a model of enlightened subjectivity who is attractive both sexually and philosophically— an appealing counterpart to Mangogul's sympathetic yet awkward pursuit of sexual enlightenment and lubricious curiosity. In her various contributions to the tale, which include forays into burlesque and speculative versions of philosophical argumentation, Mirzoza articulates a joyous empiricism that is both nondogmatic and eclectic. Refusing to be captured by the institutions of knowledge—and necessarily standing outside of them in her status as a woman—she is capable of effectively satirizing the conventional forms taken by philosophy at the same time as she insists on the priority of tender and loving feeling in her encounter with the world. In short, the focus of Diderot in this novel is not only the vagina as sex organ but femininity as both subjectivity *and* style. He positions the lubricious materiality of the speaking "sex" in a setting saturated with the kinds of dissipation, detachment, distraction, and dissolution that preoccupy Crébillon, Rousseau, and Montesquieu as indices of women's excessive cultural influence and of their ability to make men in their images. Yet, in this context, the figure of Mirzoza emerges as a feminine interlocutor who is not just wise but also receptive, the carrier and arbiter of both tenderness and knowledge. In many ways she appears to speak for the author himself (albeit only indirectly). Blurring distinctions between cultures and gendered voices, she speaks on behalf of an enlightened sensitivity that prioritizes the delicate pleasures of love.

In assuming *both* feminine objects of study *and* a feminine subject position, Diderot is not only demonstrating the way in which many of the qualities imputed to pleasure in general, whether softness and lushness or dissipation and waywardness, are linked in a particular cultural imaginary to women, he is also building on a legacy of libertine materialism that is powerfully invested in this connection as a spur to delight. In *Les Bijoux*, form takes a woman's shape not just to uncover the workings of desire but in order to induce the sweet pleasures characteristic of femininity. It is no accident that Diderot is interested both in writing about women and in adopting a woman's point of view. His dedication of the novel to the fictional Zima[48] also implicitly positions the reader—who was certainly just as likely to be a man as a woman, if not more so—in the same feminine role as the author assumes in making Mirzoza an emblem of a knowledge both enlightened and sympathetic—a voice that speaks in the name of both empiricism and love. Neither is it entirely a coincidence that *Thérèse philosophe* was published in the same year as *Les Bijoux*. With its pornographic descriptions, *Thérèse* proceeds quite differently, in tone and in message, from Diderot's work; the obscene novel presents, for its readers' delectation and edification, a heroine who is both the proof of pleasure's efficacy *and* the enlightened transmitter of pleasure's message. Mirzoza, an arbiter of decorum, plays a different role. Her *bijou* remains off limits to the ring until the very end of the novel, so that she stays a figure of virtuous commitment as well as tender feeling, whereas the philosophical Thérèse speaks in the name of an erotic desire whose power she conveys to the reader through both argument and example. Yet both texts are fascinated by the feminine body not only as an object of investigation but as an imaginary source of enlightened authority—one that can be passed on to a reader (or writer) whose desire is pricked by the images on display. The flexibility and receptivity of women in particular allow for the broadcasting of a new kind of materialist message, one that suggests the need for an emancipation from all doctrine but that of the heart, in the case of Mirzoza, or of the cunt, in that of Thérèse.

This seemingly natural flexibility also underwrites the capacity of bodies to submit joyfully to regulation, to discipline, and to the law—a quality that makes them modern (as Foucault famously affirms). Where Montesquieu and Rousseau deplore the effects of a contagiously feminine disposition on masculine judiciousness and reason, the materialist novel explores the way in which feminine sensitivity can become the scene of intellectual, moral, and ultimately social transformation. Femininity is positioned at the interface of nature and culture, as a seemingly innate capacity for responsiveness to social demands, and the soft malleability of feminine bodies is revealed as a source of political potential—a fundamental component of modern subjectivity that might provide the impetus for a revolution in morals. The triumph of women that is said by writers like Montesquieu and Rousseau to perversely characterize a decadent age becomes in materialist contexts a capacity for adaptation and delight that might emerge from within all kinds of bodies—a kind of dream of becoming woman that can be expressed in philosophical terms but also appears as a literary drive to explore the lifeworlds and sensations of women protagonists and feminine characters. This is another, more positive but also more disturbing, twist on Montesquieu's idea that "there is only one sex any longer." In the case of *Les Bijoux* and *Thérèse philosophe*, the literary work functions as an experimental plateau for living out the effects of a materialist turn toward feminine receptivity, a condition in which (in theory) any gender might participate.

As I will discuss in Chapter 1, Diderot is part of a cadre of materialist authors who embrace and expand on feminine figures of receptivity and flexibility in their attempts to argue on behalf of (and not against) a modern ethics of pleasure. In their writings, femininity is still particularly infectious, but it is also especially enrapturing. As this book aims to show, the radical materialism of the Enlightenment and beyond depends not so much on a ratification of the gender binary as on a universalization of a feminine position, one that wraps *all* genders in its embrace. The misogynist caricatures of Montesquieu and Rousseau thus have something in common with more sympathetic heroines like Mirzoza or Thérèse and even with the philosophy of a committed materialist like La Mettrie: They all emphasize femininity as the condition that makes pleasure both palpable and legible to bodies individual and social. This legacy crosses over into certain contemporary theoretical contexts, which continue to bear witness to a specifically materialist fascination with femininity—not only as a trope but as a way of understanding the conditions under which matter takes on shape and life. The concept of *devenir-femme* developed by Gilles Deleuze and Félix Guattari thus resonates obscurely and obliquely with Montesquieu's anxieties and more directly with Diderot's own investments in the resonance of a feminine voice. "Women," Deleuze and Guattari write in *Mille Plateaux: Capitalisme et Schizophrénie*, "regardless of their numbers, are a minority, definable as a state or subset; but they create only by making possible a becoming over which they do not have ownership, into which they themselves must enter; this is a becoming-woman affecting all of humankind, men and women both."[49] Later on in the text, they suggest that becoming-woman has a particular kind of force—an "introductory power" from which all other becomings (including becoming-animal and becoming-child) may stem.[50] This idea is part of the ancient inheritance of materialist philosophy, putting Deleuze and Guattari in contact with their eighteenth-century forebears, and, beyond them, with Montaigne and Lucretius. Where the materialist turn unlocks the energy of a matter that is always on the move, this power has long been articulated in and through the assumption of a (more) feminine form.[51]

This book posits the eighteenth century as the scene of an especially powerful reconfiguration of gender, matter, and sensation through the propagation of pleasure in the feminine. But it is not only materialists who acknowledge and endorse the connection of femininity to a newly receptive mode of enjoyment that defines and structures modern culture. Voltaire makes a similar association in his 1736 poem, "Le Mondain," which includes a defense of luxury economies and the cultivation of aesthetic delight. He writes:

> As for me, I render homage to wise Nature
> Who, for my own good, has placed me in this age,
> So decried by our poor clerics:
> This profane time accords perfectly with my manners.
> I love luxury, and even soft dissipation, 5
> All the pleasures, and the arts of all kinds,
> Cleanliness, taste, and ornaments:
> Every honest man has these same sentiments.[52]

Here, pleasure is ineluctable—the gift of a wise Nature who knows what is best. At the same time, it is modern—freed up by a "profane time" that lends value to the cultivation of delight in secular contexts. Moreover, while the poetic voice in these lines underlines the speaker's masculine status, the opulence and softness of the era surreptitiously return to the trope of femininity, here in the realm of commercial culture. Modern man seeks out and delights in the luxurious softness of an age that pleases him, naturally, with beautiful ornaments of all kinds. To follow nature is thus to endorse the poetic artifice of culture—to salute and sustain a feminine receptivity as the most notably modern characteristic of the *honnête homme*. Voltaire's fantasy of modern life is alluring—and enduring. His assertions of pleasure's cultural ubiquity, as well as his claims on behalf of its natural power, are part of a social and political context that had already embarked upon the long process of reorganizing itself around a new kind of human subject—marked in theory only by the traces of its own desire, if in practice made visible through the privileges of its position. At its heart, illusively, this subject is a feminine one. Voltaire's *mondain* might well anticipate Andrea Long Chu's assertion in the incipit of her book *Females*: "I am female. And you, dear reader, you are female, even—especially—if you are not a woman. Welcome. Sorry."[53]

But the focus of *Illusive Materialisms* is not only on the reverberating effects of a feminine ontology, whether despised or endorsed. It is also, and more crucially, an investigation of the way in which specific women and feminine persons could and did find philosophical, aesthetic, and erotic opportunities in the linkage between material pleasures and feminine sensibilities, between an endorsement of voluptuous sensuality and an experience of the artifices by which any gender is made real. In this way I also aim to carve out a place for a materialism crafted by and for subjects who experience "their" femininity as both assigned and made. The intensification of the connection between femininity and a culture of pleasure, which certainly enables an increasing objectification of women, also allows for a space to open in which certain feminine authors strive to articulate their own ethic of a materialist enjoyment that nevertheless does not name itself as such. They lay claim to the work of illusion as key not only to the legacy of femininity—a legacy that they carry at times with difficulty—but to the crafting of a pleasurable if not desirable life. In this way, they reactivate an inheritance of nondogmatic materialist speculation that grounds itself in a practice of finding and making enjoyment where it may occur. They explore femininity—their own and that of others—as a materialist artifice that makes pleasure possible. While Chapter 1 focuses on more canonical masculine authors, introducing the linkage between pleasure and femininity as crucial to eighteenth-century materialist philosophy, subsequent chapters take on the work of Puisieux, Du Châtelet, and Graffigny as feminine elaborations of pleasure's philosophical and lived potential.

In recognition of the ways in which each of these women reworks her material condition specifically through acts of reading and writing, which she undertakes as part of the development of a life engaged in and with delight, I have chosen to begin each chapter that follows with a reflection on the way in which the chapter itself came to be. These remarks will, I suspect, read in certain respects as personal, but they are intended less as a window into considerations usually left private as a way of thinking about the entanglement of scholarly writing (and knowledge) in specific histories and particular situations, including my own. They are also meant as an acknowledgment of how thought itself oscillates, moves, and evolves over time, often in the more visible act of writing and always in the invisible process of reading that lies behind each academic work. They are less an expression of the subjective immediacy of the issues I explore than of the power of mediation to lend shape and contour to perception. I have tried to recognize in each case not only the context that has shaped the questions that I ask but the effects of other texts, readers, and authors on my ability to do intellectual work—including but not limited to the writers past and present who are cited, discussed, and explored in this book. In this way, I have also attempted to remain true to one lesson that these texts have taught me—namely, that neither error nor illusion is a static object, preserved throughout time, but that both, like the matter of which all thought is made, change shape and form over and with the course of a lifetime. They thus require, like femininity itself, a constant cultivation that aims always toward what works.

1
Feminine Fictions of Radical Materialism: Diderot, La Mettrie, Helvétius

"Ah! if I deceive myself, in increasing the pleasure of my sensations and my happiness, might I always deceive myself thus!"[1]

Caroline Warman's illuminating 2020 study of Diderot's *Éléments de physiologie* opens with the following quotation from Diderot's text: "Love is harder to explain than hunger, for a piece of fruit does not feel the desire to be eaten."[2] From there, Warman's analysis invites the reader into the vertiginous set of perspectival shifts that open out from the analogy likening human beloved to fruit. Where at first glance Diderot's formulation seems to stress the distinction between the human and the plant realms, at the same time his phrasing subtly encourages his readers to consider the possibility of a vegetable point of view, with unsettling results. "So here we are," Warman reflects as she analyzes the sentence, "in agreement with the imaginary point of view of a piece of fruit."[3] For my part, contemplating this passage, I couldn't help but think of tomatoes—or rather the filmed images of tomatoes that appear in artist Jessica Rath's 2014 shorts entitled *Ripe Gambol* and *Ripe Still* (see figure 1).

In *Ripe Gambol*, the bright red fruits bounce seductively on a trampoline in slow motion, evoking luscious feminine bodies without ever being fully anthropomorphized. In *Ripe Still*, the tomatoes do not move, but shadows (perhaps of humans or other animals) appear in their highly reflective surfaces, which seem to be beckoning the spectator to bite into the flesh that lies underneath. The fruit is immobile but it is not passive: It appears to solicit our desire for it. Or is this just an illusion sparked by the polish of its surface? Rath's tomatoes, temptingly buoyant, ripe, juicy, inviting, seem to hint at the idea of a fruit that just *might* desire to be eaten, if we return to Diderot's

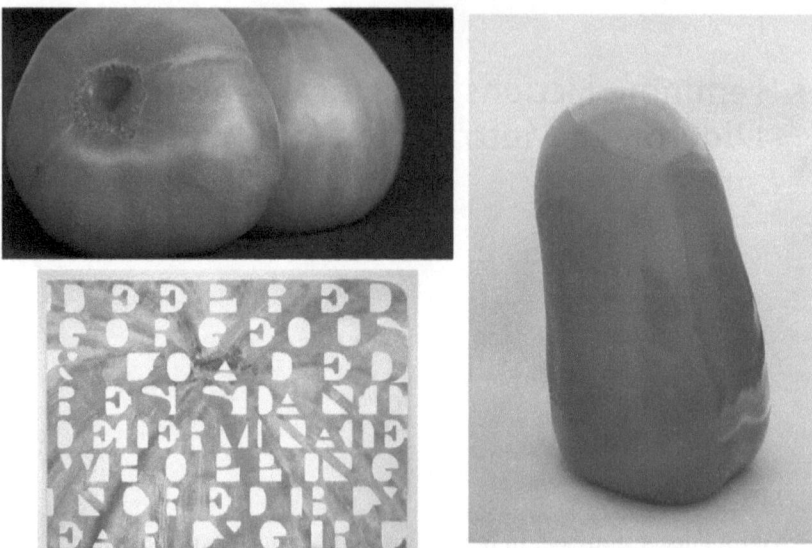

Figure 1. Jessica Rath, *Ripe Still*, 2014, still from film; *Roma #1*, 2013, ceramic and urethane, 18 in. × 12 in. × 12 in.; *Early Girl (Burst Variant)*, 2014, monoprinted lithograph, 24 in. × 30 in. Image courtesy of Jessica Rath.

analogy. But they also link this vegetal erotics to a whole history of the objectification of specifically feminine bodies—of the projection of need, hunger, and longing onto sessile forms that seem to seek their own consumption precisely because this is the purpose that has been grafted onto them. Who cares if a fruit wants to be eaten or not, as long as it is *ripe*? Diderot's "fruity feelings"—in Warman's evocative phrasing—take us to a place where the different kingdoms—vegetal, animal, mineral—begin to blur and merge, but they also suggest the ways in which sexy but insensible bodies are implicitly and explicitly gendered.

The men who are the subjects of this chapter have fascinated me for decades. They are collectively prolix writers and thinkers, bodies with little or no apparent difficulty expressing themselves. The experiences that elicit their emotions—like the emotions that mold their experiences—are often deftly and movingly invoked in their writing, putting them at odds with the tomato, whose feelings, if it has any, will always be a matter of speculation. Their words and thoughts cover pages and pages; their desires shape, inflect, and pass through the brilliance of their language. The materialisms that they represent, while very different in important ways, are invitingly lush, on occasion ambivalent, sometimes ambiguous, full of swerves and turns and the occasional contradiction that nonetheless manage to open a space for thought to expand and evolve. In my teaching and in my own reading, for pleasure and otherwise, I have been drawn to their collective exuberance, the extraordinary malleability and power of their prose, their eye for detail and their capacity to plunge themselves seemingly wholeheartedly into their work while retaining a critical sensitivity to orthodoxy. In my first book on figural materialisms, I tried, without fully admitting it, to give voice to the pleasure that I found in *their* pleasure, a zone where, as La Mettrie puts it in his description of the voluptuary imagination, "the image of pleasure that is its result, seems to be pleasure itself."[4] Across their various philosophical positions, with their distinct points of reference and their disagreements, I was taken with and taken up in the tight entanglement of matter in image—of pleasure in the forms that it assumes. I found—and still find—the interpenetration of substance and trope a source of inspiration but also of frustration: How to read something other than my own reflection in the images that they generate?

As I wrote my first book, I was struck by the way in which the poetic materialisms elaborated by these three men were so often parsed through and on the bodies of women, who functioned not only as objects of interest or analysis but as subjects made to speak in pleasure's name. Unlike fruits that do not want to be eaten (or do they?), these feminine figures often served as examples of matter's inherently voluptuous malleability or of pleasure's transmissibility from word to body and back again. Such images—of women, of feminine and female allegories, of pleasures rendered as "soft" or sweet[5] and thus communicable—proliferate across these men's work as striking instances of materialism's explanatory and poetic power, moments when pleasure becomes visible, available, and consumable for a reader who shares in the delectation of both text and writer. Femininity in this model has the power of vitality itself and the shaping force of form: It affects and sometimes infects those who witness or read about it. It also suggests a mode of identification: In writing about voluptuous women, these men sometimes seemed to me to fantasize about what it might mean to become (like) them.

For my part, I at first imagined including in the conversations I was tracking the voices of women and other persons whose femininity was assigned to them, but I did not manage to do it. I deferred this project rather than having the courage to take it on. Instead, I coauthored a book on plants and their extraordinary life, as flexible, ambivalent, and generative as the materialisms that had originally inspired me. Perhaps as a result of this swerve away from more human-centered questions, Diderot's remark on the difference between love and hunger came to resonate with me for the way in which it poses the question of desire through the figure of the plant first and only implicitly or secondarily through that of a feminine partner—thereby both stressing and evading the problem of pleasure's reciprocity. His comment also tracks my own journey from matter, to "fruity feelings," and back again, with femininity as an implication rather than a question to be posed.

In returning here to the work of Diderot alongside that of his materialist contemporaries La Mettrie and Helvétius, after a long time spent in the land of the plants, I want to more explicitly assume my own feminine point of view, thereby "lifting the veil of objectivity," as Naomi Schor writes in her collection of essays entitled *Bad Objects: Essays Popular and Unpopular*.[6] The men whom I discuss in this chapter themselves often take "the risks of subjectivity," in a phrase I borrow from Roland Barthes.[7] Far from valorizing an objective stance for its own sake, they seem fascinated by the way in which they may find (and leave) themselves in the feminine bodies that they represent, study, and ventriloquize. They are attracted to and excited by femininity as a moment in which substance and its artifices are most tightly conjoined. What might it mean to write and speak, in this context, from the position of a woman? And what does it matter? I do not want to presume that femininity itself, whether my own or another's, is in some sense a resolution or even a rejoinder to the question that these eighteenth-century writers take up over and over again, in varied and antithetical contexts—that of matter's articulation in its forms. But I do want to highlight the feminine investments of these materialist positions. And I seek ultimately to put these positions in dialogue with writing by people whose attachment to the situation of femininity was not understood, by them or others, as a concept first, but rather as a constraint to be endured, examined, and sometimes enjoyed.

This chapter groups Diderot, La Mettrie, and Helvétius together in order to show the way in which femininity becomes, for them, the "matter" of matter itself. I bring these authors into (implicit) conversation not because I want to collapse their very different materialisms into one another, but because I want to pull on the strand of femininity as a kind of "chaîne sécrete" (with apologies to Montesquieu) that binds them even in their difference and their variety. In showing how these distinct materialisms circulate around femininity—as a form that all bodies inevitably are made to take—I want to open up that circulation as crucial to the way in which these philosophers see not only themselves but the work that their thought might do. The materialisms I study here are deeply preoccupied with femininity as the very shape of matter. I want to reveal that preoccupation as intrinsic to their projects, even as I slowly and eventually make room for a feminine response—one rarely seen as philosophical, but still perhaps transmissible in the techniques that it engages.

Epicurus for a New Age

While the form that it takes in eighteenth-century France is a novel one, the association between materialism and femininity has a long history. Since antiquity, Epicurean materialists were taxed not only with immorality but with effeminacy. In her excellent book on *The Invention and Gendering of Epicurus*, Pamela Gordon explores the multiple ways in which the Epicurean sect—in its practices, doctrine, and exponents—was castigated for a feminine attachment to pleasure. This charge had specific political implications especially in the Roman context, where public life revolved around the cultivation of masculine virtue, and to be an Epicurean meant not only to be like a woman but to resemble a foreigner. As Gordon writes, "In the most virulent anti-Epicurean discourse, pleasure was the polar opposite not of pain but of a quintessentially Roman quality: *virtus*."[8] The opposition between *virtus* and *voluptas* is catchy in its pleasing alliteration, but it is also fundamental to a whole philosophy of civic virtue as a mode of manly excellence and valor. Plutarch's (ca. 45–120 CE) reiterated condemnations of the Epicureans are a *locus classicus* of this association between the Epicurean rejection of pain and an inability or unwillingness to participate not just in society but in life itself. In his critique of the Epicurean adage "Live unknown!" (or "Lead a hidden life!"), Plutarch makes explicit the connections between moral corruption and the Epicurean commitment to pleasure, writing "A repose of which nothing is heard and a life stationary and laid away in leisure withers not only the body but the mind; just as pools concealed by overshadowing branches and lying still with no outflow putrefy, so too, it would appear, with quiet lives: as nothing flows from them of any good they have in them and no one drinks of the stream, their inborn powers lose their prime of vigour and fall into decay."[9] In describing the Epicurean embrace of *voluptas*, Plutarch links the pursuit of pleasure not just to idleness, but to ignorance, sickness of the mind and body, and crucially, to a turn away from light itself and toward obscurity. This kind of life—which is not really a life at all—is lived in the company of women. Plutarch stresses this connection: "If you remove publicity from our life as you might the illumination from a drinking party, so that every pleasure may freely be indulged without detection—'live unknown.' Yes indeed, if I am to live with Hedeia the courtesan and end my days with Leontion and 'spit on noble action' and place the good in the 'flesh' and in 'titillations'; these rites require darkness, these require night, and for these let us have concealment and oblivion."[10] The rejection of virtue and the plunge into sensuality entail a mode of sociability practiced by and among women. But this life is also one that is lived *like* a woman, as Julie Giovacchini has emphasized in her article on "Sexual Freedom and Feminine Pleasure in Lucretius." In Giovacchini's words, "It is remarkable to note that historically, the hegemony of Venus and the harmonious conception of the affective commerce over which she presides will be turned against the Epicureans, depicting in them an immoral, vitiated, weak nature, at the antipodes of the *virtus*."[11] Existing under the sign of Venus, the Epicureans are taxed repeatedly for their feminine habits, their soft and useless lives, their indolent forms.

For Plutarch, to live as an Epicurean is not only to enjoy the company of women but to become womanly—hidden away, rejecting glory, without an effect on history. Relative to other philosophical schools, Epicureans were indeed notable for their willingness to tolerate or even embrace the company of both women and enslaved people, who were apparently welcomed in the Garden, even as they were turned away from other communities. But Plutarch's condemnation of the Epicurean philosopher is not just based in the historical fact of women's participation in the Epicurean Garden, it also reflects an understanding of pleasure as a force that generates a distinct relationship to the contours and densities of the body, whether masculine or feminine. Living concealed, in the company of women, the stagnant corporeal mass of the dissolute philosopher cannot access the light of glory or participate in the unfolding of history. Plutarch's "life laid away in leisure" is thus an elaboration on the old idea of Epicureanism as emasculating, which had been thematized almost from the moment of the Epicurean school's emergence. For the skeptic Arcesilaus (ca. 316–ca. 240 BCE), for example, the conversion to Epicureanism symbolized a form of castration from which the disciple could never recover: "Men may become eunuchs, but eunuchs may never again become men."[12] In Plutarch's formulation, the womanliness of the Epicurean philosopher appears across multiple dimensions: in the willingness to tolerate and seek out the society of women themselves, in the effete forms that the body takes on, and in the withdrawal from human society and human history. The Epicurean life is a life wasted in its failure to pass anything on. The Epicurean eunuch has no progeny.

In the consistent association of Epicureans with womanly softness, dissoluteness, and a refusal of "light," Epicurean materialism takes on a very different valence from Stoicism. Seneca suggests as much in *De vita beata* when he describes the Epicurean sect as resembling "a strong man dressed up in a woman's garb."[13] This image of an unsettling femininity, which veils or conceals the philosophical robustness and vigor of Epicurean materialism, is a trope that survives well beyond the demise of the Roman political system. Arcesilaus, Seneca, and Plutarch have a lasting influence on the legacy of the Epicureans; their commentary consistently inflects the reappraisal of Epicurean physics and ethics that takes place in the late Renaissance and continues into the Enlightenment. In 1641, the libertine author and critic La Mothe Le Vayer glosses Arcesilaus's remarks, reordering once again the connections linking Epicurean pleasure, emasculation, and a dissolute or wasted life. As he puts it in *De la vertu des payens*, Arcesilaus "meant to say that the voluptuousness of Epicurus made men so effeminate, that they became incapable of regaining a less dissolute way of life."[14] Epicureanism here saps the strength of will of its disciples, making it impossible for them to return to the active pursuit of virtue. "Softening" Arcesilaus's metaphor, La Mothe Le Vayer suggests that the turn to Epicureanism is a condition from which, for Arcesilaus, the Epicurean disciple can never return.

In his 1758 *La Morale d'Épicure, tirée de ses propres écrits*, an important text for the eighteenth-century reception of Epicurus, the abbé Charles Batteux likewise evokes the problem of Epicurean effeminacy in his discussion of Gassendi's rehabilitation of Epicureanism, which appears at the end of the book's preface. Batteux aims to give an account of Epicureanism that works to "confront the original, such as he is, with the portraits that others have made of him."[15] He places this project under the guiding light of Gassendi, of whom he writes, "it is obvious . . . that, if Gassendi can be painted next to Epicurus, one should not use the same colors for the one as for the other; if he is to be respected, as it appears he should be, even less should one place the portrait of a man of this merit and of this character, between those of Leontion and Ninon de Lenclos."[16] In this moment the question of form returns, first in describing the portrait of Epicurus—given a different shading from that of his disciple Gassendi—and then in forbidding the placement of Gassendi's image between those of two women, notorious for both their Epicureanism and their promiscuity. Here too the collapse of feminine company or sociability into dissolute softness recurs, and in fact concludes the prefatory remarks, as if to underscore its enduring significance.[17] The emasculating force of Epicureanism is also, at this moment, a matter of how the doctrine may be received by those who inherit it—of the contours or shape of that which is inherited or passed down, of its placement among other points of reference, of its color or shaded aspects.

In their sustained collective engagement with an ethic of pleasure, the authors whose work I will examine here all loom large in a history of the Enlightenment reception of Epicurean materialism. Throughout their careers, Diderot, La Mettrie, and Helvétius each recur in different ways and at different times to an Epicurean conceptualization of voluptuous delight, most often parsed through a reading of Lucretius. Yet unlike many of their forebears, in their reconsideration of an Epicurean doctrine, they embrace rather than shy away from the Epicurean association with femininity. They savor the potential feminization of thought itself that follows in the wake of the Epicurean corpus—routinely highlighting and even reveling in the porosity, softness, sweetness, and yieldingness of matter as a source of human (and on occasion animal and vegetal) enjoyment. At the same time, they exaggerate and accentuate the feminine dimensions of Epicurean materialism—suggesting not only that matter is in various ways feminine by nature, but that to be a material body is in some very basic sense to be a woman, or at least to take on a feminine shape and form. Unlike the classical authors who situate *virtus* in opposition to *voluptas*, contrasting a hidden and obscure femininity with a glorious and enlightened masculinity, the materialists whom I will study in this chapter all suggest at various moments that the conversion to an ethic of pleasure—that is to say, to a modern mode of Epicureanism—involves the ascription of a feminine condition to all bodies. For them, to be made up of voluptuous matter is in some real sense to become a woman. This troping of the material body in feminine terms cuts across various literary and philosophical contexts, not unlike the writing of these three materialists themselves.[18] In contrast to other natural philosophers who often argue for an inherent difference between men and women, Diderot, La Mettrie, and Helvétius hint instead at the idea that gendered subjects are different from one another by degrees, not in kind. As Diderot puts it in the *Rêve de d'Alembert*, "Man is perhaps nothing more than the monster of woman, or woman the monster of man."[19] To live the sovereignty of pleasure is in a certain sense to live as a woman, and to be a materialist suggests in yet another an acknowledgment of femininity as a crucial attribute of the body made of matter. The materialist turn of the period thus represents a turn toward femininity in both its literal and figural dimensions, as the hoary trope of the eighteenth century as a "century of woman" seems to perversely recognize.[20]

But the naturalization of femininity as the form that matter takes is not without its ambivalences or its contradictions. While the three thinkers I study here collectively recognize the material involvement of all bodies in a certain femininity, for each of them the practice of philosophy remains a masculine purview. This is to say that, while the experience of the materialist philosopher may be one of a subjective femininity, to think and act philosophically involves an extraction from this feminine condition that is also theirs—and an eventual entry into a masculine performance of knowledge by means of which the hidden life of the voluptuous Epicurean is carried out and into the illumination cast by *les Lumières*. So, while the sphere of experience is given over to matter in its divagations and its aporia, its compulsions and artifices, the sphere of thought is protected as a realm of masculinist sociability, one in which the (feminine) body (including that of the philosopher) is denied participation in the materialist philosophical project even as it is held up as a privileged material condition of *every* body. We see remnants of this split—which is both internal and external to the position of the materialist philosopher himself—in the hiving off of sensory or sensual indulgence from the work of materialist analysis. It reappears as the ever-present division between "good" and "bad" materialisms: the first a set of philosophical commitments that allows for an active and principled stance vis à vis a materiality that always threatens to capture and to captivate, the second a practice of excessive consumption linked to a weakness of both body and mind. Feminine pleasure, in this reading, is the place where illusion and matter are experienced in their conjunction, as *d*elusion or distraction, and masculine philosophy is the zone where the artifices of matter are both transmitted and arrested in thought.

Diderot and *Épicure travesti*

Denis Diderot's *Pensées sur l'interprétation de la nature*, an investigation of the methods and objects of natural philosophy, was written in 1753 and published anonymously toward the end of this same year. With an epigraph based on the *De rerum natura* (DRN)—"Que sunt in luce tuemur E tenebris" [E tenebris autem quae sunt in luce tuemur/From the darkness, we can see what is in the light]—the work is an endorsement of experimental science, which Diderot opposes to mathematical approaches that are overly reliant on abstractions for the study of the natural world. His epigraph highlights both the Lucretian influence at play in the text itself and the key role of images of light and darkness—of hiddenness and unconcealment—in organizing the approach to philosophical knowledge.[21] In Lucretius's poem, the line cited by Diderot comes as part of a discussion, in the fourth book, of the phenomenon of vision and its material organization that includes a description of how it is possible to see objects that are illuminated even when the viewer is plunged in obscurity. As Lucretius affirms, the inverse does not hold: It is not possible to see from light into darkness. The reason for this, he explains, is that "dark" air, when it strikes the eye first, can be brushed away by the "lighter" atoms that follow it, in a kind of cleansing process. Sight is "liberated" in this operation and becomes free to perceive what lies beyond the obscurity from which it originates. Looking from the light into the dark, on the other hand, involves a kind of closing up or closing off of vision, whereby the darkness rushes in to obstruct the passageways of sight, preventing any simulacra (the fine skins or *eidola* emitted by all bodies according to Epicurean doctrine) from occupying the same space. Diderot's choice of citation thus evokes the contingency of human perceptions, which are vulnerable to the material conditions in which they arise, but also depicts a physical process in which these same conditions are both enabling and (perhaps) eventually surmountable. In Diderot's placement of the line at the opening of a work on scientific interpretation, the passage takes on a clearly figurative dimension to supplement the literal one: It not only affirms the imbrication of human senses in the material situation from which these senses derive—and indeed the next section in Lucretius's text concerns instances of optical illusions that bedevil sight—it suggests a project of enlightenment in which darkness may lead to light, and the parameters constraining vision may eventually generate a freer and more expansive mode of sight.

The *Pensées* is a notoriously but productively fragmentary[22] work, organized into twelve sections (the "pensées" of the title) that deal with different questions concerning the nature of scientific knowledge, its vicissitudes, paradoxes, and potential. The focus of these sections is not only the method by which nature can be known but the nature of nature as an object of knowledge. "It is of Nature that I will write," Diderot declares.[23] He begins with a critique of "mathematical genius" for its investment in abstraction—an approach that, according to Diderot, strips from natural bodies their individuality and their material specificity.[24] For Diderot, it is only experimental philosophy that can lend substance to the speculative hypotheses of the geometers, grounding their calculations in the reality of the natural world. Still, even in this context, nature will surpass the capacity of the human mind to grasp, seize, or order it: "When one comes to compare the infinite multitude of natural phenomena with the limits of our understanding and the weakness of our organs," Diderot writes, "can one ever expect anything from the slowness of our projects, from their long and frequent interruptions, from the rarity of creative genius, than several broken and separated links from the great chain that connects everything?"[25] Nature in its infinite richness, diversity, and complexity is not given to human understanding as an object to be apprehended in its entirety. Instead, it can only be approached partially, haltingly, bit by painstaking bit. Mathematical speculation is not just detached from the workings of matter, but it disseminates a false confidence in the ability of the philosopher to make sense of a natural world that always exceeds individual human perception. The movement from darkness into light is thus not only slow but unending—with the end point ever-receding—impossible but in some very basic sense necessary. In the sixth *pensée* Diderot compares the desire to write the book of nature to the construction of the Tower of Babel—a confusion of languages that can never be untangled or resolved.

A little later on, in the twelfth *pensée*, Diderot discusses the infinite variability and fundamental interconnectedness of material bodies. He concludes this *pensée* with the following statement: "For it is clear that nature could not have preserved so many similarities in the parts and produced so much variety in the forms [of embodied beings], without having made palpable in one organized being what she has concealed in another. She is a woman who loves to dress herself up, and whose various disguises, which sometimes let one part appear, sometimes another, give hope to those who follow her assiduously to one day come to know her entire person."[26] This passage involves a troping or turning of the image from the epigraph—rendering the process of seeing out of the darkness into the light as a mode of desire that seeks to reveal that which is hidden. With this inflection, Diderot lends to scientific inquiry a libertine dimension, one in which the role of the (masculine) philosopher is to uncover the (feminine) person that would otherwise remain concealed.[27] As if to further emphasize the libertine elements at play in this description, Diderot follows this image of nature as a woman in disguise—*travestie*, having assumed the trappings of another condition or indeed of another sex—with a discussion of sexual reproduction, where he stresses the difficulty of identifying the origins and trajectory of the seminal fluids supposedly emitted by women in sexual intercourse. "It has been discovered that there is the same seminal fluid in one sex as in the other," he writes. "In the encounter of the sexes, when one compares the symptoms of pleasure in one to the symptoms of pleasure in the other, and when one has confirmed that voluptuous delight is consummated in both by bursts of the same character, distinct and spasmodic, one cannot doubt that there are also similar emissions of seminal fluid [in both men and women]."[28] From the figure of nature-as-woman (in disguise or drag) Diderot passes to the bodies of human women, who turn out to share the capacity for voluptuous pleasure with men, just as they share the ability to emit fluid. Unlike men, however, women find the very operations of "their" nature disguised (or twice concealed) within them; it is (for the moment) impossible to know how feminine semen develops, where it comes from and what it is for. The mode of "travestissement" in which nature figurally delights, as if she were a woman, is rehearsed biologically in the image of a woman's body as the site of its own "travestissement" at the very moment of reproducing itself.

Diderot concludes this discussion with the suggestion that it is through the dissection of other species that the key to the mystery of women's emissions will be solved, via the correspondence or resemblance linking small and large phenomena, animal and human bodies. This, too, is a mode of seeing from darkness into light—one in which the feminine body takes on the characteristic of opacity, an obscure zone from which knowledge may eventually be extracted. In the next *pensée*, Diderot returns to the image from the epigraph, writing "I portray the vast enclosure of the sciences to myself as a huge terrain speckled with dark places and illuminated ones."[29] If the origins and nature of woman's seminal fluids—and indeed reproduction itself—remain difficult to see, the dissection of the animal body might eventually begin to cast some light upon these shadows. Women resemble men, but in their resemblance, they suggest a difference. At the same time, nature herself is a woman or at least acts like one.

Diderot's rendering of nature as a "femme travestie" suggests a gendering of the project of enlightenment, certainly, but perhaps more revealingly it involves a shift from an emphasis on nature's illusions (optical and otherwise, as highlighted in the epigraph) to nature's artifice. Indeed, the latter transition is arguably a product of the former. In his article "'Cabinet d'Histoire Naturelle,' or: The Interplay of Nature and Artifice in Diderot's Naturalism," Charles T. Wolfe identifies the figure of feminine nature from the *Pensées* as a modern twist on the famous quote from Heraclitus: "Nature likes to hide." Wolfe reads this figure as a privileged locus for Diderot's denial of "the foundational distinction between Nature and artifice."[30] Diderot lends to nature an ontology that is "always provisional," in Wolfe's terms, and that is moreover subject to perpetual reconfiguration and "vicissitudes." Thus nature cannot be known in itself or as such, but requires human activity and engagement in order for these same humans to come into contact with it. Diderot's naturalism thereby makes capacious room for a pragmatic instrumentalism: In this sense, it is pro-constructivist. At the same time, it is an approach to nature whose most concise, and perhaps compelling, expression is lodged in the metaphor of sexual difference, a metaphor that in some sense lends the Diderotian formulation its modernity, at least as Wolfe describes it. In other words, Diderot's embrace of artifice is contingent on his "updating" of the image of nature via a sexed figure, so that the natural order is given substance and form in the disguised body of a woman. The difference between men and women becomes visible in their distinct relationship to feminine artifice. For the masculine philosopher, women's self-concealment functions as an especially generative obscurity. Still, sexed difference is not absolute, precisely because nature works her artifices everywhere. What might allow for the figure (that conceals) to be brought to light, to enable the transition of the philosopher from darkness into the place of illumination? Part of the answer to this question involves the internalization of femininity as the origin of masculine sensitivity to the world, as a proximity to nature that brings the outside in.

Diderot's image of nature as a woman disguised resonates obscurely with another such concealment—the portrayal of Epicurus, protonaturalist, as a man in drag. In 1755, the volume of the *Encyclopédie* containing Diderot's article on Epicurus (entitled "Épicuréisme ou Épicurisme") was published, two years after the *Pensées* appeared. While Seneca's rendering of the Epicurean sect as "dressed up in a woman's garb" might have been on Diderot's mind as he wrote, it does not appear in this article. It is not until the *Essai sur les règnes de Claude et de Néron* (1778–1782), composed toward the end of his life, that Diderot turns (back) to Seneca's description of Epicurus in *De vita beata*, modifying it slightly as he does so. "Epicurus was a hero disguised as a woman," he writes.[31] Where Seneca's emphasis is on the sect as a whole, Diderot narrows his focus in this rephrasing to Epicurus himself—valiant for his ethical and intellectual commitments but "travesti" or disguised under the soft forms of femininity. Like nature herself, the Epicurean philosopher hides something underneath his robes, but what he reveals is ultimately his heroic masculinity rather than his female person. Diderot's revision of Seneca's description unites in one human form the ideological or programmatic distinction between a manly Stoicism, which strives to harden body and mind against the pain of the passions, and a womanly Epicureanism, which endorses the pursuit of both softness and sweetness and thereby lends to matter itself the very voluptuous attributes that are thought to characterize the feminine figure. As it turns out, the role of the philosopher is not so much to reconcile these two positions—in fact, they may not be reconcilable—as it is to live their dynamic relation to one another.

In his article on Epicureanism, which is heavily indebted to Johann Jakob Brucker's *Historia critica philosophiae* (1742–1744), Diderot reveals how such a life might appear. He stresses the vital role that women have played in the transmission of Epicurean philosophy within France, just as they were present at the birth of Epicureanism in the ancient Garden. He affirms that Epicurus surrounded himself with women, including "Leontion, mistress of Metrodorus; Themista, wife of Leontius; Philenides, one of the most honest women in Athens; Nikidion, Erotion, Hedeia, Mammarion, Boidion, Phaedrium, &c."[32] But, unlike anti-Epicurean polemicists of the past, he makes this point in order to link the ancient Garden to a present-day mixed sociability in which men and women alike might share in the pleasures of philosophy. In this way Diderot departs from Batteux's staging of the virtuous Gassendi against the dissolute Leontion and her more modern counterpart, Ninon de Lenclos. The emphasis of the article is less on the reception of Epicurean doctrine and more on the status of Epicureanism as an expression of natural truth and universal human sentiment, but the presence of women throughout the history of Epicurean thought is itself a testament to both the naturalness and the universality of the doctrine.

Wrapping him in the chaste embrace of a circle of women, Diderot aims to present to readers an Epicurus unsullied by Stoic calumny—a man "for whom life was a continuous practice of all the virtues, & especially of temperance," a philosopher in communion with the natural world and with his disciples.[33] The genius of Epicurus for Diderot lies in the philosopher's ability to bring to light a capacity for pleasure that is never morally suspect, but instead a structuring fact of human life itself. Epicurus's precepts not only express the natural appetites of human beings; they formulate the fundamental human desire for pleasure as a need that demands to be met. "People came to his gardens from all the lands of Greece, of Egypt, and of Asia: they were drawn there by his knowledge and his virtues," writes Diderot, "but above all by the agreement of his principles with the feelings of nature."[34]

Despite the significance for Epicurus and his disciples of pleasure as a governing ideal, the *Encyclopédie* article suggests that Epicurean doctrine is remarkable less for its ability to account for natural appetites, than for the connection it makes between the practice of philosophy and the cultivation of a pleasant and meaningful life. Evidence of Epicurus's direct appeal to a universal drive toward pleasure as the necessary foundation of a broader human happiness follows directly upon the comprehensive overview of Epicureanism (divided into sections on "la philosophie en général," "la physiologie en général," "la théologie," and "la morale") with which the article opens. Diderot affirms:

> Here are the fundamental points of the doctrine of Epicurus, the only one among all the ancient Philosophers who knew how to reconcile his morals with what he could take for the true Happiness of man, and his precepts with the appetites and needs of nature; thus did he have and will he have throughout time a great number of disciples. One makes oneself stoic, but one is born *epicurean* [italics Diderot's].[35]

In this passage Epicureanism is rendered less as a specific instance of materialist theory, despite its doctrinal emphasis, and more as an orientation toward the world that ratifies the biological inheritance of animate material bodies in general—and of human bodies in particular.

Yet, despite his proximity to the "needs of nature," Epicurus himself partakes of the qualities of genius as the latter are defined elsewhere in the *Encyclopédie*.[36] His status as a philosopher of extraordinary ability is stressed: "Men of genius, such as Epicurus, lose little time; their activity takes on everything; they observe and learn without noticing it; and this knowledge, acquired practically without effort, is all the more admirable, in that it pertains to more general objects."[37] Processes of observation and instruction are depicted here as unselfconsciously set in motion by the genial Epicurean thinker. Epicurean knowledge of the world emerges from its founder's unusually heightened attentiveness to natural diversity and flux. The "general spectacle of nature" is one that requires of the genius a boundless energy if it is to be absorbed and made comprehensible, and Epicurus shows himself equal to the task.

Epicurus's capacity for acute and sustained sensitivity to sensory input goes along with a commitment to writing and the dissemination of philosophical insights. Throughout the more than three hundred treatises that Epicurus is said to have composed, "he contented himself with being true, clear, and profound," although, ultimately, he "ruined his health from working so much."[38] Yet mere awareness of the variety inherent in nature is not a sufficient condition for the emergence of philosophical truth(s). Epicurus, like other thinkers of his ilk, is presented as moving from an unwilled, yet acute, responsiveness to particular phenomena—one that is accidental in its brilliance—into a synthesis of nature in its generalities. He reconfigures the natural world as a coherent whole rather than a mere collection of phenomena. In other words, Epicurus is both exquisitely open to the multiplicity of beings in and of themselves and capable of translating this openness into transmissible knowledge, since he ultimately generates a dogma that aims to make possible the cultivation of human happiness on a massive scale. He accordingly assumes a place as a type of philosophical genius who moves reliably from observation to precept through the application of his curiosity as a kind of motive force. He translates and transfigures natural phenomena into written or spoken truth.

While Epicurus's gifts are not his alone, Diderot's Epicureanism nonetheless departs from other philosophies—and from Stoicism in particular—in the immediacy with which it is lived. If Epicurus is blessed with vast numbers of disciples, women notable among them, it is not only because of his talent for persuasion or what the encyclopedia article describes as the novelty of his approach to the question of pleasure. As an argument, Epicureanism is convincing precisely in its very refusal of doctrinal mediation as an initial means of apprehending the material universe. We are all Epicureans, the article suggests, in the sense that we are all embodied human beings; to be Epicurean is simply to be born into the world. Epicurean philosophy seems to represent, in this formulation, a kind of degree zero of human consciousness—one already available to infants, children, and of course women too. Epicurus is both notable and praiseworthy for having persuasively articulated a fundamental truth of human experience, namely, that pleasure inheres in sensitive material bodies. As the article explains, "Disturb the natural state of the parts of the body, and you will produce pain; restore the parts of the body to their natural state, and you will make pleasure blossom."[39]

The account of Epicurus given in "Épicuréisme" thus seems to raise the possibility that Epicurean materialism is less a doctrine to be embraced than a condition of experience. As it is framed here, Epicureanism does not represent an exclusive or even wholly defensible set of philosophical attachments; it is compatible with other materialisms, just as sensation is compatible with thought. Still, it remains distinct from these materialisms in its immediate connection to experience. In so far as it is identified with the brute fact of having a human body, the Epicurean position functions as a starting point out of which other more philosophical arguments may emerge. Diderot thereby sketches the possible demise of a principled Epicurean commitment at the same time as he advocates for Epicureanism's universal applicability: To accept Epicurus's doctrine as universally true is at least in part to accept its undoing as a productive mode of argumentation, just as reason melts into delight. The "natural appetites" of the Epicureans become a feature of matter in general, one that both grounds and menaces human consciousness. To be alive as a human is at once to experience the potential for reasoned intellect and, at the very moment of this experience, to acknowledge the vulnerability of the understanding to the vicissitudes of a material existence. In "Épicuréisme," Diderot once again subtly acknowledges the material pressures that render embodiment not the outside, opposite, or absence of subjectivity but the latter's constitutive condition.

What meaningful role does gender have to play in the Epicurean origins of a human subjectivity that Diderot posits as at once powerful and fragile? In some sense, the uncovering of nature's person that Diderot evokes in the earlier *Pensées* also stresses the Epicurean dimensions of all human experience, one that cuts across masculine and feminine bodies. Neither women nor men, in Diderot's schema, can escape or reliably ignore the fact that they are made of matter. The construction of modes of consciousness out of the material conditions of subjectivity is a process that consumes and constitutes life itself. Both genders must struggle to negotiate some sort of balance between the various, conflicting drives inherent in the organism—even in each organ—and the continuity upon which thought depends: Without such a negotiation, self-consciousness per se would be impossible for any human being, whether masculine or feminine. But Diderot's persistent association of nature, materiality, and Epicurus himself with femininity is not a contingent one; instead, it suggests the extent to which embodiment itself is an instance of feminization—a necessary entanglement in the artifices of matter.

In the article from the *Encyclopédie*, Epicurus himself is identified with femininity insofar as he is presented as surrounded by women, but, importantly, for Diderot the valence of this image has shifted from its classical origins in misogynist polemic. No longer a sign of Epicurean debauchery, it becomes an index of the natural truth of Epicurus's philosophy—his closeness to experience itself. This generative and often positive identification of femininity with materiality cuts across the literary and philosophical dimensions of Diderot's corpus. Women themselves, as Diderot describes them in his essay *Sur les femmes* and in works of fiction including *Les Bijoux* and perhaps most remarkably *La Religieuse* (ca. 1780), have a privileged relationship to the realm of the discontinuous, the fragmented and the diverse, to the activity and artifice of matter. Indeed, women's bodies and actions reveal the way matter takes social shape and form; they vividly illustrate in their own persons what it means to have a body at all. The distinction between masculine and feminine thus functions as one of scale rather than of nature; all humans share in these feminine aspects of experience, just as Epicurus shares in the company of women. Femininity, with its softness and sweetness, its capacity for artifice, conditions the pleasure-giving dimensions of human life and sociability. It turns out, then, that Epicurus's affiliation with women is overdetermined: He uncovers femininity as an attribute of all bodies, just as he encourages and enjoys a feminine sociability that emphasizes the pleasures of exchange between men and women, who may both relish the latter's natural receptivity as a sign of a potential inherent in matter itself.

This feminization of both matter and materialism—which takes place in and permits scenes of mixed gender reciprocity—becomes explicit in Diderot's short essay on women, entitled *Sur les femmes* and first published in the *Correspondance littéraire* in 1772. This text was penned as a response to Antoine-Léonard Thomas's (1732–1785) much longer treatise, which appears in the same year under the title *Essai sur le caractère, les mœurs et l'esprit des femmes des différents siècles* (1772). At the beginning of his essay, Diderot taxes his friend Thomas for not having written with sufficient feeling in his depictions of "the infinite diversity of a being extreme in force as in weakness." He continues, "It is especially in love's passion, the throes of jealousy, the transports of maternal tenderness, the instants of superstition, the way in which they share in popular and epidemic emotions, that women astonish."[40] Diderot's exploration of the "infinite diversity" of women is a tribute to feminine charm as well as to the unequal burden of suffering—often physical—that women are forced to bear, as mothers and as wives. He praises women for their genius, more original than that of men, even as he laments their capacity for dissimulation and excessive curiosity. Throughout the text, he invokes the violence of feminine passion alongside the ease with which some women may embrace libertine hypocrisy. How is it possible to account for the uncanny ability of women both to feel too much and to appear to feel nothing at all?

As it turns out, they are inadequately civilized—"for want of reflection and principles"[41]—and thus more superficial than men, in that their virtues never quite "take." They are also more profound in their enthusiasms, in that their capacity to feel is less mediated by culture.

Feminine subjectivity, as Diderot renders it, is constituted at the limits of self-consciousness (and thus of the conscious self). He shows women to be remarkably susceptible to the pull of their passions: "I have seen love, jealousy, superstition, anger, carried in women to a point that no man will ever experience."[42] Yet they share this vulnerability with men, even as they figure its extremes; the thinking self, generally speaking, is always on the verge of dissolving into the multifarious sensations that make it possible. The wild sensitivity characteristic of femininity is nonetheless difficult to govern and filled with an almost preternatural intensity; women are extraordinarily susceptible to outside influence—by other women in particular—but arbitrarily so. In this way, they appear to be like children. Diderot writes, "Women are subject to an epidemic ferocity. The example of one pulls a multitude along with her. Only the first is criminal; the rest are sick. O women, you are most extraordinary children!"[43] If humans are all born Epicurean, women remain in this condition throughout their lives.

As Diderot describes them, with some sympathy, women are regularly at the mercy of men, both because they are naturally more "delicate"[44] and because they are the victims of tyrannical masculine impulses. They are often poorly educated and ill-prepared to weather the suffering that is so frequently part of their lot—as young girls subject to their parents, as wives subject to their husbands, and as mothers subject to the "infirmities" that accompany pregnancy and delivery. But, even in their weakness, women retain a particular force, an energetic vitality reminiscent of the constructive power of nature herself, not only sexed but raced. As Diderot explains:

> Nothing penetrates beyond a certain depth of conviction in the understanding of women; . . . ideas of justice, of virtue, of vice, of goodness, of wickedness swim on the surface of their soul; . . . they have preserved their self-regard and self-interest with all the energy of nature, and . . . more civilized than we are on the outside, they have remained true savages within.[45]

The consequences of women's heightened sensitivity are dire—for them and for those who might fall under the spell of their irrational and damaging enthusiasms—but these effects, public and private, arise from the fact of embodiment in general. At the same time, the phenomenon of embodiment is limned here in both gendered and racialized terms. The natural plasticity of matter undergirds and threatens women's capacity to take on the attributes of the "civilized" subject. Simultaneously, women reconcile the conflicting tensions of nature and culture by giving a specific form to the intensities of desire.

Diderot's account of femininity stresses women's difference from (white) men at the same time as he implies that the feminine condition is in fact at one point or another universally shared—an index of matter's malleability. This means that it is masculinity that becomes the exception to the rule. Epicurean materialism seems to find in matter itself the artifices, energies, and vicissitudes of a femininity that is present at the point of origin of the Epicurean Garden, to which women are invited. If feminine characteristics cannot be excluded from the account of human subjectivity in general, women themselves should not be de facto shut out from the materialist enterprise more generally. The Epicurean Garden becomes a prototype of a "new" kind of philosophy in which desiring bodies are both present and restrained, in which men and women might share in a reciprocal understanding of nature's work, both powerful and delicate. But women's role in this undertaking is a specific one. They are there to serve as particularly generative examples, partners in the project of philosophy by virtue of the inspiration and exchange they provide and elicit. As Diderot points out in *Sur les femmes*:

> While we read in books, they read in the great book of the world. In this way their ignorance inclines them to receive truth promptly when one shows it to them. No authority has subjugated them; whereas truth finds at the entrance to our skulls the figure of a Plato, an Aristotle, an Epicurus, a Zeno, standing sentinel, and armed with pikes to push it back. They are rarely systematic, always at the mercy of the moment. Thomas says not one word of the advantages of a traffic in women for the man of letters; and he is an ingrate. The soul of women is not more honest than ours, but decency not allowing them to explain themselves with our frankness, they generate a delicate kind of warbling, with the help of which one says honestly all one wishes once one has been called into their aviary. . . . They still accustom us to add appeal and clarity to the most dry and thorny matters. One speaks to them incessantly; one wants to be heard by them; one fears fatiguing or annoying them; and one acquires a particular facility of expression, that moves from conversation into style. When they have genius, I think its marks are more original in them than in us.[46]

Here the image of traffic in women, already discussed in the Introduction, returns as a positive mode of exchange. Unlike Montesquieu, Diderot embraces and celebrates the ability of women and feminine persons to command masculine attention. Far from being a source of corruption, they are in a real sense a source of philosophic energy and appeal. Femininity as an attitude of responsiveness—unhindered by philosophical convention—stands at the origin of empirical knowledge. But, unlike Epicurus, women remain governed by the dictates of the moment, beholden to the demands of decency, infantile in both their responsiveness and their lack of systematicity. Interaction with them has intrinsic interest for the man of letters, just as the ability of Epicurus to surround himself with women reveals the fundamental *rightness* of his conception of human happiness—its universality and simplicity. But this interaction is not sufficient for philosophy to emerge.

While the recognition of femininity as a kind of universal condition may be at the beginning of the materialist project, as Diderot figures it, it is not at the end of it. Epicurus himself is not fully feminine; he remains "in disguise" as a woman. Beneath this disguise, he is nonetheless recognizable as an authentic philosopher. But can materiality be understood outside or beyond its connection to the feminine? How does one make oneself a Stoic, to follow the terms of Diderot's formulation in the *Encyclopédie*, which suggests that the transition from a first (Epicurean) materialism to a second (Stoic) one tracks the movement from being to becoming? In the *Eléments de physiologie*, which he worked on up until his own death, Diderot gives a compelling—and in its own way haunting—answer to this question. He writes:

> A fantasy that is quite common in the living, is to imagine oneself dead, to be standing next to one's cadaver and to follow the funeral procession. It's like a swimmer who looks at his clothes spread out on the shore. Men that we fear no longer, what have you heard?
>
> Another apprenticeship for death is philosophy, a habitual and profound meditation that removes us from everything around us and annihilates us. The fear of death, says the Stoic, is a handle by which the strong man seizes us and leads us where he will. Break the handle, and evade the hand of the strong.[47]

Death is presented in these paragraphs as the end of the threatening receptivity that is one condition of material existence in general; the dead are no longer vulnerable to the pressures of anxiety or the injunctions of the powerful.[48] In its philosophical incarnation as in our fantasies, the experience of death is ultimately different from the instances of dissipation (of self-destruction and obliteration) to which we all—and women in particular—are prone as material bodies. The dream of attending one's own funeral appears here as the desire for a self that is both materially present to itself and capable of reflecting on this self-presence. The philosopher, in his meditations, is finally released from the constraints that typify embodiment; his own body becomes part of a panorama of objects, viewed from afar and with detachment, as clothes strewn upon the shore, part of the "general spectacle of nature" perhaps that Epicurus himself was so readily able to apprehend. He realizes, in this way, a fantasy that is "common in the living"—a ghostly materiality that resembles the flight of the genius into knowledge. Where Epicurus disguises himself— initially concealing his masculinity with his feminine appeal to pleasure—the Enlightenment materialist haunts himself—dreaming of disembodiment in a world made relentlessly of things. But in this haunting he casts those first feminine garments aside. The turn to Epicureanism, for Diderot, may help us to make sense of our birth—and of our common origins. But the Stoic materialism to which he increasingly turned toward the end of his life invites us to make of our own inevitable annihilation the condition of a more virile knowledge. In this way it remains inaccessible to those whose special genius is sutured to the discontinuity, diversity, and multifariousness of nature herself.

La Mettrie's Fluid Voluptuaries

The relationship between Diderot and his fellow materialist Julien Offray de La Mettrie has been the object of a certain amount of scholarly attention, most notably and productively in work by Aram Vartanian and, more recently, Ann Thomson. As Thomson and Vartanian both point out, it is unclear whether the two men ever met, although they did know of one another and, to a certain extent, traveled in overlapping intellectual and social circles. They may even have been inspired by one another at various junctures in the evolution of their materialisms, as Vartanian argues. Certainly they were linked in the general treatment of their writing as scandalous and anti-orthodox, united in the perceived audacity of their thought. In 1746, the Parlement of Paris condemned both the *Histoire naturelle de l'âme* (La Mettrie, 1745) and the *Pensées philosophiques* (Diderot, 1746) to be lacerated and burned together. Around the same time, La Mettrie wrote admiringly of Diderot, in the *Supplément à l'Ouvrage de Pénélope* (a satire of the medical establishment composed in the late 1740s): "What genius! what talents! and at what an age! *Homo magnae spei*."[49] Yet Diderot also takes pains, later in his career, to distance himself from La Mettrie as the author of texts often invoked as ciphers for the ethical scandal of materialism. In the *Essai sur les règnes de Claude et de Néron*, he writes that "La Mettrie is an author without judgment . . . : whose head is so troubled, and whose ideas are so detached from one another, that on the same page a sensible assertion abuts a crazy one, and a crazy assertion abuts a sensible one, so that it is as easy to defend him as it is to attack him. . . . He died as he should have, victim of his intemperance and madness."[50] For Diderot, the "trouble" in La Mettrie's thinking leads to a troubled mode of argumentation; the absence of judgment extends from the works themselves to a dissolute and intemperate way of life. La Mettrie's materialism is "bad" not only because it is poorly argued but because it is lowly, groveling, concerned more with things than with ideas.

Their differences notwithstanding, the two authors have in common a sustained interest in femininity, presented sometimes as an experience, sometimes a mode of embodiment, and sometimes a receptive style, but always as a key site of materialist inquiry. This interest takes on different forms at different moments in the two bodies of work, acquiring in La Mettrie's accounts a personal dimension that implies not just a desire for women or an investment in matter as a feminine form but a dream of feminine becoming that implicates the philosopher himself. La Mettrie's variant of *devenir-femme* evokes a through line extending from the Lucretian source text, through Cyrano de Bergerac, who like La Mettrie worked to conjoin Epicureanism with a perverse Cartesianism, and ultimately up to the radical empiricism of Deleuze and Guattari. Throughout his corpus, La Mettrie elaborates on his own philosophical position as a feminine or feminized one, suggesting on various occasions that the endorsement of materialism is also an investment in an exquisite receptivity or penetrability typical of feminine persons and feminine bodies. Where Diderot experiments mainly in literary contexts with the possibility of fully articulating a feminine subjectivity or taking on a feminine voice, La Mettrie plays with the elaboration of a feminine epistemology as the privileged work of philosophy itself. It is perhaps for this reason (among others) that Diderot is able to accuse him of the sort of disordered and contradictory thinking that was so often ascribed to women, despite Diderot's own appreciation for feminine sociability as a zone of materialist exchange.

La Mettrie's emphasis in his natural philosophy on fluidity and porosity as key attributes of all bodies generates a materialism in which men are free to explore a certain femininity that traverses diverse states of being and disparate functions, including the act of generation.[51] Not only might women acquire or demonstrate a seminal capacity, but the seed-bearing body of the ejaculating man can, under the right conditions, also be or become a feminine one.[52] As in Diderot's discussion of the Epicurean dimensions of all human experience, however, it is not clear that this flexible exchange of attributes works in all directions. That is to say, it remains ambiguous whether feminine bodies could, for La Mettrie, take up the most salient qualities of masculinity, or indeed whether they might ever assume the position of the philosopher who is both immersed in the materiality that he depicts and capable of reflecting on this immersion, often as a spur to his own desires.

In his 1746 essay *L'École de la volupté*, which he reworked throughout his short life (and which predates the composition of his most famous work, *L'Homme-machine*), La Mettrie celebrates the power of the voluptuous imagination as "the art of self-deception" [*l'art de se tromper*]. This capacity, described as both a means and mode of perception, heightens and enhances pleasurable experience by redoubling it. "It is [the imagination] that gives value to everything, it warms the heart, where it helps to create desires, and inspires the means of satisfying them. In examining pleasure, which it inspects, as it were, the microscope that imagination appears to use enlarges and exaggerates it."[53] Voluptuousness is thus intrinsically linked to the ability of literature to cultivate the effects of pleasure within and on the body. As Hal Gladfelder has discussed, and as I have explored in an earlier book, the voluptuary as La Mettrie imagines him is a figure not only of sensual flexibility but of fluidity, at ease with (and even seeking out) masculine and feminine forms of responsiveness to a world that is always parsed through the imagination. The voluptuous reader is not constrained by gender in his appreciation of sexual objects that retain a poetic dimension. To take one example of this absence of constraint, at one point in his essay La Mettrie breathlessly describes the tale, from the *Satyrica* 85–87, of the Pergamene ephebe. Of the author Petronius he writes, "How he tells the story of the Pergamene schoolboy! great gods! the lovely child! would beauty be for all the sexes? does nothing limit its empire?"[54] As La Mettrie reads him, Petronius is capable of inspiring desire in mainly masculine readers for bodies of all kinds and all genders, although he always does so with finesse and with delicacy. Petronius's prose is in itself voluptuous—lively yet elegant, restrained yet impassioned—and thus generates a voluptuous response in the readers who enjoy him, no matter the object that it takes up.

The art of voluptuousness is an inherently poetic art, based in the capacity to reflect and rework sensations in the body of the sensing subject, so that the latter exist simultaneously as material effects and as images of themselves. *Volupté* is also a fundamentally receptive condition. But the fluid responsiveness of the *voluptueux* is more than just an ability to appreciate beauty in its various forms. It is also, in itself, a kind of softness—a *mollesse*, as La Mettrie puts it, that allows both body and mind to become porous, penetrable, malleable in form and in essence. As La Mettrie describes a certain group of voluptuous authors, "they don't have a single sensation into which they fail to withdraw softly, as it were, and this softness [*mollesse*], through which a more profound impression penetrates intimately into the senses, is true sensuality."[55] In this context, women serve as both an inspiration and an example for men, since voluptuousness is the ability to be seduced—to give oneself up to perception as an image of the sensation that it activates. It is true that La Mettrie describes this kind of pleasure in terms that evoke masculine conquest, but in doing so he places the putatively male reader in the position of the feminine object of desire: "How to resist it!" he exclaims of *volupté* itself. "In the entire universe, everything cedes to its power. How could our hearts be secured against it? Thought does not have time to put them on the defensive; but if there is more pleasure in being conquered than in conquering, such a defeat is worth a victory, the senses triumph in the bosom of voluptuousness."[56] There is increased pleasure in the losing than in the winning—with this remark La Mettrie frames voluptuousness as itself a kind of seducer (perhaps a feminine one at that, given the term's association with the Lucretian Venus) and positions the *voluptueux* at the delightful mercy of pleasure's force. Later on in the essay, La Mettrie will double down on this inversion of roles by inviting women to seduce their sleeping lovers (who remain, in this situation, incapable of consent). In his description of a sleeping man stimulated by a wakeful woman, La Mettrie underscores first the passivity of the masculine body, which lies "assoupi" or drowsy on the breast of his beloved. He enjoins the feminine partner to take her own pleasure in imagining her lover dreaming of her, invoking the abandon that will result, only to then turn back to the more conventional scenario in which the sleeping body of the woman offers itself in turn to the admiring gaze of the man. In both instances, however, the ideal voluptuous state is one of "demi-réveil," a suspension between waking and sleeping, where *mollesse* reigns and the body fails to master or possess itself.

Unlike his more famous *L'Homme-machine*, *L'École de la volupté* is explicitly poetic in its investments, interests, and framing. Yet the voluptuous imagination, receptive and yielding, plays a key role *L'Homme-machine* as well, tempting as it might be to understand the titular machine-man as a figure of cold rigidity, in the model of a contemporary android or automaton. La Mettrie begins the text with a letter to the Swiss scientist Albrecht von Haller (1708–1777) that (maliciously) stresses the analogy between the work of science and the sex act, comparing the "catalepsy" of study, in which the mind gives itself entirely to that which it wishes to understand, to the ecstasies of love. "In the end Study has its Ecstasies," he writes, "like Love. If I may be permitted to say so, it's a Catalepsy, or immobility of the Mind, so deliciously drunk on the object that fixes and fascinates it, that it seems detached through abstraction from its own body and everything that surrounds it, in order to be entirely at one with that which it pursues."[57] Like the lover, the scientist is utterly enthralled by the objects of his interest—so much so that he is no longer himself. Instead, he merges with that which he wishes to know, in an image of scholarly cathexis that also evokes the moment in *L'École de la volupté* where the bodies of two lovers dissolve into one another, "where the soul seems to leave us to pass into the adored object, where two lovers make only one heart, one mind animated by love."[58] As La Mettrie points out, the potential intensity of intellectual enjoyment is such that it too must be managed and regulated, like the sensual pleasures that it resembles. If the philosopher is in a sense disembodied in and by his attachment to knowledge, the effect of this "abstraction" is not to project him into the realm of ideas, but to anchor him more securely to the object that he desires to understand.

Yet it is not only the sensation of pleasure that cuts across the domains of scholarly and sexual activity. La Mettrie also suggests, in the preceding paragraph, that the act of thinking is itself analogous to that of generation. "What is this generation, this birthing of Ideas, that the taste for Nature and the search for Truth produce?" he asks. "How to depict this Act of Will, or of Memory, by which the Soul reproduces itself in a way, by joining an idea to another similar trace, so that through their resemblance and as if through their union, a third is born: for do admire the productions of nature. Such is its uniformity, that almost all of them occur in the same way."[59] In this cheeky—and certainly tongue-in-cheek—analogy, the mind of the philosopher/scholar becomes the womb in which new ideas are generated. Like the body, the soul is capable of reproducing itself—activating the same kinds of natural mechanisms in order to engender progeny.

While the comparison between scholarship and sex is certainly at least in part a jab at Haller, who was known for his religious devotion, La Mettrie continues to develop the analogy in the body of the essay, where he refers at least twice to the brain as the "Matrice" [womb/matrix] of thought. In the second of these references, he echoes the point he first made in the dedication, returning to the image of the act of thinking as a reproduction of the soul, an "enfantement" of ideas. But in this instance he develops the analogy in two directions, masculine *and* feminine. He writes:

> But also what would be the fruit of the most excellent School, without a Womb/Matrix perfectly open to the entrance, or to the conception of ideas. It is just as impossible to give a sole idea to a Man, deprived of all senses, as it is to give a Child to a Woman, toward whom Nature would have been so excessively distracted as to have forgotten to make her a Vulva, as I witnessed in the case of one woman, who had neither Slit, nor Vagina, nor Womb, and for this reason was disavowed after ten years of marriage.[60]

Here, as in *L'École de la volupté*, thought becomes a form of seduction. The senses of the philosopher are depicted as the means by which ideas enter the body, rendering the work of philosophy a libertine zone of generation. More specifically, the "open" mind of the masculine thinker is directly and explicitly compared to the "open" uterus, transforming the male philosopher into the figure of a libertine woman. The receptive intellect is a space of conception in a dual sense. Within this same framework, La Mettrie also explores the negative example of the man deprived of sensory perception, comparing him to a woman who not only cannot conceive, but cannot be penetrated. The doubled comparison to the feminine body—in one instance, perfectly opened, and in the other, unnaturally closed—underlines the masculinity of the philosopher himself, even as this masculinity shows itself to be capable of taking on a feminine position. This passage suggests that the dissolution of the male philosopher into a state of feminine receptivity—a situation that allows for ideas to germinate—does not work in reverse. The "open" woman is not, in her openness, a source of conceptual innovation or discovery, but rather an instance of matter's thoughtless generativity. On the other hand, the example of the impenetrable woman is not a positive demonstration of nature's vitality and variability, but rather is presented as a moment of distraction—a slip or error analogous to (but not the same as) the production of a man unable to feel or think.

The image of a woman without a vagina has a brutal offhandedness about it, but it also preoccupied its author. La Mettrie underscores the monstrousness of this same woman's body in *Système d'Épicure* (1750), where he returns to her example in language that is both more dehumanizing and more direct.[61] Here he writes of having seen this person with his own eyes, describing her as "without sex, an indefinable animal, totally castrated in the maternal bosom."[62] "It was necessary to give up on the project of making a vulva for her," he writes, since she had no uterus at all—a discovery that was made by introducing a scalpel into the place where her vulva would have been. Her husband had continued to have sex with her over ten years of marriage, believing that "the passageway of the bowel movements was that of generation," a mistake that La Mettrie attributes to the mutual stupidity of both husband and wife (the latter seeking to hide something unconcealable, the former credulously trusting her).[63] Her body, described as unproductive and ambiguous, is also portrayed by La Mettrie as the ultimate example of nature's capacity for error—a singular kind of forgetfulness that justifies and explains the existence of other, lesser imperfections. According to La Mettrie, not only is this woman lacking the capacity to generate other bodies, she is also without the ability to experience sexual pleasure. In her nature "sleeps" [*s'endort*], errs, "plays," and "forgets."[64] The gratuitous violence of the experiments done on her body—including the introduction of the scalpel, the stimulation of her clitoris, and the disavowal of her marriage—is justified by the (assumed) insensibility of the person upon whom they are performed. La Mettrie reveals here how an emphasis on gender fluidity may coexist with a transphobic position on gender identity.

"This woman without a sex" is portrayed as monstrous on the one hand—in a way that notably positions her as an "unnatural" woman rather than as trans or nonbinary—but at the same she expresses attributes of nature itself as unthinking or unselfconscious. La Mettrie's discussion of her in *Système d'Épicure* appears as the fourteenth entry in a series of fragmentary thoughts, inspired in part by Lucretius, that are organized around an extended critique of finalist accounts of nature. *Système* opens with a comparison of natural bodies to the soap bubbles blown by a child—produced simply, without thought or even real intention, on the fly. In this instance nature herself is portrayed as insensible, as La Mettrie puts it in the fourth fragment: "How to *catch nature in the act*? She has never caught herself there. Stripped of knowledge and of feeling, she makes silk, like the *Bourgeois gentilhomme* makes prose, without knowing it."[65] Lacking conscious awareness and feeling, personified nature acts without intelligence. The supposed "imbecility" of the woman with neither vulva nor uterus, a figure of nature's distraction, is thus anticipated in the image of nature herself, who also fails to think and feel. Yet, in this failure, nature, unlike the woman (who appears later in the text), remains astonishingly, even hauntingly, generative. In a series of reflections of obviously Lucretian influence (from fragment 5 through fragment 13), La Mettrie paints a portrait of a natural world from which emerges a swirl or flux of bodies—engendered in the air, in the earth, in water, and only belatedly in the uteruses of humans. On the one hand, this portrait at first seems to emphasize the primacy of an explicitly seminal model of reproduction: The air, La Mettrie explains, is rife with seeds that are carried hither and thither with the wind. From these small bodies—reminiscent of the atom—come not only the plants that cover the earth but the insects that inhabit it. In the seventh fragment, however, the seed-based model morphs, perhaps unexpectedly, into a uterine one: If seeds are transported across the earth by the air, the air itself is "their first womb," La Mettrie writes. But this matrix is not alone: In fact it is only the first in a tripartite series that includes, "the spermatic vessels, the testicles, the seminal vesicles," and only after these the "third and last womb": that of woman (as La Mettrie himself puts it).[66]

The portrayal of the air as a domain of seminal dispersion shifts here into a depiction of the world and its inhabitants as matrices (regardless of gender).

In the tenth fragment, with an image drawn directly from Lucretius, La Mettrie suggests that the earth itself might have "served as a *uterus* for man," becoming thus the common mother of all animate bodies.[67] Uteruses seem to occur everywhere, including in the male organs of generation, and beings proliferate thanks not only to the mixing of seeds but to the multiplication of hospitable environments that are designed to receive and to nurture. In fact, sperm needs the matrix of the testicle in order to become, itself, capable of generation. La Mettrie uses these multilayered descriptions of ever-shifting and transmogrifying matter in order to justify his critique of final causes: Bodies, as he points out, are chaotic, various, imperfect, and ever-changing. As the seminal figure of the seed morphs into the uterine image of the matrix, the reader might recall how machine-man softens into a receptive and malleable body as he puts his imagination to work, while the masculine sphere of the philosopher opens up to reveal the femininity of matter itself, of which both thoughts and bodies are made. Femininity is not just one position accessible to men among others: It is the very condition of a materiality that is anti-finalist, changeable, yielding, and ultimately voluptuous. The ideal materialist philosopher, who seeks to cultivate his connection to matter's pliability, is in some basic sense, for La Mettrie, affirmatively and actively feminine.

However, the generative chain of a natural world pulsing with reproductive verve—in which uteruses nest within one another like so many Russian dolls—is interrupted by the instance of the "monstrous" woman whose body can engender *neither* children *nor* thoughts, and who stands out as a primary example of nature's distraction (even in a situation where nature is characterized to a certain extent by "her" distractibility, as in the analogy of the child with the soap bubbles). La Mettrie thereby reveals that, for him, the condition of malleability does not apply equally (or equitably) to all bodies. The "monstrous" woman, who fails to exhibit the primary characteristics attributed to her gender, is presented as closed off, physically and intellectually, and in her closure becomes an object of particularly brutal modes of experimentation. If the attributes of femininity are accessible to the masculine philosopher as a form of fluidity, a zone of play and pleasure, the invitation to penetrability turns, in the case of the "woman without a sex," into violence. As in Diderot's comparison of the Stoic adult to the Epicurean infant, the "becoming-woman" of La Mettrie's materialist philosopher invites men both to contemplate and enjoy their femininity—as a condition of what it means to be a materialist—and thereby embraces Epicurean effeminacy as the very nexus (or even matrix) of philosophy. At the same time, La Mettrie remains deeply ambivalent about how bodies presumptively gendered as women might participate in the delicious receptivity that he sees as fundamental to both thought and being and that extends, for him, across both texts and bodies, figures and matter. The "monstrous" woman cannot make up for the absence of a uterus by accessing other modes of generativity: Indeed, her lack of receptivity becomes an inability to think or understand, in a disordered or forgetful image of nature herself. Under these conditions, can any person assigned a feminine gender effectively play the role of a philosopher?

To begin to answer this question I would like to turn to three moments in La Mettrie's corpus where he appears to engage directly with one of the most famous (if not *the* most famous) woman philosophers of his era—namely Émilie Du Châtelet, whose corpus is the focus of Chapter 3 of this book. La Mettrie's first published philosophical work, *L'Histoire naturelle de l'âme*, initially came out in 1745, prior to its condemnation (alongside Diderot's *Pensées philosophiques* as mentioned earlier) by the Paris Parlement in 1746. In 1747, a new edition of *L'Histoire naturelle* appeared, with the place of publication indicated as "A Oxford, Aux dépends de l'Auteur." This 1747 edition is prefaced by a document entitled "Lettre critique de Mr de La Mettrie sur *L'Histoire naturelle de l'âme* à Madame la Marquise du Chattelet." In a gesture that other critics have often seen as ironic, presuming it to be made by La Mettrie himself, the author of the letter praises Du Châtelet for her dissemination of the Leibnizian system in France and criticizes the text to which the letter itself is appended for its materialism. The letter concludes by reinforcing the compliment to Du Châtelet at La Mettrie's expense: "In any case his history resembles the majority of Philosophical Books; it's a real spectacle offered to the imagination, even while railing against it. Few Physicians know, Madame, as you do, how to join the severity of reasoning with the elegant dignity of Style."[68] But this is not the only piece of correspondence that has been taken as evidence of a connection, whether intellectual or physical, between the two philosophers. Also in 1747, a "third edition" of *La Volupté* appeared (with place of publication given as "Londres"), with a dedication to "Madame la Marquise de ****," an anonymous lady who has been identified by a number of critics (including notably Aram Vartanian and Ursula Jauch) as Du Châtelet.

Ann Thomson, in an article investigating the nature of La Mettrie's links to Du Châtelet, gives a convincing argument against the attribution of the "Lettre critique" to La Mettrie himself, and moreover contends that the dedication, in which La Mettrie reflects on a shared experience of sexual pleasure with the unnamed dedicatee, does not provide on its own any indication of a connection to Du Châtelet. As part of this more general critique of the tendency of scholars to presume a relationship between the two authors, Thomson also cites another passage in La Mettrie's corpus that has sometimes been taken to refer to Du Châtelet, once again debunking the ascription. The passage, taken from the 1750 edition of La Mettrie's *Anti-Sénèque*, reads as follows:

> And who, at the sight of such a well-done book, would not boo this ridiculous *petite maîtresse*, who, wanting to set her voice of a witty little gossip against so many enlightened advocates, standing on the shoulders of he who lends her something other than his pen, only rose up against the first man of his age because, apparently placing happiness there where she often finds it, she thought him as common and, to say it in the terms of my art, as *vulgivagous* as she.[69]

As Thomson correctly points out, the woman referenced here is not Du Châtelet but Madeleine de Puisieux, whose materialist leanings and association with Diderot I will discuss in Chapter 2. La Mettrie is here rather viciously denigrating Puisieux for her criticism (in her moral work *Les Caractères*) of Maupertuis's *Essai de philosophie morale* (1749), to which she claimed to prefer Fontenelle's rather more literary essay on happiness. As Thomson points out, "At this time Mme de Puisieux was Denis Diderot's lover, and Diderot was said to have contributed to, if not completely written, *Les caractères*, which is what La Mettrie is also referring to in the above quotation and not to Voltaire, as has been supposed. This reference raises therefore the question of the author's relationship not so much to Émilie Du Châtelet as to Diderot."[70] In his description of her, La Mettrie depicts Puisieux as empty-headed and meretricious, a social climber and a liar. At the end of the passage, with which he concludes the body of *Anti-Sénèque*, he settles on the term *vulgivagous* (which he italicizes) to condemn Puisieux as both a failed author and a slut.

While it is not necessarily surprising that La Mettrie should draw a connection between Puisieux's literary ambitions and her promiscuity—since this kind of slur is (and to a certain extent remains) standard misogynist fare—the use of "vulgivague" in this context is interesting for its connection specifically to the long history of materialist philosophy, since it is a term originally coined by Lucretius in the *DRN*. In book four of the poem, in which Lucretius explores the experience of erotic desire (among other topics), he refers to "wandering," "undiscriminating," or "vagrant" Venus—*vulgivaga Venere*—in his endorsement of promiscuity as a cure for the wounds of love.[71] Notably, Lucretius's deployment of the term at this moment has a positive valence (unlike La Mettrie's): Promiscuity is recommended in order to resist attachment to a single partner. Basil Dufallo has argued for the use of the term in this context as a way of reinforcing a distinction between journeys or wanderings that may bring or sustain pleasure and other forms of motion that are erroneous or errant. Moreover, while the qualifier is associated with prostitution—literally,

Venus is "crowd-wandering" here—the lack of discrimination in erotic practice does not connote for Lucretius an absence of philosophical attitude—on the contrary. *Vulgivaga* or "vagrant" Venus is one dimension of Venus among others. As Julie Giovacchini has put it in reference to the Lucretian epic, "The great lesson of this text is probably that these disparate conceptions of sexuality are not contradictory; rather, they correspond to distinct 'measured' ways, in the sense that they are subjected to the rational calculation of pursuing pleasure."[72] In the Roman context, where chastity was considered a significant aspect of male civic virtue, the endorsement of the wandering Venus as an important signifier of sexuality is all the more unusual since it reinforces the association of Epicureans with effeminacy, understood here as an absence of sexual continence and a capitulation to bodily desires.

La Mettrie's deployment of "vulgivague" is quite different. He uses the term in order to stress the failure of Puisieux to adhere to philosophical norms and standards and to identify her as a bad sort of materialist—someone who finds her pleasure (and thus her happiness) in the wrong place. In contrast to his celebration of masculine voluptuousness, in its fluid and wandering dimensions, he uses this term evocative of a Venusian vagrancy to denigrate a feminine person whose writing (and thought) are inappropriately proximate to the erotic sphere. Unlike the masculine thinker who can be penetrated by ideas just as he is receptive to sexual sensations—who can find in the tropings of his pleasures across various kinds of texts and artifacts an expression of the movement of matter across the cosmos—the woman author is sullied by virtue of the way in which she combines intellectual and sexual enjoyment. (Indeed, her sexual enjoyment negates and vitiates her intellectual claims.) In returning to the Lucretian term—but as a denigration rather than a positive qualifier—La Mettrie suggests that the voluptuous woman remains, at best, a philosophical object rather than a subject. If the *femme manquée* is closed off (and imbecilic), the *philosophe manquée* is too open (and as a result too common) to be taken seriously. Feminine form is thus accessible to men—in fact, it is the means by which bodies emerge as such—but feminine philosophy remains inaccessible to women. It requires a masculinized, indeed masculinist, sociability—a momentary extraction from the exigencies of materiality—in order to be made fully legible. If it is in pleasure that matter and image come together in voluptuous delight, it is the masculine subject that anticipates, enjoys, and surveys this conjunction, in a movement that anticipates and rehearses the passage of time toward death (as in Diderot's comparison of the philosopher with the dead man observing his funeral procession). As La Mettrie writes in *L'Homme-machine*, "Always carried away by the whirlwind of blood and the Spirits; a wave makes a mark, erased by the one which follows;

the Soul runs after, often in vain: It must expect to regret that which it hasn't seized and fixed upon quickly enough: and it is thus that the imagination, authentic Image of time, ceaselessly destroys and renews itself."[73]

Helvétius and Feminine Enlightenment

My argument thus far has been that the feminization of embodiment—and thus, in some sense, of the object of philosophy—cuts across and binds together the work of Diderot and La Mettrie, notwithstanding the differences in their ideas about the nature of matter itself. For both of these thinkers, albeit in distinct ways, feminine receptivity is the primary condition of having a body—thereby bringing into the open the "obscure" existence of the Epicurean philosopher, whose life lived in pleasure is said by Plutarch to be no life at all. If both of these philosophers write gender as fluid, at least to a certain extent, in the end they also both endorse the triumph of masculinity over femininity as the only way in which an always contingent continuity of thought, memory, and experience can be assured. They arrest the material crossings that they underscore in the intellectual work and community of the masculine philosopher.

For his part, Claude-Adrien Helvétius, another materialist writing around this same *tournant*, transfers the productive potential of feminine receptivity—and the delight and interest it inspires—into the sphere of historical periodization. He positions femininity as not just the primary spur to enjoyment, but the impetus of enlightenment itself, thereby transposing the generative capacities of feminine form from the individual to the social body. Helvétius composed a poem on happiness, entitled *Le Bonheur*, in the 1740s, at a time when he was frequenting the Parisian salons of women including Claudine de Tencin (1682–1749), Marie-Thérèse Geoffrin (1699–1777), and perhaps most notably for the purposes of this book, Françoise de Graffigny, who introduced him to his future wife and with whom he remained close. The poem predates the more famous (and controversial) materialist texts for which Helvétius remains known: namely *De l'esprit* (first published in 1758) and *De l'homme* (published posthumously in 1773), but it did not appear in print until 1772. It was Jean-François de Saint-Lambert, lover of Du Châtelet and member of the Académie française, who took charge of eventually publishing the poem following the death of Helvétius in 1771. *Le Bonheur* thus stems from a relatively early moment in Helvétius's thought and career, at a time when he was immersed in salon culture, on the verge of falling in love with the woman who would become his wife, and not yet known for his contributions to the more radical materialism that would slowly emerge in and around the late 1740s and the 1750s (a transition in which all of the men discussed in this chapter participated).

If Diderot and La Mettrie position the femininity of matter—and the *douceur* of the materialist philosopher—in some sense at the level of the material particles that make up bodies and their faculties, Helvétius in *Le Bonheur* is interested in the softness and sweetness of voluptuous pleasure as, first, a moral problem, and second, a political and social one. He deals with this problem in allegorical terms, narrating an encounter between the lyric voice of the poet and the feminine figure of Wisdom that becomes an exploration of not just personal but collective happiness. The poem is divided into four sections, or songs, and concludes with the fable of Oromaze and Ariman, two divinities who preside over a first age of human happiness, on the one hand, and a subsequent period of human suffering on the other. In the final song or *chant*, the poem suggests that benevolent political rule—focused on the cultivation of knowledge and the arts as opposed to the conquest of land and territories—might bring back that "age of happiness" with which human history opens. (At this point, the setting is not in France or even in an unspecified pastoral garden but on the banks of the Indus River, where the human race is said to have originated.) Throughout, Helvétius makes clear that pleasure is the key to happiness, but by this he does not simply mean following desire where it may lead. Love, as he suggests, is perhaps the most intense delight to which humanity is privy, but the first song of the poem is devoted to exposing the limitations of both erotic (or voluptuous) pleasure and ambition where happiness is concerned. In the poet's description of the pleasures of love, Wisdom takes the lyric speaker to a bosky grove where *la Mollesse*, the goddess of softness, reigns supreme. Reclining half naked, her dress and scarf lifted by the promiscuous breezes at play about her, the divinity is clearly meant to stimulate the voyeuristic interest of reader and poet alike. Fictional lovers Rinaldo and Armida, alongside the mythical couple Omphale and Hercules, swoon in one another's arms. The space is dedicated, above all, to erotic enjoyment: "In this place, everything is engaged in voluptuous delight./It is here that Love, prolonging its intoxication,/Discovers a new art for stimulating desire/And for multiplying the form of the pleasures."[74]

But this degree of intensity cannot be preserved indefinitely: As Wisdom points out, love is of necessity a fleeting delight, vulnerable to boredom and eventually to the infirmities of old age. The trick to sustaining happiness is thus to turn, with the passage of time, to other pursuits, namely philosophy and the arts, which can continue to be enjoyed even as the body fails and the power of attraction wanes. Unlike ambition, which Helvétius rejects as consistently a source of suffering and unmet desires, love represents the opening of the human subject—and by this is meant for him a masculine person—to the voluptuous pleasures of life, rendered in the form of a beautiful woman, whose body, more often than not, merges with the natural world that frames and encloses her. Gender here is naturalized in one sense, but only in a context where nature itself is rendered in highly artificial terms, a lushly animate yet always figurative setting where all bodies (human, animal, and vegetable) conspire to awaken and stimulate delight, in an image of the Lucretian invocation of Venus that opens the *DRN*. As the lyric speaker describes the grove of Softness: "There by the song of the birds my ear is charmed;/There by flowering bushes the earth is perfumed./Their fragrant spirits, their shadow, their freshness,/Everything invites my senses and my heart to love:/In these enchanted realms everything breathes intoxication."[75] The work of Wisdom is not to refuse love, or even to deny its power, but to modulate its effects; the youth of the philosopher may be dedicated to erotic pleasures, but always with the knowledge that these are finite, fleeting, and liable to slip or morph into the vicissitudes of ennui. Art and scholarship are present to supplement and to nurture the capacity of the human subject to seek enjoyment across the changing landscape of a life, in different modes at different moments.

The final song, which enjoins rulers to treat their subjects justly and with love, returns to the dynamic through which love becomes amenable to and finally joins with the pursuit of knowledge and truth. The couple Élidor and Netzanire are described as beloved by the benevolent god Oromaze, a charming example of erotic and marital felicity. Netzanire's beauty is burnished and heightened by the edenic natural setting that she inhabits, yet her effect on Élidor is incomparably more powerful than that of any natural phenomenon. In a moment that recalls La Mettrie's depiction of the voluptuous dissolution of one lover into another, Élidor cries out: "'How different I am when I see you!/All my being transforms in approaching you./The heavens link my love to my existence;/It's through you that I feel, it's through you that I think.'"[76] Where the beauties of the universe leave him fully master of his own emotions, the charms of Netzanire undo and transport him. But the couple cannot remain in their idyllic, erotic garden, since the era of Oromaze is soon followed by the ascension of Ariman, who sets about destroying all that is good. It is in this context that Netzanire begs Élidor to confront Ariman and to devote himself to bringing back human happiness to the earth from which it has disappeared: "'I feel in this moment all the evils of absence/But never mind; I desire that in my agitated heart/Love gives way to humanity for several moments.'"[77] Love here takes on a social and eventually political function, whereby erotic investment is diverted and sublimated into an attachment to the collective. The role of voluptuousness is thus not only to awaken the masculine partner to the centrality of pleasure to human experience—and to the capacity of desire to knit together human and nonhuman bodies, galvanizing and eroticizing the natural world—but to ease the transition from subjective enjoyment to the pursuit of a better life for all. Thus Netzanire in her beauty enlivens nature and in her sympathy for human suffering spurs Élidor's confrontation with evil. Ultimately, Helvétius affirms, it is up to the rulers of humankind to decide whether they will rule with terror or with love, in the name of Oromaze or Ariman, either to extend and expand the pursuit of happiness or to spread cruelty and suffering.

Yet Helvétius does not end the poem with an address to kings. The last lines of Le Bonheur read: "Charming sex, it is you who once, on earth, / Armed the children of war for combat: / You can do even more for the sons of Apollo; / You give pleasures: glory is a vain name. / Through new good deeds be worthy of our homages: / You made heroes: now make wise men."[78] Here the work of femininity becomes the impetus for enlightenment—the engine of a history that contains within itself the potential for a return to a more virtuous age of human existence that is also more voluptuously inclined. If love needs to be rendered in literature in order for the power of pleasure to be known—and to be disseminated across the various readers of the work—it eventually becomes not only the impetus for a turn to the collective body but the very mechanism of history itself. Women are on the one hand positioned as the avatars of a lively and receptive nature: They are the emblem of a natural world that exists to enhance and vivify their appeal to men. On the other hand, they are given as the means by which human social life will reorient itself away from ambition and the wars that accompany it, back toward a more philosophical mode of existence in which lovers will also be wise men, in which the myrtle of Venus is intertwined with Apollo's laurels.[79] With this poem, Helvétius suggests the feminization not only of pleasure but of enlightenment itself, whereby the penetrability and receptivity of the beautiful feminine body will orient and guide the awakening to pleasure and then the search for truth. Here the feminine dimensions of experience are once again embraced, in order to allow for the retrieval of a happier and more philosophical masculinity in the name of pleasure and in the work of the text itself.

In short, Helvétius's enlightened materialism of the 1740s, like that of his fellow philosophers La Mettrie and Diderot, is also in dialogue with femininity, as a privileged trope, as an object of study, and as a form that bodies may assume (and shed). Yet this aspect of their thought is often obscured, perhaps because the feminine still remains too closely linked to the "bad" materialism of the meretricious, "wandering" woman, emblematized for La Mettrie by Madeleine de Puisieux (operating in disguise as Émilie Du Châtelet). In the chapters that follow, I want to make room for the way in which Puisieux and other eighteenth-century women react to, modify, and revise the privileging of femininity in a materialist *milieu* that is in the process of radicalizing itself. This *milieu* embraces the prestige of feminine receptivity, but it also excoriates the practice of philosophy by (certain) women. What does it mean not just to value but to experience pleasure in the form and situation of a woman, as a person to whom this gender has been assigned? How is this pleasure legible (if it is) as materialist? What might these particular feminine authors make of the productive nexus of femininity and materialism? The next three chapters will explore these questions in detail.

2
Volupté in a Ruined World: Puisieux's Libertine Images

"One ordinarily bestows upon *inclination* an honest objective; but one thinks of the objective of *penchant* as more sensual, and sometimes even shameful. Thus one says that a man has an *inclination* for the arts and the sciences, and that he has a *penchant* for debauchery and libertinism."[1]

Madeleine d'Arsant de Puisieux's writing is lucid and sometimes unforgiving, stark in its assessments of the relative pleasures afforded or denied to women in her society—even elite women like her. In her eloquent but sometimes painful accounts of how to navigate a world at once privileged and desolate, her writing consistently illuminates the way in which concepts and experience interpenetrate and inform one another. What was I hoping to find as a reader in Puisieux's work? I first discovered Puisieux when I was in search of a feminine variant of the kind of libertine materialism that had preoccupied me early on as a graduate student and later as an assistant professor writing what became my first book. La Mettrie, Diderot, even Sade—in their thought the pursuit of pleasure intertwines with radical institutional critique. Indeed, critique becomes for these authors its own mode of pleasure just as pleasure in its many forms—generous, open, cruel, unyielding, lascivious, terrifying, serene—animates thought. This entanglement of writing and feeling was something that attracted me not only to the eighteenth century but to intellectual work itself, especially at precarious moments in my career, in the absence of institutional validation. Troubling and fascinating to me in the Enlightenment interest in pleasure and its effects is the way this preoccupation modulates what criticism might set out to do—galvanize bodies, stir sentiments, transmit and intensify sensation, inspire and upend forms.

Even though Puisieux has sometimes been identified as taking up the banner of a progressive Enlightenment that speaks in the name of women and their desires, I found it difficult to position her as part of a libertine legacy of thought. Her 1752 short story entitled *Le Plaisir et la volupté*—which I read many times over many years, struggling with what appeared to be its failure to think in recognizably libertine ways—seems stilted and allegorical, uninviting to a contemporary reader in search of a contemporary message. Her materialism, such as it is, is neither lively nor vibrant. Yet Puisieux is a savvy critic, particularly regarding the intellectual and social constraints operating on women of her era, even rich and well-connected ones. She is clear-eyed about the ways in which men lay claim to women's bodies, often as a means of propelling themselves toward a version of freedom that comes at the price of feminine complicity. In fact, from very early on, her corpus takes shape around this recognition. Her short story, *Céphise, conte moral*, unpublished and of uncertain date, existing only in manuscript, is a tragic narrative about a young woman who has two children with a lover who eventually marries another woman for money, leaving the eponymous heroine to die in a hovel in the forest. What begins as a coming-of-age tale turns into a tragic narrative of social marginalization and wronged motherhood. Puisieux consistently challenges the radicalizing potential of pleasure considered as a force immune to the situations in which it arises. It is in this challenge that Puisieux's engagement with the tropes and figures of libertine fiction—including an allegorized Volupté and her beloved Plaisir—eventually became more meaningful and legible to me.

Reading a digitized version of the manuscript with some effort, eyes straining to make out the curves of the letters, I wondered if Puisieux's Céphise might be an ironic reflection on other Céphises, including Montesquieu's heroine in the short narrative piece *Céphise et l'amour* (published in 1725 as an appendage to the libertine *Temple de Gnide*), who betrays her lover rather than being betrayed by him. Puisieux's focus, in her early story, on the wrongs visited upon women in the name of desire does not explicitly function as a thematic horizon for her later writing. Still, in her moral treatises and her novels, she continues to work through the difficulties, contradictions, and painful strictures attendant upon women in her social circle. At the same time, in these more mature texts, she is regularly thinking about feminine enjoyment, a response wrought slyly if not shyly, all the more intense for carrying within it an awareness of the limits that it cannot or will not transgress. In *L'Éducation du marquis de ***, ou Mémoires de la comtesse de Zurlac* (1753), Puisieux asks of her main character, the comtesse de Zurlac, who is in love with a man not her husband: "Who will dare to affirm that love, contained within the boundaries of decency, is not itself a virtue, or does not at least give some exercise to wisdom?"[2] And indeed the Comtesse eventually finds her reward, not in a pleasure that renders her free (or that she is able to take freely), but in a new relationship with a younger man whom she trains to reconcile desire and virtue, in a feminocentric rewriting of Crébillon fils's *Les Égarements du cœur et de l'esprit*. In short, Puisieux holds few illusions about the opportunities afforded to her, and to women like her, even as she retains a materialist investment in pleasure as a human impulse and a human good—and even as she values illusion, taken in its most capacious sense as both artifice and deception, as a means by which pleasure might recur. As she writes in her moral treatise *Les Caractères*, "I prefer an error that makes me happy to a truth that makes me despair."[3]

The modes of voluptuous delight that Puisieux fosters through her writing and her moral advice are not always recognizably libertine, although she often writes about sex and desire. Yet her works at their best uncover fleeting moments when her heroines, and the other women she invokes in her moral writings, might succeed in crafting a momentary pleasure out of the strictures and limitations that so often define their existence as desiring, sensate beings. In this present day, when refusing to see the forms of violence inherent in eighteenth-century narratives of seduction can become its own exercise in willful misreading, informed by a specific attachment to patriarchal modes of power, Puisieux's sober analysis of the erotic and sentimental possibilities afforded her and other women, tipping as it does into moments of intense delight, is a strange and sometimes heady mix of the contemporary and the archaic. Her vision is both resonant beyond her period and rooted, as she may have hoped it would be, in the considerations and constraints of her own peculiar and particular world.

Puisieux Among the Materialists

In a manuscript collection of short texts by Puisieux, written in a looping, clear hand perhaps some time around 1746–1747, there is a poem entitled "Le Printems" [*Spring*] that reads in its entirety:

> Winter flees and love, caressing Nature,
> With his divine breath engenders the Zephyrs,
> Creators in their turn, they decorate the greensward
> Soon to raise altars to the pleasures.[4]

These four short lines, probably from very early on in the author's career, follow the longer poem "L'Hiver" [*Winter*] and precede another entitled "Bouquet," so that the progression from barren winter to blossoming spring is repeated in the order of the poems as they appear in the manuscript. In "Le Printems," Puisieux describes a personified nature stirring and rekindling her generative energies in response to the caresses of love, an encounter that gives rise to the setting for more (human?) pleasures yet to come. In many respects the verse is banally allegorical, typical of romantic lyric of its period. At the same time, Puisieux's four short lines resonate with a specific ancient source: the opening of the *De rerum natura* (DRN; cited in French in the endnote to highlight the echoes between the two works). Lucretius's opening lines, addressed to Venus, read in part:

> O goddess, from you the winds flee away, the clouds of heaven from you and your coming; for you the wonder-working earth puts forth sweet flowers, for you the wide stretches of ocean laugh, and heaven grown peaceful glows with outpoured light. For as soon as the vernal face of day is made manifest, and the breeze of the teeming west wind blows fresh and free, first the fowls of the air proclaim you, divine one, and your advent, pierced to the heart by your might. Next wild creatures and farm animals dance over the rich pastures and swim across rapid rivers, so greedily does each one follow you, held captive by your charm.[5]

In both poems, it is love that awakens a verdant nature to fecundity, inspiring diverse but always delectable feelings in bodies vegetal or animal. Set alongside Lucretius's cosmic vision of a natural world bursting with voluptuous delight, Puisieux's quatrain is highly restrained. Her poem is decorous and contained; Lucretius's vibrating with materialist enthusiasm. Still, for both poets, the pleasures of nature intertwine with and invoke more human forms of enjoyment—including, prominently, that of reading and writing poetry. This intertwining—wherein nature both sets the stage for pleasures to come and actively participates in them—does not immediately position either the lyric voice or the addressee amid a hierarchy of bodies and emotions. Instead, it allows the reader to feel the ways in which the forms and postures that pleasure assumes are transmissible across different kinds of beings, including the body of the text in its materiality. Puisieux, like Lucretius, invites us into a scene in which figures and sensations intermingle. But she does not exactly allow us to linger there, nor does she extract from this scene a principle.

Clearly, these two poems meet very different fates. Lucretius's materialist epic continues to serve as a touchstone for anti-orthodox critics and philosophers; Puisieux's short verse has left no obvious trace on the history of literature or philosophy. On the surface, this difference in reception is hardly surprising. Lucretius thinks big: The *DRN* inaugurates a materialist journey through the atomic world and across the visible one, where Puisieux's "Le Printems" remains a bagatelle, a fragment even in the context of her own understudied corpus. To various modern critics and readers, Lucretius in the *DRN* has seemed to beckon toward a time emergent, as in Stephen Greenblatt's presentation of the poem as an augur of modernity in *The Swerve: How the World Became Modern*.[6] Puisieux's short verse reads instead as a token of her era and little more, so tightly is it bound to the lyric conventions of her moment. The pleasure of encountering her poetry today is less that of the voyage toward a speculative future than one of immersion in a long-gone past. In short, her work does not obviously extend beyond itself—whether to invite the reader on a mind-bending philosophical trip (as Lucretius might be said to do) or even to invoke a world external to the time and place of the poem. Lightly and swiftly, her verse wraps the reader into it and just as quickly sets that reader free again—presenting on the manuscript page a series of mysteries (whose hand copied the poem? to whom might the work be addressed?) that it does not care to solve. Nadine Bérenguier has written of Puisieux's moral treatises that her cynicism does not "pass the test of time," unlike the works of some of her more famous contemporaries including Louise d'Épinay (1726–1783), Anne-Thérèse de Lambert (1647–1733), and Marie Leprince de Beaumont (1711–1780).[7] The same could certainly be said of "Le Printems," whose eternally floral spring is anything but timely. Is it possible to read this poem as part of a Lucretian inheritance?[8] Could Puisieux's work be an instance of what Gerard Passannante calls "the circulation of materialist patterns of thought beneath the threshold of conscious awareness"?[9] It is difficult to answer yes to this question, since the poem is in style *and* content almost too light, too insubstantial to be worthy of sustained notice. If it does not seek to transmit the pleasures that it limns, might it not still, in its very delicacy, put pleasure itself to work? A consideration of Puisieux's corpus suggests that her interest in the contingent deployment of pleasure's image was nonetheless sustained over a lifetime.

It is not clear to me whether Puisieux could have been reading Lucretius when she penned "Le Printems," although she was at least passingly familiar with the philosophy of Epicurus, which she discusses in her moral work *Les Caractères*, where she calls herself an Aristippean. Another moment in the same text suggests her interest in *voluptas* (in passages I will return to). But Puisieux clearly associated with another famous materialist, Denis Diderot, himself a preeminent reader of Lucretius, as mentioned in Chapter 1. Puisieux was involved romantically with Diderot while he was doing some of his most important early work, including the *Pensées philosophiques* (1746), *Les Bijoux indiscrets* (1748, sometimes said to have been written at the instigation of Puisieux herself), and perhaps most notably the *Lettre sur les aveugles* (1749). She may have penned "Le Printems" during the five years of their liaison.

The intimate scene of Puisieux's involvement with Diderot unfolds during a period that witnesses what Jonathan Israel calls in *Enlightenment Contested* "the eruption of full-scale intellectual warfare" among the *philosophes* and the radicalization of Diderot in particular.[10] But what does Puisieux's proximity to these developments mean for her work? Puisieux's relationship with Diderot certainly shaped the reception of her corpus by eighteenth-century commentators, often in predictably misogynistic ways, as contemporary feminist critics including Alice M. Laborde and, more recently, Nadine Bérenguier and Laurence Vanoflen have demonstrated.[11] As these critics point out, Diderot's influence on Puisieux's standing as an author and critic was more often than not to her detriment, his proximity to her serving to highlight Puisieux's own deficiencies as a writer and thinker rather than her own merits. Read in the shadow of Diderot's materialism, Puisieux's corpus seems beholden to generic and ideological convention precisely where Diderot is probing and risk-taking, although Puisieux is also taken to task by critics of her time for her reluctance to embrace orthodox conceptions of feminine virtue. Worse, where her relationship with Diderot is concerned, Puisieux continues to be portrayed—even in very recent criticism—as grasping, nasty, superficial, and unattractive—in short, a bad influence on Diderot, who is sometimes said (including in the *Dictionnaire de Diderot*, published in 1999) to have been forced by her to write for financial gain. Once again, as with the comparison to Lucretius, Puisieux comes up short.

If Diderot represents "good" materialism—polyvocal, flexible, delighting in his own contradictions, epistemologically modest but stylistically and philosophically daring, engaged where necessary[12]—Puisieux is here too his inverse—greedy, thoughtless, hungry for personal gain. Ironically, though, Puisieux is a bad materialist not because of overly speculative flights of fancy or even a latent idealism but because she is too preoccupied with the material world, whose disorganized and contradictory impulses wreak havoc on her ability to make a consistent case. In her self-conscious femininity and her care for the nuances to which delight is subject, any ethic of pleasure she espouses remains resistant to recuperation as a political or theoretical position. She rejects not only systematizing but to a certain extent organization itself. As she cautions the reader at the opening of *Les Caractères*: "Don't expect an admirable order here; I have never inserted one anywhere. The spirit of arrangement does not yet dominate me. I incur Debts, and I give to my Works neither beginning, nor middle, nor end."[13] She concludes, "This is all thus; and it is thus that it will stay."

Puisieux's corpus therefore takes shape within the gap between a materialist philosophy—formulated around a set of pleasure-giving principles—and a materialist practice—attentive to the materiality of its own production but unfaithful to precept. As an author, she often defines herself as specifically interested and invested in women's situation. As she writes at the beginning of the 1761 *Réflexions et avis sur les défauts et ridicules à la mode*, her third conduct book and the sequel to her successful *Conseils à une amie* (1749): "I will include a vast terrain in my morals: I will most often put them to work on the state of woman."[14] To be clear, at this moment Puisieux is not positing the "state of woman" [*l'état de femme*] as somehow the counterpoint or complement to that of men. Instead, she is intent to distinguish an interest in girlhood as a moral and social condition from that of womanhood, since she claims to find women (rather than girls) to be a more rewarding, enlightened, and enlightening study. But her insistence here is suggestive, especially since it is somewhat at odds with the moments when she underlines the disordered particularity of her own thought. Her consideration of women's "state" indeed threatens on occasion to bump up against a history of materialist speculation in which both Diderot and Lucretius are participants, but these conjunctions remain unsystematic, even involuntary, often covert or clandestine.

Yet as her thought swings between conceptual disorder and thematic insistence, Puisieux reactivates specific materialist encounters in a feminine key, not by laying claim to a woman's point of view in opposition to a masculine one, but by revealing how a voluptuous practice might develop out of a particularly feminine context at least partially supplied by and illustrated within the works of art and moral reflection that she produces. She is thus not writing specifically as a woman who philosophizes. Instead, she explores how a certain set of modes of comportment activated in the feminine— including those of *amour propre*, *délicatesse*, and *volupté*—might gain purchase on a masculine philosophical legacy. Across her corpus, she tacks back and forth between a register that modern readers might be inclined to think of as personal—that of an elite *ancien régime* woman whose inspiration and examples are drawn from her own life—and one that is deliberately generalizing—that of the maxim or moral sentence.[15] This oscillation between concreteness and abstraction, which is also in a sense an oscillation between a particular scene of experience and an impersonal set of experiential possibilities, mirrors the movement between sensation and figure into which she invites her reader.

Puisieux's materialist preoccupations, or what some critics have called her "sensualism," reveal themselves at different moments across her corpus. Marie-France Silver writes eloquently of Puisieux's "rationalist Epicureanism" in her article, "Madame de Puisieux ou l'ambition d'être femme de lettres," although Silver is careful to point out that Puisieux, unlike Epicurus, celebrates passion deeply felt—and love in particular—as a potential source of happiness. As Silver affirms, "Madame de Puisieux makes happiness depend on the intensity of states of feeling."[16] At the same time, Puisieux's œuvre reveals her to be acutely aware of the passions as a source of suffering and trouble, for women in particular. As she puts it in the *Réflexions et avis sur les défauts et ridicules à la mode*: "Without passions, no pleasure; with them, certain sadness."[17] Puisieux seeks then not the suppression of the passions or their sublimation into a state of *ataraxia* (following Epicurus) but their careful management and cultivation. In the *Réflexions*, she writes, "We have nothing real beyond pain and pleasure: all the rest is the child of our imagination or of our desires; even the passions derive from these principles: the less we desire, the less we have of them. Pain causes the same movements in everyone; pleasure the same sensations; and if the passions have different effects, they only vary by their degree of intensity."[18] Pleasure, then, is at the heart of her moral project; it is also a key aspect of her literary writings. Yet the ethical position she maintains emerges not from a set of dogmatic investments, but from an effort to cultivate and sustain specific modes of enjoyment and to foster particular readerly and writerly inclinations. In this way she might be said to embrace a libertine ideal, but one that is always aware of and attentive to the workings of femininity on the forms that pleasure may be allowed to take.

Puisieux's presentation of herself as an Aristippean is a case in point. In a passage that occurs late in *Les Caractères*, which evolves into her commentary on Fontenelle's and Maupertuis's analyses of happiness,[19] she rejects both Stoicism and Epicureanism as inflexible: "Let it be true, as [Epictetus] pretends, that it is easier for us to subtract from the sum of our pains, than to add to that of our pleasures; or maybe on the contrary that Epicurus is correct? It makes no difference to me. I see clearly that he who only assigns to himself one or the other of these goals does not understand his own happiness. This was the feeling, I believe, of a certain Aristippus, and it is also mine."[20] In this discussion, she celebrates Aristippus for his ability to adapt himself to circumstance, to "faire bonne contenance" wherever he might be. He is thus responsive to the vicissitudes of fate but not overwhelmed by them, playing the role of the Stoic or the Epicurean as context might suggest. Puisieux continues, "Is it necessary to endure pain, or to taste of pleasure? My philosopher plays by turns the role of Epictetus and that of Epicurus; thus I will not give this name to someone who can only sleep on the hard ground or on soft surfaces. A well-made head adapts itself to all the pillows that fortune presents to it."[21] Puisieux follows in the ancient tradition of understanding philosophy as a kind of therapeutics while rejecting adhesion to any specific dogma. The Aristippean philosopher as she describes them is not someone who works to dissociate themselves from the circumstances of their existence—to sublimate pain into the pleasures of thought—but instead accommodates themselves to these very circumstances, difficult or sweet as they may be.

Puisieux carries this focus on contextual adaptation into her reading of the work of philosophy itself. If the philosopher as she sees them is characterized less by a particular set of arguments than by a specific attitude or style, one that responds intimately to the place in which it finds itself, their work will tend to disseminate this attitude almost regardless of its content. Developing this idea, the analysis that follows the passage on Aristippus, on the difference between Fontenelle's and Maupertuis's approaches to the question of happiness, once again turns away from the problem of doctrine—Puisieux is not primarily interested in the truth claims that either philosopher is making—and focuses instead on the effect of the writing upon the reader, one that is determined by the philosopher's position vis à vis their own work. She writes, dryly, of Fontenelle's short treatise: "You will leave his work perhaps less enlightened than you would be by Maupertuis's *Essay on Moral Philosophy*, but you will leave happier. You will love life more after having read Fontenelle; after having read Maupertuis you will almost wish for death."[22] What matters about the definitions of pleasure that either author provides is not so much their accuracy as the enjoyment that they are capable of feeling and thus conveying. Fontenelle, who has lived a happy life (according to Puisieux), transmits his own happiness through his prose to the reader, his treatise like a "bonbon" that melts deliciously in the mouth. Maupertuis, on the other hand, is a "noisette" [hazelnut]—dry and dusty.

In her approach to the problem of philosophy and the pleasures that it expresses and analyzes, Puisieux refrains from openly embracing the role of a philosopher for herself yet remains philosophical in her approach: She is suspicious of generalities and especially resistant to what she presents as Maupertuis's proto-utilitarian calculus, even as she aims to communicate to her readers the means to negotiate the difficulties that they might face in their attempts to live more joyfully. Her attention to pleasure is anti-utopian and at various moments reactionary; she is dubious about the possibility of feminine solidarity and attached to her own class status. At the same time, she lucidly carves out a space for a certain voluptuous sensuousness as both a material need and a materialist aim. In her rejection of critical abstraction, quantification, and even of arrangement itself, Puisieux stresses the way in which feminine pleasures emerge unpredictably in the moment but also require management and forethought, since, for the women whom she writes about and addresses herself to, pleasure is not a natural condition. It requires a canny preparation in order to come to be—a training that is something other than a discipline. As she describes the difference between men's and women's experiences of pleasure in the *Réflexions*, "Nature, moreover so just, so equitable, has not at all equalized pain and pleasures: she has destined us to spend our best years in horrible suffering; and for our only recompense she has placed in men a greater or lesser degree of desire, which is not for those whose ugliness puts them off, and who nonetheless do not experience the pains attached to our sex."[23] In this passage, pleasure is not something there for the taking—a condition to which women might return or be released into, as in libertine narratives of women's sexual awakening. The scene of men's sensual delectation is for women a zone of ruin and devastation. But this does not mean that pleasure is absent from feminine experience.

If her moral writings often emphasize the difficulties inherent in cultivating a feminine persona, in her fiction and her poetry Puisieux suggests that there is still enjoyment to be had in the careful work of creating a situation where a woman might momentarily lend herself to voluptuous delight, playing deliciously with the constraints under which she operates to deliberately make room for a fraught and fleeting submission to the flow of things (a momentary "undoing," even in complicity, of the text of desire).[24] This delight must be approached with caution, since it holds perils for women in a culture that ignores and negates their agency at every turn. But it also reserves a certain promise. At these moments, Puisieux rewrites a naturalist *libertinage*—according to which a flexible sensuousness comes from the shedding of attachments—to accommodate and even prioritize a femininity to which the capacity for pleasure is never given but comes instead as the result of a creative labor. This labor includes the work of thought upon the perceptions but always takes place under specific sensual circumstances to which the work of art might contribute. Here it is possible to see Puisieux's preoccupation with pain not so much as an attraction to Stoicism—or even an essentialism—as an acknowledgment of the particular conditions in which enjoyment really becomes available for (certain) women. This acknowledgment accompanies and is fostered by creation.

A different kind of materialist practice emerges at this point, one both critical and, to use a word beloved of Puisieux, delicate. Pleasure as Puisieux describes it lies in a state of gorgeous suspension—a condition that she sometimes describes as an oscillation between sensual "penchants" and thoughtful "inclination"—that is radically dependent upon the present where she dwells, even as it is informed by the history that determines this present's contours. In this way, Puisieux couples a sensitivity to women's experience and the constraints under which they act with a rejection of philosophy as an identitarian discourse. She engages a materialist practice in which her writing functions as both effect and cause. And she inhabits a split or break—the place where need becomes desire, where the senses are taken up in thought, where art and artifice converge—that resonates with what poet and critic Lisa Robertson has called a "complicitous nilling"—a slight, sometimes invisible adjustment that is also a willed assertion of the delight of refusal, the (limited) freedom to quietly err.[25] In a context where women's "penchants" may lead them irretrievably on to destruction, as Puisieux stresses throughout her corpus, the embrace of pleasure can never be unselfconscious or natural: It must be carefully and attentively fostered. Puisieux thus revises a certain libertine materialist story that conceives of the progression to pleasure as a regression back to nature. She is clear that no such movement is possible where women are concerned, since the "return" to pleasure cannot be a turn *back* to a set of natural impulses waiting to be uncovered or reclaimed: For women as feminine persons, subjectivity is constituted in constraint. Instead, Puisieux makes room for a materialist practice that is limited in scope but firm in its conviction that pleasure must be made, not taken, enduringly entangled as it is with artifice and craft, with the capacity to briefly slip the bonds of the social scene that animates without for all that engaging a lost or absent nature. Puisieux herself is an instance rather than an example of this point. Perhaps this instance might travel through time even in its specificity—its particularity—to engage other moments, other experiences, in the management of perception and sensation that pleasure in the feminine requires? In a ruined age, maybe her apparent cynicism holds a lesson after all.

Volupté et délicatesse

How does Puisieux conceive of pleasure if not as an abstract concept or a measurable force? In what sense is hers a feminine or feminized project? Here I want to return to an extraordinary moment early on in *Les Caractères*, the second of her moral treatises and a work that not only enjoyed a relatively wide readership but was translated into English shortly following its publication in 1750. After an initial assertion of the key significance of pleasure for human nature—"The love of pleasure is in all men" —Puisieux begins the next paragraph: "Voluptuousness; everyone talks about it, thinks they know it, and few people are in a condition to feel it."[26] What to make of the distinction between *volupté* and *plaisir* that she is exploring here, one that will recur in her 1752 short story *Le Plaisir et la volupté* and for which this passage perhaps sets the stage? The same difference is parsed both in the *Encyclopédie*—in the entry on *volupté*[27]—and of course by La Mettrie himself, as I discuss in Chapter 1. The *Encyclopédie*'s entry on *volupté* opens with its own reference to Aristippus: "*Voluptuousness*, according to Aristippus, resembles a magnificent queen adorned in her beauty alone; her throne is golden, and the Virtues, in celebratory dress, rush to serve her," it begins.[28] The author goes on to remark that both Epicurean and Aristippean ethics "aimed at *Voluptuousness* without wavering," with the important difference that Epicurus recommends a withdrawal from public life while Aristippus embraces participation in society and sociability. The focus of the entry as a whole is on voluptuousness as an *illicit* pleasure—one that works against reason to draw men (following the usage in the entry) toward sensuous and creaturely realms. Here *volupté* is certainly libertine, but libertinism itself is disavowed.

La Mettrie's position on the question is quite different, and close enough to that of Puisieux to suggest that she may have known or heard of his essay on the topic, although she does not mention it outright (and even suggests that no such treatise exists). For La Mettrie, as I have hoped to show, voluptuousness is distinct from pleasure *tout court* for its involvement with art, particularly literary or poetic form, and its connection to (rather than detachment from) wit or *esprit*. Yet La Mettrie's *volupté* is also a libertine concept that plays on the connections among reading, critique, and eroticism. Where the *Encyclopédie* skirts around the overtly sexual connotations of the word—emphasizing them primarily to decry them as salacious and "empoisonnée"—La Mettrie delights in them. How does Puisieux's meditation on *volupté*, which receives its own entry in her index, navigate the libertine context in which the word operates, one deeply intertwined with patriarchal ideas about the availability of feminine bodies for men's pleasure? Here is her definition:

> This name is given to all the movements of pleasure. But pleasure is far from voluptuousness: they come together sometimes; but they are felt separately. Voluptuousness comes from the soul, pleasure from the senses; thus everyone takes pleasure, because everyone has senses. But voluptuousness is a delicate feeling, dependent on the mind, and on taste; thus three quarters of the world has never felt voluptuousness.[29]

For Puisieux as for La Mettrie, voluptuousness is pleasure conjugated in the mind or the soul, rather than deriving only from the senses. It is therefore in a sense pleasure intellectualized, but it is also, crucially, pleasure passed through the filter of delicacy or *délicatesse*, a capacity often said to be more highly developed in women than in men. It is moreover limited by class or social status—unavailable to those seemingly without refinement. While La Mettrie too makes the association between voluptuousness and delicacy (although somewhat less emphatically than Puisieux does), he does so primarily to invite men into femininity rather than to reshape the norms that govern women's particular relationship to feeling. He offers up a theory of delicacy to men rather than remobilizing it in the service of women's specific relationship to their conditions.

Puisieux's own defense of an ethic of delicate *volupté*, in a book written for a feminine public and by a feminine author, is implicitly a revision of an emergent sensualist norm according to which the intricacy of constitution thought to be inherent in women is associated not just with an inferior capacity for thought but with an impaired responsiveness to certain powerful pleasures, including most notably erotic ones. As Lieselotte Steinbrügge puts it in her commentary on the Montpellier-trained physician Pierre Roussel (1742–1802), for Roussel, "The superior softness and mobility of women's bodily organs resulted in a greater sensitivity of the nerves and thus in quicker and more subtle sensory perceptions. . . . Woman, thus, has more sensitive perceptions than man, but it is precisely this superiority which hinders her from grasping broader connections, because she is dominated by immediate sensory impressions."[30] The flexibility of feminine physiology as it is conceived here renders women liable to be overwhelmed by strong or persistent sensations, so that their delicate natures sever them from pleasure in its intensity. In this context, the invocation of feminine delicacy becomes an instrument of objectification. As an example of how this works, take the *Encyclopédie* entry on "Femme (Morale)," where Desmahis (Joseph de Corsembleu) reflects in deeply fatuous terms on the nature of the female soul. "The soul of *women* is like their beauty," he writes, "it seems that they only appear in order to make us imagine. . . . *Women* have little else but mixed, intermediary, or variable characters; whether it be that education alters their natural way of being more than ours; or that the delicacy of their organization makes of their soul a mirror that receives all objects and reflects them vividly, but preserves none of them."[31] In the entry as a whole and in this passage in particular, Desmahis presents women first and foremost as objects of masculine interest. They stimulate imaginative reverie in both appearance and essence. While their beauty stokes desire, their minds are impossible to plumb because of the intrinsic complexity of their "organization." Their souls are not receptive but reflective—the site of a proliferation of images and objects that are "returned" without being sustained. They are difficult to study, because they animate the observer, and they are impossible to know, because, like mirrors, they reflect desire back to those who desire them, rather than receiving or responding to this desire in kind.

While Desmahis's entry was notable even at the time for its stale compilation of gallantry and *idées reçues*, his description of women's delicacy of constitution anticipates Diderot's more famous (and inarguably more eloquent) portrayal of women's relationship to pleasure in *Sur les femmes*, published well after the conclusion of his relationship with Puisieux. Early on in the essay, Diderot describes women's general difficulty in achieving orgasm, writing that they are "Less mistresses of their senses than we are, the reward the latter bring is less immediate and less sure for them. Over and over again their expectations are betrayed. Organized in the opposite way from us, the motive that stirs voluptuousness in them is so delicate, and the source so far away from them, that it is not surprising that voluptuousness does not arrive or that it gets lost along the way."[32] For Diderot, feminine constitutional delicacy interrupts rather than intensifies voluptuous experience; women are alienated from their own bodily sensorium, less able to manage the content of their own experience. Nonetheless, as for Desmahis (and, later, for Roussel), delicacy in Diderot's description retains its connection to the material organization of women's bodies—an organization that is weaker, less gratifying, and ultimately more mysterious than that of men. Women's *délicatesse* not only produces suffering for them—a "fuzzy" or obstructed relationship to pleasure that contrasts negatively with that of their masculine counterparts—but makes necessary a whole literature of commentary and explanation. For Desmahis, women are machines for generating masculine desire; for Diderot, this generativity explicitly becomes a source of poetic and intellectual production and a site of enhanced sociability from which both women and men might benefit.

Puisieux's binding of *délicatesse* to *volupté*, on the other hand, counters the kinds of assumptions that make of women both the more superficial sex—the more alienated from their bodies and indeed from their very nature—and the less philosophical one—unlikely or unable to sublimate their desires in thought.[33] For Puisieux, *délicatesse* is fundamental to women's ability to feel, sense, and imagine voluptuously; they are more Epicurean than men in their disposition, but not in the sense that they are more fleshly or more concupiscent. Nor does their delicacy suggest an incapacity to connect with or perceive their own sensations, as in the pronounced ability to dissociate that Diderot both highlights and deplores. Through the scrim of *délicatesse*, Puisieux lays claim to a certain specificity in women's experience of pleasure, as an inclination that is both potentially erotic and implicitly philosophic. For her, this inclination is not necessarily the product of an alienated relation to the body. Rather, it intensifies and expands the capacity for pleasure, routing sensation through a series of networked faculties—the imagination, the senses, the "movements" of the soul—that serve to heighten and diversify delight. As I will explore later in this chapter, she delights in narrating the effects of this routing on the feminine characters that populate her fiction.

Puisieux, like La Mettrie, is interested in voluptuous pleasure for its connection to poetic modes of discourse and thought, including those generated by the imagination as a material faculty. Unlike "plaisir," which may be entirely self-interested and self-enclosed, "voluptuousness" for both of these authors is part of a relay—a dynamic interchange among bodies, concepts, and sensations. But, unlike La Mettrie, Puisieux explores these interchanges in specifically feminine contexts, whether imagined or derived from her own experience, that depart in important ways from classic scenes of libertine desire. Puisieux continues in her description:

> I don't even know if one can give to the movements one feels when self-love is satisfied the name of voluptuousness; that is an enjoyment of oneself; it is thus no more than a pleasure. When I see that which I love, the movements that happen to me having been generated by sight, and my eyes finding nothing to reproach me with in the object that pleases me; wit and taste being in agreement with the senses; one can call what I feel a voluptuous pleasure. If that which I love is ugly, it is pleasure without voluptuousness.[34]

This passage establishes *volupté* as generated within a social and aesthetic context that has two intercalated dimensions. On the one hand, voluptuous feeling is produced by the sight of the beloved, whose image inspires feeling as it passes into the lover by means of vision. (Puisieux returns to this scene—where the "mouvements" engendered by an adorable image seize hold of the one who views it—over and over again in her work, including in her early poems.) On the other hand, voluptuousness is connected to the aesthetic principles and social norms that govern beauty as an ideal; these are given a quasi-materialist aspect in Puisieux's description, wherein the pleasing dimensions of the beautiful beloved are described as agreeable specifically for the eyes themselves, as if these organs were also animated through the sensation of enjoyment.

Here the elitist and class-bound aspects of the voluptuous imagination are once again obvious, in that the ability to love voluptuously is one that is only accorded to a few, even if it is not self-interested in essence. At the same time, Puisieux's embrace of "taste" as a key element of women's desire might remind the reader of the extent to which the question of beauty, for women, is never *just* an aesthetic one. As is clear from this passage as well as from her description of ugly women in the earlier excerpt on pain and pleasure, relative degrees of beauty materially affect any given woman's experience of herself and her social world, both in the pleasures that are available to her and in the pains that she can anticipate. In the passage above, Puisieux suggests that loving an ugly partner or thing diminishes the enjoyment the lover takes in her own desire. In the opening sections of the book, she asserts that ugly women are left out of heteronormative sociability but as a result are less likely to experience the pain of becoming an object of masculine interest. In each case beauty appears to Puisieux not only as an aesthetic norm but as a material condition.

Puisieux's depiction of *volupté* might at first suggest that she is doubling down on a set of idealist distinctions—mind/body, beauty/ugliness, taste/instinct—that serve among other purposes to inhibit women's agency, linked as they are to the differentiation between genders. But the binding of voluptuousness to *esprit* and its range of denotations—including soul, taste, spirit, and wit—takes on a different function as part of Puisieux's analysis of *ancien régime* gender relations. Years after *Les Caractères* was published, in the 1761 *Réflexions et avis sur les défauts et ridicules à la mode*, she writes of women: "We are the masters of our soul & of our reputation, & we do not master our life, nor our liberty, nor our happiness; however, one commonly lives without thinking that one has a soul; & being fairly little concerned with good reputation: on the contrary, one does everything one can to conserve one's life, one's liberty, & to procure happiness"[35] This passage is a condemnation of her time and her *milieu* that operates, like the earlier definition of *volupté*, on multiple levels. Puisieux sees clearly the constraints that are put on women, even aristocratic women, who are not permitted to be the "masters" (as she puts it) of their lives, their liberty, or their happiness. In an echo of Graffigny's diagnosis of French women's situation in *Les Lettres d'une Péruvienne,* Puisieux suggests that most women live *as if they had no soul*—doggedly pursuing that which it is impossible for them to attain (including freedom, happiness, and indeed life itself, if by the latter is meant a life that is led actively and in consonance with a basic need for pleasure). When "reputation" enters into this formulation, it does so to reveal Puisieux's inherent conservatism: She does not give a Wollstonecraftian denunciation of the dependence of women's virtue on the regard of others. In fact, she accepts this dependence, despite the challenge it poses to women's happiness. On the other hand, in asserting soul [âme] itself as a value, she is not necessarily following a strictly metaphysical approach, since she has established earlier on, in a way that she returns to in her literary work, the entanglement of the soul (and the feminine soul in particular) with pleasure. *Volupté* is the name of this entanglement.

When Puisieux affirms the connection of voluptuous pleasure to "âme," then, she is affirming its relationship to women's particular mode of agency, which must lie in the mind (that has the potential to act in freedom) and not in the person (that is bound by convention). But this "âme" is not the Cartesian soul—the *res cogitans*—that exists separately from the material situation in which the body might find itself and serves to direct or control this material situation in specific ways. Instead, the feminine soul becomes a zone of material delight—an embodied sensuousness—that is not consistently subject to manipulation and direction by men or even by the self that it distills. (She thus transforms an Epicurean theme of retreat into the Garden as a withdrawal into feminine subjectivity.) At the same time, this pleasure must be constructed within women's situation or *état*—not extracted from it—since it is made in the work of the mind on the sensual body and vice versa. Puisieux continues in her definition of voluptuousness:

> There is none in *jouissance*, because at that point one is beyond the state of reason. Everything that strips from us the capacity to feel our happiness cannot merit this name. One must see, one must hear, one must touch, one must feel beauty to know voluptuousness. The purest kind comes from imagination & from delicacy; for without it there is nothing but pleasure. I even contend that virtue has its voluptuousness. Beautiful actions procure for us a voluptuousness of a kind that is all the sweeter for not being momentary like that of passion, & and whose proceeds are never regrettable.[36]

Here Puisieux detaches voluptuousness from *jouissance*, as a state in which reason is no longer operative, and thereby introduces the possibility of a virtuous *volupté*, all the while stressing the material, physical connection to beauty from which such a pleasure emerges. This voluptuousness cannot be experienced unconsciously or ecstatically; it arrives out of an awareness of beauty in the fullness of its materiality and requires the operations of imagination and delicacy in order to be consummated. Virtuous action, to the extent that it is both experienced and then recollected, can be an important source of voluptuous pleasure, if not the only one. As Puisieux's fiction makes clear, women are the exemplary subjects of *volupté*, not insofar as they *are* beautiful (pace Desmahis) but insofar as they have an exquisite sensitivity to beauty's effects, as the latter make themselves manifest in bodies, actions, artworks, and experiences.

Puisieux ends her commentary on *volupté* with a reference back to antiquity, revealing therein both her erudition and, with a certain knowing wink, her ignorance. She writes:

> No one has yet dared to give a Treatise on voluptuousness. Ovid was not voluptuous; he was nothing more than libertine; La Fontaine was even worse. There is only one whom I don't dare cite; I would be afraid that someone would suspect me of knowing Latin. For my own part, if I undertook this Treatise, women would accuse me of experience, & and I am not yet of an age to be able to show any without consequence.[37]

She denies the rights of Ovid or La Fontaine, whom she disparages as libertines (and worse), to lay claim to voluptuousness as she conceives of it (and in the process suggests that she could not have known La Mettrie's work on the topic, which was originally written in French rather than Latin). Could her reference to the text that she dare not cite be to Lucretius? The initial mention of Ovid—also of course a Roman epic poet—makes the possibility seem more likely. In this context Puisieux returns again to the problem of the constraints that operate upon women who seek to write about pleasure. If she were to write such a treatise herself, other women would accuse her of having "experience," a term that suggests the difficulty that women authors confront in taking an overtly or even covertly materialist position. "Experience" in the sense that Puisieux uses it refers to sexual knowledge—inadmissible at least in a younger woman, not meant to be versed in such matters. But the term also potentially denotes an empiricist scientific perspective that derives from both observation and experimentation.[38] With a certain finesse, Puisieux sketches out the limits on women's participation in any discourse on pleasure: Not only can she not be expected to write her own treatise on *volupté*, thereby demonstrating too extensive a knowledge, she cannot admit to knowing how to read Latin (and thus, possibly, Lucretius). She endorses women's right to feel and perceive voluptuously but she does not dare embrace their right to discuss this experience.

The limit that Puisieux presents to her reader at this point might lead them to anticipate that the topic of *volupté* remains blocked or forbidden in her other writing, but I want to suggest that in this moment we find a passageway that leads from her moral treatises, where *volupté* can be mentioned but not fully investigated as a philosophical problem, into her fiction, where specific situations conducive to women's pleasure can be constructed, revised, revisited, and reworked. Her literary writing thus gives the reader access to a world brought into being through the efforts of a voluptuous imagination (following La Mettrie's claim that whoever would write voluptuously must himself be a voluptuary) and itself generative of voluptuous effects. Moreover, if Puisieux's short poetic works remain bagatelles or (returning to the metaphor she uses to describe Fontenelle) bonbons, as opposed to epic masterworks or philosophical treatises, it is precisely in these writings that voluptuous pleasure may be both explored and disseminated, for it is in the text's ability to elicit the reader's enjoyment that this same reader may be convinced of the author's own capacity for pleasure. And indeed we find in Puisieux's fiction a consistent preoccupation with the ability of the image—both poetic and visual—to transmit and amplify pleasurable sensation in its ability to arrest the imagination, however momentarily. While Puisieux may never have been able to write the treatise on voluptuousness to which she alludes in *Les Caractères*, I want to suggest in what follows that it is in her literary writings from the 1750s, shortly after the publication of *Les Caractères*, that the reader finds an extended meditation on the question of pleasure in the feminine (which is not to say pleasure as it is felt exclusively by women) and thus a negotiation with the more radical or overt materialisms—perhaps they could be called materialisms of "experience"—of this same moment in the French Enlightenment. It is in her writings from this period that Puisieux works through the connection of pleasure both to a specifically feminine situation and to the creative power of an imagework led and undertaken by the imagination.

Pleasure as Envoy, Pleasure as Allegory

How is pleasure cultivated within a feminine condition that forbids the pursuit of life, liberty, *and* happiness, leaving only "âme" and "réputation" in their wake? How can this ensouled remainder be conceived in materialist terms at all? Puisieux's short story *Le Plaisir et la volupté* (1752) is directly concerned with parsing the answers to these and other questions. Its preoccupations are anticipated by another of her short unpublished poems, entitled "Aux Plaisirs" [*To Pleasures*], which appears in the same manuscript collection as *Céphise* and "Les Printems." As Puisieux's discussion of *volupté* from *Les Caractères* suggests, her purpose in both poem and story is less to excavate *volupté* as a category of experience—a principle to be adopted or endorsed—than to reroute voluptuous sensation across a particular set of bodies, texts, and images. As Puisieux understands the effect of voluptuous writing, its goal is to act upon the reader with an arresting force, relaying mind to body (and vice versa) as this force is transmitted through the image. Women possess a special sensitivity to these effects, but they are also capable of deploying them with specific energy. Puisieux distills the workings of this process in "Aux Plaisirs," where the speaker addresses herself to pleasure directly:

> Pleasures, divine children, what has become of you,
> I do not find you around me any more
> You abandon me like the object of my love
>   You deliver me to my extreme sadness
>   And vainly do I seek to call you back.   5
> My most tender desires seem to drive you away.
> At least follow in the footsteps of the lover I adore.
> Offer yourselves to his eyes, so that he might caress you.
> Banish pain and torment far from his heart,
> Render him happy, but never unfaithful.   10
>   To interest him more,
>   Present yourselves in my image,
> Paint my love for him and hide from him my regrets.
> Bring closer your transports, your charms, your allures.
> And to make yourselves finally the master of his soul,   15
> Reinscribe them in letters of flame
> These happy days, these lucky moments
> When in your arms and burning with love
> Only existing through our tenderness,
> We both desire to die of your drunkenness.   20
> Eh! What . . . . . this memory brings about your return.
> Ah! Flee from me Pleasures, let love weep.
> I don't want to see you until you are offered by a cherished hand.
> Bring back my Lover, if you want to please me.[39]

On the one hand this poem is a lament, close to the ancient genre of the heroid, albeit with a more explicitly sensual twist.[40] It deploys certain conventions of a poetic form that expresses, communicates, and exposes feminine ruin, but it does so with an investment in the pleasures that bear this ruin on their wings. "Aux Plaisirs" might also stand as a counterpoint to the preface with which La Mettrie opens his essay *La Volupté*, likewise invoking a beloved whose charms he recalls with nostalgia, wishing to reanimate their memory in and through his writing. Yet, if both pieces traffic in the metaphor of erotic recollection, the differences between them remain stark. The narrator of Puisieux's poem addresses not her absent lover, but pleasures personified, and the gender roles are reversed, so that it is the man rather than the woman whose absence is recalled. Moreover, the poem's speaker never fully exits the position of lamentation from which the poem emerges. In contrast to La Mettrie's account of the delights of a seduction in which the writer takes the more active role, conjuring up the image of the beloved in order to stimulate his own imagination, Puisieux assumes the voice of the one left behind, seeking to return her lover to her. Still, the lyric address in the poem is not directed to the beloved himself but mediated through the personification of pleasure as a troop of "divine children." The speaker hopes to animate these allegorical figures in an attempt to reanimate the person of her lover—to bring him back to her so that the figural delights of love will become literal once again. Instead, she succeeds in galvanizing only her own desire. The effect that she had hoped to have on her lover—to whom pleasure might carry her image in order to reignite the memory of happier days spent together—is one that redounds back upon her. The speaker conceives of pleasure as a force detachable from persons—a messenger or agent with a special power to beguile and charm—at the same time as she emphasizes the subjective power of pleasure's image—not only over her lover but over herself. It is then in her realization of pleasure as a particularly energetic trope, one that transmits a condition by distilling an image, that the speaker (unwittingly) calls pleasure back. Her undoing is her own doing, a situation that seems to underscore rather than resolve her state of loss.

Probably written several years before the short story, "Aux Plaisirs" introduces the reader to the problem that will continue to preoccupy Puisieux in *Le Plaisir et la volupté*—namely, how to "marry" Pleasure to Voluptuousness, which is to say, how to ensure that love relationships for women do not devolve into misery (a question around which *Céphise* also revolves). The fact of women's suffering in love is not a self-evidently libertine theme: On the contrary, according to the generic categories dominant at the time, the motif of feminine abandonment is primarily a sentimental one. From this perspective, the fantasies of constancy that seem to inform women's regret serve to counter a libertine logic of desire in which one partner is never enough and habit is the death of eros. Indeed, from a libertine point of view, the sentimental endorsement of fidelity functions as anti-naturalist and ideological—leading back to orthodoxy rather than away from it.[41] Puisieux nonetheless refuses to inhabit this binary, or to portray disappointment in love as either false consciousness or naïveté. Instead, she uncovers a series of sensual pleasures that emerge in response to women's experiences of loss rather than in resistance to them. Acknowledging that limitations on women's freedom affect their ability to pursue both sex and love, Puisieux's fictions, poetic and literary, endorse the search for pleasure but refuse to embrace the right to follow one's *penchants* as the only natural resolution to the problem of desire. By knitting together portraits of human couples in congress with their allegorical counterparts—who become actors in the human dramas that they oversee—Puisieux manages to create a space where the artifices of illusion interrupt and divert the conventional narrative of heterosexual romance—thereby setting it on a different course. Pleasure is cultivated here in the context of art, rather than as a return to nature, and often to women's advantage. An illusive materialism flickers in its images.

In both Puisieux's poem and in the short story that may have derived from it, her allegorical personae function less as normative models of love's pursuit than as a set of envoys or messengers that can be sent back and forth, from the human world and into the allegorical one (and vice versa), allowing pleasure to cut across gender and type and scrambling the codes that would otherwise govern erotic encounter. In both texts, human characters are just as capable of agreeable communion with allegorical figures as they are with other humans. Tropes thus become agents of pleasure as well as pleasure's representatives. In "Aux Plaisirs," the intensification of voluptuous delight through the means of images is ultimately portrayed as a sad substitute for the enjoyment that might be attached to the lover's own person: Figure supplements a distressing reality but does not overcome it. In *Le Plaisir et la volupté*, however, it becomes clear that the same hierarchy does not hold: The body of the lover no longer operates as a privileged referent, the point to which all pleasures return. Instead, the allegorical figures themselves embrace and revel in their own capacity to stimulate, carry, and translate sensations and emotions across pages and persons; they are ultimately desirable in and of themselves.

"Aux Plaisirs" represents the beginning of Puisieux's interest in allegory—an interest that will take on a fuller and more intensive form in *Le Plaisir et la volupté*—but it does not (yet) function to retrieve pleasure from the scene of disappointment and melancholy that appears to be women's lot. In the poem, a feminine perspective organizes the verse—deploying pleasure across the body (and mind) of the masculine lover—only to resist the tropic power that the lyric speaker has unleashed in the writing. The poem thus represents a kind of intermediary step between the sentimental tragedy of *Céphise* and the libertine allegory of *Le Plaisir et la volupté* in that it recurs to the formal devices of the latter but does not entirely depart from the hopelessness of the former. The poem uncovers both the vulnerability of women's pleasure to disappointment and the energies that gather within the poetic image, whose voluptuous effects will be more vigorously underscored in *Le Plaisir et la volupté*. Intervening between the short story and "Aux Plaisirs" is the reflection on *volupté* from *Les Caractères*. The conduct book itself seems to serve as a relay for pleasure's passage, out of precept and into poetic form: Fiction becomes pleasure-giving thanks to the work of moral reflection.

Puisieux's use of allegory in "Aux Plaisirs" might once again seem dated or quaint in comparison to more overtly sensuous depictions of pleasure that emphasize bodies in their suffusive and effusive materiality—living, breathing, collapsing, reviving. Here, too, the contrast with Diderot is notable. As Florence Lotterie writes, "Diderot chooses the genre of the dialogue all the better to extract it from its most abstract forms, where the identities of the actors are fixed and their discourse compartmentalized."[42] Puisieux's personification of pleasures embraces the kind of abstraction that Diderot will increasingly eschew. For her, pleasure retains a key link to literary or visual image rather than to embodied experience; indeed, the sensation of delight is severed from the very fact of having a (human) body. Puisieux's pleasure thus comes across as highly formalized—a matter of position rather than emotion—giving it something of the trouble (following Lisa Robertson) of pornography,[43] yet from a position marked as feminine. Puisieux's writing does not mobilize the sensuous body as a scene of delightful dissolution and dissipation; instead, it momentarily subjects the person to the arresting force of the trope. This instance of subjection recalls the process by which feminine subjectivity itself comes to be. Femininity functions as an allegory of embodiment itself, but not in order to return form to nature (as is often the case for Diderot and La Mettrie); instead, nature remains exquisitely and powerfully vulnerable to the formal operations that make it real.

When Puisieux deploys allegories as relays of desire, the personification of pleasure in fiction comes to serve a feminine cultivation of *volupté* as a practical ideal. Pleasure may take a masculine form on occasion, but he is not only *for men*. Her texts resist the typical libertine argument according to which the function of fiction is to uncover the social constraints that operate upon pleasure in order to do away with or evade them. Instead, literary writing comes to work as a technique for the cultivation of a pleasure that patriarchal culture is reluctant to recognize; it does so not by bypassing the constraints of representation but by renegotiating them. In this sense, *reality* operates as the primary obstacle to women's pleasurable feeling, one that only textual and visual forms can shift. This approach to the critique of women's oppression might seem artificial and idealist by definition—a form of *préciosité*. But Puisieux's preoccupation with voluptuousness suggests her materialist affinities, once we accept that the human experience of nature is itself entangled with the images, illusive and elusive, that make it palpable to us.

In *Le Plaisir et la volupté*, the allegorical elements that interested Puisieux in her poem are still in place, but their relationship to a once-intractable sentimental reality has changed. The opening scene of the narrative is erotically charged and conventionally libertine—a beautiful country house where an experienced and attractive woman is staying with her lover. Whereas in *Les Caractères* Puisieux suggests that she does not want to explore pleasure in too much detail, for fear of what other women would make of her, *Le Plaisir et la volupté* features a personified Volupté as a main character. The title page of the work gives the location of publication as Paphos, a town in Cyprus famous as the birthplace of Aphrodite and the site of a sanctuary dedicated to the goddess. As Nadine Bérenguier points out in her entry on Puisieux from the *Dictionary of Literary Biography*, "With this incursion—however brief—in the genre of allegorical erotic tales, Puisieux singles herself out among other female contemporaries, who rarely adopted this genre, preferring instead to use the novel as a conduit to analyze relations between the sexes."[44] In tone and to a certain extent in setting, the story hearkens back to other pieces of libertine fiction, including Montesquieu's *Le Temple de Gnide* (previously mentioned as a possible intertext for Puisieux's tale *Céphise, conte moral*), Crébillon fils's short story *Le Sylphe* (1730) and his novel *Le Sopha* (1742), and Diderot's *L'Oiseau blanc* (written around 1748)—on which he may have collaborated with Puisieux—as well as the *Les Bijoux indiscrets*.[45] By the end of the tale, the character Volupté is finally able to find a solution to the problem that remains unresolved in "Aux Plaisirs," recalling her lover (who as it turns out is Pleasure himself) but also revitalizing pleasurable sensation as the latter passes through the grid or screen of voluptuous perception. In the narrative, Puisieux uses stock libertine allegory not only to intervene critically in a materialist ethics but to suggest a vision of femininity shaped by and within voluptuous experience. In tracing this arc, Puisieux deploys concepts and figures drawn from an explicitly libertine tradition, one that was dominated almost exclusively by men, and diverts them toward a feminine end. But the divagation represented by the tale is also a formal one. The moment in *Les Caractères* where Puisieux bars herself from the project of writing a treatise on pleasure suggests the need to reroute the examination of *volupté* away from philosophy and into literature. This double *détournement* allows her to reanimate the question of pleasure in a newly productive way.

Le Plaisir et la volupté opens with a dedication—perhaps to the comte d'Argenson—that begins: "There is a God that one cherishes in France/That one thinks to grasp, but rarely holds/But that everyone knows upon seeing you./Pleasure is his name, and his taste is for Inconstancy."[46] The author begs the dedicatee to "Attach this flighty God near Voluptuousness"—a task that, she suggests, will be nothing but a "game" for him, even if "for us"—referring presumably to women—the attempt to force Pleasure to settle down is unlikely to be successful.[47] "It would be too much for us," she writes.[48] The tale will attempt this reconciliation or marriage nonetheless, rehearsing what will become a familiar scene in Puisieux's literary writing: The effort of a specific woman to craft pleasure from within a scene of disappointment, to make the impossible attempt to secure delight in a context that all but ensures the persistence of women's suffering. The making of pleasure out of a situation of betrayal, abandonment, or simply disillusionment will reappear at several instances through the text, so that the narrative reworks on several occasions, literally and figuratively, the scenario that is evoked both in the poem and in the dedication (in which the relationship of women to pleasure is of necessity mediated by their confinement within patriarchal roles that require their apparent passivity). It gradually becomes clear that the task for women is not to *avoid* disappointment, however, but to wrest a renewed relation to illusion from the scene of feminine despair; it is in this renewed relation that pleasure can be called back. At issue for Puisieux is not the eventual liberation of women from their constraints—suggesting a pessimism about the possibility of social change that Bérenguier refers to as a form of cynicism—but the momentary experience of pleasure *in* constraint, both an opening out and a seizing hold. As such, this crafting of pleasure is not a flight into idealism—pace Plato—but a potentially materialist project in which women might and do engage. Puisieux's story affirms that the question—what is my desire?—is impossible to answer even on its own terms; desire is never "mine." Instead, a better question might be: How can I make pleasure for me and others, here and now? The image turns out to play a key role in this scene of affective and sensual production.

The first episode in *Le Plaisir* is narrated not from the perspective of the allegorical figures named in the title but from that of Love, making his way to the home of the gorgeous Aminte, who journeys there from Paris to cure herself of the vapors that beset her in the city. Like Aminte, Love travels to the countryside with the intent of shaking off the fatigue induced by his sojourn in Paris. The bucolic location, in which art and nature harmonize with and complement one another, not only embodies calm and aesthetic equilibrium but allows both characters to leave the preoccupations of the city behind, thereby crafting a space not just for pleasure, but for romance and dreams to converge in a pastoral framework. The setting recalls the beginning of Crébillon fils's libertine tale, *Le Sylphe* (1730), in which the pleasures of the countryside are weighed against those of the city, with the latter found wanting. For both Crébillon and Puisieux, it is in the exit from the constraints of urban life that illusion will take on its full weight and erotic power (a libertine twist on an ancient association of the countryside with sexual freedom). The city thus becomes the space of habit and social obligation with the country the zone where duty dissolves into oneiric pleasure—a pleasure that might nonetheless be sustained in the work of fiction on and with the bodies it imagines. As the narrator of *Le Sylphe* writes, "You will no doubt make fun of me, when I admit to you that the pleasures of which I boast so much to you, are nothing but dreams; yes, Madame, they are dreams; but among them there are those of which the illusion is a real happiness, and of which the flattering memory contributes more to our felicity than do those accustomed pleasures that ceaselessly return, and that weigh on us even in the middle of the desire we have to really taste of them."[49] Something of the same dynamic—wherein dream becomes real and reality takes on the texture of a dream—is operating in *Le Plaisir et la volupté*, which suggests that pastoral artifice, in its very detachment from reality, might revise the restrictions that in fact govern women's experience, inclining them deliciously toward happiness even in the midst of specific unhappy obligations.

As it turns out, Love makes his way to Aminte's opulent country estate only to find Pleasure already in her bed. (He soon replaces Pleasure there, allowing the latter to return to Cythera, to the relief of his mother Venus, who has been looking everywhere for him.) As it proceeds, the narrative alternates between scenes of erotic encounter involving putatively real people— albeit "disguised" behind classical pastoral names—and descriptions of the adventures of the allegorical characters, which include Pleasure, Love, and finally Voluptuousness (the sole woman of the trio). The narratives of human sex—including the story of Aminte and her two lovers Lisis and Damis, and, later on, the concluding scene of erotic satisfaction featuring Théagene and Églé—reflect and refract the allegorical ones, in which Pleasure serves as a disappointing, inconstant husband to Voluptuousness, who despairs of reforming his libertinism until the very end of the story. Throughout, the work criticizes a personified Libertinage—portrayed as a repulsive exemplar of debauchery—but it does so in favor of a defense of the passions that "marries" Pleasure to Voluptuousness, ultimately happily.

While the two narrative dimensions (allegorical and more literal) are in one sense distinct—Pleasure, Love, and Voluptuousness are rendered as gods and goddesses, capable of flight and natives of Cythera, while the human characters are earthbound, in more ways than one—they are also consistently intertwined. For instance, while Pleasure is able to animate Aminte with desire for Lisis—who turns out to be a fop unworthy of her attentions—he is also described as "charmant" in his own person. Aminte first meets Pleasure at the home of her friend Philis, who has fallen in love with him. For her part, as Pleasure explains, Aminte "became in a moment impassioned for me. She asked Philis for me instantly . . . [and] carried me off in her arms."[50] Whereas in "Aux Plaisirs" pleasures are capable of taking on the feminine shape of the speaker, here they remain in the form of a man (or, rather, young boy), who is himself subject to the kind of possession that is typically described as the lot of women. Ravished and ravishing, Pleasure nonetheless regularly galvanizes those who seek to grasp him; he possesses those who possess him, men and women alike. In presenting Pleasure as a young boy who is described as an object of desire for more mature women, Puisieux prefigures the later encounter between Aminte, a mature woman, and Damis, who is young but philosophically inclined; it is this relationship that compensates Aminte for the boredom and contempt that permeate her relationship with Lisis, whose intellect she finds as unimpressive as his anatomy. "I believe your resources to be as limited as your . . . [ellipsis Puisieux's]," she tells him.[51]

While Aminte's attraction to Lisis is purely a matter of "penchants" and thus proves unsatisfying, her interest in Damis brings with it a commitment to reflection, an inclination that bends her will in a new direction. Damis's effect on Aminte ensouls her (in terms that presage Puisieux's insistence in the *Réflexions et avis* on the autonomy of the feminine "âme") even as it delights her. Puisieux writes:

> Aminte was enjoying for the first time the most complete victory; her self-esteem triumphed: she was making a comparison, during the besotted ardor of Damis, between the conduct that her lovers had had with her, and that which Damis was going to have. Everything was new to her; the reserves, the tenderness, the respect, the tears, and the silence of Damis, everything had become for her the object of the most serious reflections: her situation was so sweet, that this time she forgot the pleasure that had distracted her up until this day in order to dream of nothing but the delights [*douceurs*] that Love would bring. "It's you then," she said to Damis, lifting his head softly [*doucement*], "it's you then who is the first to make me feel that I have a soul?"[52]

While Aminte's rejection of Lisis for Damis suggests a move toward a quasi-Platonic idealism (reminiscent of the *Symposium*), it is also linked to the reaffirmation of *amour propre* for Aminte. The consummation of Aminte's and Damis's desire for one another does not so much represent a sublimation of eros in thought as it does an intensification of erotic pleasure through reflection (in other words, voluptuousness). This intensification is made possible both by Aminte's realization that Love is necessary to ensure an enduring felicity and by Damis's submission to Aminte's will. The relationship between a more mature woman and a boyish lover is one that will reappear in the *L'Éducation du marquis de ***, ou Mémoires de la comtesse de Zurlac* (1753) as a potential solution to the problem of feminine misery. The difference in experience allows for feminine self-esteem, pleasure, and reflection to come together in order to ensure that both delicacy and reason are respected.

From this first example of a happy scene of feminine desire, the story shifts (back) into the allegorical scenario, following Pleasure on a journey through various social conditions and situations. The erotic encounter between human figures leads the reader into the portrait of Pleasure as himself subject to the demands of love and to the prodding of a certain dissatisfaction. *Le Plaisir et la volupté* uses the device of a personified Pleasure not just to suggest that both men and women may be equally subject to his charms but to revise the reader's sense of who might be inclined to erotic and amorous possession and who might remain free from it. As he travels from household to household, he finds that the poor have never heard of him and the rich are too committed to libertinism to embrace him. Puisieux writes of his wanderings:

> Pleasure flitted for some time from house to house. He passed through all the social classes, and found everywhere reasons to get away more or less quickly. With some it was stupidity that made him flee. With others it was avarice, self-interest, bad faith, and especially the lack of delicacy. Often he found himself in the company of *Libertinage*, to whom he soon ceded his position.[53]

As Puisieux never ceases to remind her readers, women are particularly vulnerable to forms of inconstancy that are socially acceptable (indeed, valorized) in men. This is not to say that women are less subject to desire: Aminte and, later, Églé are, if anything, *more* passionate than their male counterparts. Puisieux's allegorization of Pleasure is thus not so much a dematerialization of sensation or idealist abstraction of the body—on the contrary, her characters are collectively receptive to Pleasure in his various forms—as a denaturalization of pleasure's effects.

If Pleasure takes hold without warning, he also departs without concern. This is the case both for the allegorical figures themselves—Voluptuousness is disappointed by Pleasure in her desire for constancy—and for the men and women whom he visits on earth. As Pleasure moves from place to place, he meets Voluptuousness and falls in love with her. But instead of this relationship being a more perfect version of the couplings that might be found in the human sphere, it too is subject to the forces that constrain and bedevil the human characters. The other gods are distressed at Pleasure's devotion to Voluptuousness; They fear that he will abandon the mortal world entirely. The solution? Have the couple marry in order to guarantee that they will no longer love one another. This works, but only for a little while, since Voluptuousness remains enamored of Pleasure even as he falls out of love with her. In her desperation and sadness, Voluptuousness consults an oracle, who says to her: "Return to .... You will find there two Lovers, who will bring together in their worthiness and their tenderness Pleasure and Love; then your Husband will be faithful to you."[54] This prophecy ends up being fulfilled, in part thanks to the operations of Venus, Pleasure's mother, who sends him out to live with a series of libertine couples who disgust and exhaust him by turns. Finally, with the aid of Love, acting on behalf of Venus and Voluptuousness, Pleasure travels to the house of Églé, who is writing a letter to her lover Théagene. In contrast to Aminte and Damis, who are unequal to one another in status, Églé and Théagene are perfect counterparts.

In the concluding scene of the novel, the coupling of the human lovers is accompanied by that of the allegorical figures that inspire and animate them. It is here that the ultimate work of the image of pleasure is both illustrated and carried out. Puisieux describes the reunion of the human lovers as foreshadowing that of Pleasure and Voluptuousness, so that the scene of human erotic delight flows into the consummation of the allegorical tale:

> The happy Lovers had tasted of their happiness for two hours, when Love thought that it was time to go in search of Voluptuousness. These Lovers had been too preoccupied with the presence of Pleasure to dream of all the refinement and delicacy that follow in the wake of Voluptuousness. They began to desire her, when she appeared before their eyes. What moments for Théagene & for Églé! What joy for Voluptuousness in finding in such good company her Husband, a Lover so tenderly beloved! She threw herself into the arms of Pleasure, who, seized by an equally delicious feeling [*mouvement*], responded to the transports of Voluptuousness with all the signs of the most ardent love. Pleasure rediscovered Voluptuousness with all the graces that she had had before he became her Husband. Love that had wished to soothe their unhappiness, warmed them with new fires, and accomplished the prophecy of his Oracle. No reproaches, no clarifications came to trouble such sweet moments; it was nothing but tender sighs, flattering compliments, delicate caresses, voluptuous feelings, transports, assiduous concerns, distractions, drunkenness, sweet rages.[55]

At this moment the reader bears witness to the sexual encounter of Théagene and Églé, which is then doubled and redoubled by the sexual encounter of Pleasure and Voluptuousness. This mirroring—whereby the characters galvanize the allegorical figures that in turn work their effects on the characters, in an endless exchange of passion for image, and image for passion—represents its own solution to the problem of inconstancy, effectively combining an endorsement of erotic satisfaction in love with an acknowledgment of the suffering wrought by and through romantic attachment. Pleasure is too mobile to endure; he is portrayed as constantly on the move, to the dismay of his mother and his wife, not to mention the humans he abandons without thought. His inconstancy—pleasure's malleability—in some sense puts women in particular at a disadvantage, in part because they cannot as openly embrace promiscuity as men can. But here, the image, in its capacity to transfix and transport the bodies that it energizes, comes to the rescue. The appearance of the allegorical figures incites desire in the human characters, whose passions in turn crystallize in poetic tropes that galvanize the sensations of the personifications. The images return, but in their return, they multiply, intensifying enjoyment and transfiguring bodies. The staging of human passion—the presentation of the characters as their own embodied allegory—enables the loving marriage of Pleasure and Voluptuousness to be consummated once again, and, in theory at least, to endure. If Puisieux is committed to exposing a certain kind of libertine fiction—that of the perpetually, naturally receptive body (most often a woman's body)—as its own material illusion, it is through the manipulation of this illusion that her allegory generates its own version of reciprocal, perpetual sensation. Where the speaker in "Aux Plaisirs" refuses pleasure's illusory effects, seeking to recall to herself "the real thing" (her lover, in human form), the characters in *Le Plaisir et la volupté* embrace them: The illusion, here, is the realest thing of all.

Puisieux allows the relationships among the allegorical figures to enhance the tensions running through the human world, but she also presents the humans as models for the allegories. The final scene, in which Églé and Théagene are joined by Voluptuousness and Pleasure—the most overtly erotic moment in the narrative—involves an intermingling of art and nature that both echoes and revises the opening moments in which Love and Pleasure function as objects of desire for Aminte (and vice versa). At the end of the short story, the dissolving of the allegorical world into the actual one is complete. The comingling of Églé and Théagene, Voluptuousness and Pleasure, presents the reader with the scene of a marriage that is not juridical but sensual—resulting from the interpenetration of bodies both actual and virtual. The pleasure that is envisioned here is one in which artifice heightens and enriches nature in specific embodied ways, and in which illusion stimulates, shapes, and then revives sensation. The story thus presents itself as a possible resolution to the dilemma posed to women in particular by the wandering lover's eye. But this ending is something other than an escape into artifice as a means of forgetting or effacing the demands of a cruel or unforgiving world. Rather, the image operates as its own instrument for the cultivation of sensation—not just as a model but as a tool. Pleasure, Puisieux suggests, needs to be managed, finessed, and worked—gradually generated from within scenes of difficulty and disillusionment—not because pleasure is what remains after ideology falls away, but because sensation is generated by form. Artifice and illusion are the zones in which feeling can and must take shape. Feminine persons thereby remobilize and reanimate a "quaint" and outdated libertine allegory.

A Voluptuous Education

If *Le Plaisir et la volupté* remains overtly allegorical in tone and mood, the voluptuous techniques that this story parses are carried over into Puisieux's more realistically (and moralistically) inclined fiction—including, perhaps most strikingly, her novel *L'Éducation du marquis de* ***, *ou Mémoires de la comtesse de Zurlac* (1753), written two years after the short story. This novel, as Marie-France Silver has discussed, represents a rewriting of Crébillon fils's libertine classic, *Les Égarements du cœur et de l'esprit* (1735–1738), from the point of view not of the young man but of the older woman who initiates him into social life.[56] The novel tells the story of the comtesse de Zurlac, originally Silvie de Valance, who is married off to a man she does not love. The young Mademoiselle de Valance is described in idealized terms, but Puisieux makes it clear from the outset that the narrative interest lies less in preserving the heroine's virtuous exemplarity than in articulating the merger of passion and happiness from within a feminine situation. The first sentence of the work reads, "Happiness begins with the age when passions make themselves felt," thereby delineating an innocent girlhood from an "état de femme" that is both fraught and productive.[57] At the same time, the novel endorses constancy as a means of lending substance to love, moving it away from the realm of illusion and into the domain of the real: "without constancy love is nothing but an illusion that flatters the senses like a dream."[58] The term "illusion" is used here in a negative sense that emphasizes its link to deception and *tromperie*, but the text itself retains a commitment to the image as an instrument of voluptuous satisfaction and indeed enlightenment. *L'Éducation* embraces the passions as a source of happiness but does so in a way that maintains a (sometimes uneasy) equilibrium between virtue and desire, between the constraints enacted by the world and the delicious interplay of concepts and emotions animated by the encounter with the beloved. Nevertheless, Puisieux affirms that there is a risk in insisting upon the possibility of a happiness in love: "It has so often been said that the great passions are the source of all pain," writes Puisieux, "that there is perhaps a certain temerity in insisting the opposite."[59] But the heroine is notable for her respect of social mores to which she never issues an open challenge; her pleasure occurs in the crack or gap opened up by a "jouissance de la vûe" [delight in sight] that is unpredictable and arresting. If the novel is not fully libertine in the sense of openly challenging specific social codes or ratifying the pursuit of pleasure for pleasure's sake, it is consistently erotic; the text dwells on and in the heroine's oscillation between desire for a younger man and the couple's mutual recognition that this desire should not be sexually consummated, even as it is ratified and intensified over and over again in their encounters with one another. It is here that the pleasures of the narrative *mise en scène* intervene; a series of encounters between Zurlac and Me*** — in a carriage, on a boat, in Zurlac's bedroom — allow both the heroine and the reader to become suspended in a state between activity and passivity, momentarily at the mercy of images that generate a suffusive and abiding pleasure without ever tipping into the domain of a permanent sexual possession.

The comtesse de Zurlac is both delicate and discerning, almost to a fault: "The senses in her case followed the penchant of the heart, and voluptuousness only emerged from the delicacy of her ideas and of her organs; it was easy to tell from her portrait that her taste was exquisite, that it was difficult to captivate her."[60] She is an admirable woman of her time — the *consœur* of Églé in her ability to think philosophically and feel both intensely and with discrimination. The text itself is designed to cultivate and respond to the same sort of delicacy of thought and "organ" in its reader. Zurlac's exquisite taste and striking intelligence do not mean that she is invulnerable to romantic disappointment, however. Instead, in *L'Éducation*, Puisieux returns to the narrative structure that gives shape to *Céphise*, "Aux Plaisirs," and *Le Plaisir et la volupté*, one in which love is never happy in its first instance, but instead requires maturity, wisdom, and a certain amount of luck to evolve into a source of joy rather than tragedy. As Mademoiselle de Valance, the youthful heroine is charmed by an inconstant lover and must find a way out of romantic suffering and into a lasting happiness that is built on the management of specific moments of pleasure; her philosophical inclinations cannot save her from this fate. Married off by her parents to an unappealing and unsuitable man, she is betrayed by her first beloved, the perfidious chevalier de B***, to whom she vows to remain loyal despite her marriage to the comte de Zurlac. Her vow of fidelity is described as a dedication to the Chevalier's image, which alone suffuses her heart: "At least no one will share my heart with you: your image alone will fill it, and I will have for my husband only the consideration given by friendship."[61]

As it turns out, the Chevalier's power over her does not endure. His displacement from her affections is a result of the forceful impression that *another* striking image makes on her heart and mind, that of a handsome young friend of her brother's, the marquis de Me***. "Only through new impressions could she cease to love the Chevalier," the narrator remarks, and indeed it is a set of "impressions nouvelles" that cures her of her initial unhappy passion: The energy with which the figure of the Marquis acts upon her imagination eases the pain that she endured in her previous relationship.[62] The next time she sees de B***, then, she is unaffected. Puisieux's narrator seems to puzzle over the exact nature of this process, but suggests ultimately that it has to do with the relationship between the soul and the senses. The narrator explains:

> I have often asked myself about the emotion that the sight of the beloved causes: why, I wonder, this shock, this warmth that travels to the heart and to the chest at the unexpected appearance of an object that is dear to us? Why is one troubled, at the end of an allée in the Tuileries, upon perceiving this object; is it the senses that are moved? Is it the soul? Is it the effect of surprise? The distance from one person to the other ought to suggest that sensory impression has nothing to do with the emotion of the heart. What is it then? However we are not moved in the same way with the approach of a disagreeable object, even when the surprise is the same: if one sees the person whom one hates, one feels as agitated as when one sees another who is dear to us: but these movements are cruel to feel, while the presence of the beloved object causes pleasure. This question has never been decided. Let anyone who may decide it.[63]

This passage suggests that the question of love's origins may be an unanswerable one—since the effects of the image of the beloved person are both intimately, viscerally felt and somehow transmitted over a distance—but it remains of crucial importance to the Comtesse. Why is her heart no longer moved at the sight of the Chevalier? Is it because sight is not a concupiscence of the eyes but a "jouissance de l'âme," and the soul is not capable of receiving multiple impressions at once ("quite different from the senses," the Comtesse seems to muse)? The sensuality of the encounter with the lover is preserved in the language of this paragraph—her lover's presence brings "heat" to her heart and chest—but the effects of desire seem to transcend physicality, even as they suffuse the body. In both form and content of the passage, the reader is confronted with a moment of oscillation. As Puisieux interrogates the mechanics of love, the text vacillates between the perspective of Zurlac herself and the perspective of the narrator in a way that brings the reader very close to a kind of free indirect discourse *avant la lettre*. The explanation Puisieux attempts to give hesitates between a physiological and a metaphysical rendering of the effects of love, ultimately refusing to settle on either one. Love seems to be a matter, the passage continues, of the "images engraved in our mind," which are recalled and reanimated by the sight and sound of the beloved person.[64] Either way, the narrator asserts, these speculations may be best left to the metaphysicians. Yet the dynamic in question remains of urgent interest to the narrative.

Zurlac goes on to find love and happiness with her new younger lover, who dedicates himself to her with an earnestness that almost surpasses his beauty. While the narrator hints in the final paragraph that the couple may have acted on their desires, their relationship is framed as an education of the young man by the more mature woman, a process that is not governed by the logic of seduction but instead relies on the power of the image to stimulate and to inspire the heart and mind. In her honor, her thoughtfulness, and her probity, Zurlac is the equal of any *honnête homme*. "Even men only have one justified reproach to make to us," affirms the narrator, "which is the lack of reflection; but they willingly agree that those of us who think, are indeed their equals. Let us remove any idea of seduction by Madame de Zurlac. The only difference between her and M. de Me*** was the experience of several years that turned entirely to the advantage of the Marquis through the seeds of virtue and of greatness that this experience was able to give him, and that he appeared to benefit from beyond his hopes."[65] Zurlac galvanizes the Marquis in both body and mind, operating through and on her own image in order to ensure his commitment to her, but she does not exploit him. Throughout the second volume of the novel, Zurlac and her lover are described as both irresistibly drawn to one another—overcome by pleasure in their interactions with one another—and exquisitely capable of self-management and self-control (Zurlac more so than the Marquis). In respecting the Comtesse's desire that their relationship not be consummated, the Marquis is often reduced to contemplating her beauty in a kind of helpless ecstasy—often while she sleeps. When the Comtesse gives the Marquis her portrait, he creates a shrine to her and prostrates himself before it. "No Indian ever adored the Sun with such fervor," the narrator exclaims, in a moment that both underscores and disavows a potential parallel with Graffigny's *Lettres d'une Péruvienne*.[66] At the same time, the Comtesse herself is drawn to the Marquis by forces that she does not entirely control—including her own response to his beauty and virtue—but retains the right to define the nature of their love affair. With the Marquis beholden not only to the Comtesse but to the wishes of his father—and the Comtesse a woman of maturity who is free to decide her own fate—the conventional masculine and feminine positions are inverted to generate a situation of shared ecstasy in which the pleasures of *amour propre* are cultivated even as the self dissolves in delight: "Both given over to their happiness, they could have ceased to exist without even noticing. How worthy of envy is this happy situation!"[67] The sexuality on display here is neither appetitive nor possessive; it acknowledges constraint to tarry on the edge of coming undone, and it cherishes illusion as a means of sustaining shared voluptuousness.

Coda: From and Out of Ruin

Puisieux's corpus creates a zone where a feminine *volupté* is momentarily possible, where aristocratic women initiate men into the management of desire and the deployment of artifice toward the ends of pleasure. In her fiction as in her moral writings, she imagines not a progression toward a zone of enlightenment or a "critical maturity," to echo Kant, but a situational response to a set of constraints that can be acknowledged but never fully bypassed. As such, her writing is indeed beholden to its *milieu*, not least because it is profoundly imbued with a form of class privilege that is also structured, as in the comparison of the Marquis to a nameless Indian, by racist and racialized assumptions. As a materialist in something other than name, Puisieux does not appear to anticipate a better future for women of her class or to consolidate for herself a more worthy position than her masculine counterparts. Instead, she carves out the conditions in which pleasure briefly becomes possible and imaginable as an attribute of elite femininity, thereby revealing how delight is always anchored to the situations that render it palpable. In so doing, she suggests a redeployment of the relationship between the "natural" artifices of matter and the cultural tricks to which the feminine self is heir. Her practice as an author is one that operates on bodies through images and on images through bodies: She generates pleasures and Pleasure by putting text and art to work. Using figures as the envoys of sensations, she creates scenes, tropes, and allegories that situate her heroines on the edge between willing and nilling, action and passion, substance and illusion, in a relation of *papillotage* to themselves and the world that confines and enables them. Her relationship to philosophy is not one of an enlightened progression toward truth and self-realization, but of a sometimes hesitant cultivation of pleasure that emerges from a survey of an often desolate landscape.

As she aged, Puisieux's reflections became at once more sharply critical of women's (and her own) plight and ostensibly more resigned to it. In the *Réflexions*, she writes that "A beautiful and well-organized machine, who would feel nothing and think of nothing, would be, in my view, preferable to the most spiritual person, who would be constantly at war with her desires.

I know some of those very machines; and I admit that it is not without envying them."[68] Profoundly critical of the *savants* who refuse women admission to the Académie française, she notes the double standard for women's authorship that leaves her jealous of the kind of women who resemble insensible and insensitive automata, neither feeling nor reflecting. She even expresses skepticism about forms of enjoyment available in writing, which she feels strikes the imagination less vividly than do statues or other monuments. Women's *délicatesse* is also more clearly a source of suffering in this final installment of her moral writings; if delicacy heightens delight, it also makes pain more palpable. She muses:

> I remember my pains better than my pleasures: it must be that suffering or chagrin make more of an impression on the senses, or that chagrins last longer. The soul is not enough for lively and continuous pleasures: it stands up to suffering better. I leave it to the Metaphysicians to work through this line of thinking, and to derive results from it.[69]

Once again a resolution to a problem—this time that of memory and the capacity of sensation to endure—is left to the metaphysicians. The inability of the soul to sustain itself in the face of intense pleasure—combined with its resilience in the face of pain—suggests the difficulty and not the satisfaction of orienting a life toward pleasure's cultivation. The inclining of women's experience toward pain is an injustice, but one that Puisieux seems unsure how (or whether) to combat. The *Réflexions* concludes with a discussion of her own inability to achieve glory or any lasting reward despite her talents. "So true it is that pleasure and idiocy govern all men," she writes.[70] These passages heighten the speculative quality of her earlier work of the 1750s. If a space seemed to have opened there for a particular endorsement of pleasure in the feminine, by the time she writes the *Réflexions* that portal appears to have closed. Are her writings a failed effort? If they are judged as part of an inexorable movement toward a more certain knowledge, the answer can only be yes. But if they are read as an experiment that is also an experience—fleeting and substantial—they might communicate not only the limitations of other ways of conceiving pleasure but a certain suggestive potential—a moment when disappointment could be both acknowledged and all too briefly overcome.

Puisieux is deeply entangled with the history of modern (and ancient) materialism in certain respects while in others she seems to touch upon this history only lightly, obliquely. In reading her "bad" materialist ethic—inconsistent, wavering, and ultimately uncertain—through and against the "good" materialism of her masculine interlocutors, I have tried to show how this opposition, as much as it reveals, also obscures certain dynamics and possibilities, and not just because it traces the distinction between feminine and masculine as a difference between those who are easily swayed and those who are doggedly or riskily critical. Puisieux's work suggests not only that "good" materialists might yet embrace the specific and timely pleasures of aesthetic construction and creation, but that artificial and illusive spaces, places, objects, and bodies might become productive zones of materialist effect. Can materialism be expansive enough to take into its ambit the encounter with a delicate craftiness that might subtly shift the way in which the world is known or perceived? Puisieux's answer to this question is both affirmative and negative. She oscillates.

3
Illusions Without Error: Du Châtelet Loves Enough for Two

"I have spent my life in a state of independence. . . . I only want to depend on my taste and on my pleasures."[1]

"What I'm proudest of, I guess, is having a life where work and love are impossible to tell apart."[2]

After a furious spate of reading—rediscovering her moral writings, making my way slowly through her scientific work (at turns edified and dazzled), and ending up in her astonishing love letters—I still find the prospect of writing on Émilie Du Châtelet daunting. Of the three women whose work I discuss in this book, her corpus engages fields and bodies of knowledge most distant from my own. Although she loved theatrical performance and participated in it with gusto throughout her life, Du Châtelet's approach to philosophy and her engagement with the world do not pass through literary or poetic texts first and foremost.

But the main challenge for me in thinking with Du Châtelet lies elsewhere. As a brilliant and renowned mathematician and woman of science, her success positions her as both exceptional and authoritative. As an aristocrat and manager of a large and costly estate, she was comfortable with the exercise of power. Reckoning with her corpus also means reckoning with its belated reappraisal as a cornerstone of the Enlightenment, present in the *Encyclopédie*, influential for the course of scientific history. This reappraisal is in large part the result of the work of feminist scholars who have labored to uncover and recover the significance of Du Châtelet's contributions to eighteenth-century science and philosophy. Its effects have been powerful—reestablishing the divine Marquise as a metaphysician of verve, inventiveness, and lasting influence, sometimes described as a progenitor of Kant.³ Du Châtelet participated in key Enlightenment debates and her contributions to the fields of mathematics and metaphysics were acknowledged by some of Europe's most prominent intellectuals; in her family and social life, she cultivated relationships with members of the highest nobility and was adept in advancing the prospects and careers of those closer to her. In other words, she is not a marginal figure.

How to approach the enmeshment of knowledge and pleasure, in Du Châtelet's case, while remaining attentive both to the complexity of her thought and to the effects of her unique social position on the enjoyments she pursued? As a woman of science, she did not benefit from the forms of institutional prestige to which some of her male counterparts had access. In these contexts, her femininity becomes the limit of her intellectual authority. Is it possible to write about pleasure in Du Châtelet's thought without effacing her metaphysics, without sidelining her scientific accomplishments, and without forgetting in the end how an enlightened science dovetails with a desire to exploit and master? She herself formulates a powerful reading of the way in which her life shapes and informs her work, but her biography alone cannot fully resolve these questions.

The unsteady oscillation between marginalization and privilege that marks Du Châtelet's life and work feels especially acute to me in her correspondence. Reading her love letters to the marquis de Saint-Lambert, it is clear the extent to which Du Châtelet used her social status and influence with great flair and precision to attempt to forward the career of her lover. At the same time, it is hard to read those letters—by turns passionate, aggravated, despairing, proud—without being painfully aware of what awaits the woman writing them, who would die of puerperal fever shortly after giving birth to a daughter with the marquis, a daughter who herself died in infancy. In these letters the pleasure that the Marquise takes in her love and in her writing, including the famous translation and commentary on Newton that she works desperately to complete before what she fears (correctly) is her impending demise, can easily be overshadowed by the tragedy to come, as if her death shines a light on the errors that sustain her, all too fragilely and in the end, to no avail.

Remembering my own pregnancy with its attendant fears and hopes, it is hard for me to resist reading Du Châtelet's attachments, both to her writing and to Saint-Lambert, in relationship to her death, as if the latter illuminated the meaning of the life *and* the work, a final dispelling of error in the cold hard light of truth. But it is also clear in the letters—in their intensity, passion, and specific insistences—that meaning emerges not in the conclusion to the narrative but in the very making of it. The significance of her love affair is not just in its sad end but also in the way in which Du Châtelet works through her obsessive, excessive writing to activate her own desires and those of her lover—a lover whose voice, throughout, is now gone, lost to history. Saint-Lambert's absence from the exchange underscores the ways in which love for Du Châtelet seems to represent both utter dependence *and* a strange kind of autonomy—one in which she desires—and writes—forcefully enough to fill in the gaps that the Marquis leaves, both as a partner and as a correspondent. "I spend my life making monologues with you," she reproaches Saint-Lambert, but in her letters he emerges not as her love's limit but as its very emanation—the formal materialization of erotic need in the character of a male coquette.[4] Pleasure cuts across her intellectual and her sentimental life and makes of her letters another expression of the force of her creative imagination.

In the sometimes frantic labor of her writing—the gargantuan effort to cultivate and maintain a sense of Saint-Lambert's responsiveness and to complete "her Newton" before giving birth—the connections binding the work of thought and the work of love are worked and reworked again. These are both the purest forms of happiness, according to Du Châtelet herself, and they are both grounded not in the search for truth alone but in a specific cultivation of illusion in the name of pleasure. Like her thought, Émilie Du Châtelet's desire can be animating, reestablishing for a moment a speculative openness, an array of possible futures, notwithstanding the fact of her early death. As her corpus makes palpable, delight may be found and sustained in an awareness of the gap between illusion and a reality sometimes difficult to bear. This cognitive mode might be very difficult to read positively or optimistically today—it seems to call out to be dispelled—but in her attachment to illusion's hold over time—an attachment that traverses both her scientific projects and her romantic experience—Du Châtelet generates an alternate version of how enlightenment (and its pleasures) might work. In science and in passion, she seems to suggest, we confabulate delightfully with that which is beyond our ken and outside of our control, with our futures, in other words. With her reflections on the entanglement of study and desire in the illusions that sustain them, Du Châtelet reveals pleasure not as a disruptive force but as the weaving together of life and work in an act of love. That she does so as a woman of means and power foregrounds not only the potential of this model but its limits.

Love and Work

Du Chatelet's reflections on pleasure, scattered throughout her corpus, suggest that the pursuit of knowledge and the pursuit of love come together to form her life's project. This comingling of passions—erotic desire and *curiositas*—implies a certain kinship with the enlightened naturalisms of her time, in which pleasure operates so often as a means of apprehending the world, shaping what and how it is possible to know. But as is the case for the other two women about whom I write here, Du Châtelet's approach to the question of enjoyment—her sense of love and work as intertwined sources of specifically feminine satisfaction—does not fit easily into standard accounts of eighteenth-century materialism or libertinism, or even of the French Enlightenment as an age preoccupied above all with pleasure. In contrast with some of her less orthodox interlocutors, she retains a commitment to virtue as a social ideal and to freedom as a uniquely human capacity. At the same time, she embraces metaphysics.

In her scientific writing, Du Châtelet takes on with great originality some of the most crucial Enlightenment debates around matter, but she does so as a thinker who explicitly believes that "physics cannot get along without the metaphysics upon which it is founded."[5] In fact, Du Châtelet's most obvious involvement with the materialisms of her day often takes place in work that did not appear in print until many years after her death—as is the case for the *Discours sur le bonheur*, which was first published posthumously in 1779, or her translation of Bernard Mandeville's *Fable of the Bees*, made available by Ira O. Wade in 1946.[6] Indeed, it is only fairly recently that Du Châtelet has been ascribed an independent status as a philosopher and scientist at all. As critics including Judith Zinsser, Felicia Gottmann, Ruth Hagengruber, Véronique Le Ru, and Anne-Lise Rey have shown, Du Châtelet's contribution to the history of philosophy has not only been underestimated or effaced; it has also been misunderstood as "merely" a form of translation or "vulgarization" of the works of great men.[7] But to reclaim Du Châtelet for the history of eighteenth-century thought is not just a matter of validating the originality of her arguments or her intellectual bona fides. Reading Du Châtelet in the wake of her reinvention has also meant rereading—and revising—a history of enlightenment in which her philosophical commitments can seem idiosyncratic or incompatible with one another. Such a revision also makes it possible to uncover within her work a sometimes cryptic variant of materialist thought and practice that is sustained with and alongside her metaphysical orientation, as a means of heightening and enriching the pleasures of philosophy.

For Anne-Lise Rey, the difficulty in acknowledging Du Châtelet's contributions to metaphysics appears as a structural problem emerging from within the history of philosophy itself. As Rey shows, this history tends to give a central role to the opposition between Cartesianism and Newtonianism as part of the passage of enlightened thought away from an archaic rationalism and toward a modern experimental science (represented in this narrative by the ascendant

Newtonian paradigm). Du Châtelet's work is illegible within this system, since for her, as Rey puts it, "acknowledging the epistemic revolution that newtonianism entails does not signify giving up metaphysics, and, in particular, that version which seems to her the most effective: the one she designates as the metaphysics of Leibniz."[8] Du Châtelet is thus working in a blind spot constructed within the history of philosophy. While in one way she may appear ahead of her time—specifically, in her embrace of Newtonian experimentalism—in others she appears to be out of step with what is to come—namely, in her insistence that this experimentalism be metaphysically justified.

In short, Du Châtelet's work fits uneasily into narratives touting modernity's "rise." This untimeliness—the gap between the possibilities actualized in the work and the positions that come to define the period—is also characteristic of the writing of Puisieux, albeit in a different mode. In Du Châtelet, the archaism appears structural—a matter of clashing paradigms. In Puisieux, her unreadability often emerges first as a problem of style—a deficiency stemming from the genres or voices in which she chooses to work. But if both women appear as outsiders to a conventional history of enlightened thought, their exclusion from this history also does not automatically lend their work the contestatory force that is traditionally ascribed to libertine materialism. Their engagement with an ethic of pleasure is thus doubly obscure in that this engagement is legible neither within a set of metaphysical commitments nor as a gesture of radical critique. In either case, the grand narratives of enlightened modernity cannot fully reckon with these women's efforts to present pleasure in its vicissitudes, as the contingent symptom of a femininity that oscillates from agential to receptive, from experience to style, and that operates as a "second nature" that may only be recovered in the cultural contexts that make it visible. They reveal (feminine) pleasure as recurrently evasive, not for its resistance to thought or reason but for the way in which it is wrapped in time.

As with Puisieux, the challenge of reading Du Châtelet as a theorist of pleasure is compounded by the patriarchal social context in which she works and lives—a world accustomed to representing women not as agents of desire but as delight's (and science's) handmaidens. The Epicurean dimensions of Du Châtelet's thought appear most explicitly in her moral writings, but they take on a form unlike those preferred by her male peers and associates.[9] At the same time, Du Châtelet's position is not that of a protofeminist *avant la lettre*, as critics who have also wrestled with the ambivalences and contradictions inherent in Du Châtelet's approach to gender would attest. She sometimes argues on behalf of women's equality, but also on occasion seeks legitimacy as an exception to the rule. Her reliance on networks of patronage often obliges her, as Mary Terrall has explored, to navigate the sexist expectations of her time with a certain finesse. Her contributions as a philosopher in her own right also regularly collide with an eroticization of the scene of knowledge, not uncommon in naturalist and libertine texts, according to which feminine or feminized pupils are portrayed as eager for tutelage from masculinized authority figures. This is the role in which she appears on the frontispiece of Algarotti's *Il Newtonianismo per le dame*, in an illustration that places her in the position of the desiring and desirable student.[10]

Du Châtelet herself will revise this particular scene of knowledge transmission in her magisterial introduction to the science of physics, the *Institutions de physique*—where she writes in the voice of a teacher addressing a young boy (her son), in a formal reversal that brings to mind Puisieux's reformulation of the older woman/younger man pairing dear to Crébillon fils.[11] While Du Châtelet does not emphasize her gender in the first edition of the *Institutions*—which was initially published anonymously in 1740—the frontispiece of this text reveals a subtle shift away from more conventional representations of masculine authority in the sciences (see figure 2).[12]

In this image, a woman, maybe Du Châtelet herself, ascends the clouds toward the female figure of Truth; she is observed and helped along her way by allegorical women representing Botany, Astronomy, Physics, Medicine, and Chemistry. Above her and out of the primary frame of reference, three men appear as portraits—perhaps Descartes, Leibniz, and Newton. The scene within the frame—focused on the active pursuit of knowledge—is entirely inhabited by women or feminine persons. This image presents a striking contrast to the frontispiece to Voltaire's 1738 *Eléments de la philosophie de Newton* (see figure 3), which he dedicated to Du Châtelet and composed in her company.

Here Du Châtelet appears as a muse, reflecting the light of truth received from Newton himself onto Voltaire at his writing desk. Voltaire's version of Du Châtelet, enmeshed in the exchange among masculine figures, displays one breast and is surrounded by cherubim; the light of truth passes through her on its way toward Voltaire. In the image from the *Institutions* on the other hand, Du Châtelet's woman philosopher, dressed in flowing robes, is arguably gendered but not clearly sexed. This figure's pursuit of knowledge is arduous but seemingly joy-inducing; the three men ornament the frame but do not participate in the process it depicts. Like Epicurean divinities, they observe the scene but do not affect it. Femininity no longer stands as the form that mediates between the manly scientist and the artifice of nature, or between the masculine philosopher and the male authority from which he draws. The women, allegorical and real, appear in active relation to one another.

In her letters and her occasional writing on ethics, Du Châtelet often remarks on the connection between the pursuit of knowledge and the

Figure 2. Frontispiece of Gabrielle Émilie Le Tonnelier de Breteuil Du Châtelet, *Institutions de physique* (Paris: Prault, 1740). Engraving. Image courtesy of BIU Santé Médecine.

Figure 3. Frontispiece of François Marie Arouet de Voltaire, *Élémens de la philosophie de Newton, mis à la portée de tout le monde par M de Voltaire* (Amsterdam: Etienne Ledet, 1738). Engraved by J. Folkema. Image courtesy of BIU Santé Médecine.

cultivation of libidinal and affective bonds, but she does not represent this connection as solely or even primarily the product of heterosexual *badinage*, an instrument of seduction. Instead, for Du Châtelet, pleasure inhabits and animates the intellectual work itself. It drives the production of scholarship (particularly by women) and it is attendant upon the whole system of physics as a mode of knowledge grounded in both experience and metaphysical speculation. Mary Terrall, in her classic article on "Émilie Du Châtelet and the Gendering of Science," writes that "The ties linking femininity and pleasure already permeated Du Châtelet's culture; in broadening the definition of pleasure to include rational and critical thought and even mathematical calculation, she realigned the gendered associations of pleasure."[13] What are the effects of this realignment on the way in which women might pursue an intellectual life? Might the revision Du Châtelet undertakes be considered a form of materialist practice? Du Châtelet's reconfiguration of the relationship between gender and pleasure in philosophy inheres not only in her idea of pleasure but in her sense of what femininity itself might pleasurably *do* to and with the production of thought. Still, if what Terrall calls Du Châtelet's "pleasure-based rationalism" is illegible as libertinism, because it seems to bypass or evade the titillating transmission of knowledge as a sexual relation, it is also illegible as materialism in a traditional sense, since Du Châtelet preserves a strong commitment to the metaphysical architecture of a world where human perceptions only manage to catch "traces" of reality and not reality itself. Du Châtelet reworks the characteristic position of women (and the feminine) in the scene of philosophy at the same time as she formulates a theory of matter grounded in Leibnizian metaphysics. In each case she seems to drop out of a conventional history of materialism that can only "see" her as inadequately engaged with or insufficiently committed to the questions that it foregrounds. Terrall identifies Du Châtelet's efforts to "broaden the definition of femininity to include rationalism and mathematical accomplishment" as a failure, in part because of the Marquise's own ambivalence about her performance of gender identity.[14] But the failure, as Terrall makes clear, is not hers alone. Du Châtelet's attachment to an ethic of pleasure that seeks to ratify both feminine scholarly prowess and feminine experience in love seems incidental to metaphysics; yet her theory of matter remains too metaphysical to be retroactively assimilable within a libertine culture of critique.

Ongoing critical debates around the relationship between Du Châtelet and her contemporary La Mettrie have not resolved the difficulty of incorporating Du Châtelet into the field of vision of a materialism that foregrounds pleasure as its *summum bonum*. While La Mettrie recognizes Du Châtelet's philosophical prowess in the *Histoire naturelle*, in the sense that he borrows from the *Institutions de physique* to make some of his arguments, he does not explicitly acknowledge Du Châtelet as a legitimate philosophical interlocutor, although as I have discussed later critics will read the letter prefacing the 1747 edition of this text in such a way as to make of her both an icon of metaphysics and an object of the author's sexual desire.[15] Where Du Châtelet is proximate to La Mettrie's discussion of the nature of matter, the nature of this proximity remains a matter of considerable discussion—and even today tends to engender critical assumptions about her sexual as well as social connections to materialist men. Still, as I hope to show in what follows, Du Châtelet's attachment to pleasure, as a mode of interaction with the world in which thought and experience encounter and shape one another, is both sustained and diversely configured. It is this attachment that allows for her work to cut transversely across various fields of apprehension sometimes understood to be mutually exclusive. For her, pleasure does not interrupt or illustrate the thought that she generates; it emerges from and in it, as a reconciliation of a situation of dependence with a joy that is absolutely for her if not hers alone. It is also centrally concerned with femininity, not just as a constraint (fixing her in a particular position) but as a zone of imaginative possibility. Finally, it is tightly bound to love. For Du Châtelet, the tie between thought and desire makes of both a mode of illusion, but in this illusion the work of love and the work of philosophy can jointly rediscover a relationship to the material conditions that make them possible.

Translating Mandeville with Lucretius: Pleasure in Relation

In the 1735 preface to her translation of Bernard Mandeville's the *Fable of the Bees* (1714), composed between 1735 and 1738 at her estate in Cirey, Du Châtelet opens with a reflection on getting older: "Since I started living with myself, and paying attention to the price of time, to the brevity of life, and to the uselessness of the ways one spends one's existence in the world, I was surprised at my having taken extreme care of my teeth and my hair and having neglected my mind and my understanding. I felt that wit rusts more easily than iron, but it is much more difficult to get its first polish back."[16] In this passage Du Châtelet describes a transition from a world of feminine preoccupations in which the body is a matter of primary concern to a life of philosophical engagement in which her mind—"mon esprit et mon entendement"—is the principle object of her care and cultivation. Du Châtelet often evokes with striking and moving precision the situations in which she works and thinks. In these moments, she gives readers a sense of the material conditions framing her activity as a woman intellectual even in the absence of direct references to feminine attributes or bodies.[17] Her transition to philosophy is not just a turn away from frivolity but is also compelled by the passage of time, which "rusts" the wit and lends a certain rigidity to thought, as she will later suggest in her evocation of a similar transformation at the beginning of the *Institutions de physique*. This acknowledgment of mortality anticipates a distancing from earthly concerns, including not just the parts of the body that need to be dressed and presented in a particular way but the world and its pleasures. It becomes more important to cultivate the understanding than the teeth or hair since all human parts are liable to wear out. The passage from body to mind suggests an exit out of self-incurred immaturity, as Kant will put it in "What is Enlightenment?," toward a more spiritual and enduring knowledge. In this movement, femininity seems to be at least partially effaced.

But the turn from bodily matter ("my teeth, my hair") to mental capacity ("my mind, my understanding") belies a persistent need for activity that is described in surprisingly concrete and material terms—as a form of exercise. Du Châtelet continues:

> Such sensible reflections do not give the soul that flexibility that the lack of exercise strips from it once one has passed the first blush of youth. The *fakirs* of the Indies lose the use of their arm muscles by leaving them in the same position and not employing them. It is thus that one loses one's ideas in neglecting to cultivate them. It's a fire that dies out, if one doesn't continually throw wood on it to keep it up. In wanting to repair, if possible, such a great error, and to try to train this tree that is already too far along, and to make it bear the fruits that could still be hoped from it, I searched for some kind of work that could, in attaching my mind, give it that consistency (if I may express myself thus) that one never acquires without proposing a goal for one's studies. One must conduct oneself as in civil life, knowing well what one wants to be. Lack of resolution producing in the one case false ways of proceeding, and in the other confused ideas.[18]

This paragraph emphasizes first and foremost the necessity of mental focus and intellectual cultivation. But Du Châtelet's description of her efforts to give her mind "consistency" is composed of a series of analogies that liken the soul to the body, the mind to a substance, ideas to muscles. The impression that this passage leaves, then, is less one of the departure from physicality than the latter's reassertion at the heart of thought itself. Like teeth or hair, the mind needs to be polished, cared for, and nourished. The diverse images that propel this passage—from that of the tree that must be trained to the fire that must be fed—evoke the rituals of daily life that are not so much left behind in intellectual work as they are transposed into it. The practice of fussing over teeth and hair becomes the daily mental exercise of an understanding that seeks a substance for itself. If the idea of knowing well what one is suggests both independence and determination—a rejection of uncertainty and ambivalence—the emphasis on the labor of thought, a labor not unlike that of caring for the body, means that this independence is never simply given but emerges over time and in practice. From the opening invocation of the "inutilité" or uselessness of worldly devices, Du Châtelet's comparison of her understanding to other bodies that require nourishment and care brings the emphasis of the preface back around to the material conditions that sustain thought. She asserts her right to the cultivation of autonomy as a mental exercise that lends material weight and power to the actions of her mind. In so doing, she highlights the importance of thought as a mode of being in the world.

Du Châtelet's translation of Mandeville, which she most likely discussed with Voltaire as she wrote and which she never published,[19] stands out among the rest of her works for a number of reasons. Perhaps most strikingly to a modern reader, the preface includes a strong defense of women's right to education and an endorsement of their intellectual potential. As Du Châtelet puts it, "I would have women participate in all the rights of humanity, and above all in those of the mind."[20] Her choice of the *Fable of the Bees* as a translation exercise was unusual on its own, given the association of Mandeville's book with danger and scandal. As Elisabeth Wallmann points out in her article on Mandeville and Du Châtelet, the uproar that accompanied the publication of the text in England informed its French reception as well; following its initial publication in French in 1740, Mandeville's text was ritually burned in Paris and placed on the Index of Prohibited Books.[21] Du Châtelet provides a generally sympathetic reading of Mandeville in her translation, but also revises the original argument significantly, to such an extent that she feels obliged to highlight the "liberté" of her version in the preface. While it was not unusual at the time for translations to be less than faithful, Du Châtelet renders the text with a particularly free hand, transposing the introductory poem into prose, changing English references to French ones, and adding passages of her own (set off by quotation marks in Wade's edition). The result is an ambivalent recuperation of Mandeville, as both Elizabeth Wallmann and Felicia Gottmann discuss,[22] even as it brings into focus Du Châtelet's own ethical commitments.

As Gottmann shows in a particularly nuanced reading of the source text against the translation, Du Châtelet revises Mandeville's criticism of the passions and their role in modern society in part by placing an emphasis on the pleasure that both can provide. For Du Châtelet, virtue is not only compatible with the passions but a source of social cohesion and utility—a universal good. It is tempting to understand Du Châtelet's revisions as leading away from a properly materialist conclusion, at least according to the terms that the original text sets for itself. After all, Du Châtelet is clearly unwilling to endorse Mandevillean self-interest as the primary means by which the social body coheres. Yet the intertexts that Du Châtelet evokes suggest her text's relationship to a materialist past, since her turn toward virtue in the translation occurs not only in the name of pleasure (as Gottmann points out) but through the invocation of Lucretius as a key Epicurean authority. In her reference to the Roman poet, Du Châtelet embraces voluptuous delight as part of an argument on behalf of love as a key social relation. Moreover, her particular use of Lucretius suggests that it is in the production of knowledge—through the work of the philosophical text itself on author and reader—that the solitary cultivation of thought and understanding can transmute itself into the strengthening of social bonds. In scholarship as in love, as Du Châtelet will explicitly affirm in later texts, the pleasure of the individual—in this case, an individual woman—can take flight or bear fruit.

While Du Châtelet's reference to the *De rerum natura* (DRN) is in one sense a glancing one, it plays a crucial role in shifting the tenor of Mandeville's argument. She interposes two paragraphs of her own composition at the beginning of the first chapter, "De l'origine des vertus morales" [*On the Origin of the Moral Virtues*]. These paragraphs render the origins of human society as follows:

> Love appears to have been the beginning of all society. Man, like all other animals, has an invincible penchant for the propagation of his species.
>
> A man, having fallen in love with a woman, will have children with her. The care of their family will have caused the union to outlast their taste for it. Two families will have had a need the one for the other out of which they will have been formed, and these mutual needs will have given birth to society. Thus Lucretius was right when he said to Venus: *nec sine te quicquam dias in luminis oras exoritur*. Mutual needs having brought men together, the more capable among them perceived that man was born with an untamable pride, and it is from the empire that this passion has over him, that the first lawgivers extracted the greatest remedies to arrive at civilization.[23]

As Felicia Gottman points out in her analysis of this passage, the changes to Mandeville's account of the beginnings of human social life are particularly noteworthy here. They include the emphasis on love and the focus on natural sociability and mutual need, both enabled by the turn to Lucretius.

Gottman emphasizes the fact that Du Châtelet is more or less summarizing the Lucretian anthropology of book five of the *DRN* in her discussion of the development of social bonds out of those of love.[24] Du Châtelet's insertion of Lucretius at this point sits uneasily with Mandeville's portrayal of early humans as fundamentally self-interested; it is also inconsistent with a tradition of Augustinian neo-Epicureanism that highlights the asocial nature of humankind.

In the quote that she selects from the *DRN*, Du Châtelet is not only engaged in a revision of a neo-Epicurean position that sees humans as wholly motivated by selfish passions, she is also knitting together two specific passages from the Lucretian source text in an unexpected way. The quotation that she includes—*nec sine te quicquam dias in luminis oras exoritur* ["since without you nothing comes forth into the shining borders of light"]—is drawn from the first section of the first book of the epic poem, at a moment where Lucretius links the ability of Venus to animate the cosmos with love to his own capacity as a poet to bring his work into the world. In the invocation, Venus lends to the poem the same kind of galvanizing and pleasure-inducing force that she uses to cause the earth to spring to life. The full passage from Lucretius reads: "Since therefore you alone govern the nature of things, *since without you nothing comes forth into the shining borders of light,* nothing joyous and lovely is made, you I crave as partner in writing the verses, which I essay to fashion on the Nature of Things, for my friend Memmius, whom you, goddess, have willed at all times to excel, endowed with all gifts. Therefore all the more grant to my speech, goddess, an ever-living charm" [italics my own].[25] Lucretius suggests an analogy at this moment between the ability of Venus to generate life and her ability to animate the poem, to lend it stimulating charm. In this context, the goddess acts to enliven and intensify the social tie between poet and his addressee Memmius, ratifying the conversion to materialism and sustaining the friendship built on patronage. But this tie is also imbued with the energy that circulates through nature as a scene of voluptuous pleasure. Lucretius specifically calls to Venus as a "partner" in poetic production, so that the joy of the reader who receives the materialist message is likened to the erotic joy that Venus disseminates throughout the natural world in the very first lines of the poem. In contrast, the Venus of the anthropology brings into being human society itself. Thanks to her, men and women first come together in "violent force" and "vehement lust"; later, she acts to cause them to "grow soft" so that children are able to compel their proud and hardy parents to care for them.[26] It is at this point that friendship and mutual sociability begin. Children, requiring nurture from their parents, allow "invincible" erotic need to be transformed into a shared sociability. Under the aegis of Venus, erotic desire and social cohesion are not in opposition to one another but interconnected; the one animates the other.

In both the first and the fifth book of Lucretius's epic, then, pleasure reveals itself as capable of traversing distinct types of relationships that bring together different kinds of beings. Du Châtelet's summary condenses these various models of human and nonhuman relationality, which shift with the shifting emphasis of the poem, into one narrative. In quoting from the opening of the *DRN* and then turning to a summary of the anthropology, she is thus combining not only two distinct moments in the Lucretian text but multiple conceptions of love that turn out to be co-constitutive. The juxtaposition of the Venus of the invocation with the Venus of the anthropology suggests the entanglement of different modes of love in the figure of the goddess, who gathers together and integrates them with one another. Du Châtelet's portrayal of the origins of human society thus stresses the capacity of Venus to modulate and modify the workings of desire to serve multiple purposes. In contrast to the more individualist reading of human desire emphasized by Mandeville—in which the passions operate to set humans against one another—Du Châtelet's focus is on the relational aspects of love—whether in the erotic encounter, the care that parents bestow upon their children, or the love of the author for her work. In her endorsement of pleasure as a motive force, Du Châtelet moves away from a conventionally libertine position, which tends to condense diverse modes of desire into a scene of seduction and conquest. Instead, she implicitly proffers a concept of love in which the pleasure animating the world, the delight taken by the couple, the care experienced by the parent, and the joy galvanized by the writer herself intermingle with one another, to various effects.

Lucretius himself suggests that it is not just sensually animated bodies that produce pleasure but the poetic work that generates a new and vital source of delight. This enjoyment, which stems from a textual encounter and expresses a transformed relation to the world, is in a sense self-augmenting and self-sustaining, disseminating and proliferating through the reader's engagement with the Epicurean poem. In this context, Du Châtelet's choice to undertake a *translation* resonates as yet another pleasurable relation that might serve an Epicurean purpose. Halfway through the preface, she writes of her luck in being able to meet and become friends with notable *gens de lettres*; thanks to their early recognition of her potential. "I began to believe that I was a thinking creature," she writes.[27] Yet, despite the unusual support she has received, she still presents herself as lacking in "that creative genius that allows new truths to be found."[28] In her terms, her labor as a translator allows her to clearly render that which other minds have already uncovered, thereby making useful to the reading public works that would otherwise remain out of their reach. At this as at other moments in the preface, and later in her essay on happiness, she foregrounds the need for women to cultivate an intellectual life not just as a source of personal enjoyment but as a mode of sociable interaction. For all of her text's ambivalence around her status as a woman author, Du Châtelet's emphasis throughout her discussion of philosophical translation is on a network of connections that provides the impetus for the scholarly work, which subsequently generates its own set of relational entanglements and satisfactions.

The tie between the individual pursuit of thought and a more collective social good, which takes shape in both theory and practice, is likewise central to Du Châtelet's defense of women's education. If women are given the tools they need to participate in the "rights of the mind" [*les droits de l'esprit*], as she puts it, "This new education would be all in all a great good for the human species. Women would be the better for it and men would gain from it a new subject of emulation; and traffic [*commerce*] with us, which in polishing their mind too often renders it weaker and smaller, would then only serve to expand their knowledge."[29] To be a *créature pensante* or "thinking creature" is not only to be engaged in an act of self-cultivation that strengthens and fortifies the substance of the mind, it is also to become a source of inspiration and strength for others. Here the image of a traffic in women returns once again. Du Châtelet appears to echo Montesquieu's and Rousseau's concerns about the detrimental or feminizing effects on men of feminine sociability. Yet in making a claim for women's right to education, she proposes that the contagious effects of femininity might be redeployed for a more expansive and indeed enlightened social purpose. Rather than proffering an image of infection, she suggests a new mode of emulation that might arise from a changing social scene. Throughout this discussion, Du Châtelet highlights the way in which mental activity may be put to work in various contexts, shaping and molding the circumstances in which thought emerges and operates. It is crucial for her to recognize how scholarly production redounds back upon the situations in which it is produced. The transition that she invokes in the beginning of the translation—a turn away from preoccupation with the body to a concern with mental activity—is also a transition from one mode of sociability, organized around feminine desirability, to another in which pleasures continue to serve to solidify social bonds but women might as a result be accorded the recognition and respect that they deserve. In this transition neither the body nor desire are effaced; rather, they are themselves translated into multiple forms, colluding with one another to lend consistency to the project at hand.

Du Châtelet thus extracts from her project of translation, which significantly revises the thrust of Mandeville's own text, an Epicureanism that combines the pursuit of pleasure with an attachment to love and relationality, thereby undercutting the libertine focus on individual desire as a motive force while retaining a materialist orientation. This attachment makes of intellectual production its own mode of pleasure-giving—whether by advancing the project of knowledge, stimulating the emulation of others, or exercising the mind—and suggests (once again following Lucretius) that the creative figuration of the world in philosophy can become its own kind of generative act. And indeed, the thread that connects pleasure to philosophical work can be followed from her translation into Du Châtelet's metaphysics. Mary Terrall contends that Du Châtelet's embrace of pleasure extends to her conception of God himself: "Where Leibniz had grounded his philosophy on God's infinite wisdom, Du Châtelet attributes the divine choice to the pleasure God takes in his creation, a pleasure linked to the rational process of optimization. The best of all possible worlds is that 'which pleases him the most'; the contemplation of perfection is a source of pleasure to God."[30] In the passage from the *Institutions de physique* that Terrall cites, Du Châtelet affirms that "the contemplation of perfection is the source of pleasure in intelligent Beings, for that which has more perfection pleases more, and a reasonable Being only desires things in proportion to the perfections that he finds in them."[31] As Du Châtelet explains, the reason for God's creation of the earth as it is lies in the satisfaction that he takes in this world's perfection. Human intelligence follows the same principle, although our understanding is limited in comparison to that of the divine creator and we are thus more likely to be led astray in our assessments of what is good, taking "an apparent perfection" for a "real" one.[32] Du Châtelet locates pleasure both in the act of creation itself—"he has thus chosen the proceedings of the things that make up this Universe to bring it into being, according to that which pleased him the most"[33]—and in the contemplation of this creation by the divine being.

As in her account of God's delight in this best of all possible worlds (following Leibniz), Du Châtelet's sense of the pleasure involved in human intellectual activity is linked to the organization and shaping of reality as we perceive it. Science, directly concerned with apprehending the matter of experience, may thus become the source of sustained delight. Du Châtelet is more dubious about the effects of poetic texts on readerly pleasure. In the preface to her translation, she stresses that her interest lies specifically in works of philosophy [*ouvrages de raisonnement*], since reason is universal while rhetoric is local—tied to place and custom. "The genius of the language,"[34] as she puts it, should be of little concern to philosophers, who dispense with style in favor of ideas, and whose work is thus eminently capable of being shared across linguistic traditions. She presents imagination as in a basic sense untranslatable and, as a result, difficult if not impossible to convey from one language to another: "it is impossible to have faithful accounts of the imagination of men," she contends.[35] Reason, on the other hand, provides the foundation for human connections across culture. Du Châtelet stops short of rejecting the need for poetic translation—she claims that the translators of poetry must be great poets themselves—but she does not see this work as contributing to collective human good in the same way that philosophy may.

In the *Institutions*, Du Châtelet sharpens her dismissal of the flowers of rhetoric, specifically by emphasizing the pleasure to be taken in the actions of reason, which she distinguishes from the products of wit. She writes to her son, "I didn't dream in this work of displaying wit, but of displaying reason; and I believed in yours enough to think that you were capable of seeking truth free from all the foreign ornaments with which one burdens it these days."[36] Her rejection of literary ornament here seems to accord with her turn away from personal decoration in the preface to her translation; both begin with a dismissal of frivolity and superficiality in favor of the more substantial delights that inhere in the pursuit of truth.[37] Yet it is not the austerity of reason but its capacity to sustain human interest and to promote human enjoyment of the world that lend philosophy its allure. As Du Châtelet explains in the *Institutions*, "I have contented myself with removing the thorns that could have wounded your delicate hands, but I did not think myself obliged to replace them with strange flowers, and I am persuaded that a good mind, as weak as it might still be, finds more pleasure, as well as a more satisfying pleasure, in a clear and precise form of reasoning that it grasps with ease, than in a misplaced witticism."[38] Beginning as she does with a conventional distinction—cleaving the rigors of reason from the pleasures of rhetoric, the honey from the bitter draught of philosophy—Du Châtelet proceeds to displace it, ending the passage with an insistence on the heightened pleasure to be gained from "a clear and precise form of reasoning."

Her rationale for the turn away from rhetoric thus lies not in the refusal of pleasure but in the embrace of it. Reason becomes a source of intensified delight rather than a means toward delight's sublimation. As Du Châtelet declares to her son, "You must accustom your mind to thinking early on, and to being sufficient unto itself, you will feel in all the periods of your life what resources and consolations one finds in Study, and you will see that the latter can even generate delights and pleasures."[39] This formulation might seem muted. It positions scholarly work as a supplement or a substitution for livelier pleasures once the time for the latter has passed. But it also suggests a form of sensuous delight that is consistently accessible through this work. This enjoyment takes both individual and collective forms; it emerges out of networks of relationships that it feeds into and maintains over time. In the next section of the foreword Du Châtelet confirms, without hesitation: "The study of Physics seems to be made for Man, it deals with things that are always around us, and on which our pleasures and our needs depend."[40] She contends that the study of geometry, with its intrinsic connection to sensory apprehension, is particularly appropriate for young students, and she insists on physics as a form of knowledge with direct ties to human satisfaction. Yet she also acknowledges the cares that she, like other parents, must take in preparing the way for their children to make pleasure where they may and can. In a passage that recalls her invocation of the Lucretian anthropology from her translation's preface, Du Châtelet informs her son that, even if the production of this text for him has caused her pain, "I will think it [la peine] well spent if it can inspire in you love of the Sciences and the desire to cultivate your reason. What pains and what cares does one not take every day in the uncertain hope of procuring honors for one's children and of enhancing their fortune! Is the knowledge of truth, and the habit of seeking it out and following it, a less worthy object of my cares; especially in an age when Physics crosses all ranks and begins to participate in the science of the world?"[41] It is both the knowledge of truth and the desire to find it out that benefit the child here, an advantage that extends outward toward society as a whole. Like the parents in the Lucretian poem, who are inspired by Venus to soften the violence of their desires in order to tend to their offspring, Du Châtelet dedicates herself to her text in the hope of guaranteeing the future happiness of her son through the love of study. The shared taste for physics forms part of her bond to her child but also part of this child's eventual bond to the world that will receive him.

In the *Institutions*, Du Châtelet connects the pursuit of pleasure to the work of science, both as an activity undertaken by human reason and as a series of acts that generate effects on the world in which they occur. Read in tandem with her invocation of Lucretius in the translation, the *Institutions* reveal scientific instruction as part of a project of transmitting pleasurable feeling across generations and over time. In these texts, Du Châtelet explicitly and implicitly connects the labor of reason to the work of love, but not because both satisfy an erotic compulsion (as in the Augustinian model that is heavily satirized and reworked by libertine thinkers). Instead, thought represents an enduring source of pleasure in being itself—a pleasure that might be communicated through scenes of instruction and acts of translation. At the same time, scientific experimentation represents its own mode of productive fabrication—a project within which selves might be shaped and sustained, as Julie Candler Hayes has discussed.[42] Science responds actively to human need—it allows us to negotiate our dependence on one another and to affirm our obligations to one another—but it also functions as a potential zone of human autonomy, specifically in the delight that emanates from the work that it requires.

But there is another sense in which reason and love converge for Du Châtelet—and that is in their connection to illusion. Illusion as she presents it operates in the gap between the phenomenal world—the world as it is received by the human senses—and reality as it is organized in ways fundamentally inaccessible to our limited perceptions. It makes of the very encounter with the world a creative act—a mode of artifice in which our pleasure works upon the stuff of life. And it has specific ties to femininity, not because of women's helplessness in the face of desire (their own or others), but because of their acute understanding that pleasure is not simply there for the taking. Enjoyment emerges in the interstices between what is and what is known or felt, crafted out of the gaps that inform our knowledge. Illusion is one way in which the relationship between these strata—the noumenal and the phenomenal—may be adjusted or accorded to maximize delight. This is an urgent task for women in particular, who lack the opportunities afforded to men to inhabit their passions with intensity and conviction. In what follows, I will explore some of the different zones in which Du Châtelet herself carried on this delicate but delightful labor.

The Matter of Artifice

In 1738, Du Châtelet secretly submitted an entry to the prize essay competition sponsored by the Paris Academy of Science. When Voltaire had decided to enter the competition, the two of them worked alongside one another at Cirey conducting experiments on "the nature and propagation of fire," the assigned subject. Du Châtelet wrote up her findings and submitted her own entry without telling Voltaire. In the end, neither of them won the prize, but ultimately the academy published both essays, even though they disagreed with one another. Françoise de Graffigny, who was reading Du Châtelet's essay in December 1738, wrote to Antoine Devaux that "[Her essay] is the best that can be written on this subject, with a cleanness, a precision, and a resonance; begging Mr de V.'s pardon, but it's well above him."[43] Voltaire argued that fire must have a weight, while Du Châtelet took the position that fire was an imponderable—"the soul of the world" that throws parts of bodies into motion, like the breath that God spreads over the universe.[44] In the *Dissertation sur la nature et la propagation du feu*, as Du Châtelet eventually entitled her published text, fire is thus poised somewhat uneasily between the world of matter and that of spirit, responsible for animating all sorts of bodies but receding from human attempts to know or grasp it. As she writes in the first sentence of the treatise, "Fire manifests itself to us through such different Phenomena, that it is almost as difficult to define it by its effects, as to know its nature entirely: it incessantly escapes the grasp of our mind, although it is within us, and in all the bodies that surround us."[45] If fire here eludes intellectual apprehension in significant ways, it also resists sensory perception in certain respects, since, as Du Châtelet argues, the attributes that we tend to assign to fire (heat and light) are two modes that fire assumes rather than essential properties of it. As she points out, other beings, organized differently from humans, might perceive fire in a different way entirely. Yet fire is a universal force, fundamental to the order of the cosmos. In enlivening bodies, it functions as something of the antagonist to gravity. She affirms, "The rarefaction that fire operates on all the bodies that it penetrates seems to be one of the primitive laws of Nature, one of the springs of the Creator, and the reason for which Fire was made; without this property of Fire everything in Nature would be compressed; all fluidity, and perhaps all elasticity, come from Fire, and without this universal agent, without this breath of life that God has spread over his works, Nature would languish in repose and the Universe could not last for a minute such as it is."[46] Indeed, it is only thanks to divine intervention that fire does not destroy that which it has animated; God puts limits on fire's power just as he guarantees its distribution across the many bodies that populate the universe.

In the *Dissertation*, fire's activity cuts across matter and spirit; it is both formally and physically generative. Du Châtelet presents the elusiveness of fire not as a spur to voyeuristic curiosity—since fire is always something other than it appears to us to be—but as a rationale for intertwining speculative hypothesis with pragmatic experiment. At the same time, fire deploys specific powers that reveal themselves to humans in consistent ways. We are galvanized by these moments of discovery—where hypothesis meets empirical investigation, where metaphysical speculation meets the elasticity of material bodies[47]—as knowing subjects who cannot ever fully perceive the forces that shape us most powerfully. "Within us, and in all the bodies that surround us" —Du Châtelet's description marshals the ubiquity and power of an energetic force that persistently evades our grasp but nonetheless puts us, and everything around us, in motion. Fire is at once multiple in its effects—phenomenologically varied and variable—and singular in its power. The more tightly it is intertwined with material bodies—the more intensely it moves us—the more productively it intervenes in our attempts to account for it. It is made palpable and visible to us in the phenomena it mobilizes, even as it puts us into motion. Moreover, fire in the *Dissertation* takes on a combinatory force. As Du Châtelet writes, "Without this perpetual action and reaction of Fire on bodies, and of bodies on fire, all fluidity, all elasticity, all softness would be banished, and if matter were deprived for a moment of this spirit of life that animates it, of this powerful agent that fights ceaselessly against the unification of bodies, everything would be compressed in the Universe and it would soon be destroyed."[48] Fire is active, but, crucially, it is not itself sensate. There is thus a gap between its abstract power and the phenomenal world, which science may work to bridge through speculation and experimentation. Fire's artifice is in a sense matched and met by human artifice; fire ensures the elasticity of matter *and* of the thought that seeks to account for it.

While Du Châtelet herself sometimes portrays her essay as a mere foray into the topic set by the academy rather than a definitive statement, her preoccupation with fire's potential to create and combine—and her insistence on the interpenetration of metaphysics and experiment—anticipate the revisions of Leibniz and Newton that she will undertake in the *Institutions*. In the latter text, as Julie Candler Hayes has beautifully shown, matter itself demonstrates a "labyrinthine potential" that echoes fire's combinatory energy.[49] In the chapter "De la Figure, & de la Porosité des Corps," Du Châtelet writes, "The different orders of particles of which I am presuming here Bodies to be composed, are only in truth in the order of things that some experiments make probable, and of which it is necessary to find the confirmation in other experiments: but, however may be generated the innumerable number of combinations necessary for producing the diversity that reigns in nature, one cannot admire too much the artifice by means of which so many things of such variety come from the assemblages of first Bodies."[50] The evident diversity of the natural world, in all of its possibilities, is a product of the capacity of nature to make combinations from among the different orders of particles of which substance is composed: Artifice is constantly at work, allowing for a passage from the metaphysical to the physical realm.[51] But this same diversity—generated through the figurative power of particles—also produces and requires the reiterated work of experimentation. Du Châtelet's embrace of hypothesis thus functions as an impetus for scientific practice, enabling the transition from thought to matter and back again, in a process analogous to that which brings bodies themselves into being. Where the particles of the first order, imperceptible and unknowable as such, produce the astonishing variety of the natural world, which we can perceive and enjoy, hypothesis produces experiment after experiment in an effort to find confirmation for itself.

Nature for Du Châtelet is thus the expression of a mode of artifice in which human and nonhuman agencies may collude. But there is another force at work here—that of God, who, in the *Dissertation* and the *Institutions*, ascribes specific limits to the power of matter. In the *Dissertation*, it is God who ensures that the enlivening energy of fire does not simply consume that which it brings into being. It is in part because of God's activity—which lends to humans a capacity for freedom that is denied other bodies—that Du Châtelet's metaphysical position does not end up tipping into animism or vitalism. As the letter that prefaces the *Histoire naturelle de l'ame* intimates, Du Châtelet's particles come very close to acquiring activity in and for themselves; her fire-as-world-soul has clear affinities with Stoic materialism if not also with the Epicurean position that La Mettrie would espouse. But, as is also obvious in the *Dissertation* itself, Du Châtelet retains her metaphysical commitments to the organizing power of the divine creator, who is responsible for managing the capacity of fire to destroy just as, in the *Institutions*, he "has set out the limits of each Being, and these limits are never crossed."[52] In a universe in motion, God lends regularity and order to the operations of matter with the boundaries that he places on its potential.[53] As she writes in the *Dissertation*, "If the power of Fire over bodies were not limited, Fire would soon destroy the universe, the limits that the Creator has imposed on it and that it never crosses are one of the great proofs of the design that rules in this universe."[54] She continues, "Thus Fire is the most powerful and perhaps the only agent of Nature for uniting and for separating."[55]

Both the *Dissertation* and the *Institutions* underscore the tension between matter's abstract power to smudge and blur the boundaries between beings and the stability of the universe as humans observe it. It is God who resolves this tension in favor of coherence. In the *Institutions*, Du Châtelet points out, "If Matter were infinitely soluble, it would be impossible for the same sprouts and the same seeds to produce the same animals and the same plants . . .: for if the sap that nourishes them were sometimes more refined and sometimes more crude, . . . it would be impossible for them not to be subject to perpetual variations . . .: thus, the form and the manner of being in composites would be subject to a thousand changes, and the species of things would be constantly confused. Now, there is none of this disorder in the Universe."[56] Each being persists in its essence because of the limits that God ascribes to it. Matter is at once indescribably subtle in its arrangements—to such an extent that human imagination struggles to compass it—and finite in the shapes that it takes. Yet this finitude appears to us as a form of infinity; the diversity of matter is such that we are unable to distinguish its primary particles, Du Châtelet explains.[57] The limits placed on matter's power thus remain for us both hypothetical and necessary.

The workings of God allow for the workings of the universe as a whole to accord with human need and lend pertinence to human observation, restricted as the latter is. They guarantee not only the perfection of creation—that activity in which God himself takes delight—but the persistence of human enjoyment.[58] God's creative power intervenes to ratify a certain rational order of things and to enable pleasure to be sustained in a cosmos that otherwise would collapse in chaos. Du Châtelet's recourse to divine agency is thus suggestive not only of her need to retain a certain optimism about the way in which the universe should function, but of her pessimism about what it might mean to embrace without hesitation the motive force of substance. Reading the *Dissertation* alongside the *Institutions*, we can see that it is not just reason that needs to be underwritten by divine intervention—this is the point of the "principle of sufficient reason" that she borrows from Leibniz and that she will develop at length in the *Institutions*. Pleasure also requires this guarantee, in a universe where the power of matter to destroy and confuse, to burn down as well as to create, is such that it could threaten to obliterate the world. Human enjoyment, like human intellection, is ratified by a divine power infused throughout the visible and invisible worlds. Yet the divide between this world as humans perceive it and matter as it is still requires human ingenuity to bridge. Our pleasures, too, emerge from artifice—but in the very energy of this artifice lies its fragility. In the face of an Epicureanism that might be too sanguine about the capacity of the natural world to satisfy us, Du Châtelet reveals that pleasure requires its own metaphysics to be assured. Even in the face of the metaphysical guarantee, however, this pleasure is not simply extended to us; it must be brought into being as part of a constant ongoing crafting of our own relationship to the world, whether in the laboratory or in society. In this process, our human artifice may echo the divine one, resonating through the workings of nature itself. The energies of the scientist, the energies of particles of which nature is made up, the energies of God—all of these combine to animate the world in accordance with human delight, but they also reveal the vulnerability of this delight, which is never given over, always only emerging in the moment when matter engages with its limit.

Illusion Without Error: The *Discours sur le bonheur*

Du Châtelet returns to this complex interplay between pessimism and optimism, strength and vulnerability, independence and dependence in her *Discours sur le bonheur*, which she probably worked on in stages throughout the 1730s and 1740s.[59] Here she makes clear the particular importance for women of the cultivation of pleasure in artifice—a means to operate upon matter as matter works upon the bodies that it shapes. In the *Discours*, which is perhaps the least metaphysical of Du Châtelet's writings, God more or less drops out as an active force. In his place stands a feminine figure: A woman who studies and loves, and, in love as in study, seeks to sustain the illusion of pleasure to be taken in the world—to wrest enjoyment from potential chaos and yet to preserve delight's guarantee. In the *Discours*, Du Châtelet is not simply ratifying a model of feminine intellectual accomplishment or positioning women as naturally more responsive or receptive to nature's impression. Instead, she is suggesting that it is precisely because women's pleasures are so vulnerable that they need to dedicate themselves with particular attention to the cultivation of those artifices in which they might make a fragile and elusive satisfaction for themselves. Since pleasure is not easy to come by, we must always be crafting it—wresting it from within the divide between the world as we perceive it and the world as we desire it to be. In the *Discours*, Du Châtelet hews most closely to an Epicurean ethics, but at the same time she asserts that pleasure is not free for the taking, particularly for women. What we enjoy must come to us through artifice—whether divine, natural, or human. In this acknowledgment a small space opens for women to remake their own enmeshment with and confinement in an often harsh world, to knit together reason and love, and to marshal a creative force that will stretch delight over time.

The *Discours sur le bonheur* is on the one hand part of a proliferation of treatises on happiness for which the eighteenth century is well known.[60] It shares preoccupations not only with Fontenelle's essay on happiness (cited by Puisieux), which Robert Mauzi likens to Du Châtelet's essay in its focus on the author's own experience, but with La Mettrie's *Anti-Sénèque ou Discours sur le bonheur* (1748); Helvétius's poem *Le Bonheur*, published posthumously by the marquis de Saint-Lambert himself and discussed in Chapter 1; and Voltaire's *Discours sur l'homme* (1734–1737), initially entitled *Épître sur le bonheur* and inspired in part by Alexander Pope.[61] It is clear from this list of influences—almost all men whom she would have known personally—the extent to which Du Châtelet was enmeshed in an enlightened philosophical milieu, both intellectually and affectively. Yet the *Discours sur le bonheur* stands out among these other examinations of happiness not just because it was authored by a woman. In the *Discours*, Du Châtelet is less interested in a theory of happiness in the abstract than she is in linking a particular experience of happiness to the conditions in which happiness might emerge. While she frames this emphasis in a pedagogical context that will be familiar to readers of the *Institutions*—she writes of her hope that younger readers of her work will find in her writing reflections that might guide them in their own pursuit of a happy life—her recommendations are couched in a description of her specific feelings, moods, tendencies, and desires that remains remarkable for its forthrightness. The essay also makes regular reference to Du Châtelet's own experience in her elucidation of the "machines of happiness," as she puts it.

Throughout the essay, the themes that I have been tracking in this chapter recur, including an emphasis on the consolatory delight of scholarship, a commitment to love, and an investment in pleasure as a universal good. But they do so in persistent relation to Du Châtelet's own situation: They take shape as part of her reflection on femininity as a lived condition. Perhaps this more personal or subjective emphasis helps explain why the essay is resolutely secular, with little to no mention made of divine agency. In the absence of God's authority, it is the autobiographical subject who must step in to shore up the truth claims that the essay makes. In this context, it becomes clear from the outset that pleasure is fragile. It is not given to everyone to be able to cultivate delight, whether theirs or that of another, in the world. This limitation on the human capacity for pleasure leads Du Châtelet to the second remarkable aspect of the *Discours*—notably, its explicit endorsement of illusion as a principle of happiness. Here another path opens up for the "adjustment" of the world in accordance with feminine desire, a mode of realignment that recalls the work of God—who takes pleasure in his creation—but also invokes the figure of the philosopher, whose speculations seek to make contact with the reality of the world as it is, to pull this reality into the service of human enjoyment and human need. In the *Discours*, her attachment to scholarship on the one hand and love on the other operate in tandem to put illusion to work for pleasure—and for women's pleasure in particular. Where Puisieux seeks to mobilize the poetic or visual image for this purpose, for Du Châtelet the twin crafts of scientific investigation and amorous devotion open up a space for enjoyment to persist.

Du Châtelet prioritizes illusion in her very definition of happiness, which opens the essay. In the third paragraph, she writes,

> In order to be happy, one must have freed oneself of prejudices, one must be virtuous, healthy, have tastes and passions, and be susceptible to illusions; for we owe most of our pleasures to illusions, and unhappy is the one who has lost them. Far then, from seeking to make them disappear by the torch of reason, let us try to thicken the varnish that illusion lays on the majority of objects. It is even more necessary to them than are care and finery to our body.[62]

The conclusion to this passage recalls Du Châtelet's evocation of bodily cultivation and adornment in her translation project. But, in this instance, the role of reason, which she also stresses in her preface to Mandeville's *Fable*, is more ambivalent. She likens illusion to a "varnish" that is painted over the objects that humans encounter and then asserts: We must work not to strip the world of this decorative sheen but to augment it. Just as clothing and jewelry adorn our bodies—and the "we" here is implicitly feminine, if not feminized—illusion adorns reality with a coating that pleases us. If we are to cultivate our pleasures, we must be careful not to feed reason's dissipating flame—to set our world on fire with our desire for a truer knowledge.

Illusion as a mode of perception is distinct from error or mistake, both of which should be actively combatted, and it is not a form of prejudice, since it is defensible even when technically false.[63] It activates sensory and sensual perception as a way of coming into contact with a world that does not always please, but it is not a refusal to see things the way they are. In the next line of the text, Du Châtelet emphasizes the role of pleasure in the happy life: "One must begin by saying to oneself, and by convincing oneself, that we have nothing to do in the world but to obtain for ourselves some agreeable sensations and feelings."[64] The positioning of this claim after her strong endorsement of illusion suggests that the turn to pleasure might require its own mode of self-deception. As it turns out, happiness involves both a liberation from falsehood—the dissipation of prejudice—and a cultivation of receptivity to the illusions that lend life worth. The latter are the source of intensely pleasant feelings and may be actively fostered or rejected, even though we do not decide on the power they hold over us. Du Châtelet compares these "illusions of happiness," as Marcy P. Lascano calls them, to optical illusions, which may still work their effects even if we know, rationally, that they are deceptive. Eric Schliesser has speculated that "On an epistemic level Du Châtelet's category of an illusion is close in spirit to the character of Spinoza's universal tenets of faith, which can be beyond rationally knowable, but ought to avoid knowable falsehood."[65] Might this resemblance suggest a distinctive genealogy for an illusive eighteenth-century materialism, one in which femininity holds a central place? Perhaps we could find at this moment the stirrings of a feminine counter-Enlightenment, with influences from both Epicureanism and Spinozism, that imagines a community of feminine persons actively remaking the affective, imaginative, and eventually political possibilities available to them through the work and pleasures of writing, research, and conversation.

Either way, in Du Châtelet's account of the importance of illusion for ensuring her own happiness and potentially that of others, it is clear that what engages and sustains her may come not in the rejection of artifice but through its specific and tactical embrace. In keeping with her reflections in her translation of Mandeville, Du Châtelet contends that the passions are of primary importance in life: "One is only happy because of satisfied tastes and passions," she affirms.[66] Her interest in the passions follows from her investment in pleasure; even if the former produce more unhappiness than happiness in the world, they are worth pursuing for the liveliness of the delight that they generate. "I say they are still to be more desired, because they are a necessary condition for the enjoyment of great pleasures. Now, the only point of living is to experience agreeable sensations and feelings; and the stronger the agreeable feelings are, the happier one is."[67] Here Du Châtelet doubles down on an unusual acknowledgment that she has already made in the fourth paragraph of the essay—namely, that the passions are not available to everyone equally, nor are they universally felt. Instead, they emerge from a context: "So it is desirable to be susceptible to the passions, and let me say it again: passions do not come for the asking."[68] A given person's impassioned experience is thus tightly linked to "state" [*état*] and "fortune." As Du Châtelet will demonstrate, gender and class play an important role not just in determining whose passions may be satisfied but in shaping what it is possible to feel. Illusions, in this context, can function as a kind of prosthetic—a means to heighten and intensify passions that are unevenly distributed across society. "It is for us to make them serve our happiness, and that often depends on us," she affirms.[69] But from this supplement is forged the substance of experience.

How does illusion engender delight? A bit later in the essay, Du Châtelet parses more finely the distinction between illusion and error, with an eye toward discovering how the former operates on us. She writes, in a passage already cited in the Introduction to this book:

> Finally, I say that to be happy one must be susceptible to illusion, and this scarcely needs to be proved; but, you will object, you have said that error is always harmful: is illusion not an error? No: although it is true, that illusion does not make us see objects entirely as they must be in order for them to give us agreeable feelings, it only adjusts them to our nature. Such are optical illusions: now optics does not deceive us, although it does not allow us to see objects as they are, because it makes us see them in the manner necessary for them to be useful to us.[70]

At this moment Du Châtelet acknowledges illusion as a specific technology of pleasure—a mechanism inciting our enjoyment by means of an artifice that is inherent in rather than external to nature more generally. The stimulation that illusion provides accommodates objects to our perceptions of them, without doing violence to those objects "as they must be." Indeed, illusion operates in the fissure that divides reality from our perception of it. In making "adjustments" to what is, illusion smooths the passage between inner and outer worlds, interweaves our perceptions with the environments that we inhabit, and makes available to us a range of sensory and imaginative possibilities that would otherwise remain out of reach.

If nature contains within itself its own illusion-making power, one that generates delight in those who encounter it, performances or spectacles can exploit the same potential. As Du Châtelet continues,

> Why do I laugh more than anyone else at the puppets, if not because I allow myself to be more susceptible than anyone else to illusion, and that after a quarter of an hour I believe that it is Polichinelle, the puppet, who speaks? Would we have a moment of pleasure at the theater if we did not lend ourselves to the illusion that makes us see famous individuals that we know have been dead for a long time, speaking in Alexandrine verse? Truly, what pleasure would one have at any other spectacle where all is illusion if one was not able to abandon oneself to it? Surely there would be much to lose, and those at the opera who only have the pleasure of the music and the dances have a very meager pleasure, one well below that which this enchanting spectacle viewed as a whole provides.[71]

Here activity and passivity coexist in a momentary deception to which the spectator must know how to lend herself, a dynamic that echoes Puisieux's literary explorations of the workings of tropes and images on feminine desire. The pleasure to be taken in spectacle involves both a knowledge of the performance as artifice and a willed suspension of disbelief, by means of which the spectator solicits the transporting effects that will delight her. But this oscillation between awareness and enchantment is not characteristic of art alone, as it turns out. Du Châtelet continues:

> I have cited spectacles, because illusion is easier to perceive there. It is, however, involved in all the pleasures of our life, and provides the polish, the gloss of life. Some will perhaps say that illusion does not depend on us, and that is only too true, up to a point. We cannot give ourselves illusions any more than we can give ourselves tastes, or passions, but we can keep the illusions that we have; we can seek not to destroy them. We can choose not to go behind the set, to see the wheels that make flight, and the other machines of theatrical productions. Such is the artifice that we can use, and that artifice is neither useless, nor unproductive.[72]

And she sums up: "These are the great machines of happiness, so to speak."[73] It is through the ability of illusion to provide and maintain the "gloss of life" that nature works upon our pleasures, not independently of our will, but enmeshed in our very perceptions. In engendering these pleasures in us, illusion thereby exposes the interconnections binding self to world, but it also highlights our own ability to cultivate or nurture these networks—and thereby to modify the nature of our participation in them—even if we do not voluntarily choose to enter them in the first place. Du Châtelet's consolatory project in the *Discours* entails not only the promotion of an enlightened rationality in the form of scholarly research and reflection but an endorsement of the sweet artifice by means of which a second nature, an "other" nature that nonetheless reverberates in tune with our own, becomes available to us in its actions on our senses. It is in our illusions that we see the extent to which the artfulness of nature—an artfulness comparable to and recurring within that of spectacle—allows any one of us to cultivate both our enjoyment of and engagement with the world. Du Châtelet intimates that the figures through and by which the world reaches us may tell us something about our own nature, in animating or pricking our pleasures in particular ways. With this knowledge, agreeable in itself, we may activate our delight more effectively.

Du Châtelet's injunction to cultivate illusion involves not only a set of philosophical propositions but also, as the *Discours* affirms, a response to personal moments of joy and disappointment, desire and heartbreak, including the end of her relationship with Voltaire and the beginning of her affair with Saint-Lambert. She invokes her own experience in scholarly work and in love in order to reflect on the power of illusion to mediate women's experience in particular—not as a form of escapism, but as a means of aligning a sometimes terrible and unjust reality with the passions that animate a feminine subject. If women in particular need to embrace the cultivation of illusion, it is both because their pleasures tend to be more vulnerable than those of men—less various, more fragilely constituted, but also threatened by the norms that deny them pleasure's pursuit—and because they might find in this cultivation a chance for creative fabrication that is its own delight. In their artifice, they might make a world for themselves, intertwining scholarship and romance. It is in this context that the individual woman takes on an almost divine power, responsible for her own pleasure's guarantee despite the imperative to recognize this pleasure as fundamentally relational in nature. As in the negotiation, in illusion, between activity and passivity, here the woman in question—necessarily of an elevated class status, according to Du Châtelet—shuttles back and forth between a kind of autonomous self-construction and an assertion of her dependence on pleasures that come from elsewhere. In this space Du Châtelet comes very close to ascribing a kind of poetic power to both love and study—or at least to the capacity of both of these activities to sustain pleasure over time, even in the face of vulnerability, disappointment, and loss.

If pleasure is not easy to come by—thanks to the uneven distribution of the passions—then feminine persons must always be seeking it out, crafting it little by little in the space where perception and reality meet. Scholarship and love are two sites of this intensive energy, which is not just a form of self-fashioning but a way of reimagining relationships to others, a remaking and reusing that extends from the past into the future.

Perhaps surprisingly, Du Châtelet asserts that "If we value independence, the love of study is, of all the passions, the one that contributes most to our happiness."[74] This love is especially important for women: "Undeniably, the love of study is much less necessary to the happiness of men than it is to that of women. Men have infinite resources for their happiness that women lack," she writes.[75] Scholarship then becomes a place where women can cultivate the pleasure of independence as well as what Du Châtelet refers to as "the love of glory" or *l'amour de la gloire*—the prospect of a future recognition by generations yet to come. Study is thus a consolatory delight: It makes up in a certain sense for all the forms of exclusion and dependence that are visited upon women in their present. And it too retains a complex relationship to illusion, which in some sense constitutes it. Du Châtelet contends both that the love of glory is "entirely founded on illusion" and that this love of glory, denied satisfaction in every other context, is particularly key to women's enjoyment of scholarly pursuits.[76] The pleasure that emerges from this love, however, is anything but illusory: It is real. She writes: "This pleasure is not an illusion, for it proves to us the very real benefit of enjoying our future reputation. If our only source of good feeling were in the present, our pleasures would be even more limited than they are. We are made happy in the present moment not only by our actual delights but also by our hopes, our reminiscences. The present is enriched by the past and the future."[77] In this moment, Du Châtelet revises an Epicurean message—which condemns the pursuit of glory and future acclaim as vain desires—in order to accommodate the constraints of women's situation, which do not allow for the expansive cultivation of pleasant feeling. If illusion drives the love of glory that motivates study—as a mode of imagining self-worth in social relation—the pleasure that "l'étude" produces may nonetheless be deeply felt, "inexhaustible," as Du Châtelet states, and in some sense in defiance of the passage of time.[78] The embrace of this pleasure, which removes women from situations of real dependence on men while engaging them in a kind of virtual dependence on the judgment of posterity, nonetheless succeeds in revising and recasting some of the limitations that women face in pursuing an enjoyable life.

In a sense, then, the scholarly relation is the inverse of that other great pleasure that Du Châtelet names in this second portion of the essay—that of love.

Du Châtelet explains, "I have said that the more our happiness depends on us, the more assured it is, yet the passion that can give us the greatest pleasures and make us happiest, places our happiness entirely in the hands of others. You have already gathered that I am speaking of love."[79] Unlike study, love is not available when and where we might want it, and it does not enhance autonomy, yet it is the greatest and most profound of pleasures when it arrives. Du Châtelet suggests that it is indeed the only pleasure that can "make us wish to live," an idea that recurs in Françoise de Graffigny's very different effort, in the *Lettres d'une Péruvienne*, to weave together the joys and intensities of both love and the pursuit of knowledge.[80] At this moment in her text Du Châtelet cites a libertine source, the Earl of Rochester, and gives her own distillation of the thrust of his verse, one that once again significantly alters the message of the original: "One must love, it is that which sustains us. / Because without love, it is sad to be man."[81] It is love that enables an attachment to life itself, imbues itself in our perceptions of the world, compensates us for our suffering. And in the operation of this sense, too, the role of illusion is primary, "for where is illusion more important than in love?"[82]

Does illusion in love then represent another way through the problem of dependence? In a sense, it does. Or, at least, it might. In an extraordinary paragraph, Du Châtelet writes:

> A tender and sensitive soul is made happy by the sheer pleasure it finds in loving. I do not mean that unrequited love could make one perfectly happy; but I say that, although our ideas of happiness are not entirely satisfied by the love given us, the pleasure we feel in giving ourselves up to our feelings of tenderness can suffice to make us happy. And if this soul still has the good fortune to be susceptible to illusions, it is not impossible that it should not believe itself more loved perhaps than it is in fact. This soul must love so much that it loves for two, and the warmth of its heart supplies what is, in fact, lacking in its happiness.[83]

At this moment Du Châtelet gestures toward the possibility of a love caught happily in its own illusions, a love that in fact resembles her own passion for Voltaire, in which, she claims, "I was loving for two, I spent all my time with him, and my heart, free from suspicion, delighted in the pleasure of loving and in the illusion of feeling myself loved."[84] Even if a reciprocal passion—of overwhelming intensity and power—is an illusion, *as an illusion* it may still be enough to satisfy. While humans may only be happy as a result of fulfilled desires, Du Châtelet claims, perhaps we are able not only to modify our desires to fit our circumstances but flatter our illusions to respond to our needs. As her description of a self that loves for two reveals, the susceptibility to illusion that art and nature both engage ultimately enables a kind of multiplication of the amorous soul. If enjoyment proliferates, it is not because of the capacity of the beloved woman to generate a reciprocal desire, but because of her ability to abandon herself to her own feelings: She becomes, in this sense, her own spectacle, one in which she may (for a time, at least) remain absorbed. The woman in love is split in two, but it is this very doubling that, paradoxically, guarantees her self-sufficiency; the image of tenderness proliferates within her, suggesting an exchange of sentiments that may be in fact self-generated. With this consolatory image of a technics of desire, Du Châtelet intimates that sensual nature, responsible for our pleasures, is not inflexible, but tractable, available for adjustment by means of fantasy; for better or worse, illusion is the foundation upon which our most instinctual delight may be built.

Du Châtelet draws from her own experience in her discussion of the work of illusion in and on love, asserting that she herself has received from God a soul of great tenderness and constancy that seeks in vain to temper its passions. In some sense this soul is artless, in that it is incapable of deceiving others. But it is nonetheless exquisitely designed to overwhelm itself with love. As she explains, while for many years she "delighted in the pleasure of loving and in the illusion of feeling myself loved," she also eventually discovered an unhappy truth — namely, that her lover was incapable of responding to her love in kind. Du Châtelet evokes here the impossibility of a mutually binding passion; in the end, she is unable to find a partner like herself, and thus is obliged to bear witness to the slow dissolution of her lover's desire for her. Because her ideal is precisely one of reciprocity, it is exceptionally vulnerable to disappointment, to the intrusion of an unbearable absence into the space formerly filled, and intensely so, by the energy of her imagination. The reader sees again in this discussion that, if passion can entail a startling capacity to multiply the self in its images, the ability to nurture fantasy over time is its own form of privilege.

For Du Châtelet herself, then, illusion ultimately constitutes its own scene of struggle, personal and social; at stake is not the accuracy of the images formed by and within desire, but the conditions under which they may be allowed to circulate. She recommends to young women, not that they avoid love but that they be ready, at any time, to cure themselves of their attachments, sounding, in the conclusion to the *Discours*, a bit like the Lucretius of book four of the *DRN*, who suggests promiscuity as a remedy against the pangs of desire. She writes, "one must not pride oneself on a constancy that would be as ridiculous as it would be misplaced."[85] This is in a sense a libertine lesson — as the reference to Rochester that precedes it perhaps underscores. But it is a libertinism that is grounded in an awareness of the imbalance between men's and women's rights in love; the difficulty of sustaining passion over time; and the need for women to cultivate their own autonomy not just as a ratification of their pursuit of pleasure but as protection against despondency. Her suggestion that it might be possible to love enough for two—to solve the problem of waning masculine desire when faced with feminine longing through a careful preservation of illusion—concludes in a much starker recognition that "experience must at least teach us to rely on ourselves and to make our passions serve our happiness."[86] In a way, Du Châtelet seems here to be searching for another lover like herself; her autonomy—her insistence that it is crucial to know who and what one is—tips over into isolation. From the pleasures of love she returns in the end to those of study, "a taste which makes our happiness depend only on ourselves."[87] The speculation that it might in fact be possible for one woman to love enough for two—to create a relational happiness in the void left by a man's desire—remains a speculation.

Coda: Isolation in Love and Work

Du Châtelet's letters to Saint-Lambert reveal in a different key the way she lived the interpenetration of love and study as a mode of creative fabrication. As a reader, I find in her correspondence a strong sense of her own autonomy as well as her cultural and economic power. If she is a defender of luxury as a social good, her letters make clear the extraordinary privilege of her patterns of consumption. In this framework she seems a forerunner of a certain liberal idea of the subject—the feminine libertine as a precursor of the practiced consumer: another bad materialist, in other words. But, read in tandem with the *Discours*, her letters excavate other dimensions of her embrace of pleasure, a project that is not undertaken in the service of independence alone, or simply as a way of justifying her own desires. Thus her plangent claim serving as the epigraph to this chapter—that she would like to depend upon her *own* taste, beholden to no other—is only part of the story. In her writings to Saint-Lambert, it is possible to see her working hard to craft not just independence but new modes of being-in-relation, to call into existence through her writing, her thought, her pleasures, and her care a set of bonds that will sustain her desire for life itself and attach her to the course of her own experience. In addressing Saint-Lambert, she attempts to hold together her sense of inevitable disappointment with her knowledge of the irresistible force of her longing: "It is easy for you to reanimate in my heart the invincible desire [*goût*] that draws me to you. Perhaps it would be difficult to snuff it out, but I always try to keep my soul in such a situation that I find a resource in my courage, in my philosophy, and especially in my taste [*goût*] for study, if you abandon me."[88]

Her courage, her philosophy, and her passion for study—these are substitutions, but potentially delightful ones. They work upon her, like her love, amid her fears for her own life, as a pregnant woman of forty. Her will brings a set of connections into being in the face of her own mortality; her love and her scholarship maintain the illusions of relationality that banish, for a moment, the death to come. "I admit to you that I want to finish my work, especially on the eve of giving birth, and being very likely to die in the process," she writes. "I will lose this idea when I am with you, sadness and terrible thoughts then being able to find no purchase on my soul."[89] These pleasures are hard-won and hard-fought. If her desire for recognition and connection resonates over time, she still remains in many ways a figure of exception—alone in her authority.

In her letters, as in her physics, her powerful voice carries: Its imaginative force generates a posterity for itself, as she perhaps hoped it would. It transmits itself toward other pleasures, toward distinct futures that she could not have envisioned. Still, it is remarkable that what Du Châtelet sometimes appears to be seeking—her own double—remains out of reach, elusive and illusive, and not just because she was a person of exceptional prestige and intelligence. In her effort to imagine a love that is held up and maintained in its illusions, as a remedy to the waning passions of men, she only rarely makes reference to her relationships with other women. She remains singular—immutable in the independence of her will. This absence of feminine solidarity suggests the limitations of her vision, wherein the pleasure that women take in and for one another only rarely finds a place. In her thoughtful meditation on Du Châtelet's physics, Julie Candler Hayes lingers on the moment in the manuscript of the *Institutions* where Du Châtelet wonders if another version of her might exist on another planet; could she find her equal—her counterpart in love and in work—there? The marginal notation to the text reads in Du Châtelet's hand: "Could there be someone just like me in another world?"[90] As Hayes points out, the answer must be no, since "within the Leibnizian scheme ... the possibility of two entities differing in number only is resolutely denied."[91] There can only be one of her, even as, in the *Discours*, she dreams fervently of multiplying herself. If there is a real possibility of this multiplication—of the proliferation of hearts of such true and lasting commitment that she might in fact find her equal in love—it is not available to her in life. Nor does her physics enable it. Hayes eloquently finds in this marginal question a coming-to-voice that is part of an act of self-creation, but the query also reveals the limits of Du Châtelet's will to pleasure, a will that can only dream of others like itself, who might share amply and always in its projections.

Perhaps, if the possibility of a *semblable* is denied her, the possibility of pleasure disseminated—a reciprocal delight, ruptured by time but still palpable—might still come to be through her writing and the readers it has engendered. In this transmission of enjoyment across the gap of history and geography, the correspondence, the physics, and the moral texts all have their part to play. As a philosopher, Du Châtelet may not succeed in advancing rationalism as a pursuit for women, but she successfully reactivates a pleasure-based ethic for feminine experience as she conceives of it, while affirming that love and scholarship complement and enhance the enjoyment each affords. Women's contingent attributes, including the centrality of love to feminine experience and the importance for them of intellectual work, suggest that femininity may become a key source of creativity in pleasure—a means of remaking not just the self but the social ties that sustain it. This project is never complete. As an author, she sets it into motion again and again, but she also charts its limitations and aporia. Du Châtelet's work shows the tension inherent in her exceptional status as an aristocratic woman of science with no real peers: She valorizes her own autonomy at the same time as she highlights pleasure as a relational condition. Although she is aware of the way in which delight emerges in social contexts, she still wants to craft pleasure as a resource for herself. Yet in her turn to the illusions of love and study, she also opens a small space for other feminine persons—her future readers—both to receive and to extend the artifices that once sustained her.

As Du Châtelet contends, nature is incessantly mediated to us, then, but it is also its own kind of mediatic force. Artifice and fact are deeply entangled, which is not to say that error is impossible, or that truth cannot be uncovered or made newly palpable. Although Du Châtelet does not explicitly make this particular connection in the *Discours*, perhaps we might see in the category of gender itself, always both concept and experience, a key instance of the imbrication of matter in the various means by which it can be apprehended and of the potential for illusion and error to mold and shape our most natural attachments. This potential may be resisted in the pursuit of a more rational knowledge or an indifference to what seems to be, but it may also be embraced in the name of a future yet to come. We know gender only by its effects, but these effects may galvanize us in both body and mind, putting a new kind of materialist practice in motion. The laboratory and the *cabinet* are not the only possible scenes of this work that is always ongoing, but also yet to be. Du Châtelet's ethic of pleasure might thus find some resonance with a feminist project of fostering, sustaining, and reimagining a feminine craft that is vested in the embodied acts of sensing, touching, feeling yet nonetheless makes room for artifice to do its work.

4
"I am, I live, I exist": Graffigny's Pleasure of Being

"It is enough to be."[1]

When I first read Graffigny's eighteenth-century bestseller *Lettres d'une Péruvienne*, published in 1747 and reissued in 1752 in a luxe edition overseen by the author herself, I did so more out of obligation than interest. As I was planning a new course on pleasure in the eighteenth century, I wanted to include more texts by women. Graffigny's text did not strike me as a natural fit for this topic, so I turned to her famous novel a bit grudgingly, as a kind of necessary stopgap. It is easy, on a first encounter with her work, to see Graffigny as an avatar of sentimental suffering, both in her writing and in her own experience. Her sustained focus on trauma, emigration, and forced cultural assimilation in *Lettres d'une Péruvienne* can be read as the antithesis of libertine irony. While Du Châtelet and even Puisieux may be forced into a certain model of aristocratic femininity—arch, sophisticated, mostly in on the joke—Graffigny resists this kind of association. Du Châtelet and Graffigny even had a famous falling out, complete with nicknames that seemed to distill two divergent but equally stereotypical modes of femininity: Du Châtelet was "la Monstre" where Graffigny was "la Grosse." A cursory glance at Graffigny's life story, as the victim of a brutally violent husband who ended up having to make a way for herself as an author, exposes right away the limitations of a brittle image of *ancien régime* aristocratic womanhood as primarily insouciant and pleasure-seeking.

Then I started teaching *Lettres d'une Péruvienne*, which became over time a staple of my syllabi—the one eighteenth-century novel that I have returned to again and again in the classroom. I can't say that my students took to Graffigny immediately either, but they saw something more expansive in her vision than I originally thought any of us would find there. And their readings were not bound, as mine at first had been, by the artificial distinction separating a libertine corpus from a sentimental one. My students were often interested in Graffigny's novel for its critique of institutions, which resonates at times with the genre of feminist complaint as Sara Ahmed has named and defined it. As Ahmed contends, "making complaints teaches us about how institutions work."[2] This is also the case for Graffigny's Peruvian heroine, Zilia, who comes to her knowledge of French social life—and French culture—through abduction. In her situation it is the classical form of the heroid, recrafted within a culture of sentiment and sensuality, that allows her unhappiness to distill itself into a shape and to generate a social and political analysis that cuts across temporal limits. Like Puisieux, she remakes lamentation for more sensualist ends.

It is tempting to read Zilia's experience as a kind of allegory of Graffigny's own, but to do so would efface Zilia's particular status as an outsider: She is an immigrant to France and Peruvian-born. As a foreign observer of French customs and foibles, Zilia stakes her claim to a place among the many travelers and Indigenous interlocutors who proliferate across the eighteenth-century French literary canon. The preface to the novel names its intertexts, which include most famously Montesquieu's *Lettres persanes* (1721) and Voltaire's play *Alzire* (1736), as points of reference in a history of French efforts to grapple specifically with the question of cultural difference. But in one important way, Graffigny and Zilia do hold a resemblance to one another. Their complaint does not emerge from their position as critics or philosophers; instead, their philosophical positions take shape from within their complaint. In Zilia's case, my students helped me better see how her grief as a woman lost and abandoned, which echoes ancient motifs, not only morphs into a mode of philosophy but deliberately affirms a place for itself there—refashioning trauma, alienation, and loneliness into tools for making sense of the mechanics of power in the culture that she is forced to "discover." *Lettres d'une Péruvienne* shows over and over again not only that knowledge comes to be in moments of dispossession and undoing, but that the articulation of this dispossession may constitute its own mode of "enlightened" understanding. When Zilia transforms herself, by the end of the novel, into a kind of hybrid subject—an amalgamation of Peru and France—the novel links her assertion of identity to an affirmation of loss as a force capable of generating both thought and, somewhat astonishingly, enduring pleasures. Her life among the ruins is reworked one more time into a possible source of satisfaction, both imaginary and real.

Graffigny's nuanced and at times ambivalent portrayal of the relationship between exile and personhood, complaint and critique, emotion and self-awareness can still seem very modern, especially in what Madeleine Dobie has analyzed as the novel's insistence on the open-endedness of signifying processes that include language (both written and spoken) and translation. But, even to modern readers who might not find the idea of a woman philosopher too surprising, Graffigny's willingness to make her philosophy of and in feminine emotion can still feel strange and discomfiting; Zilia is neither at home in eighteenth-century France (her origins in sixteenth-century Peru are a sign of this) nor is she a modern *avant la lettre*—an obvious harbinger of what is yet to come. In reading and rereading Graffigny's famous text, I was reminded of Elizabeth Gumport's reflection on Chris Kraus's 1997 *I Love Dick*, another unsettling, even awkward feminine lament made in epistolary form, a postmodern updating of the heroid. In a discussion of Kraus's critique of contemporary art, Gumport quotes a passage from *Video Green*, Kraus's examination of the Los Angeles art world in the 1990s. Kraus writes, "I think that 'privacy' is to contemporary female art what 'obscenity' was to male art and literature of the 1960s. The willingness of someone to use her life as primary material is still deeply disturbing, and even more so if she views her own experience at some remove. There is no problem with female confession providing it is made within a repentant therapeutic narrative. But to examine things coolly, to thrust experience out of one's own brain and put it on the table, is still too confrontational."[3] Gumport's analysis underlines the way in which Kraus approaches vulnerability and emotional excess not as pathological symptoms but as socially determined and creatively generative forces. "Could it be, then," Gumport asks toward the end of the essay, "that what Kraus is at work on is a kind of philosophy, philosophy that simply goes unrecognized as such?"[4] Zilia's own narrative at first seems anything but "cool." Her letters to her lost lover Aza are often lyrical and formally complex, suffused with lush sentiment that my students tend to see as excessive—too stylized and too emotional all at once. But ultimately Zilia's voice shifts, revealing the fusion between a way of feeling rendered in desolation and the critique that emerges from this rendering. Graffigny is in sympathy, it seems to me, with the project of making philosophy out of a feminine life—albeit a life that is neither the author's nor the reader's own.

Zilia thus stands in a kind of breach—here again generating a certain unease. She appears clearly as a trope, a figment, a fragment of the author's imagination, just as much as she functions as the expression of a voice, a specific point of view and a particular set of experiences, often involving oppression and ethnic prejudice. In my classrooms, students have reacted to this double positioning of Zilia as both "typical" sentimental heroine and ultimate outsider, victim of genocide and a double abduction (first by Spanish captors and then by French rescuers), with a criticism of Graffigny's use of cultural appropriation to make a series of points about French society. They are not wrong about this aspect of the work, which reaches outside of and beyond its own cultural context, and in doing so both brings colonial history to bear on the question of enlightenment and reifies this history in the service of critique. Graffigny's novel comes to be in the gap between the possessive pronoun ("her" story) and the indefinite article ("a" story), and indeed it is in this space—in her final emotional dispossession due to her betrayal by her betrothed—that Zilia discovers the pleasure of a relationality without dependence, perhaps because she realizes that her love was never hers at all, and thus, finally, a fiction to do with as she pleases. But the shadow of Peruvian genocide falls heavy on the love story; empire is at work in the artifice of Zilia's authenticity.

Lettres d'une Péruvienne works so well as a teaching text not because it imparts a series of lessons—I don't find it a particularly didactic novel, certainly not by the standards set by Voltaire's Peruvian play *Alzire*—but because it suggests that the capacity to generate philosophy in feeling might be transmissible and eventually shared. But this feeling is not fully personalized, as it might be in a modern novel. Graffigny's feminine complaint emerges in narrative as one story among others—the beginning of a conversation. At the end of the novel, Zilia arguably constructs a world in which her pleasures finally circulate for her and not only for others, but her ability to find this delight is predicated on her recognition that her story is not her own, that all that is left of the desires that once defined her is the narrative that she made of them. In this realization, she paradoxically affirms her pleasure in being, an affirmation not of selfhood as such but of a right to exist and to persevere. Her tale of dispossession, discouragement, and disappointment echoes strongly at the moment at which I write—a moment of global pandemic, political violence, the end of abortion rights in the United States, and a time of deepening ecological despair. Zilia still provides readers with a kind of map for crafting something out of nothing—although the "thing" that she makes is not really a possessive personhood, but an intense and weirdly abundant feeling—a *sentiment de l'existence* that is also a *plaisir d'être*—out of which a more collective joy might one day spring. At the same time, she comes to this feeling through the evocation of a Peruvian subject whose function resembles that of the feminine body passed through the filter of a masculine materialism—the avatar of a shared embodiment whose origins lie outside of both history and politics. In her dispossession but also in her strength, she forces us to ask the question: Who are these pleasures really for?

Erring Two Ways

From one vantage, Françoise de Graffigny's *Lettres d'une Péruvienne* is a novel about errancy. Even so, it begins and ends with the heroine Zilia in situations of stasis, immobile and constrained, although the conclusion confirms that this position is ultimately chosen rather than forced upon her. In her first letter, written in Peruvian *quipos* (Graffigny's spelling) or *quipus* (from the Cusco-Collao Quechua word *khipu*)[5] and later translated by Zilia herself into French, Zilia calls out for her betrothed Aza, her cries dissolving in the air "like a morning mist."[6] As the reader soon discovers, she is the prisoner of Spanish abductors, who have ripped her from her home in the Temple of the Sun, which they have invaded and plundered. The image of words dissolving into vapor conjures a scene of barely comprehensible chaos, but it also invokes the fundamental malleability of the method of writing that Zilia uses, since the *quipus* take on diverse forms as they pass from one author to another—allowing for the transmission of sentiment across distance and time. Crafted by Zilia into a series of love letters, these knotted threads, woven, unraveled, and woven again, are designed to change shape in the hands of her beloved Aza, morphing from her emotions into his as he reweaves them in his reply. By the end of the novel, though, Zilia's means of communication seem to have acquired a certain solidity, one no longer quite as vulnerable to dissolution. In her final letter, she writes to the Frenchman Déterville to invite him to join her in her fine home built from looted Peruvian treasures, restored to her partly in the form of gold, partly in that of the house itself. In refusing Déterville's offer of marriage, she evokes her "resolutions, which unlike yours will not be shaken."[7] And she issues him an invitation, suggesting that he come "learn to appreciate innocent and lasting pleasures."[8] Is this alchemy—whereby vapor becomes solid—an effect of enlightenment? Her sentiments, like her words, appear to have acquired a new capacity to endure. But what has brought about this transformation? Separating these two moments from one another is the narrative of her unwilled voyage; she is taken first from her Peruvian homeland by the Spanish and then from the Spanish ship by a French vessel, which carries her to Paris, where she lives with the family of Déterville, including his mother and his sister. Her isolation, too, has changed. Her relative solitude is shared the second time around, and not horrifying, but delightful. Is it then her journey—and the new company that she has cultivated in the process—that has given substance to her words? What desublimation is here at work?

Zilia is both a prisoner—constantly enclosed and confined, both with and without her consent—and a traveler—moving across oceans, continents, and worlds in a way that she initially finds bewildering and later considers as a potential source of knowledge. She is often compared to Montesquieu's more famous Persian voyagers—although Montesquieu only made his authorship of the *Lettres persanes* public *after* the success of Graffigny's novel[9]—but unlike Montesquieu's protagonists Usbek and Rica she does not initiate her own travels, even nominally.[10] Her journey of discovery is unchosen and unwanted; it remains this way throughout the novel. What's more, she does not come to a realization that the constraint under which she suffers hides within it a lesson to be learned, a decision that she should or would have made; her inability to choose her fate is simply the fact of her situation as a victim of genocide, as an Indigenous person in a foreign country, and as a woman. Indeed, the final section of the novel, when Zilia learns that her long-lost beloved has betrayed her by converting to Christianity and marrying someone else, involves not an acknowledgment of her agency but another unwilled disappointment. If this is the story of an education, with her increased knowledge of the world does not necessarily come an increased capacity to act. Rather, it is the return of some of the Peruvian plundered wealth to her possession—as a result of Déterville's decision to restore her treasures to her—that provides her with a buffer from the vicissitudes of fortune.[11]

Zilia's travels, however far they take her, eventually return her to a place of relative immobility—not a convent, but a fine manor home, where she can read and observe nature and share the results of her studies with Déterville, whom she invites to join her in friendship rather than in love. At the same time, the narrative of her physical travels is doubled by that of her mental journey, in which errancy takes on a different connotation, regularly revealing its links to misunderstanding, mistake, and even falsehood as Zilia struggles to understand what has happened to her. Yet here too, a certain ambivalence arises. If Zilia's mobility always stands in relation to stasis—the possibility of remaining where she is or prefers to be—her epistemological journey toward the truth always preserves its connection to error, which wanders and circles back on itself, refusing to leave or to stay put.

In the opening letters, Zilia emphasizes her ignorance—of the language of her captors, of her location, of what is happening to her—as one of the many deprivations that afflict her. After her kidnapping, her world shrinks: "locked away in a dark prison," she writes, "the space I occupy in the world extends no further than the confines of my own being."[12] Yet, even as she is prevented from accessing the knowledge that she needs, she also depicts movingly the mistakes and illusions that sustain and fortify her. In her fourth letter, she evokes her struggles to make sense of her situation: "Everything around me is unfamiliar, everything is new, everything stirs my curiosity, and nothing can satisfy it. In vain I concentrate and strive to understand, or to be understood; both are equally beyond me."[13] In this letter, which masterfully unfurls a panoply of images of light and shadow, illumination and obscurity,[14] Zilia points out that her efforts to communicate are blocked by her inability to understand the language of her captors, who are at this point French. Her torment is so great that she closes her eyes—voluntarily condemning herself to darkness, as she puts it—in order to still the agitation of her soul. But this attempt fails. Her internal suffering, although invisible, is even more acute than "pains which might seem more real."[15] Her only recourse to assuage these pains lies in her *quipus*. She describes the effect of writing to Aza on her state of mind: "I spend as much time doing this as my feeble state allows. These knots which touch my senses seem to make my thoughts more real; the kind of resemblance I imagine them to have with words creates an illusion which brings relief to my suffering. I fancy that I am speaking to you, telling you that I love you, assuring you of my devotion, of my affection; this sweet delusion is my sole possession and my life."[16] In the act of writing to Aza, the words that she is knotting strike her senses as if they were spoken out loud, conjuring the figure of Aza perhaps but more immediately supplying the illusion of a conversation, an interchange that lends reality to Zilia herself, who locates her very substance in this relationality. This is an animating fantasy—indeed, it is described in this letter as a life-preserving one—that enables her to survive her transport across the seas. But at the same time it is an *de*lusion and a mistake—an error, sweet as it may be. As Zilia moves through these early accounts of her abduction, she seems to be navigating precisely the divide opened up by Du Châtelet, between the life-sustaining effects of illusion on the feminine person, and the life-negating properties of error.

This negotiation is at play not only in the figure of Zilia herself, but in the mode of address that the novel assumes. The preface to the *Lettres*, which some critics have suggested (without evidence) was written by Graffigny's lover Antoine Bret,[17] emphasizes the difficulty of communicating, in fiction, a truth that fails to conform to the reader's expectations, diverging either from verisimilitude or prejudice. It opens, "If truth deviates from what is considered plausible, it normally loses its credibility in the eyes of reason, but this loss is not irreversible; but if it runs counter to prejudice however slightly, it is rarely granted leniency in that court."[18] Where reason might allow the reader to find the way toward a truth that seems unlikely, prejudice presents an obstacle that is more difficult to conquer. As a result, the "Avertissement" affirms, the "editor of this work" has everything to fear from the public's reaction, since both the style and content of the text will fail to conform to the prejudices the French hold regarding Peruvians. We only see merit in resemblance, the

"Avertissement" continues, and not in difference—hence Montesquieu's famous question, "How can one be Persian?" [*Comment peut-on être Persan?*]. The author of the "Avertissement" is invoking not only the problem faced by Montesquieu's Persian travelers in encountering the French, but the constraints of the novel as a form that solicits the reader's identification at the same time as it exposes identification's limits: The practice of reading is at stake here, beyond the problem of what the text strives to represent. We cannot become like that which we can neither see nor understand; difference requires a moment of recognition in order to be legible and receivable as such. Still, as the author goes on to confirm, testaments to the sagacity and wisdom of the Indigenous Peruvians continue to circulate globally; their history is available and accessible. The *Lettres d'une Péruvienne* thus aims to contribute to a more general archive that has been developing over time around Peruvian "caractère" and culture, leading the reader to assume that the narrative that will unfold is one of knowledge countering error, illuminating and improving. The education that will take place here is thus presumably not only that of Zilia herself but of the reading public, whose ignorance concerning Peru mirrors the heroine's ignorance of France. The work is placed, then, under the sign of enlightenment—although the progress of this enlightenment will soon be shown to be fraught with peril and ambiguity.[19]

Illusion plays a constitutive role in this progress. At the same time as the heroine's errant journeys conclude with her (re)placement in a situation of relative confinement, Zilia's struggles to fully understand her situation shift: Her rejection of the sweet mistake that at one time guarantees her survival ends not with a coming-to-truth but with an embrace of error on different grounds. The novel does not reliably take her away from illusion but sometimes leads her deeper into it; in either case, it remains a mode of sustenance on which she relies.[20] This is not to say that certain prejudices that Zilia carries with her are not dispelled. On the contrary, Zilia's deployment of reason serves a distinct purpose, as many astute readers of Graffigny have noted, as a moral position, linked to Graffigny's own investment in promoting women's education.[21]

Still, the conclusion to the novel, which avoids the typical strategy of simply marrying the heroine off, allows Zilia not only to remain attached to the illusion of fidelity with which the novel begins, but to enhance and fortify this illusive attachment in a new way. The process of enlightenment, as it unfolds through the novel, is not simply one of dispelling error; instead, the struggle against prejudice, and the *va-et-vient* between disappointment and hope,[22] serve to strengthen Zilia's commitment to her origin—not just in Peru but in Aza's regard and love for her. At the same time, this origin emerges as a fiction, one that Zilia preserves despite her recognition that Aza will never return her devotion for him, that he is lost to her as a potential partner both in marriage and in love. It is precisely in this commitment to Aza-as-illusion that Zilia finds the possibility of a lasting pleasure of being [*plaisir d'être*]—a sensation proximate to the *sentiment de l'existence* that critics have situated at the heart of Rousseau's writing in particular, but have also traced through the political philosophy of the period as a key component of an emergent modern self. In Graffigny's case, this pleasure is the result of Zilia's shaping of the conditions of her experience through writing and conversation. Zilia experiences her subjectivity as primarily and fully relational, but this relationality is transformed and reconfigured through her epistolary labor, thereby generating a fragile kind of freedom. Her attachment to exchange and to the communication of emotion is transformed, as the novel goes on, from an exquisite vulnerability to a receptivity to the world that fortifies rather than depletes her, giving her words their substance.

But it is not reason alone that makes this transformation possible. Zilia's independence arrives belatedly, on the wings of illusion recognized and cultivated as such. And this arrival is premised both on the loss of her beloved and on her refusal to recognize this loss—her realization that it is she who can deploy the production of illusion as sustenance *for her* first and foremost. It is this realization that in fact generates the narrative itself, which notably comes to be in its edited and translated form *after* the betrayal by Aza. As readers, if we have been swept away by the enormity of Aza's treachery, and earlier undone by the intensity of Zilia's suffering as she is ripped from her homeland, we too may have been deceiving ourselves as to the true nature of the text, whose ending implicitly invites us to circle back to the beginning, reading again with an eye to the power of the illusions that once sustained us, too. We who would reread do so with a sense of Aza's tenuousness as a kind of simulacrum of himself—or of who he is meant to be—but also with a knowledge of his force. In this sense Zilia invites us to remain with her after the work concludes, since its ending, as she suggests, turns out to be its beginning after all.

Perhaps Zilia, with her words that are both solid and scintillating, changing sense as the scene changes around her, fulfills Du Châtelet's dream of a love that endures through the imaginative work of a woman who reads, writes, and feels for two rather than one. Even after her betrayal by Aza, she commits to him, and from this commitment manages finally to derive a consistent pleasure, no longer subject to the vagaries of his desire for her. In his book *Regressive Fictions*, Robin Howells reads Zilia's position at the end of the novel as infantile—a willful regression to ignorance that is prefigured in the framing of Zilia in the "Avertissement" as a faithful translator of her own story. He writes,

"Zilia's final letter, apparently balancing Peruvian past and French future, assigns to the past not only affective privilege but even intellectual parity. Her ambitions are carefully limited, with gender roles strongly differentiated and her own self-image of naivety. She may have developed but she declines to change."[23] Reading Graffigny's Zilia alongside the work of Puisieux and Du Châtelet on the interpenetration of pleasure and illusion, however, we can see the way in which Zilia's "naïveté" is artfully and carefully crafted and maintained—an attachment to the sensed relationality of being and to the sensuousness of the world—which does not require her total submission. This is not the willful assertion of a break with reality or a retreat into the pre- or semiconscious self. Like Du Châtelet and Puisieux, Graffigny locates feminine pleasure in an encounter with the world that arrives *after* knowledge of this world's vicissitudes, in a recognition that illusions may be transmuted into abiding sources of substantial enjoyment. In this knowledge, which results from a careful parsing of prejudice and error, and an equally nuanced control over the fictions that make feminine selfhood possible and sustainable, pleasure can finally come to be.

In other words, while Graffigny is quite different from Du Châtelet and Puisieux in her investment in the expressive potential of the novel form, she ultimately locates her heroine at the same kind of conjunction of illusion and materialism, artifice and substance, that her two contemporaries also explore, one in science and metaphysics, and the other in moral writing and the allegorical tale. Within the framework supplied by the work of these other women, both writing around the same time and in contact with overlapping *milieux* (despite their disagreements with and even dislike of one another), Graffigny's heroine seems an example not of regression toward infantilism but of movement toward pleasure as an ethical and intellectual situation that she can reasonably cultivate and sustain. If she withdraws from marriage and from the social scene, it is in order to preserve her capacity to persist in a delightful relationship to the world, one that does not require only her dependence. Marriage ironically suggests the end of mutuality, a mutuality that might otherwise be productively generated as a key effect of femininity—the latter's own tenuous image.

Is it possible to understand Graffigny's novel as the emergence of an illusive materialism from within a sentimental form? Does Zilia's errancy reach a materialist end? I suggest that Graffigny's novel reveals not only the complexity and interest of *sensibilité* as a term and condition, as Ann Lewis has incisively demonstrated, but also the intimate moral and physical entanglement of sensitivity with pleasure, and feminine pleasure in particular.[24] In short, I see Graffigny as working in tandem with Puisieux and Du Châtelet to revise and rewrite the pursuit of delight in often covert dialogue with materialist concepts and ideals. Taken in this context, the novel not only upends certain contemporary critical expectations of what sentimental texts may be expected to accomplish but loosens the long-standing association between materialism and masculinity. In a sense, *Lettres d'une Péruvienne* does what a libertine novel might be expected to do: It locates pleasure at the heart of experience. But because this experience is painted in resolutely feminine terms, and because Zilia remains attached to norms of virtue and reason throughout the text, Graffigny's work is rarely read as a contribution to the kind of materialist critique that is often seen as informing libertine thought and philosophy. If Graffigny is sometimes said to be building a feminine enlightenment that exists alongside or as a supplement to a masculine one,[25] her presence in the eighteenth-century canon becomes a matter of inclusion, a stretching of the corpus to bring in the works by women that ought to have been there all along. But what if the pleasure upon which Graffigny insists is both distinctively feminine *and* an invitation to readers of any gender to reconsider the terms by which pleasure as such comes to be? What if she revises the association of femininity and pleasure in order to open a space for all feminine persons to do what works?

In what follows, I argue not so much for the novel's singularity as for its particularity—its connection to a specific situation from within which it crafts a certain delight that encompasses both heroine and reader. In making Zilia Peruvian, Graffigny imagines a lost world where virtuous norms may not be at odds with women's autonomy, but this is not a world that is immediately accessible either to Zilia herself or to her readers. Instead, it is a speculative fiction, akin to a utopia. Nonetheless, Zilia's Peruvian origin provides her with an imagined point of departure from which to negotiate her relationship with a society that is all-too-often committed not to pleasing but constraining her (and often both at once). Zilia's abduction from Peru preserves the kind of alongside-ness that allows her to envision a breach with the world as it is: It is in this breach that she constructs her own distinct relationship to reality, setting illusion in delicate relation to critique, reason in contact with speculation. Zilia's experience—of love, of nature, of the act of writing—involves learning not just to organize and account for her perceptions in a particular way but to aim toward pleasure as a position that she might on occasion fully assume. By the end of the novel, Zilia undergoes a quasi-materialist conversion in which she manages her relation to Aza not as a source of distress but as a continued spur toward delight. The pleasure of being with which she is left—the remainder that precipitates out from her fiction—derives from her navigation of a traumatic past, her passage through a mode of critique (enabled by the positioning of Peru as a lost paradise), and her embrace of a life-sustaining mode of enjoyment that is maintained through what Du Châtelet would call the preservation of her illusions.

The conclusion of the *Lettres* thus blurs the boundary dividing a libertine ethics from a sentimental one by showing to what extent these generic taxonomies are linked to contemporary ideas about what pleasure entails and who it is for. Zilia's position in her fairy-like manor house, immune to the disappointments of love but exquisitely sensitive to the world around her, suggests the kind of situation that both Du Châtelet and Puisieux posit as a prospective feminine ideal. In response to the trauma with which she is faced, Zilia learns to deploy images and illusion (both textual and visual) in order to create another kind of "second nature" that allows her relationality without dependence—and thus the capacity to reliably cultivate pleasure on her own terms. Her critique of superficiality—once again, the specter of "bad materialism" with which women in particular are forced to contend—is thus not a critique of artifice per se; it is a means toward a more delightful end. Her journey concludes in the cultivation of an illusive and infinite movement that doubles back on itself to incite joy.

Zilia and the Pleasure of Being

In the 1740s, while she was in the process of writing *Lettres d'une Péruvienne*, Françoise de Graffigny (see figure 4) was also cultivating contacts with the Parisian literary world. Her correspondence reflects the fact that she began to concentrate seriously on her novel in early 1745. A few years earlier, in 1742, she had moved into her own house on the rue Saint-Hyacinthe in Paris. She also began attending gatherings at what would become an informal salon hosted by the comte de Caylus and Mademoiselle Jeanne Quinault, a star actress of the Comédie-Française. While Graffigny would go on to maintain a salon of her own, it was at Mlle Quinault's dinners that she received her introduction to Parisian literary life, and it was here that she would develop relationships with Crébillon fils, Charles Pinot Duclos, and Claude-Adrien Helvétius (who would go on to marry Graffigny's first cousin once-removed, Anne-Catherine de Ligniville, known as Minette).[26] As English Showalter describes in his excellent biography, Graffigny was in contact with some of the most celebrated figures of the French Enlightenment as a result of her participation in salon culture; she was also in regular conversation with Helvétius as he developed what would become his sensationist magnum opus *De l'esprit*, published in 1758 and condemned to be burned in February 1759. It was in the 1740s that Helvétius was meditating on the composition of

Figure 4. Henri Levêque, "Françoise de Graffigny (née d'Issembourg Du Buisson d'Happoncourt)," circa 1800–1825, line engraving, 10 ⅝ in. × 7 ⅜ in. Image courtesy of National Portrait Gallery, London.

this work, but he had also been sharing more occasional unpublished pieces with Graffigny, including his poem *Le Bonheur* (read to Graffigny and friends in 1744) and perhaps a play (never found). In her correspondence, Graffigny refers to Helvétius as "le Génie" [the Genius], writing in a letter to Antoine Devaux from May 1744: "He is certainly the most excellent wit and the best taste of this century and many others, but you will see such force, such vigor of the soul, of the depiction of feelings and of expression free from mechanical poetry! This is what I call genius."[27] Later in the same year, Graffigny describes to Devaux a conversation that she had with Helvétius regarding his project for a philosophical book (that would become *De l'esprit*):

> I do not know through what trick of fate I dared to name metaphysics. This is the string that makes all the rest dance. He speaks, he bares his soul. He summarizes for me the book that he is going to have printed. Ah, what a book! Locke is not worthy of knocking the mud from his boots. The great Locke, this man who up until now was the only one I admired, he will always be great, but it will be because he showed what the Genius needed to say. His book will be accessible to everyone through its details and the dexterity with which he writes. Everything he says to me about it proves this to me as if I had read it.[28]

Graffigny's admiration for Helvétius is clear, especially in her assertion that John Locke is not fit to clean his shoes. Like Puisieux and Du Châtelet, she takes eager part in a *milieu* that is actively engaged in working through specifically materialist questions around pleasure.[29] Whereas English Showalter describes her public engagement with the ideas of the *encyclopédistes*, among others, as nonpartisan and her approach to social change as "gradualist," he notes the enthusiasm with which she greets Helvétius's proposals for *De l'esprit* (and the early versions of what would become *Le Bonheur*).

This context provides an impetus for reconsidering the *Lettres*, while often read under the sign of sentimentalism, as in fact proposing an ethics of shared pleasure that at once resonates with a materialist vision of communal harmony and modifies the cultivation of enjoyment or self-satisfaction in a feminine direction. At the end of the novel, Zilia even proposes her own pleasure as a model for her community, in a way that both makes good on Du Châtelet's vision of an ever-multiplying feminine self, capable of sustaining her own passionate investments, and reconfigures Puisieux's dream of a feminine trope that, once disseminated, might return again and again to generate delight. With this conclusion, Graffigny retains an emphasis on the relational aspects of the self, but she posits feminine experience as a locus of pleasure that could vibrate out from her heroine, as this experience is taken up and registered by others, including the (ultimately rather hapless) lover Déterville. Zilia's hard-won "return" to sensuousness—not a return at all but a reconfiguration of her capacity for feeling through the work of writing—guarantees her own substantial pleasure at the same time as it could serve as a spur to a more enduring delight for Déterville, should he be so bold as to accept her invitation. It also invites the reader into a different relationship to the text, which suddenly takes on the shape not of a progression toward marriage but of a journey through and with the power of fiction.

The final letter of the novel, addressed by Zilia to Déterville, asserts Zilia's right to refuse Déterville's offers of love at the same time as it affirms her fidelity to him in friendship. In the aftermath of her discovery of her beloved Aza's conversion to Christianity and marriage to another woman, she invites Déterville to come join her in her country house, to share with her in the pleasures not of impassioned love but the study and observation of nature, which she portrays as both external and internal to her. She writes to him:

> You are wrong to fear that solitude might impair my health. Believe me, Déterville, solitude is only ever dangerous when it is idle. Always occupied, I shall be able to create new pleasures for myself from everything which habit makes dull.
>
> Without delving into the secrets of nature, the mere examination of its wonders is surely sufficient to bring infinite variety and freshness to occupations which are always a pleasure. Is one lifetime enough to acquire even a slight, if engaging knowledge of the universe, of what surrounds me, of my own existence?
>
> The pleasure of being, this pleasure which has been forgotten, is not even known by so many people in their blindness; this thought which is so sweet, this delight so pure at saying to oneself, *I am, I live, I exist*, is enough to bring happiness, if we were to remember it, if we were to enjoy it, if we knew its true worth.[30]

The situation that Zilia describes here—and the attitude toward nature that she cultivates within it—invoke a modern version of the Epicurean Garden where friends meet to exchange knowledge in the service of a shared enjoyment, with Zilia in the role of the Epicurean sage. Zilia presents both "the universe"—the environs surrounding her—and her own being—"my own existence"—as proper objects of study and interest. But her goal is not the production of an objective science. Instead, the knowledge that she obtains is to be set in the service of pleasures old and new, including that remarkable *plaisir d'être* that might, all on its own, generate a perfect happiness. With a lyrical invocation of the delight of existence—a thought so sweet that its effects resonate across both mind and body—Graffigny makes two unexpected moves. First, in her refusal to find in marriage the self-evident conclusion to Zilia's story, she exposes the mechanics of the sentimental novel as themselves a form, not of consolidating "natural" imperatives and drives, but of cultivating particular attitudes and affections that then take on a nature of their own. Zilia locates in the resistance to marriage the possibility of a more intimate connection not only to the world she inhabits but to her existence *in* that world, both of which become legitimate objects of her own interest. Second, Zilia's endorsement of the happiness that comes from enduring—"I am, I live, I exist" [*je suis, je vis, j'existe*]—suggests not that she has transcended suffering but that she has finally attained a form of substantial delight that had eluded her in her previous errancy. She describes this sensation—both mental and physical—as an inherent pleasure in being that animates her and allows her to persevere, to sustain herself, and ultimately to reach out to Déterville in friendship to invite him to share in her situation. This mutual enjoyment may be activated by means of writing and reading, or through collective study and in conversation, yet it always springs from a percipience deliciously immersed in the environment from which it stems, a materiality that is only fully felt in form, a solicitation taking the shape of a letter that aims with its reception to redouble the delights of which it tells.

What Zilia asserts here as *plaisir d'être* is very close to the *sentiment de l'existence* that will take on perhaps its most definitive form in the works of Jean-Jacques Rousseau, although the idea is expressed by Graffigny in a resolutely feminine if not feminist key. In a recent analysis of Rousseau's "first philosophy," Christophe Litwin takes up a moment in Rousseau's *Lettres morales* (1757–1758) where Rousseau comments on the Cartesian *cogito*: "It is necessary to finish where Descartes started," Rousseau writes. "*I think, therefore I exist*. This is all that we know" [italics Rousseau's].[31] Litwin is particularly interested in the way in which Rousseau privileges the verb *exister* over that of *être*, shifting the valence of the famous Cartesian formulation. For Litwin, "Saying 'I think, therefore I exist' thus implies that I never exist without existence already being of singular importance to me, the I who thinks. The immediate datum of my existence, as a self, is that it is never originally of indifference to me that I myself exist. And this immanent interest in the feeling of the existence of the self, Rousseau calls *amour de soi*. The first philosophy of Rousseau lies in the immanence of the *amour de soi*."[32] As an immanent affective situation, the *sentiment de l'existence* sits at the heart of Rousseau's philosophy without itself being philosophical: Existence is not first of all an idea or concept for Rousseau, as Litwin shows, but a feeling. Of course, this feeling may be overwritten or forgotten thanks to the nefarious effects of civilization, as Graffigny likewise suggests, but even this forgetting is for Rousseau not a departure from the *sentiment de l'existence* but its corruption—the turning of the *amour de soi* against itself rather than the denial of this feeling as the grounds of existence itself. Graffigny, in her invocation of Zilia's *plaisir d'être*, modulated by the sudden, explosive anaphora *Je suis, je vis, j'existe*, seems very close to presaging this Rousseauvian affect—a zero-degree mode of being that subtends all cognition. In the famous letter 34, in which Graffigny criticizes the superficiality and cruelty with which the French treat women, Zilia frames the *plaisir d'être* in these very terms: "The first feeling which nature inspired in us is the pleasure of being," she writes. But, as the sentence develops, Graffigny's stress is not on the "moi" in isolation; instead, she is interested in the "nous" that both emerges from this "moi" and makes the latter legible to itself. She continues, writing of the *plaisir d'être*: "and we experience this more and more intensely as we recognize the esteem in which we are held."[33] This is a primordial feeling, but it is one whose intensity (for Zilia) is always felt in relation, relative to the extent that others perceive us as worthy of consideration.

There are two distinctive aspects of Zilia's assertion worth underlining here, both of which suggest a specific genealogy for the affective declaration (and subsequent invitation) with which the novel ends. The first is that Zilia herself uncovers or discovers this pleasure only at the conclusion of her story. Her initial emphasis, in the letters that recount her abduction from the Temple of the Sun and her introduction to French culture, is much less on the self and its pleasures than on love as a scene of dependence and loss. It seems, then, that Zilia's *plaisir d'être* is not so much the foundation of her narrative—or the basis for her self-expression—as the place in which she ends up, in a way that resonates strongly with the idea (characteristic of both Puisieux and Du Châtelet) that women tend to come to a full recognition of their situation belatedly, through the action of thought in a context that is not hospitable to them. Even when Zilia acknowledges the *plaisir d'être* as fundamental—a "premier sentiment"—she suggests that the activation of this pleasure occurs over time and in context, in the fullness of a sense of love. Yet Zilia's own capacity to eventually accede to the *sentiment de l'existence* also comes as a result of (and not in spite of) moments of dispossession that strip her of her homeland, her culture, and finally her beloved, before she is able to locate a place where her happiness might endure. This dispossession is perhaps not inevitable, but it is nonetheless intimately connected to her position as an Indigenous woman faced with the fact of imperial domination.

Zilia's concluding account of the extraordinary pleasure of her belatedly uncovered sensations suggests a kinship with other more or less contemporaneous formulations of the *sentiment de l'existence* that highlight the way in which this feeling is embodied, fleshy, voluptuous—a matter of sensory organs just as much as of mental awareness or of imaginative impressability.[34] As an example of this more obviously sensualist rendering of this feeling, Roland Mortier finds in Diderot's article "Délicieux" from the *Encyclopédie* a reflection on the *sentiment de l'existence* that anticipates Rousseau while also expanding on the potentially libertine dimensions of this affective condition—its enmeshment with a sensuous pleasure. Diderot writes that "Rest also has its delights [*délice*]; but what is a *delicious* rest? He alone has known its inexpressible charm, whose organs were sensitive and delicate; who had received from nature a tender soul and a voluptuous temperament; who enjoyed perfect health; who found himself in the flower of youth; whose mind was troubled by no cloud, and whose soul was agitated by no overly lively emotion; who emerged from a sweet and light state of fatigue, and who felt in all the parts of his body a pleasure that was so equally distributed among them, that it could not be located precisely in any of them."[35] For Diderot, the *délices* of rest or *repos* are rooted in a physical situation; he describes these pleasures as corporeal—part of a physical condition of receptivity (and indeed *délicatesse*) that is coupled with an emotional and intellectual experience of untroubled tranquility.[36] Yet the immobile softness—somewhere between sleep and wakefulness—that he depicts takes on an ethical dimension too, for those who are capable of cultivating it. Here Diderot's formulation seems to echo that of Zilia: "If one could fix through thought this situation of pure feeling . . . , one would form the notion of the greatest and purest happiness that man can imagine," he writes.[37]

Diderot's voluptuous languor differs from Zilia's *plaisir d'être*, though, in that it is a fundamentally passive state: "he enjoyed it with a completely passive delight, without being attached to it, without thinking of it, without rejoicing in it, without congratulating himself for it," Diderot explains. For her part, Zilia actively reflects upon her happiness in writing—formulating the latter as a call or injunction to Déterville—in order both to communicate it and to recall it. Her final epistolary assertion of her right to be, to live, and to exist functions, then, a bit like the memory of Aza himself, which operates to immunize her to passionate love and to give her the possibility of managing her own pleasure without letting go of the fundamental relationality from which all pleasures spring. Graffigny also differs significantly from Diderot in her stress on dispossession and disappointment. For Diderot, the *repos délicieux* is a privilege extended by nature to a person with a sensing, responsive body who is young, in good health, and untroubled of mind and heart. While Zilia perhaps meets the first two criteria, she is inarguably excluded from the third. Indeed, her penultimate letter highlights at length the extent of the pain and sadness that accompanied Aza's betrayal. "As I emerged from the long and devastating lethargy into which Aza's departure had plunged me, the first impulse which nature inspired in me was to withdraw to that retreat which I owe to your far-sighted kindness,"[38] she writes to Déterville. Her *plaisir d'être* is one that is deliberately cultivated—extracted from a scene of disappointment in which she submits to the laws of destiny (as she puts it) at the same time as she gives in to the charms of freedom.

What does this deliberate oscillation between constraint and emancipation look like? How does it promote an ethics of shared pleasure? Zilia's reaction to Aza's betrayal initially involves a sort of second childhood, a return to "the weakness of our earliest years" in which "objects alone have power over us."[39] But rather than returning too to the passivity or indeed ingenuity of the infant, Zilia cultivates a kind of "second nature" here that doubles and corrects for the original one, a mode of being that is both immanent and the result of craft. Her realization of the "pouvoir des objets" suggests her capacity to manage and manipulate this power to her own ends. She continues:

> If the memory of Aza comes back to me, it is in the same guise as I imagined him at that time. I see myself awaiting his arrival. I yield to this illusion for as long as it gives pleasure to do so; when it fails, I turn to books. It is difficult to read at first, then, imperceptibly, new thoughts cloak the terrible truth hidden in the depths of my heart, and in the end bring some relief to my sorrow.
>
> Shall I confess it? The sweet pleasures of freedom sometimes offer themselves to my imagination, and I give way to them; surrounded as I am by delightful objects, possessing them has a charm which I make an effort to enjoy; at one with myself, I do not rely much on my reason. I indulge my weaknesses, I can only combat those of my heart by giving in to those of my mind. Maladies of the soul will not submit to violent remedies.[40]

Here Zilia takes control of the production of the illusions that both sadden and fortify her. She moves from a situation in which she was at the mercy of her passions to one in which she is capable of lending herself to the delights of Aza's memory, up until the point at which this memory distresses or disturbs her. She supplements its force with books and with agreeable or delightful objects that allow her to indulge her weaknesses. In so doing, she actively resists the call of romantic love—the happy ending that would otherwise seem to be dictated to and for her. But she does so in the name of pleasure and not as pleasure's deferral and sublimation.

At the same time as she softens in the face of her own weaknesses, Zilia remains remarkably obdurate in the face of others' demands on her. Her willingness to uphold the memory of Aza suggests that he is a more natural object of interest than Déterville, the man who in fact stands before her. This memory preserves Zilia's attachment to nature, and importantly to her own ethnic identity, while detaching her from the imperatives of the marriage contract; yet it is also, profoundly, an artifice. Zilia's enduring investment in Aza as a narrative persona—indeed, the Aza whom she imagined was a more appropriate love interest than Aza himself turns out to be—is what enables her to lay claim to her own autonomy, not as an independence from nature (in which she remains invested and by which she remains fascinated) but as a freedom from men's demands (particularly those of European men) on her person. Zilia's turn to her library and to the pursuit of knowledge is also enabled by her indifference to Déterville's romantic claims, an indifference that is itself premised on her sustained cultivation of an impossible love for Aza as both the most natural of bonds—he is, after all, both promised to her and possibly her brother—and the most artificial of ties. The satisfactions promised by love may still be consummated in her memory of Aza, now assuming its full character as a fiction, while the pleasure of being receives its own enhancement and augmentation in the company of sympathetic subjects. We might return to Diderot's *repos délicieux* in this context. His description of the body emerging from a sleep or fatigue, suffused with pleasure and in the bloom of youth, suggests not only internal sensuality but desirability, a sensuous receptivity to pleasure. But in Zilia's case her embrace of the *plaisir d'être* coincides with her total rejection of romantic rapture or a specifically erotic sensitivity. Her special *sensibilité* remains relational—it is for this reason that she invites Déterville to come share in her delight—but it is not erotically impassioned. Her feminine variant of the *sentiment de l'existence* is predicated not on the assertion of desire but on the withdrawal of the woman from the scene of marriage, all while she remains substantially receptive to her environment. In fact, the conclusion goes further than this. Zilia's receptivity to the world around her is determined by her retreat from the solicitations of Déterville, which threaten to interrupt her pleasure. Her experience as a woman is not severed from the forms that constrain it, but her relationship to these forms has changed.

Illusion and Autonomy

How does Zilia arrive at a delicious independence that also allows her to preserve a practice of responsiveness and exchange—a sensitivity to feeling that lends itself to communication? How does her pleasure become a model for others? To ask this is also to ask: How does the novel itself take shape? For the text arrives belatedly, thanks to Zilia's translation of her original letters, a labor that she undertakes after the narrative's end. In one sense, the letters in their entirety are organized around a mistaken belief: Zilia's erroneous conviction that her love for Aza is reciprocal. This mistake, which engages, moves, and compels the reader, is an internal fiction that nonetheless provides the motivating force for the narrative. But the reliance of the novel on illusion for its substance is even more comprehensive than this, extending from the work's content to its form. As I have discussed, the *quipus* themselves generate their own particular deception. As Zilia describes their resemblance to speech, these knots suggest to her that she is in fact addressing Aza and that her expressions of love are received by him. Yet she knows, at this point in the story, that this cannot be the case: She is also aware of her "sweet delusion."[41] In this sense, her dream of reciprocity—a mutual communication of feeling—is a fiction that she deliberately cultivates for its sustaining power. It carries both her and the reader across the narrative of her abduction and gradual enlightenment.

In the beginning of the novel, Zilia asserts that both knowledge and pleasure arise from the charms of love, which are transporting and motivating. As she puts it, in terms that stress an initial, erotic form of dispossession in the face of her feeling for Aza: "Just as the rose draws its brilliant colours from the rays of the Sun, the charms which please you in my mind and heart are simply the fruits of your own luminous inspiration; nothing is truly mine except my love."[42] It is this tenderness, and not an intrinsic desire for enlightenment, that serves as her goad or impetus for the cultivation of knowledge. It is also this tenderness that gives her access to a voluptuous delight in the very act of pleasing the one she loves: "But, oh light of my life, had it not been for my desire to please you, would I have had the resolve to give up my blissful ignorance in exchange for the painful activity of study? Without the desire to earn your esteem, your trust, your respect, with virtues which strengthen love, and which love turns to sheer delight, I would have been no more than the object of your gaze; absence would already have erased me from your memory."[43] This statement from the second letter, read with the ending of the work in mind, seems ironic: Clearly Aza's memory (and devotion) are not as steady as Zilia would like to believe. Moreover, the suggestion that her learning is only a result of her submission to her prospective fiancé's wishes troubles any argument on behalf of Zilia's protofeminism. Her path to enlightenment is born not out of a free inclination toward reason (or learning) but a constrained and determined desire for pleasure. The problem of the text is not how to subdue love by rational thought but how to put love to work in order to generate a critical and affective purchase on the world—and how to shift the feminine relation to the image so that the latter retains its therapeutic value in the absence of he to whom it refers.

In other words, it is precisely in her acknowledgment of the power of her fictive attachments—and their ongoing life-sustaining force—that Zilia finds the ability to persist and eventually thrive. To return to the image that Zilia herself employs, the seeming passivity of the flower—and its utter need of the sun for survival—do not obviate the fact that the bloom of the rose is also *for it*—a sign of its unique mode of life and the pleasure that it takes therein. In the same letter where she recounts her first meeting with Aza, Zilia describes her love for him as deeply sensual: "I draw from it a feeling of intense joy which intoxicates my soul," she exclaims of the treasures of love. She suggests that he abandon his kingdom to be with her, so that his empire would extend over her alone: "You will be more a king ruling over my soul," she writes, "than you are now, doubting the affection of countless subjects."[44] Aza's freedom from the cares of ruling would be bought at the price of her (perfect) obedience to him. She goes on to evoke the confusion of hearts, the instantaneous exchange, that is a result of a love that is most likely incestuous, in which a similarity of thought appears to resonate with a likeness of body. Her desire for Aza is so intense that she mistakes its origin as a godly one. "My mind was full of the sublime theology of our *Cucipatas*, and I took the fire which inspired me to be divine rapture; I thought the Sun was manifesting his will to me through you, that he was selecting me for his preferred wife: I sighed at this thought, but once you had gone, I looked inside my heart and found nothing there but the image of you."[45] The power of Aza's image is overwhelming, sublime, dominating, and seemingly transcendent. But it is also, eventually, liberating, precisely because of the way in which Zilia anchors its force in the intensity of her attachment to her beloved. For the image is indeed not metaphysical in origin but material. And because it is material—sensuously evocative rather than divinely given—it is subject to reconfiguration and redeployment.

Zilia's ability to survive—and to consciously cultivate her pleasure—depends upon her capacity to maintain the illusion of Aza's love; it is through this labor—of writing, of feeling, and of thinking—that she learns to redirect the mediatic power of his sign, as if the rose were to provide its own light. This process is described in starkly material terms—as a literal matter of life and death. After the French "rescue" her from the Spaniards in a sea battle that she only vaguely understands, Zilia begins to lose hope; indifferent to her future, she contemplates the end of her life without regret. At this moment she is weakened in body and mind; her relationship to the image, her ability to receive and respond to impression's marks, becomes attenuated: "already, the images taken in by my enfeebled imagination were no clearer than the faintest of drawings, sketched by a trembling hand; already objects which had once moved me the most now excited in me nothing more than that kind of vague sensation which we experience when we let our mind wander in aimless dreaming; I was almost gone," she explains to Aza.[46] The indeterminate dream-state into which she enters at this moment is very different from the active manipulation of illusion that she puts to work elsewhere in her correspondence, a process in which the image bears with it and engenders sentiment and sensation. As she reveals in this third letter, the latter requires a certain strength of both mind and body for it to operate as sustenance; it is an active rather than a passive condition. Or rather, it is a situation in which receptivity to the world alternates with an attention to the effects generated by this world, in which the feminine subject oscillates between sensitivity and self-assertion, in a substantiating *papillotage*.

In a corporeal situation of extreme weakness and destitution, Zilia's imagination ceases to be able to receive the images of the objects around her, which become vague, ethereal, and "light"—dematerialized, in other words. Their effects are life-draining rather than life-sustaining. Yet even at this moment when she hesitates at the edge of death, a certain reciprocity returns: "I discovered, however, that the natural instinct which impels us during our life to delve into the future, and even into the future which we shall not live to see, seems to acquire a new strength at the very point of death. We cease to live for ourselves; we want to know how we shall live on in the object of our love."[47] The stimulating and animating energy that serves to propel Zilia toward her own future—a version of the Spinozan *conatus*, perhaps—projects her instead, in the absence of mental vigor, into a kind of dreamworld in which she imagines Aza learning of her death. Given her weakness and her withdrawal from the world—her inability to receive the images that come to her from outside—this is a scene not of illusion but of delusion—a *délire*, as she puts it. She imagines Aza on his throne, taking on the form and figure of a lily burned by the equatorial sun: The passivity of the flower that was once Zilia's own passes in this scene to him. At the same time, her love for him becomes sadistic, a desire for his suffering: "Is love then sometimes brutal?" she asks.[48] The answer is clearly yes, but more crucially Graffigny reveals with this vignette the way in which the receptivity of the feminine subject to the images that allow it to persist must be managed in reflection, as a concrete position vis à vis the world rather than a susceptibility to the powers of reverie. The letter concludes: "the weightless cloud of my thoughts will never cease to hover about you."[49] In light of the scene she has just described, this assertion seems both promise and threat. In the utter loss of her sense of self—her disorientation within a world that she neither recognizes nor understands—the desire to be loved and remembered morphs easily into cruelty. In a fantasy where imagination operates without constraint, Zilia expresses a need for possession and domination that is enacted through the transmissibility of thought. Her grief at the absence of Aza becomes his suffering in the light of her loss. He assumes her position, wilting.

Zilia will continue to explore the link between pleasurable sensation, illusion, and (self-)possession while she resituates herself in France. As she moves out of the dreamworld fabricated from her disorientation and despair, she does not cease to reflect on the pleasures that images can communicate. These pleasures are linked to the function of illusion, but not exhausted within it; they also affect the relationship of the feeling subject with the world, and vice versa. In letter twelve, Zilia finds herself in a coach traveling from the provincial city in which she has disembarked to Paris. As she looks out the window, buoyed by the motion of the coach that she describes as a kind of moving house ("this machine, or hut"[50]), she remarks upon the charms that unfurl before her. For four days, she contemplates "the beauties of the universe," to which she was forbidden access as a virgin cloistered in the Temple of the Sun. Their effect on her is stunning, striking, ravishing: It also induces an error. "Our eyes at once scan, embrace, and come to rest on an infinite number of objects, as varied as they are delightful," she writes to Aza.[51] "We believe that there are no limits to what we can see other than those of the world itself. This error flatters us; it gives us a comforting sense of our own stature, and seems to bring us close to the Creator of so many wonders."[52]

In this passage the unobstructed view of the delighted spectator is identified with the divine perspective on a world that God both creates and controls. This is a dangerous association for the human viewer, since it threatens the reciprocity of feeling that allows the relationship to the image to inflect both perceiver and perceived in pleasurable ways. It may also generate reverie, both sweet and painful. Zilia describes the transition from night to day as she watches the setting sun; the appearance of the moon induces in her a state of calm, in which "we delight in the universe as if we were its sole possessor, we see nothing in it which is not ours."[53] This situation is sweet, but it must come to end, "and if some regrets come to disturb [pleasant thoughts inspired in us], they arise only because we must tear ourselves from this delightful reverie and shut ourselves away once more in those prisons without sense or reason which men have constructed for themselves, and which all their efforts will never make anything other than worthless when compared with the works of nature."[54] The delight of this dream-state is necessarily intermingled with the trouble of its ephemerality; from her position as a privileged spectator that the coach permits and enables, Zilia is thrust back into a situation of constraint. Her sense of possession is in error.

But in her discovery of nature as a source of aesthetic pleasure Zilia also recounts a different kind of relation to the environment that she has been traversing. Every day, Déterville allows her to leave the coach in order to observe the beauties of the world from a new perspective. It is at this point that she describes the appeal not of the landscape spread before her but of the forest into which she may enter. She writes, "How delightful the woods are, my dearest Aza! as you enter them, their pervasive spell touches every one of our senses and seems to confuse their function. You have the impression of actually seeing the cooling breeze before you feel it; the different shades of colour in the leaves soften the light that penetrates them, and seem to impress our feelings at the same time as our sight. A scent, pleasant but indistinct, scarcely allows us to tell whether we are tasting or smelling it; even the air, unperceived, brings to our entire being a feeling of the purest delight, which seems to give us an extra sense, without our being able to locate it in our body."[55] This invocation of aesthetic pleasure is quite distinct—in its mechanism and its effects—from the description of the transports of the scene that precedes it. In the first instance, the setting sun and rising moon are set out before Zilia as she moves through the world in her coach; they induce in her the thrill of possession, as if the cosmos arrayed before her were hers to do with as she liked. The forest, on the other hand, is an immersive experience, akin not to viewing a painting but to entering a virtual reality that is indeed not virtual at all—or rather that is both virtual and material all at once. Among the trees, brightness changes to softness, sensory impressions melt one into the other, and human faculties of perception lose their specificity while still retaining their acuity. The forest, where the light does not so much strike the leaves of the trees and other plants as blend and merge with them, is the zone of *volupté*, which is evoked here in a manner reminiscent of La Mettrie (and indeed of Puisieux too). For Zilia, sensations of pleasure infuse her body as if they traveled through the medium of the air, which is tasted and smelled all at once. As the light moves into and across the leaves, the air moves through Zilia, binding her synesthetically to the place she discovers.

The critique of possessive desire that accompanies the setting of the sun is thus followed by an endorsement of the appeal of *volupté*, as an attitude or relation in which the objects perceived and the perceiving subject exchange positions with one another. When Zilia views the sun from the coach's window, she is a spectator positioned before a landscape that she grasps through the faculty of vision; her descent from the coach allows her to be voluptuously incorporated into the environment through which she moves. Rather than carrying her away into a situation of reverie, the forest stimulates and animates her — seeming in the freshness of its air and the nuanced hues of its foliage to enhance her own ability to feel it. Zilia's contact with plants in this scene might call to mind the earlier image of her and Aza as flowers. In this instance, however, Graffigny depicts a different kind of interpenetration of human and vegetal bodies: Where the botanical intermingling from the second letter took place on a purely metaphorical scale, in her description of the forest the entanglement has a explicitly physical dimension. And the effects on Zilia herself are quite distinct. Unlike the rose who seems beholden to the sun that illuminates and sustains it, in the woodland scene Zilia retains her capacity for action while still receiving nourishment from the environment that she traverses. Moreover, this pleasure is not hers alone — it is not a feeling that results from the instance or fact of possession — and because it is not only hers, it is capable of being passed on: It suffuses the epistolary exchange between the two lovers, moving through the correspondence and galvanizing Zilia as she creates and imagines yet another scene of contact in which Aza will receive the outpourings of her heart. At the end of the letter, she addresses him with fervor: "Oh, my dearest Aza! such perfect pleasures would be lovelier still if you were here! how I have longed to share them with you! As the witness of my loving thoughts, I would have you find in the feelings of my heart delights which are even more powerful than those bestowed by the beauties of the universe."[56] The sentiment engendered in the forest can move out again toward the world: It is transmissible, fungible, shareable. If only Aza were there to receive it. In his place, at this moment, is the reader, for whom the scent of the forest air, so delicious and refreshing, might linger past the conclusion of the letter.

But there is another interlocutor present, lurking in the background of the scenes that Zilia admires, describes, and inhabits, and that is Déterville. The same letter where Zilia rapturously recounts her encounters with nature begins with a very different kind of meeting — namely, the moment when Zilia catches sight of herself in a mirror, this "ingenious machine" to which she has only recently been introduced.[57] Zilia's surprise at seeing herself in the form of an image, "as if I were actually standing opposite myself," is echoed by Déterville's own amazement at viewing the Peruvian princess in European rather than Indigenous dress. The *vis-à-vis* constituted by Zilia and her own reflected figure, where she stands as separate from herself, is swiftly followed by another *vis-à-vis*, where Déterville stands facing her, motionless in the doorway as if frozen in place, unable to speak. At this moment, he enters into his own state of reverie, a term that will of course recur in Zilia's description of her reaction to the moonrise, so that the letter as a whole suggests a complicated web of interwoven sights, metaphors, and sensations, a crux of its own where images both stand apart from and merge with the sensing subjects who perceive them. In Déterville's case, "He was so lost in thought that he stood aside to let the *China* pass and then returned to his position without realizing it; his eyes fixed on me, he looked over my whole person with the closest attention, which made me feel uncomfortable without my knowing why."[58] If the reason for Déterville's distraction is unclear to Zilia, however, it is all too obvious to the reader, who understands that, transformed by her new clothing into the image of a Frenchwoman (another *vis-à-vis*, since she both is and is not this image), Zilia suddenly appears as an appropriate object of Déterville's desire. This transformation, the result of a racist logic, is only heightened by what happens next: Zilia, concerned to show her gratitude for the gift of the new garments, repeats to him the words that he taught her shipboard, when they first met one another: *yes, I love you, . . . I promise to be yours* [italics Graffigny's].[59] On the one hand, these phrases seem to solidify the illusion of Zilia's Frenchness (and thereby both her desirability and availability for marriage). On the other hand, Déterville is fully aware of their emptiness, since they serve not to carry Zilia's sentiment toward him but merely to echo his own voice back to him (down to the very tone in which Zilia speaks, a tone that, she affirms, is an imitation of Déterville's own). This instance of failed reciprocity anticipates Zilia's communion with the setting sun, which for all the transports it engenders represents another failed or missed connection driven by a mistaken relation to the image, since from her delightful fantasy of possession Zilia can only fall back into the world of "those prisons" made by humans. Both she and Déterville must wrest themselves from a dream state that interrupts rather than fosters the exchange of signs and sentiments. But the immersion in the forest world seems to represent a very different kind of pleasure, quite unlike the contact with an "empty" or unattainable image that solicits desire only to leave it unsatisfied.

In other words, there are two relationships with materiality—and materialism—on display in this letter, which appears at a kind of hinge in the plot. On the one hand, Zilia articulates a relationship to the image whereby the latter inspires the need for possession by preserving the distinction between perceiving subject and object of perception. Because Zilia observes the first landscape from a window, the varied elements of the natural world are presented before her as if they were set in place, static artifacts available for her delectation. Her vision travels across these objects but is not caught, retained, or shaped by any given one of them; she is thus tempted to believe in her own omnipotence as a spectator, detached from a world of her own making, as if she were in the position of an idle god. On the other hand, in the case of the forest, Zilia experiences a connection to the scenery around her in which the qualities of the woods themselves "melt" into her, dissolving the boundaries that separate one sense from the other at the same time as they heighten the mechanisms of her perception. Two forms of pleasure are also perceptible in these two examples: The one sparked by a possessive drive that generates a fiction of the self as both detached and powerful, the second involving a more "delicious" or voluptuous exchange in which Zilia becomes part of the sensually engaging forest world. These two modes are introduced by her encounter with Déterville as she is observing herself in the mirror wearing the dress or costume of a Frenchwoman, another moment in which reciprocity is dramatically absent and a thwarted need for conquest both draws the observer closer to the object observed (in this case Zilia's person) and acts as an insuperable barrier between the two.

Graffigny's formulation of this double relationship to materiality has a clear Epicurean antecedent in the form of the Lucretian critique of erotic passion, wherein the need for possession similarly drives an increasingly painful pursuit of an impossible consummation. In Lucretius's terms, a relation to the image *as object* both pricks or spurs desire and dooms this desire to failure on its own terms. He writes in the *De rerum natura* (*DRN*) of the lover perceiving the beloved:

> For food and liquid are absorbed into the body, and since these can possess certain fixed parts, thereby the desire of water or bread is easily fulfilled. But from man's aspect and beautiful bloom nothing comes into the body to be enjoyed except thin images; and this poor hope is often snatched away by the wind. As when in dreams a thirsty man seeks to drink, and no water is forthcoming to quench the burning in his frame, but he seeks the image of water, striving in vain, and in the midst of a rushing river thirsts while he drinks: so in love Venus mocks lovers with images, nor can bodies even in real presence satisfy lovers with looking, nor can they rub off something from tender limbs with hands wandering aimless all over the body.[60]

Errantes incerti [wandering aimless] — in this expression the body of the lover becomes the zone of endless errancy, where substance fails to satisfy. The desire to possess the image of the beloved is a desire to consume, subdue, and dominate this image, which nonetheless resists possession in its very lack of consistency, so that the encounter between the lovers takes the shape of combat rather than exchange.

Moreover, while the "thin images" of the beloved body never acquire enough substance to satiate the urge to take hold of or master it, the substance of the lover's body also dissipates, becomes tenuous and feeble: Lucretius writes, "Add this also, that they consume their strength and kill themselves with the labour; add this, that one lives at the beck of another. Duties are neglected, good name totters and sickens. Meanwhile wealth vanishes, and turns into Babylonian perfumes."[61] Déterville confronts this precise problem of desire pricked and unsatisfiable in the scene of Zilia "disguised" as a Frenchwoman—where the image that he receives stimulates him with its femininity and its coded ethnic identification (staged here as yet another fiction). Zilia, for her part, describes the feminine role in the Lucretian coupling from the first-person: She first experiences *herself* as an image, in the initial moment of *vis-à-vis* with the mirror. Notably, she does not seek to trap or exploit Déterville's interest on this occasion—presenting her pleasure in her French apparel as a result of her dislike of the attention that her Peruvian garments incite. In the second half of the letter, Zilia transposes the relation to the image into a context framed as aesthetic rather than amatory (one that seems to anticipate in some sense the Kantian sublime). At first relishing her newfound sense of mastery over the scene that she observes from the coach, Zilia also emphasizes its negative *dénouement*: "we must tear ourselves from this delightful reverie and shut ourselves away once more in those prisons without sense or reason which men have constructed for themselves."[62] The communion with the forest, which involves senses other than sight and a kind of synesthetic dissolve into the environment that she appreciates, concludes differently however, with a call to the beloved: In the end, her words suggest, Aza's presence might embellish even the charms of nature, enhancing and augmenting their effects. In sharing thoughts and feelings, mutual sensitivity might be heightened, rather than frustrated. Here there is also a Lucretian model, albeit a scabrous one: *Quare etiam atque etiam, ut dico, est communi voluptas.* "Therefore, again and again I say, the pleasure is for both."[63]

Zilia too frames voluptuousness as necessarily mutual. Her experience in the forest suggests a way back to the human world in which human artifice is not only the source of constraint but of enjoyment, where the loving transmission of sentiments (rather than the fruitless pursuit of the composed figure as an image to consume) might endlessly fortify the appreciation of natural beauty. The wonders of the forest mingle with the sensory pleasure that Zilia takes in the exchange of letters, imagined as a conversation that enables the translation of her thoughts into "delights which are even more powerful than those bestowed by the beauties of the universe."[64] The alchemy of sentiment that takes place here is still material and materialized: It is in the loosing and the losing of her feeling toward Aza (who is not only absent but will always remain so) that Zilia imagines an infinite extension of her pleasure. The articulation of her thoughts would have on Aza an effect even more delicious than the "volupté pure" that transpires via the sylvan air. But, tellingly, this possibility is even at this moment framed as a loss, not an eventual gain, in the past conditional. Zilia is already speaking the language of her future dispossession.

In the famous letter 34, which Graffigny added to the 1752 edition along with an introduction focusing on the history of Peru and the Peruvians (an aspect of the text to which I will return), Graffigny extends this contrast between two materialisms—and two relations to materiality—into an explicitly political and social context. Where an ancient critic like Lucretius is interested in the turn to materialism as a therapeutics, Graffigny reveals the potential of a voluptuous mutuality for generating a social critique that takes seriously women's exploitation precisely as objects of exchange among men. Zilia confirms that, in France, women's objectification is tightly linked to their social role as image-bearers: They function primarily as symbols of familial wealth and social prominence, whose beauty is meant to stimulate and exacerbate a desire for seduction and conquest. She writes:

> Regulating the movements of one's body, adjusting one's facial expression, composing one's outer appearance, this is the essence of their education. It is on the basis of their daughters' ability to comport themselves more or less awkwardly that parents take pride in having brought them up well. They instruct them to be stricken with embarrassment if they commit any offence against social decorum; they do not tell them that an honest countenance is mere hypocrisy if it does not spring from the honesty of one's soul. They constantly encourage in them that despicable feeling of self-love which is concerned only with their outer appeal.[65]

This passage describes a moral and physical education that impedes an exchange between partners and prioritizes feminine ignorance. It produces girls and young women who are incapable of self-understanding because they have always served the interests of others: "In their infancy," Zilia notes, "children seem destined to do no more than entertain their parents and those responsible for their upbringing."[66] Girls are deliberately kept away from the truth; denied the use of their senses as a source of knowledge; duped about that which they cannot see. "They mislead them about the evidence of their senses."[67] In this context, how are they to correct their errors? The pleasures that they take are short-lived, insipid, puerile. Feminine virtue here is not grounded in any kind of human relation whatsoever; indeed, it emerges in the *absence* of such relation—as a commitment to chastity that forms the sum total of what it means to be an honorable woman.

In this extraordinary letter, which echoes many of Puisieux's complaints about the vacuity of French culture that sets women up to fail, extending them the possibility of erotic and sensual pleasure only in a situation where they are least able to achieve or demand it, Zilia presents her commitment to Aza as an antidote. "It is you, my dearest Aza, it is your boundless love, it is the honesty of our hearts, the sincerity of our feelings, which have revealed to me the secrets of nature and of love."[68] Aza's love for her stimulates her sense of self-worth, sparks her latent *plaisir d'être*, solidifies her idea of her own importance in another's eyes. It is a counter to the desire for possession but it is also the ultimate expression of this desire, differing from friendship in the intensity of its preference and the singularity of its aims. She continues:

> Friendship, that wise and tender bond, ought perhaps to fulfil all our desires, but it can share its affections among several objects without dishonour or scruple; love, which makes and requires an exclusive preference, gives us such an elevated and rewarding sense of our being that it alone can satisfy the avid desire for primacy with which we are born, which is apparent in us at all ages, at all times, and in all states, and our instinctive appetite for possession strengthens and completes our inclination to love.[69]

This vision of love as a natural extension of the taste for property might seem astonishing in the context of Zilia's preceding critique—not only of something very like the "avid desire for primacy," which denies the right of other humans to participate in the privileges that it accrues but specifically of the hoarding of wealth and resources to the detriment of society as a whole.[70] Even more striking is her modulation of this acute, overweening impetus in the paragraph that follows: "If the possession of a piece of furniture, a jewel, or a plot of land brings one of the most pleasurable feelings we can experience, what must we feel when we know that we possess a heart, a soul, a being who is free and independent, and who willingly surrenders itself in exchange for the pleasure of possessing in us those same qualities!"[71] At this moment Zilia seems fully transformed from the cloistered princess of her Peruvian past into someone recognizable by and within a French culture of production and consumption: She lauds possession (of an object, of a land, of a jewel) as the foundation of a love that only belatedly enters into mutuality. Ownership is the basis for desire, so that the sentimental exchange in the love relationship is really a transfer of freedoms—a mutual enslavement. Relational exchange in this situation takes on a different cast; it is not flexible but imperious. Zilia asks: What might be the pleasure to be had from a dynamic of joint submission, the one partner to the other and vice versa, so that the distinction between either might be effaced in a give-and-take of hearts, souls, bodies, and independence? Is it in this instance that equality might be assured? In fact, the answer to this question is no, but Zilia moves toward this realization over time, in a process that obliges her to parse the difference between delusions to be countered and illusions to be cultivated and enjoyed.

Graffigny's reflections in letter 34 stress the link between sexual or sentimental desire and a rampant need to possess and to master that spurs luxurious consumption (and its ills) in its many forms; this connection also forms a key part of Lucretius's critique of love as a kind of sickness whereby the lover imagines for himself a power that he cannot have, finding in the body of his beloved the limit of his self-conception and the anxiety of finitude. Zilia's notion that the primacy of the self is so insistent and compelling that it grounds not only property relations but erotic ones even finds a bizarre echo in the marquis de Sade's scandalous vision of sexual despotism, drawn from the revolutionary pamphlet inserted in *La Philosophie dans le boudoir*. "No passion has more need of all the range of liberty than that one, without a doubt, none is as despotic," Sade writes of erotic desire, designating the latter as "the dose of despotism that nature places at the bottom . . . [of the] heart."[72] He too ties the libidinal impulse directly to political metaphors of domination and oppression, but unlike Zilia, he affirms not just the strength of a tyrannical desire but a uniquely human right to the freedom to refuse it: "No act of possession can ever be exercised over a free being," he asserts, in stark contrast to Zilia's claim that love is only possession reconfigured.[73] (Both men and women, he affirms, should have infinite right to all other bodies at any moment, in special state-run institutions.) Unlike Sade (and Lucretius himself for that matter), Zilia appears to be committed to the mystifying power of love to satisfy (rather than thwart) the need for primacy.

And indeed the next letter in the sequence seems to confirm her in this error, for she soon finds herself in delicious possession of a kind of fairy tale palace, bestowed upon her by Déterville who, in quasi-alchemical fashion, has transformed part of the Peruvian spoils from the Spanish ship into a house for her. Given what has come before, this satisfaction of the need for property—a manor house of Zilia's very own—seems designed to consolidate Zilia's transition to a more European identity; it also would appear to anticipate a happy conclusion to the correspondence with Aza—one that, notably, fails to arrive. In letter 37, the reader discovers that Aza has converted to Christianity and married a Spanish woman. Zilia once again finds herself utterly dispossessed. "My life belongs to him," she writes to Déterville, "let him take it from me, and let him still love me."[74] From the sweet reverie that constituted the idea of a shared submission—a mutual exchange of freedoms and dependency—Zilia is thrust back into another kind of prison—that of a living death. At this moment, Zilia sees her error and longs for her lost ignorance (but not innocence). She addresses the French women whom she has pitied: "How fortunate you are, women of France, you are betrayed; but you can long enjoy an illusion which would be a real comfort to me at this moment. Dissimulation prepares you for the fatal blow which is now killing me."[75] Zilia misses her shattered fantasies, which she has been unable to protect and nurture. In her despair, she sees dissimulation as a lesser evil than the suffering induced by the terrible honesty of her beloved: Aza has remained Peruvian at least, in his directness. His betrayal of Zilia reveals that the mutuality she had expected and fostered in her correspondence was its own kind of deluded mistake. The possessive model of desire has failed her.

Zilia's dispossession as a Peruvian—her abduction from her homeland and her transport to France—gives her critique of French culture and gender norms its heft and power. As an outsider, she sees clearly the errors that inform the mores of the society in which she finds herself. But she remains vulnerable to her own errors. As a case in point, her relationship with Aza comes closer and closer to that sustained by the Epicurean lover with the figure of the "thin image"; even as it exerts a dazzling power and influence over her, his simulacrum functions increasingly in total detachment from the material conditions that have generated it. This detachment reaches a kind of fever pitch in the letter in which she produces her most detailed critique of French society, suggesting that acute social analysis can and does coexist with the cultivation of a romantic illusion of possession. But this copresence of critique and error can persist only until the circumstances helping foster her mistake shift, at which point Zilia is thrust back into a position of near total vulnerability—seeking death as her only respite. Graffigny reveals here the way in which the use of reason as an instrument of social analysis is not a sufficient condition of either self-transformation or liberation from constraint. At this moment, as Zilia describes it (and as Robin Howells emphasizes in his reading), she reverts to a weakened and childlike stage, one in which she is at the mercy of her impressions: "An excess of grief," she writes to Déterville this time, "takes us back to the weakness of our earliest years. Just as in infancy, objects alone have power over us; it seems that sight is the only one of our senses which can reach the secret depth of our soul."[76] In the grand novelistic tradition of feminine suffering that seems to find its inaugural modern moment with *La Princesse de Clèves*, Zilia withdraws to her manor house, into solitude.

But this infancy is distinct from the first one—the original moment of immersion in the object world—precisely because it comes after: It can be recalled, recollected, remembered, and reshaped as a second origin for a self that stands in intimate, interconnected relation to a world of which it is nonetheless capable of taking stock. This time around—unlike the first—the pleasure of being (itself associated with the condition of the child) entails not an unconscious receptivity to the object-world but a set of material conditions and a deliberate cultivation of illusion in response to those conditions. *Le plaisir d'être* means knowing what being is and how pleasure might emerge in and from it: It requires a stripping away of error and the painstaking construction of illusions in which pleasure might reemerge. Notably, these illusions must be fought for. Zilia thus retravels the path toward adulthood again, following Aza's betrayal, but this time around in full *connaissance de cause*. She is clear, too, that the state of dispossession in which she now finds herself—one that is both imagined and real—is also the space in which she must build her own fleeting sense of freedom, where pleasure can finally be her guide.

In her critique of French society, Graffigny eloquently points out that the ideology of woman's nature operates as a self-fulfilling prophecy to create the feminine attitudes and practices this same society appears to deplore. But her solution, for Zilia, is not so much to point to a "real" nature that undergirds the false one as to reveal the ways in which women's most apparently natural feelings and attributes are themselves deeply linked to the forms, including language, through which they enter into contact with the world. The passive theory of nature—as essence, or unselfconsciousness—denies this linkage at the same time as it makes use of it to shape the very contours of feminine experience. Such a shaping, unexamined, is something other than just a mistaken belief; it operates materially to the detriment of the subjects it captivates. Still, this power may (indeed, must) be countered on the ground of figuration itself, where Zilia has been operating all along.

Zilia is savvy about her needs, and marriage is not among them. The illusion that she makes, tucked away in a dwelling that resembles something from a fairy tale, is real and genuine: It is not a simulacrum in the ordinary sense of the term, although it may still be one from a Lucretian perspective. As Zilia explains to Déterville, "It could be that your nation's grand sense of decency does not allow one of my age to live alone in this independent state; at least, whenever Céline comes to see me, she tries to persuade me so. But she has not yet provided sufficiently good reason to convince me; true decency is in my heart. It is not to the image of virtue that I pay homage, it is to virtue itself."[77] This rejection of virtue's fictions (and embrace of its reality) is dependent upon the preservation of Aza as a fiction of another kind. Zilia's moral status becomes visible and tangible as a set of practices that allow her to retain her independence while remaining responsive to the environment she inhabits, not to the norms that are dictated to her as the truth of her nature, veiling the fictions that sustain them. And it is true that Zilia, in her manor house, is by no means playing a part, acting upon the stage of femininity. Rather, she is gently, sweetly, and softly lending herself to the *faiblesses* that she calls her own in order to share them, *douceurs* that might have appeared before as supplemental pleasures but are now all that she has left. From here something else extraordinary happens. When Zilia invites Déterville to come participate in the "innocent pleasures" that she has willfully and deliberately made for herself, offering him the happiness of simple friendship, she positions herself in the final paragraph of the novel as his teacher: "Come, Déterville, come and learn from me how to use wisely the resources of our soul, and the gifts of nature."[78] This is a household economy that is both materially situated and philosophically oriented, taking the ancient association between women and domestic management and transforming it into the principle that lies behind the cultivation of the Epicurean Garden, where the cultivation of pleasure is transmitted from one student to another. An exchange may be constructed from the wreckage here—Zilia remains committed to relationality throughout—and in the delicate attention to the constraints laid upon subjectivity, a form of freedom can be crafted. This is a position that must be fostered: It is not natural, but becomes so. If femininity is the position of being made to be, why can't the capacity for that making change hands?

Coda: Fictions of Empire

In *Lettres d'une Péruvienne*, dispossession becomes a situation from which a self can emerge, but a self that remains in a flexible, contingent, and fragile position. Critique allows for the recognition of vulnerability, not for the hardening of an autonomous will. While Graffigny's novel is formally innovative, her thought nonetheless resonates with that of the two other women whose work I have analyzed here. Puisieux and Du Châtelet are likewise invested in the ways that pleasure can emerge from (but not precisely in reaction to) constraint and trauma, from a susceptibility to illusion and from a knowledge that betrayal is all too soon to arrive. Graffigny adds a new element to this dynamic with the fact of Zilia's being Peruvian. Her ethnic identity (like her fidelity) seems by the end of the tale to both exist and not exist in the world—to function as a form of belonging but also as something else, as a position that promotes and commands her separation from the society that has abducted and received her. In contrast to Du Châtelet and Puisieux, whose references to racial others (including the *fakir* and the Indian worshipper) crop up as brutal signifiers of alterity, Graffigny's strategy is different: She promotes Zilia's Peruvian "nature," sometimes as a cipher for feminine abandonment and exclusion writ large, sometimes as a distinct mode of being to which historical documents can give access. The fact of Zilia's apparent but undiscussed time travel from sixteenth-century Peru to Enlightenment France both gives a kind of consistency to her difference—Graffigny was notably unusual in including a historical introduction to her text (and footnotes, as Aurora Wolfgang discusses) that aim to give Peruvian culture its due—and lends to her origins the status of a speculative fiction. It is both plausible and impossible that she could be Peruvian in the way she is. To ask what may be carried forward from Graffigny's novel into the present time is a question that is staged in the novel itself as the problem of what Zilia may transport out of and away from her own culture, which had already been destroyed in an act of mass murder, plunder, pillage, and rape. The historical introduction brings readers closer to precolonial Peru, at the same time as it delimits this origin as a fiction.[79] Recognition is possible here because ancient Peru is gone, not in spite of this disappearance. *Comment peut-on être Péruvienne?*

While in Du Châtelet and Puisieux the world of the other remains primarily that of men, in Graffigny this difference is also cast in racial and ethnic terms, a difference that forms the "heart" of Zilia's sense of who she is, both before and after her rebirth. And it is this consistency that is troubling, for it subtracts from the "fact" of ethnic origin the flexible relationality that Zilia crafts in her feminine solitude. If her pleasure is in many ways made in the ruins of what has come before it, her Peruvianness seems to cohere as a denial of that ruined history—as a fetish, in other words, that both reveals and conceals her story. Ethnic difference is here conceived as whole and integral in a way that femininity is not; at the same time, exchange is inconceivable with a Peruvian culture that has vanished from an earth that Zilia, as an Incan, can only haunt. In the evocation of ethnicity as a zone of dispossession to which there can be no return—a point of identification but also an absolute and in some sense incomprehensible difference—Graffigny fails to recreate the oscillation between willing and nilling that characterizes Zilia's own position vis à vis Aza. Unlike for instance Diderot's Tahiti in the *Supplément au voyage de Bougainville* (written in 1772), a society that exists both in its colonial despoliation and outside of it, Peru as Graffigny portrays it is *only* lost, *only* gone, and because it is lost and gone, it functions to solicit a relationality that takes place in the absence of material enmeshment. Graffigny's text is also striking for the ease with which it allows the ethnic other to function as a cipher for white, metropolitan women's fantasies of self-transformation. And it is here, in this too-easy slippage toward domination, that the contemporary reader might be invited to reflect on the delusion of possession once again. For if the fantasy of ownership is subjected to reconfiguration and remaking in the face of the depredations of love under patriarchy, this fantasy is *not* subject to such reworking in the face of empire, at least in Graffigny's case. On the contrary, it is empire and its depredations that sustain the fiction of Zilia's perfect integrity as a character. Her identity as a Peruvian is shored up by historical fact but remains untouchable and unchangeable, lost to craft: It exists outside of the domains of artifice that structure both gender and the matter of the novel itself. In a sense, Zilia's Peruvianness does for Graffigny what femininity is meant to do for the materialists who dream of becoming woman but nonetheless are in a position to refuse feminine attributes as the latter are made and lived. It resists productive reactivation, since it is inaccessible to the workings of both time and thought.

Zilia at the end of the novel imagines herself in community—and indeed community, intellectual, amatory, sociable, was a crucial ideal for Graffigny herself until the end of her life—but the collective she envisions and evokes, with her gesture to Déterville, is emphatically not a Peruvian one: It cannot be. If the pleasures of her heart are reanimated and transformed in and as fiction, Zilia's own Peruvianness cannot be restaged in this way, for to what can Zilia return? Only a smoking ruin. We can imagine the exchange that Graffigny desires as one knitting together a local community of readers and writers, or even a community of women and the men who love them, but we cannot imagine it as a global solidarity, precisely because the material conditions for this solidarity have been attacked in and under imperial domination. Zilia's Peruvian subjectivity becomes static in order to make its way to France: Her history would need to be reopened, rendered contingent once again, so that its full effects could be felt. Graffigny's novel ultimately suggests the need for a return to the fictions of empire that the work itself cannot enact.

Postscriptum
Olympe de Gouges chez Ninon

How might the particular entanglement of femininity in materialist artifice shift as it moves into other contexts, both political and social? Toward the end of 1787, Olympe de Gouges (born Marie Gouze in 1748, just as the materialist turn of the Enlightenment was getting underway) wrote a five-act play entitled *Molière chez Ninon ou le siècle des Grands Hommes*.[1] Never performed, the play was nonetheless published by Gouges in 1788, in a volume that included her correspondence with the Comédie-Française, with which she was engaged in an extended quarrel. A review of the publication, appearing in the *Journal encyclopédique* of August 1788, emphasizes the play's deft and vivid portrayal of a specific *milieu*—namely, the group of authors, courtiers, and freethinkers who gathered around the famous intellectual and *courtisane* Ninon de Lenclos in her salon on the rue des Tournelles in the Marais. As the reviewer describes Gouges's work, "The goal of the author was to present the great characters of the last century: could she find a meeting place that was more stimulating and more in line with the mores of the time? This play comes close to the most illustrious truth, and never feels like art; it is the product of a natural talent who paints with frankness."[2] Drawing on a mid-eighteenth-century source, the *Mémoires sur la vie de Mademoiselle de Lenclos* by Antoine Bret (first published in 1751 and revised in 1763), Olympe de Gouges herself confirms the historical investments of the play, claiming in the preface to have "stripped History of the most interesting facts, and put them into action, without forgetting the most minor circumstance."[3] Indeed, in several instances she incorporates passages from Bret's text into the dialogue, with many of the play's episodes drawn directly from the accounts given in the *Mémoires*.[4] Like the *Maison de Molière*, written by Gouges's friend

Louis-Sébastien Mercier and performed at the Comédie-Française in 1787, *Molière chez Ninon* represents an homage both to the period in question and to its most eminent personages, with Molière chief among them.

The review in the *Journal encyclopédique* stresses the extent to which Olympe de Gouges is able to bring into focus the conversations and interests of the "grands hommes" of the title, who include Molière himself (1622–1673); the author, dramatist, and wit Paul Scarron (1610–1660); Louis II de Bourbon, the prince of Condé (1621–1686, known as le Grand Condé for his military prowess); and the poet and libertine Nicolas Vauquelin des Yveteaux (1567–1649). In this sense, Gouges's play clearly participates in and extends a longer tradition of representing Ninon de Lenclos as an exceptional woman in a company of men (see figure 5).[5]

Yet among the "greats" of the title Gouges also incorporates a number of women, most notably philosopher and patron Christina, queen of Sweden (1626–1689), at one time Descartes's correspondent; Madame Scarron (1635–1719, Françoise d'Aubigné, the future Madame de Maintenon and secret wife of Louis XIV); and of course Ninon de Lenclos herself (1620–1705), whose name had in the eighteenth century become synonymous with the

Figure 5. Nicolas André Monsiau, *Molière Reading Tartuffe in the Apartments of Ninon de Lenclos*, 1802, oil on canvas, 65 cm. × 97 cm. Paris, Bibliothèque de la Comédie-Française. Photo: RMN-Grand Palais / Art Resource, New York. Ninon de Lenclos is pictured here listening attentively to Molière and surrounded by men.

libertinage of a bygone era. The gender confusion implied by the inclusion of these figures as part of a century of great men is underlined throughout the play, which repeatedly returns to the idea that Ninon is a gallant man in the garb of a woman and presents the encounter between Christina and Ninon as one of two exceptional figures who combine in their persons the virtues of both genders. As Ninon's servant Francisque exclaims of his mistress at the beginning of the play, "Oh! It's a woman who doesn't resemble the others!"[6] He goes on to quote Molière as saying "'Ninon is a brave man with the features of a woman,"[7] rendering considerably more polite Maurepas's famous epigrammatic description of Ninon as an illustrious gentleman nonetheless in possession of a "con" or cunt.[8]

In the context of her renown as an exponent of an Epicureanism,[9] the image of Ninon as a woman who makes of herself a man *en titre* seems to function as a revision of the classical rendering of Epicurus as a heroic man who is dressed in women's clothing. Implicitly, Gouges represents her as a specific *détournement* of an Epicurean legacy. In so doing, she is following in the footsteps of various men of the seventeenth and eighteenth centuries, who often rendered Ninon as a modern Leontion or Aspasia. Given this history, even while Gouges touches only lightly on the philosophical commitments of the various characters in the play, her celebration of Ninon implicitly endorses the cultivation of a community that is distinctive for its practice of Epicurean values (and virtues). Yet, while Gouges (like many other authors who preceded her) turns to Ninon as an emblem of an *honnêteté* that is conventionally gendered in the masculine—thus reinforcing the traditional link between a certain kind of philosophical sociability and maleness—at the same time she writes a character named "Olimpe" into the play, suggesting that the reactivation of materialist sociability by a woman of the past might serve as a spur for her own self-invention in the present. She thus makes of Ninon—and, implicitly, Christina—forebears who anticipate her own participation as a woman author in a kind of public life very different from that of the seventeenth-century salon. Gouges thus crafts an inheritance for this materialist philosophical community not so much in the form of a masculine ethos (to be put into practice by men and women alike) as in the writing and production of the theatrical work, to which she adds her name (as author and as character). The ending of the play, in which Ninon hesitates over her decision to retreat to a convent, suggests the difficulty that Ninon confronts as a woman for whom Epicurean sociability and libertine free thought can have disastrous repercussions. Yet this same moment also suggests that it is the community that Ninon has built around herself that might act to sustain (or make possible) her legacy. Here it is the "grands hommes" who enable the transmission of Ninon's inheritance, both philosophical and social, rather than the other way around. In this way, Olympe de Gouges reanimates a materialist past as a kind of material support for her own claims to authorship and authority.[10] She enables the passage of this past into a revolutionary context, not by a consistent and open materialist position-taking, but by a theatrical rewriting that makes of materialism the support for a particular version of feminine solidarity. She updates materialist craftiness for a new era.

While both the reviewer and Gouges herself emphasize the centrality of Molière to the creation and construction of the play, it is in fact Ninon—in her life, her love affairs, and her commitments both familial and moral— around whom the work is organized. Episodic in structure, the play lacks a sustained plotline, although it sketches a series of moral arguments over the course of the five acts. In its fragmented and anecdotal form, it resists encapsulation into a single position or dogmatic philosophy. While it invokes and endorses a particular way of life, it does so by means of a series of tableaux rather than through a set of dramatic dénouements. Ninon herself clearly functions as an exceptional (but also paradigmatic) *femme de lettres*, committed to the cultivation and maintenance of a literate sociability that imagines the pursuit of pleasure as including erotic love (since Ninon is introduced as a woman with many lovers, both past, present, and future), but also writing, reading, thought, witty conversation, and the enjoyment of friendship as a key mode of sentimental attachment. In some sense the libertine persona of Ninon is in tension with her embrace of a virtuous practice of *honnêteté*, but this tension, as Ninon describes it, comes from the context she inhabits, rather than from an inherent incompatibility between the two modes. In a conversation Ninon has with a potential lover, the comte de Fiesque, Gouges ascribes to Ninon a passage taken directly from Bret—given as a *réplique* that Gouges marks off as a quotation: "There is a way of imagining love, and its principles, for which esteem is not always the foundation," Ninon begins. "The disposition that I have for reflection has caused me to focus on the unequal division of attributes that we have agreed to demand of the two sexes. I feel the injustice of this, and I cannot support it. I see that we have been burdened with that which is most frivolous, and that men have reserved for themselves the right to the essential attributes. From this moment on, I am making myself a man."[11] Ninon's statement puts the emphasis on gender as a response to a particularly unjust situation—a crafted position that enables a specific right to be seized, or at least demanded. But the rest of the conversation suggests that Ninon is not only a woman who has made herself a man, but also, and still, a feminine person—inhabiting an aging body, subject to pressures and constraints that are both social and temporal. "I will thus no longer blush at the use I have made of the precious gifts I have received from nature," she continues. "If one could grow young again and I went back to the age of fifteen, I would change nothing about the path in life I have followed; but the onset of my fiftieth year . . . that surprises you, and especially that I have the strength to admit it."[12] While Ninon does not regret the passions of her youth, she is also cognizant of the shifting moral imperatives that govern specific moments in her life; as she puts it, "good Philosophy demands that we mortify ourselves sometimes with pleasure."[13]

Clearly, the passage of time is an important theme throughout the play, whose interest lies not only in the representation of history as it relates to the formation of national identity and literate culture but in the presentation of a life as it may be lived. Ninon's experience of her gender is not a static one, but neither is her relationship to the practice of philosophy. As she remarks to the comte de Fiesque, who suggests to her that he can see her as she truly is: "But as for me, I do not see myself with your eyes, and I see myself quite differently than that which I was yesterday, especially in relationship to you."[14] Ninon is always truthful, but she is also changeable—not in her willingness to play various roles or adopt disparate personae but in her recognition that different times of life require different ways of negotiating pleasure's demands and difficulties. While "greatness" here is a matter of accomplishment—both literary and military, in the case of le Grand Condé—it is also a matter of loving and being loved, and Ninon de Lenclos is exemplary in this aspect above all. As Molière puts it, "Equal with all, modest without affectation, she obtains the best wishes of all the social classes, and the love of great souls."[15] The work of the play is thus not just in imagining an exceptional woman but in constructing around her a community in which a whole variety of physical, mental, and social situations might be acknowledged as worthy of love. This effort enfolds both masculine and feminine bodies. For instance, as the *Journal encyclopédique* review underscores, the poet Scarron's disabilities are rendered on stage as a crucial part of his physical and emotional experience, without recourse to a burlesque mode. In a scene drawn from Bret but revised to give Scarron a more significant role, he decides the dispute between the maréchal d'Estrées and the président d'Effiat over the parentage of Ninon's unborn child. In a different register, the libertine poet des Yveteaux (Desyveteaux in the play) is represented as in the grips of a pastoral delusion: He imagines that he is a simple shepherd named Coridon and insists on being addressed as such.[16] Yet the "madness" to which he has fallen victim does not exclude him from the group: He is instead treated with sympathy and compassion by Ninon in particular.[17]

Finally, in a conflict that provides perhaps the most sustained plotline of the play, Ninon and Molière are called upon by the young woman named Olimpe to assist her in her plans to escape her father's wrath by joining Molière's theater troop with her lover. It eventually becomes apparent that the lover in question is Ninon's illegitimate son, the chevalier de Belfort, who has been ignorant of his origins until, in a conversation with Ninon, she reveals to him that she is his mother. By the end of the play, Ninon has prevailed upon Olimpe's father, Monsieur de Chateauroux, to allow the couple to marry with his blessing. Struck by the greatness and delicacy of Ninon, Chateauroux endorses the union of her son with his daughter, allowing Ninon to become a mother to Olimpe, as the character Molière puts it. Gouges thus concludes the play with a critique of the patriarchal family that also lends to Ninon herself a new kind of legitimacy, at the same time as she positions Ninon quite directly as her own foremother—the inspiration for the play who is also the progenitor (at least in a figural sense) of the playwright herself. Gouges is a beneficiary of the ability of Ninon to create for herself a kind of family line, one not defined by the constraints of legitimacy but rather by the alliances (both ephemeral and lasting) made possible by love (both amical and amatory). Instead of Ninon functioning here as the carrier of a legacy that she receives from her male companions, she operates at this moment as the origin point of an inheritance that she will pass down to Olympe de Gouges herself, so that the authority of the play comes not only from Gouges's willingness to honor Molière but from Ninon's willingness to adopt the other Olimpe as her own.

Yet the conclusion of the play is not without ambivalence. Fearing the effects of gossip on Olimpe and Belfort were her parentage to become known, along with other reasons that are not made entirely clear, Ninon decides to withdraw into a convent. This choice seems to stem at least in part from her acute understanding of the force of prejudice—particularly as the latter is incarnated by scolds and prudes. As she ages, she has developed not only a certain amount of nostalgia for the attachments of her youth but a heightened sense of her own vulnerability to the condemnation of other women. While Gouges proposes Ninon as a kind of model for the women of her own century, she nonetheless reiterates on several occasions the extent to which Ninon (and Christina) transcend the foibles and weaknesses of "the sex." Ninon's Epicurean morality—linked to a libertine practice—makes her subject not only to social marginalization but to the loss of those most dear to her, including Belfort himself, who remained unknown to her for the first eighteen years of his life. Her embrace of the pleasures of love—and the pleasures of friendship as they are expressed in the company that she draws about herself—is thus not without its difficulties and indeed ambiguities. Certainly it does not function systematically to create alliances with other women, even if her kisses with Queen Christina are described by the queen herself as "the beginnings of our relationship," in a rhetorical flourish that recalls Ninon's other, more erotic attachments. Instead, Gouges leaves the ending of the play in suspension. In the very last scene, Ninon has decided to depart for the convent, but Scarron drapes his body across the threshold to prevent her from leaving. Her friends, "more dead than alive," join together to attempt to dissuade her of her "fatal resolution."[18] It is not at all evident that they will succeed in this, although Gouges gives the last line of the play to Saint-Évremond, who exclaims: "Her mind takes her from us, but her heart will bring her back again."[19]

This ending, then, is not conclusive: It invokes the ability of Ninon's community to somehow come to her aid, to ensure her legacy, but refuses to determine the outcome of this intervention. Ninon's "choice" remains suspended in time. Sophie Houdard has found in the imprisonment between 1656 and 1657 of the historic Ninon in the couvent des Madelonnettes, with other women and girls suspected of immoral conduct, an example of her inability to escape her identity as a woman. Houdard writes, "Never positive, femininity shows itself in this spectacular reversal of the freedom of mind and of life as she intended to live it. A man among men, 'despite the cunt,' according to one of her admirers, Ninon de Lenclos is a woman, despite her free-thinking."[20] Gouges rewrites this position in her willingness both to embrace Ninon as a historical personage and to stray from the order of Bret's account. Instead of a victim of social expectations and unjust laws, Ninon appears at the ending of the play as an ambivalent agent of her own destiny—but also as the arbiter of the community that she has cultivated and made possible. Her choice to withdraw is not only an admission of her vulnerability—and it is not entirely certain that it is even this—it is also a demonstration of her social power.

Gouges thus expresses the inherent challenge of a feminine embrace of materialist ethics, which is inevitably subject to social censure and indeed possible persecution. At the same time, she suggests that feminine persons might revise materialist legacies to help bring into being new forms of filiation, and she derives from Ninon as a historical character a ratification of her own work as a woman artist and creator, linking the aristocratic salon to a protorepublican context. *Molière chez Ninon* shows how a feminine materialism might involve not only the activation of future potential but also the retransmission of a materialist past in the work of theatrical and poetic invention. It stresses the complexity of a community formed out of the capacities and qualities of diverse human bodies, but it also endorses the pleasures that such a community sustains. In its willingness to embrace suspension, it makes room for the work of artifice to continue.

I have tried to make the case throughout this book for an illusive reanimation of materialist legacies and questions that allows for a rethinking of femininity as an embodied practice; that prioritizes literary and poetic modes of inquiry; and that regularly turns to artifice and art-making as means of providing an opening within a confined or even desolate life. These (often covert) materialist claims do not so much involve a return to nature as a recrafting of natural impulses and inclinations within a situation of constraint. In her play, Gouges suggests some ways in which the cultivation of an Epicurean sociability, oriented around a specific woman often taken as an icon of libertinism, might enable both a remaking of community and the emergence of a feminine authorial position. Gouges thus puts to work, in her own context and for specific ends, a speculative history of women and feminine persons who may not always overtly endorse materialist philosophy but nonetheless transmit, translate, and enrich a materialist ethics.[21] Like Puisieux, Du Châtelet, and Graffigny, she tarries with the suggestion that the present system is not inevitable; that pleasure might be taken where it can be craftily made; that the entwinement of nature and artifice provides a space for experimenting with new forms of enjoyment and perhaps, eventually, new forms of encounter and connection. For all of these women, the practices that cohere around this suggestion are reactivated in different modes at different times. As a result, they do not so much reflect an unchanging legacy or inheritance to be seized as they make available a set of possibilities. Taking seriously the anti-teleological commitments of an Epicurean argument that posits only pleasure as an end, the illusive materialists I discuss here are interested in making delight where it becomes available, in a gesture that is both aleatory and determined. Even as they emphasize the way in which a survey of a ruined life might nonetheless make room for cannily constructed moments of pleasure, their femininity becomes itself a matter of strangely satisfying craft—a responsiveness to the changeability of material constraint that nonetheless can be delightfully arrested in the image, by the moment, through the actions they perform. This is an ethical position that cultivates a sense of writing, reading, conversing, observing, and loving as means of pleasure giving and receiving. And it is an endorsement of specific femininities not as expressions of an essence but as uniquely generative scenes of materialist technique. If only for a time.

Acknowledgments

For so many of the eighteenth-century writers whose thought has moved and engaged me, the labor of study and reflection is an intrinsic part of the process of living—intimately connected to the rhythms of experience. As these authors emphasize, sometimes with delight and sometimes with frustration, thought, like life, shifts and changes over time. But one persistent source of vitality—for me as well as for the authors whose works are discussed here—remains the communities that texts draw together around them. Conceived at a time of great epistemological uncertainty and often in a state of relative isolation, this book nevertheless seeks to ratify the material practices of generosity and exchange without which it would not exist. I owe much of my ability to write to the many institutions that provided me with support, but I owe my desire to do so to the people who, over many years, offered me their ideas, time, solicitude, labor, joy, and kindness.

I will always be grateful to the USC-Huntington Early Modern Studies Institute for two fellowships that came at just the right moments, and to the USC Provost's Advancing Scholarship in the Humanities and Social Sciences Grant program for funding the research that led to the idea for this project. USC-Dornsife Divisional Deans of the Humanities Rebecca Lemon and Peter C. Mancall were sources of professional wisdom and invaluable institutional support. The Albert and Elaine Borchard Foundation, helmed by Janna Beling, provided me with a semester in residence at the Château de la Bretesche. This transformative experience brought me closer to my eighteenth-century French sources in especially powerful ways, and I am profoundly thankful for the privilege of being the foundation's guest in Missillac. I feel especially lucky to have benefited from the incisive but generous comments of audiences at lectures hosted by Scripps College; the New York Eighteenth-Century Seminar; the Place Settings series in Los Angeles; Pennsylvania State University; the University of California, Los Angeles; the Université Gustave Eiffel; and the University of Oxford. My heartfelt thanks are due, as well, to Joanna Stalnaker and Caroline Warman, who commented on a draft of the project in the most inspiring, thoughtful, and incisive ways. Without Tom Lay at Fordham University Press and the anonymous reviewers of the manuscript the book could not have come to be. Lis Pearson brought extraordinary discernment and good cheer to the task of copy editing. Victoria Baker created an index that is also a work of art.

Parts of Chapter 1 were first published in an article entitled "Sexing Epicurean Materialism in Diderot," in the edited volume *Epicurus in the Enlightenment*, ed. Neven Leddy and Avi S. Lifschitz (Oxford: Voltaire Foundation, 2009): 85–104. A short section of Chapter 3 was previously published in French as the essay "Lucrèce au féminin au dix-huitième siècle: La femme épicurienne et le *Discours sur le bonheur* d'Émilie Du Châtelet," which appeared in *Femmes à l'œuvre dans la construction des savoirs: Paradoxes de la visibilité et de l'invisibilité*, ed. Caroline Trotot, Claire Delahaye, and Isabelle Mornat, in the collection "Savoirs en texte," ed. Gisèle Séginger (Le LISAA éditeur, 2020): 85–100. I am grateful for the opportunity to republish these portions here.

Illusive Materialisms owes so much to the communities of scholars, students, friends, and family who have sustained, encouraged, and inspired me. In a very real sense, this book is not my own but theirs (although I remain the source of all the infelicities and errors it contains). At USC, I am enduringly grateful to Richard Brutchey, Mia Du Plessis, Olivia Harrison, Peggy Kamuf, Neetu Khanna, Béatrice Mousli, Panivong Norindr, Kelsey Rubin-Detlev, Ruggero Sciuto, Antónia Szabari, and Jason Webb for friendship and unflaggingly supportive advice and commentary. Lydie Moudileno and Margaret (Tita) Rosenthal have been exemplary departmental chairs and mentors. Beyond USC, I appreciate the collegiality, brilliance, and care of Sarah Benharrech, Andrew H. Clark, Annelle Curulla, Polly Geller, Marian Hobson, Mimi Long, Blanca Missé, Laura Nelson, Jon L. Pitt, Marie Raulier, Jessica Rath, Anna Rosensweig, Tracy Rutler, Caroline Trotot, Anya Ventura, and Chloé Vettier. I also want to thank and acknowledge the incredible group of graduate and undergraduate students with whom I have worked over the course of many years. Their intelligence and good will have been boundless and I am moved by the faith they place in me. Among them are Reese Armstrong, Doug Cavers, Tori Champion, Hayun Cho, Bart Chu, Aidan Diamond, Brieuc Gérard, Katherine Hammitt, Mina Kaneko, Katy LeBris, Chloé Luu, Daisy Reid, Kristina Shea, Jacob Schwessinger, and Michaela Telfer. Debbie Brutchey and Anne Magruder have kept me going with patience, good humor, and the deepest reserves of generosity. Cati Jean and Kumbi Butler show me how to move even when everything seems stagnant. Mirna Aldana provides unstinting support both material and moral.

Family members are usually thanked last but really they often come first—in mind, in heart, in matter. Michael and Gesine Meeker make everything possible. Elena Meeker, Eric Wagoner, and Walter Wagoner bring the joy and ask the questions. David and Linnaea Tomkins are the reason for it all: This book is for you both. I cannot know what it will mean to you, but I hope that you will know how much it owes to your love.

Notes

Preface

1. All translations my own unless otherwise indicated. Diderot, *Éléments de physiologie*, in *Œuvres complètes*, vol. 17, ed. Jean Varloot et al. (Paris: Hermann, 1987), 468–69. In a fascinating article entitled "Diderot's Brain," Joanna Stalnaker suggests an analogy between the "deep memory" that Diderot evokes in this passage and contemporary scientific renderings of deep time. See Stalnaker, "Diderot's Brain," in *Mind, Body, Motion, Matter: Eighteenth-Century British and French Literary Perspectives*, ed. Mary Helen McMurran and Alison Conway (Toronto: University of Toronto Press, 2016), 243.

2. Diderot, *Éléments de physiologie*, 470.

3. Madeleine de Puisieux, *Réflexions et avis sur les défauts et ridicules à la mode, pour servir de suite aux Conseils à une Amie* (Paris: V. Brunet, 1761), 261.

4. Paul Thiry d'Holbach, *Théologie portative ou dictionnaire abrégé de la religion chrétienne. Par M. L'Abbé Bernier. Licencié en Théologie* (London [Amsterdam]: M. M. Rey, 1768 [1767]), 158. I am grateful to Caroline Warman for directing me to this source.

5. Gerard Passannante, *Catastrophizing: Materialism and the Making of Disaster* (Chicago: University of Chicago Press, 2019), 3.

6. I owe my belated discovery of Lisa Robertson's work to Jessie Hock's capacious and inspiring book, *The Erotics of Materialism: Lucretius and Early Modern Poetics* (Philadelphia: University of Pennsylvania Press, 2021). Robertson's poetry and prose, including *Debbie: An Epic* (a brilliant recasting of Virgil's *Aeneid*) and *Nilling* (a collection of essays that includes a meditation on Lucretius and the pleasures of reading), are exemplary instances of the redirection and reanimation of a classical inheritance in a feminist and queer vein. Ruggero Sciuto kindly made me aware of artist Jane Benson's nuanced reworkings of Paul Thiry d'Holbach's 1770 *Système de la nature* in a feminist and ecological idiom.

Introduction: The Materialist Pleasures of Femininity

1. Gabrielle-Émilie Le Tonnelier de Breteuil Du Châtelet, *Discourse on Happiness*, in *Émilie Du Châtelet: Selected Philosophical and Scientific Writings*, ed. Judith P. Zinsser, trans. Isabelle Bour and Judith P. Zinsser (Chicago: University of Chicago Press, 2009), 350.

2. Grace Lavery, *Pleasure and Efficacy: Of Pen Names, Cover Versions, and Other Trans Techniques* (Princeton, NJ: Princeton University Press, 2023), xxii.

3. There continues to be debate around the exact nature of this contribution. See Carla Hesse's *The Other Enlightenment: How French Women Became Modern* (Princeton, NJ: Princeton University Press, 2001) for a discussion of the explosion in women's publishing following the French Revolution; Joan DeJean has convincingly contested this interpretation and argued on behalf of the significance of a prerevolutionary literary tradition that women actively and prominently shaped. See not only DeJean's classic *Tender Geographies: Women and the Origins of the Novel in France* (New York: Columbia University Press, 1991) but DeJean's review of Hesse's text in *The Journal of Modern History* 75, no. 4 (2003): 958–60. More recently, Julie Candler Hayes has argued for the philosophical vigor and vibrancy of women's moralist writing in her book, *Women Moralists in Early Modern France* (New York: Oxford University Press, 2023). For a wide-ranging discussion of gender/genre and Enlightenment philosophy, see *Femmes et philosophie des Lumières: De l'imaginaire à la vie des idées*, ed. Laurence Vanoflen (Paris: Classiques Garnier, 2020). For an excellent overview of the Enlightenment period, which stresses the amplitude of women's contributions to eighteenth-century literary culture as well as the difficulties they confronted, see Christie McDonald's chapter on "Le dix-huitième siècle: 1715–1793," in *Femmes et littérature: Une histoire culturelle*, ed. Martine Reid, vol. 1, *Moyen Âge-XVIIIe siècle* (Paris: Éditions Gallimard, 2020). Women were also active in the sciences, although to a much lesser extent than in the domain of literary publishing. For recent studies of women's participation in Enlightenment science, see in particular Nina Rattner Gelbart's fantastic *Minerva's French Sisters: Women of Science in Enlightenment France* (New Haven, CT: Yale University Press, 2021) and Sarah Benharrech's important ongoing work on the botanist Madame Dugage de Pommereul, especially "Botanical Palimpsests, or Erasure of Women in Science: The Case Study of Mme Dugage de Pommereul (1733–1782)" *Harvard Papers in Botany* 23, no. 1 (2018): 89–108.

4. The identity of Choiseul-Meuse is somewhat uncertain. See Jean-Clément Martin's "L'érotisme au féminin ou la transgression discrète en temps de crise?" in *Genre Révolution Transgression: Études offertes à Martine Lapied* (Aix-en-Provence: Presses universitaires de Provence, 2015).

5. See Hayes, *Women Moralists in Early Modern France* for an illuminating discussion of the exclusion of women from a different canon, that of moralist writing. Both Du Châtelet and Puisieux feature in Hayes's analysis, which stresses the contributions of women authors to ethical, social, and moral critique in ways that were often subsequently ignored or effaced.

6. Florence Lotterie, *Le Genre des Lumières: Femme et philosophe au XVIIIe siècle* (Paris: Classiques Garnier, 2013), 16. Lotterie's examples of well-known (and highly privileged) women facing critique, slander, and censure of various types include Émilie Du Châtelet, discussed at length in Chapter 3, and Germaine de Staël.

7. Studies of women's role in early modern materialisms have often necessarily confined themselves either to the realm of fictional characters or to the domain of a social history not particularly invested in philosophical principle or debate. For an especially notable example of the latter approach, which consists of finely drawn studies of the lives of twelve libertine women, see Olivier Blanc, *Les libertines: Plaisir et liberté au temps des Lumières* (Paris: Librairie Académique Perrin, 1997). The collection *Femmes et libertinage au XVIIIe siècle ou les Caprices de Cythère*, ed. Anne Richardot (Rennes: Presses universitaires de Rennes, 2003), gives a very helpful survey of the figure of the woman libertine across the eighteenth century, with an emphasis on literary writing.

8. See Jessie Hock, *The Erotics of Materialism: Lucretius and Early Modern Poetics* (Philadelphia: University of Pennsylvania Press, 2021) and Kristin M. Girten, *Sensitive Witnesses: Feminist Materialism in the British Enlightenment* (Stanford, CA: Stanford University Press, 2024).

9. Girten, *Sensitive Witnesses*, 172.

10. James Steintrager provides a comprehensive and highly generative examination of libertine theories of pleasure's sovereignty in *The Autonomy of Pleasure: Libertines, License, and Sexual Revolution* (New York: Columbia University Press, 2016).

11. Particularly important to the current study have been Nadine Bérenguier's *Conduct Books for Girls in Enlightenment France* (Farnham: Ashgate Publishing, 2011); Heidi Bostic's *The Fiction of Enlightenment: Women of Reason in the French Eighteenth Century* (Newark: University of Delaware Press, 2010); and Isabelle Tremblay's *Le Bonheur au féminin: Stratégies narratives des romancières des Lumières* (Montréal: Les Presses de l'Université de Montréal, 2012). Nina Rattner Gelbart's *Minerva's French Sisters: Women of Science in Enlightenment France* (New Haven, CT: Yale University Press, 2021) was an inspiration for the prefaces that precede each chapter. Madelyn Gutwirth's *The Twilight of the Goddesses* (New Brunswick, NJ: Rutgers University Press, 1992) has long been a key resource for thinking about the relationship between eighteenth-century femininity and theories of desire and pleasure.

12. The Goncourt brothers published *La Femme au XVIIIe siècle* in 1862. This work, somewhere between a social history and a fantastical idealization, suggests the intrinsic connection of (elite) women to an Epicurean ethos of voluptuous cultivation.

13. Thank you to David Tomkins for inspiring this reflection on different forms of clandestinity in the context of women's writing. Margaret C. Jacob's work has been particularly notable for her investigations of eighteenth-century clandestine culture

in the context of eighteenth-century radicalisms, including her by-now classic *The Radical Enlightenment: Pantheists, Freemasons and Republicans* (London: George Allen and Unwin, 1981), which predated the publication of Jonathan Israel's *Radical Enlightenment: Philosophy and the Making of Modernity, 1650–1750* (New York: Oxford University Press, 2001) by twenty years.

14. I want to insist here on the interest of women's contributions not just to eighteenth-century philosophy—and thus to what has come to be known as the radical Enlightenment—but to a broader history of materialist critique, especially one that passes through the literary or poetic sphere. Intellectual historians Ann Thomson and Charles T. Wolfe have done particularly valuable work in clarifying and complicating the position of eighteenth-century materialism in a larger intellectual history. See especially Thomson's *Bodies of Thought: Science, Religion, and the Soul in the Early Enlightenment* (Oxford: Oxford University Press, 2008) and Wolfe's *Materialism: A Historico-Philosophical Introduction* (Cham, Switzerland: Springer, 2016). Margaret C. Jacob's *The Secular Enlightenment* (Princeton, NJ: Princeton University Press, 2019) provides a crucial study of eighteenth-century secularisms that dovetail at various moments with clandestine materialisms.

15. Du Châtelet, *Discourse on Happiness*, 350.

16. Peter Hanns Reill, *Vitalizing Nature in the Enlightenment* (Berkeley: University of California Press, 2005). See also Franck Salaün's *L'Ordre des mœurs: Essai sur la place du matérialisme dans la société française du XVIIIe siècle (1734–1784)* (Paris: Éditions Kimé, 1996).

17. As mentioned, Julien Offray de La Mettrie seems to have been the first to embrace the qualifier. See Wolfe, *Materialism: A Historico-Philosophical Introduction*, 2.

18. See Karen Green, *A History of Women's Political Thought in Europe, 1700–1800* (Cambridge: Cambridge University Press, 2014).

19. John C. O'Neal studies her work as a variant of "sensationism," in a crucial analysis upon which I build. See *The Authority of Experience: Sensationist Theory in the French Enlightenment* (University Park: The University of Pennsylvania Press, 1996).

20. Marian Hobson, *The Object of Art: The Theory of Illusion in Eighteenth-Century France* (Cambridge: Cambridge University Press, 1982), 53. Earlier in her book, Hobson cites the Epicurean essayist and philosopher Charles de Saint-Evrémond (1613-1703), who writes of the "consentement agréable" that pleasure requires in his essay "Sur les opéra." Without this consent, the soul resists the impressions of the senses. See Saint-Evrémond, "Sur les opéra, à Monsieur le duc de Bouquinquant," (1705) in *Œuvres en prose*, ed. René Ternois, vol. 3 (Paris: Librairie Marcel Didier, 1966), 151. The renegotiation of the relation to pleasure thus requires a rethinking of the relation to consent, as Puisieux in particular will explore.

21. Hobson, *The Object of Art*, 52.

22. Roy Porter, "Enlightenment and Pleasure," in *Pleasure in the Eighteenth Century*, ed. Roy Porter and Marie Mulvey Roberts (London: Palgrave, 1996), 1.

Porter and Roberts explore the ways in which pleasure is always mediatized, never given, in cultural contexts. The literature on pleasure in the French Enlightenment is vast on its own, with a good degree of overlap with scholarship on libertinism in both philosophical and literary contexts. For a wide-ranging and incisive recent treatment of the question of pleasure's social function in the eighteenth century and beyond, see especially Steintrager's *The Autonomy of Pleasure*. Other notable studies of the role of pleasure (particularly sexual pleasure) in French Enlightenment culture include Marc-André Bernier, *Libertinage et figures du savoir: Rhétorique et roman libertin dans la France des Lumières (1734–1751)* (Québec: Presses de l'Université Laval, 2001); Pamela Cheek, *Sexual Antipodes: Enlightenment Globalization and the Placing of Sex* (Stanford, CA: Stanford University Press, 2003); Peter Cryle, *La Crise du plaisir, 1740–1830* (Lille: Septentrion, 2003); Catherine Cusset, *No Tomorrow: The Ethics of Pleasure in the French Enlightenment* (Charlottesville: University Press of Virginia, 1999); Doris Garraway, *The Libertine Colony: Creolization in the Early French Caribbean* (Durham, NC: Duke University Press, 2005); Patrick Wald Lasowski, *Dictionnaire libertin: la langue du plaisir au siècle des Lumières* (Paris: Gallimard, 2011); Jean Mainil, *Dans les règles du plaisir…: Théorie de la différence dans le discours obscène, romanesque et médical de l'Ancien Régime* (Paris: Éditions Kimé, 1996); and Julie Peakman, *Amatory Pleasures: Explorations in Eighteenth-Century Sexual Culture* (London: Bloomsbury Academic, 2016). For studies with an emphasis on visual culture, see in particular Frederick Ilchman et al., eds., *Casanova: The Seduction of Europe* (Boston: MFA Publications, 2017); Susanna Caviglia-Brunel, *History, Painting, and the Seriousness of Pleasure in the Age of Louis XV* (Oxford: Liverpool University Press, 2020); and Philip Stewart, *Engraven Desire: Eros, Image, and Text in the French Eighteenth Century* (Durham, NC: Duke University Press, 1992).

23. Thomas Kavanagh, *Enlightened Pleasures: Eighteenth-Century France and the New Epicureanism* (New Haven, CT: Yale University Press, 2010), 2.

24. Kavanagh, *Enlightened Pleasures*, 1.

25. Michel Delon, *Le Principe de délicatesse: Libertinage et mélancolie au XVIIIe siècle* (Paris: Éditions Albin Michel, 2011), 31.

26. The terms "two-sex" and "one-sex" model were coined by Thomas Laqueur in *Making Sex: Body and Gender from the Greeks to Freud*, rev. ed. (Cambridge, MA: Harvard University Press, 1992).

27. It is difficult to translate this quotation, with its erasures and doublings back, so I give the French version here. "On me demendoit pourquoy on n'avoit plus de gout pour les ouvrages de Corneille Racine &c. je repondis c'est que l'on n'en a guere pour ne peut plus souffrir les choses pour lesquelles il faut de l'esprit cela est devenu ridicule et on s'y s'est tellement livré a cette façon de penser qu'on n'a plus de gout pour rien il est averé que l'on toutes les choses pour lesquelles il faut de l'esprit sont devenues ridicules et l'on le mal est plus general on ne peut plus souffrir les choses aucune des choses qui ont un object determiné, les gens de guerre ne peuvent souffrir la guerre les gens de cabinet le cabinet [*trois mots biffés non*

déchiffrés] ainsi des autres choses on ne conoit que les objets generaux ~~ce qui~~ et dans la pratique cela se reduit a rien c'est le comerce des femmes qui nous a menés la car c'est ~~leur l'esprit et~~ leur caractere de n'estre attachées a rien de fixe ~~aussi nous somes nous devenus come elles~~ il n'y a plus qu'un sexe et ~~et si une~~ nous somes touts femmes par l'esprit et si une nuit nous changions de visage on ne s'apercevroit pas que du reste il y eut de changement quoy que les femmes eussent a passer dans touts les emplois que la societe donne et que les homes ~~dans~~ fussent privés de touts ceux que la societe peut otter ~~a un autre sexe que le leur~~: aucun sexe ne seroit embarrassé." Montédite, *Édition critique des Pensées de Montesquieu*, ed. Carole Dornier (Caen: Presses universitaires de Caen, 2013), [online], pensée 1062, http://www.unicaen.fr/services/puc/sources/Montesquieu/ [consulted on 06/12/2023].

28. Clearly, his preoccupations would not be entirely out of place in a contemporary critique of the effects of social media on the human brain.

29. Anthony J. La Vopa also opens his study of gender in intellectual work and life, *The Labor of the Mind: Intellect and Gender in Enlightenment Cultures* (Philadelphia: The University of Pennsylvania Press, 2017) with Montesquieu's quote. For La Vopa, Montesquieu is struggling with "the emasculation of the male mind" as an effect of both commercialized print culture and polite sociability (1). Joan DeJean discusses Montesquieu's note in *Ancients Against Moderns: Culture Wars and the Making of a Fin de Siècle* (Chicago: University of Chicago Press, 1997). She reads it in the context of Charles Perrault's suggestion, in the last decades of the seventeenth century, that to be truly modern it is necessary to think like a woman (75). While "the Moderns herald the superiority of female literary judgment," as DeJean puts it, she asserts that Montesquieu's misogyny gets in the way of his acquiescence to this project. Elena Russo's book on *Styles of Enlightenment: Taste, Politics, and Authorship in Eighteenth-Century France* (Baltimore, MD: The Johns Hopkins University Press, 2007) returns to Perrault's remark in her excellent discussion of the gendering of the *goût moderne*.

30. Karen M. Offen, in her *European Feminisms, 1700–1950: A Political History* (Stanford, CA: Stanford University Press, 2000), refers to the "feminocentrism" of Enlightenment intellectual life (31). Critics who have explored in depth the fascination of the eighteenth century with femininity and feminization, particularly vis à vis its ramifications for women's social status, include, in addition to DeJean, La Vopa, and Russo, Adéline Gargam, in *Les Femmes savantes, lettrées et cultivées dans la littérature française des Lumières ou la conquête d'une légitimité (1690–1804)*, 2 vols. (Paris: Honoré Champion, 2013); Madelyn Gutwirth, in *Twilight of the Goddesses*; Joan B. Landes, in *Women and the Public Sphere in the Age of the French Revolution* (Ithaca, NY: Cornell University Press, 1988); Florence Lotterie in *Le Genre des Lumières*; Mary McAlpin, in *Female Sexuality and Cultural Degradation in Enlightenment France* (Farnham: Ashgate Publishing, 2012); and Lieselotte Steinbrügge, in *The Moral Sex: Women's Nature in the French Enlightenment* (New York: Oxford University Press, 1995). For a wide-ranging and nuanced examination of the representation of feminine spaces and femininity in the eighteenth-century

French novel, from a perspective informed by psychoanalysis, see Christophe Martin's *Espaces du féminin dans le roman français du dix-huitième siècle* (Oxford: Voltaire Foundation, 2004). Martin's discussion of softness or *mollesse* is particularly enlightening. Two classic discussions of femininity and the French Enlightenment include Paul Hoffmann's *La Femme dans la pensée des Lumières* (Geneva: Éditions Slatkine, 1995) and Pierre Fauchery's *La Destinée féminine dans le roman européen du dix-huitième siècle, essai de gynécomythie romanesque* (Paris: Armand Colin, 1972). Lotterie gives a judicious critique of the tendency of the latter two critics to rely on an idealized vision of "la Femme" in their explorations of eighteenth-century femininity.

31. Montesquieu, *Persian Letters*, trans. Margaret Mauldon (New York: Oxford University Press, 2008), 145.

32. The reference to "machine" here could also refer to a theatrical illusion.

33. Indeed, across the canon of French Enlightenment literature, the privileged space of masculine distraction—and male impotence in the face of cryptically exercised feminine influence—is the harem. This is an image that travels, despite its seeming cultural specificity, since it functions as a cipher for political corruption and for a depleted national body. For a more openly libertine version of this dynamic, see Crébillon fils's orientalist tales, in particular *Le Sopha* (1742), deftly analyzed by Madeleine Dobie in *Foreign Bodies: Gender, Language and Culture in French Orientalism* (Stanford, CA: Stanford University Press, 2001), and to a certain extent *Tanzaï et Néadarné, histoire japonaise* (1734). As I will discuss, Diderot will also trade in related orientalist tropes, setting the wise and witty courtisane Mirzoza against her bored and on occasion befuddled partner Mangogul, in *Les Bijoux indiscrets* (1748).

34. Jean-Jacques Rousseau, *Letter to M. d'Alembert on the Theatre*, trans. Allan Bloom, in *Politics and the Arts: Letter to M. d'Alembert on the Theatre*, ed. and trans. Allan Bloom (Ithaca, NY: Cornell University Press, 1968), 100.

35. In *Queering the Enlightenment: Kinship and Gender in Eighteenth-Century French Literature* (Liverpool: Liverpool University Press, 2021), Tracy Rutler persuasively analyzes the development of queer kinship models in eighteenth-century fiction as a response to an ongoing crisis in patriarchal authority. In the *Letter*, Rousseau ratifies this sense of crisis, not in order to endorse queerness, but to shore up sexual difference in the face of a modernity that negates and erases it.

36. Rousseau, *Letter*, 101.

37. Elena Russo explores the political, social, and epistemological implications of this relation in *Styles of Enlightenment*.

38. Rousseau, *Letter*, 101.

39. Rousseau, *Letter*, 137.

40. A specific kind of "traffic in women," to echo Gayle Rubin's famous essay, is at issue here. The *commerce des femmes*, for both Montesquieu and Rousseau, involves a traffic *with* women—which ends up turning men into women, through an adoption of their habits, attitudes, and "characters." See Gayle Rubin, "The Traffic in Women: Notes on the 'Political Economy' of Sex," in *Deviations: A Gayle S. Rubin Reader* (Durham, NC: Duke University Press, 2012), 33–65.

41. Mary McAlpin analyzes in depth the link between eighteenth-century theories of female physiology, especially in the work of the Montpellier vitalists, and fears about cultural decadence or "regression."

42. Crébillon fils, *Les Égarements du cœur et de l'esprit*, in *Œuvres complètes*, vol. II, ed. Jean Sgard (Paris, Classiques Garnier, 2000 [online edition 2010]), 211.

43. See Jean Salem's article on Epicurean themes in Crébillon fils for a reflection on Crébillon's commitment to hedonism as a social value. Jean Salem, "Réminiscences épicuriennes dans *Les Égarements du cœur et de l'esprit* de Crébillon," in *Dix-huitième Siècle*, 35 (2003), *L'épicurisme des Lumières*, ed. Anne Deneys-Tunney et Pierre-François Moreau, 187–210.

44. For a fascinating reading of Lucretian nature as fundamentally transsexual, an idea that resonates with many of the texts and authors discussed here, see Luce deLire's "Nature is a Transsexual Woman: Lucretian Metaphysics Reconsidered," *Classical Philology* 19, no. 2 (2024), 203–33.

45. In an article on Montaigne's travel writings, Louisa Mackenzie argues that Montaigne experiments with a "remise en cause" of masculinity but ultimately reinforces masculine norms. See Louisa Mackenzie, "La masculinité itinérante du *Journal de voyage* de Montaigne," in *Théories critiques et littérature de la Renaissance. Mélanges offerts à Lawrence Kritzman*, ed. Todd Reeser and David LaGuardia (Paris: Classiques Garnier, 2020), 155–75. Mackenzie rejects Catherine Randall Coats's argument, in "Writing Like a Woman: Gender Transformation in Montaigne's *Journal de Voyage*," *Montaigne Studies* 5 (1992): 207–18, that the *Journal de voyage* involves a scene of gender transformation. On the intersection of materialism and skepticism in Montaigne's thought on love, pleasure, and women, see Isabelle Krier's "Montaigne, le plaisir et les femmes. Une perturbation sceptique de l'hédonisme épicurien ou un matérialisme inédit?" in *Les Matérialistes paradoxaux*, ed. Patrice Bretaudière and Isabelle Krier (Paris: Classiques Garnier, 2023), 47–67.

46. Foucault both rehearses and revises the link between modernity and a (feminine) culture of pleasure. Michel Foucault, *The History of Sexuality*, volume 1, *An Introduction*, trans. Robert Hurley (New York: Pantheon Books, 1978), 77.

47. Whether they succeed in doing this is another question entirely. For thoughtful analyses of *Les Bijoux* in the context of enlightened knowledge, see in particular Madeleine Dobie's *Foreign Bodies: Gender, Language, and Culture in French Orientalism* (Stanford, CA: Stanford University Press, 2001) and Srinivas Aravamudan's *Enlightenment Orientalism: Resisting the Rise of the Novel* (Chicago: Chicago University Press, 2011). In *The Autonomy of Pleasure*, James Steintrager makes an excellent case for *La Religieuse* (rather than *Les Bijoux*) as a prime example of "the emergence of 'sexuality' as a pervasive and hidden force, subject to psychic repression and plastic in its expressions" (96). In *La Religieuse* (ca. 1780), set in a series of convents, the crucial role played by femininity in this emergence is even more clear.

48. The dedication also invokes a woman named Aglaé, said to have contributed to the creation and revision of the text. This figure may be an oblique reference to Madeleine de Puisieux, with whom Diderot was involved at the time.

49. Gilles Deleuze and Félix Guattari, *A Thousand Plateaus: Capitalism and Schizophrenia*, trans. Brian Massumi (Minneapolis: University of Minnesota Press, 1987), 106.

50. Deleuze and Guattari, *A Thousand Plateaus*, 248.

51. For a study of interspecies becoming in which women function as both trope and mechanism, see Jennifer Milam's fascinating article, "Rococo Representations of Interspecies Sensuality and the Pursuit of 'Volupté,'" *The Art Bulletin* 27, no. 2 (June 2015): 192–209.

52. Voltaire, "Le Mondain," in *Mélanges*, ed. Jacques van den Heuvel (Paris: Librairie Gallimard, 1961), 203–6: "Moi, je rends grâce à la Nature sage/Qui, pour mon bien, m'a fait naître en cet âge/Tant décrié par nos pauvres docteurs:/Ce temps profane est tout fait pour mes mœurs./J'aime le luxe, et même la mollesse,/Tous les plaisirs, les arts de toute espèce,/La propreté, le goût, les ornements:/Tout honnête homme a de tels sentiments." See Christophe Martin on the association of femininity with *mollesse* in particular. Martin links *mollesse* to the materialization of feminine space, contending that "son usage est récurrent au dix-huitième siècle pour désigner une qualité propre à certains espaces, en liaison étroite avec leur destination essentiellement féminine" (*Espaces*, 56).

53. Andrea Long Chu, *Females* (London: Verso, 2019), 2.

1. Feminine Fictions of Radical Materialism: Diderot, La Mettrie, Helvétius

1. Julien Offray de La Mettrie, *La Volupté*, in *Œuvres philosophiques*, vol. 2, ed. Francine Markovits (Paris: Fayard, 1987), 112.

2. Translation Warman's. Caroline Warman, *The Atheist's Bible: Diderot's "Éléments de Physiologie"* (Cambridge: Open Book Publishers, 2020).

3. Warman, *The Atheist's Bible*, 2.

4. La Mettrie, *La Volupté*, 117.

5. For a particularly inspiring reflection on the work done by materialism's sweetness, especially in nineteenth-century contexts, see Amanda Jo Goldstein's *Sweet Science: Romantic Materialism and the New Logics of Life* (Chicago: The University of Chicago Press, 2017).

6. Naomi Schor, *Bad Objects: Essays Popular and Unpopular* (Durham, NC: Duke University Press, 1995), ix.

7. Roland Barthes, *La Préparation du roman: Cours au Collège de France (1978–1979 et 1979–1980)*, ed. Nathalie Léger and Éric Marty (Paris: Éditions du Seuil, 2015), 16. Barthes writes in this same lecture of subjectivity's "lures" [*leurres*] as well as of its risks. "The lures of subjectivity are worth more than the impostures of objectivity," he affirms (16). Echoes of Du Châtelet's illusion without error seem to pass through this sentence.

8. Pamela Gordon, *The Invention and Gendering of Epicurus* (Ann Arbor: University of Michigan Press, 2012), 112. In his book *Disorienting Empire: Republican Latin Poetry's Wanderers* (Oxford: Oxford University Press, 2021), Basil

Dufallo describes the "perceived gender deviance" of the original Epicureans (199). I will return to Dufallo's description of potentially queer wanderings—specifically in the Lucretian discussion of the *vulgivaga Venus*—later on in this chapter. In a recent article on Epicurean women, Kelly Arenson stresses the extent to which Epicureanism generated misogynist critique from the inception of the sect. See Arenson, "Ancient Women Epicureans and their Anti-Hedonist Critics," in *Ancient Women Philosophers: Recovered Ideas and New Perspectives*, ed. Katharine R. O'Reilly and Caterina Pellò (Cambridge: Cambridge University Press, 2023), 77–95.

9. Plutarch, *Moralia*, Vol 14, *That Epicurus Actually Makes a Pleasant Life Impossible. Reply to Colotes in Defence of the Other Philosophers. Is "Live Unknown" a Wise Precept? On Music*, trans. Benedict Einarson and Phillip H. De Lacy, Loeb Classical Library 428 (Cambridge, MA: Harvard University Press, 1967), 332–33.

10. Plutarch, *Moralia*, 328–31.

11. Julie Giovacchini, "Sexual Freedom and Feminine Pleasure in Lucretius," in *Women's Perspectives on Ancient and Medieval Philosophy*, ed. Isabelle Chouinard et al. (Berlin: Springer Verlag, 2021), 119.

12. Diogenes Laertius, *Lives of Eminent Philosophers*, Volume I: Books 1–5, trans. Robert Drew Hicks, Loeb Classical Library 184 (Cambridge, MA: Harvard University Press, 1925), 4: 43.

13. Seneca, *Moral Essays*, vol. 2, *De Consolatione ad Marciam. De Vita Beata. De Otio. De Tranquillitate Animi. De Brevitate Vitae. De Consolatione ad Polybium. De Consolatione ad Helviam*, trans. John W. Basore, Loeb Classical Library 254 (Cambridge, MA: Harvard University Press, 1932), 132–33.

14. François de La Mothe Le Vayer, *De la vertu des payens* (Paris: Augustin Courbé, 1647), 202.

15. Charles Batteux, *La Morale d'Épicure, tirée de ses propres écrits* (Paris: Desaint et Saillant, 1758), 9. Batteux's text will be used as a source by both Giacomo Casanova and Denis Diderot, among many others. In his presentation of excerpts from the text in *Dix-Huitième Siècle* (2003, 35), Branko Aleksić notes that *La Morale d'Épicure* was widely studied and read during the eighteenth century (253).

16. Batteux, *Morale*, 12.

17. Citing Batteux approvingly in his *Essai sur les règnes de Claude et de Néron* (1778–1782), Diderot will rework Seneca's image of Epicurus in drag, not so much to underline the irreversibility of the Epicurean conversion as to emphasize the heroic aspects of a philosophical tradition that had long been concealed beneath a woman's form. I will return to this text later.

18. One of the reasons for the proliferation of narratives about women (or written from a feminine point of view) during this period is, I argue, a kind of experimentation with an articulation of femininity that is available not to women alone but to all bodies, insofar as they recognize their own involvement in materiality. This does not mean that masculinity takes on the same availability; quite the contrary.

19. Denis Diderot, *Rêve de d'Alembert*, in *Œuvres*, ed. André Billy (Paris: Éditions Gallimard, 1951), 908.

20. See Florence Dujour's *Le Fil de Marianne: Narrer au féminin, de Villedieu à Diderot* (Paris: Garnier, 2021) for an exploration of the replacement of women authors—writing in women's voices—by men—also writing in women's voices—that occurs with the onset of the Enlightenment. Dujour points out, "[L]es femmes, si importantes pour l'histoire du roman, se sont faites très discrètes dans le paysage littéraire en tant qu'auteures, dès le XVIIIe siècle, et cela même si elles continuent à tenir salon, alors pourtant qu'elles ont fourni les plus beaux personnages de la littérature de cette époque" (17).

21. Diderot was most likely citing from memory, since he indicates that the citation appears in book 6 (rather than book 4), and transposes the order of the sentence as it appears in the *De rerum natura* (DRN). See Moishe Black's articles on "Lucretius's Venus Meets Diderot," in *Diderot Studies* 27 (1998): 29–44, and "Lucretius Tells Diderot: Here's the Plan," in *Diderot Studies* 28 (2000): 399–58 for a more specific exploration of Diderot's engagement with the Lucretian poem, particularly in the context of his aesthetic writings.

22. See Andrew H. Clark's *Diderot's Part* (New York: Routledge, 2008) for a sustained and deeply evocative analysis of Diderot's relationship to fragmentation.

23. Denis Diderot, *Pensées sur l'interprétation de la nature*, ed. Colas Duflo (Paris: Éditions Flammarion, 2005), 61.

24. Diderot, *Pensées*, 62.

25. Diderot, *Pensées*, 64–65.

26. Diderot, *Pensées*, 68.

27. For a fascinating discussion that begins with the inverse figure—that is, with the disguise of women philosophers in men's clothing—see Nathalie Ferrand's article, "'C'est en habits d'homme qu'une femme peut philosopher': figures féminines du philosophe dans *Thérèse philosophe* et *La Fliosofessa italiana*," in *La figure du philosophe dans les lettres anglaises et françaises* [online], ed. Alexis Tadié (Nanterre: Presses universitaires de Paris Nanterre, 2010), generated June 30, 2023.

28. Diderot, *Pensées*, 69.

29. Diderot, *Pensées*, 70.

30. Charles T. Wolfe, "'Cabinet d'Histoire Naturelle,' or: The Interplay of Nature and Artifice in Diderot's Naturalism," *Perspectives on Science* 17, no. 1 (2009): 70.

31. Denis Diderot, *Essai sur les règnes de Claude et de Néron*, ed. Jean Deprun et al., in *Œuvres complètes*, vol. 25, ed. Herbert Dieckmann et al. (Paris: Hermann, 1986), 348.

32. "Épicuréisme ou épicurisme," in *Encyclopédie, ou Dictionnaire raisonné des sciences, des arts et des métiers*, Denis Diderot et al., vol. 5 (Paris: Briasson, 1755), 784. Consulted in *Encyclopédie, ou dictionnaire raisonné des sciences, des arts et des métiers, etc.*, ed. Denis Diderot and Jean le Rond d'Alembert. University of Chicago: ARTFL Encyclopédie Project (Autumn 2022 Edition), ed. Robert Morrissey and Glenn Roe, http://encyclopedie.uchicago.edu/. The French version of this

passage reads as follows: "Léontium, maîtresse de Métrodore; Thémiste, femme de Léontius; Philénide, une des plus honnêtes femmes d'Athenes; Nécidie, Erotie, Hédie, Marmarie, Bodie, Phédrie, &c." In her article on Epicurean women and misogynist critiques of Epicurean hedonism, Kelly Arenson points out that many of these names only appear in anti-Epicurean polemics, and that some of them have strong sexual or comical connotations. Were they to have existed, some of them may have been *hetaerae* or courtesans. Still, the fact that women were members of the Epicurean community is important on its own. Diderot is seeking here to validate the participation of women in the Epicurean Garden, which in a sense becomes a kind of salon *avant la lettre*, at the same time as he highlights Epicurus's own sexual continence. See Arenson, "Ancient Women Epicureans and their Anti-Hedonist Critics," 77–95. See also Pamela Gordon's discussion of lists and inscriptions of the names of Epicurean women in *The Invention and Gendering of Epicurus*.

33. "Épicuréisme ou épicurisme," 779.
34. "Épicuréisme ou épicurisme," 784.
35. "Épicuréisme ou épicurisme," 784.
36. See in particular the article, "Génie," which, despite its Diderotian overtones, has not been definitively attributed to Diderot. Here the man of genius is defined in the following terms: "L'homme de génie est celui dont l'âme plus étendue frappée par les sensations de tous les êtres, intéressée à tout ce qui est dans la nature, ne reçoit pas une idée qu'elle n'éveille un sentiment, tout l'anime & tout s'y conserve" ("Génie," in *Encyclopédie*, vol. 7 (Paris: Briasson, 1757), 582). Consulted in *Encyclopédie, ou dictionnaire raisonné des sciences, des arts et des métiers, etc.*, ed. Denis Diderot and Jean le Rond d'Alembert. University of Chicago: ARTFL Encyclopédie Project (Autumn 2022 Edition), ed. Robert Morrissey and Glenn Roe, http://encyclopedie.uchicago.edu/. The genius is thus notable not only for his exquisite receptivity to impressions, but for the capaciousness of his animating interest. For an analysis of the positioning of the Diderotian philosopher vis-à-vis the poet, see Christie V. McDonald's "The Sophistry of Heuristics," *Modern Language Notes* 100, no. 4 (1985), 780–88. See also Philippe Lacoue-Labarthe's *Typographies*, vol. 2: *L'Imitation des modernes* (Paris: Éditions Galilée, 1986).

37. "Épicuréisme ou épicurisme," 784.
38. "Épicuréisme ou épicurisme," 784–85.
39. "Épicuréisme ou épicurisme," 782.
40. *Sur les femmes*, in *Œuvres*, ed. André Billy (Paris: Éditions Gallimard, 1951), 949.
41. *Sur les femmes*, 956.
42. *Sur les femmes*, 949.
43. *Sur les femmes*, 954.
44. As I will explore in the three chapters to come, women writers with an interest in Epicurean ethics will take up the quality of delicacy as a key element of feminine pleasure. *Délicatesse* was indeed understood, as Lieselotte Steinbrügge discusses in *The Moral Sex*, as an intrinsic aspect of women's style, deriving from the fineness

and tenderness of their feelings. Steinbrügge, *The Moral Sex: Woman's Nature in the French Enlightenment* (New York: Oxford University Press, 1995), 17.

45. *Sur les femmes*, 957–58.

46. *Sur les femmes*, 957–58.

47. *Éléments de physiologie*, 361–62.

48. The portrayal of philosophy as an apprenticeship for death is of course not unique to the reading of Stoic materialism that Diderot is engaging in here. For one of the most famous early modern elaborations on this same theme, see Montaigne's "Que philosopher, c'est apprendre à mourir" in the *Essais*, composed in 1572.

49. La Mettrie, *Supplément à l'Ouvrage de Pénélope; ou Machiavel en Médecine*, vol. 3 (Berlin, 1750), 242.

50. Diderot, *Essai sur les règnes de Claude et de Néron*, 246–47.

51. La Mettrie's depiction of the ejaculatory delights of voluptuous pleasure has sometimes been described as masculinist. See Dalia Judovitz's claim, in *The Culture of the Body: Genealogies of the Body* (Ann Arbor: University of Michigan Press, 2001), that "La Mettrie's focus is entirely on ejaculation and the male sexual functions and pleasure" (143). Daniel Tiffany makes a similar case in *Toy Medium*. La Mettrie writes of "la semence de la femme" in *L'Homme-machine*, but he suggests that it is likely that this fluid plays no active role in the process of generation. At the same time, the feminine plasticity of the sensitive body takes on an almost liquid form at various moments in La Mettrie's œuvre, one that allows even masculine or male semen to acquire an important feminine dimension. Like Diderot, La Mettrie may have been influenced by the Lucretian depiction of generation as involving the mixing of masculine and feminine seeds. For a reflection on the relationship between female semen in Lucretius and the critique of patriarchal privilege, see Michael Pope's "Embryology, Female Semina and Male Vincibility in Lucretius, *De rervm natvra*," *The Classical Quarterly* 69, no. 1 (2019): 229–45. Pope argues that Lucretius is not interested in the emancipation of actual women, but that his model of active female semen feminizes men by "masculating" women.

52. Hal Gladfelder's article "Machines in Love: Bodies, Souls, and Sexes in the Age of La Mettrie," in *Eighteenth-Century Fiction* 27, no. 1 (Fall 2014): 55–81, develops with great verve and acumen the idea of La Mettrie's receptive and sensitive machines, whose pleasures are found in the dissolution or dispossession of the self through the action of the imagination. Gladfelder writes, "Against a rigid, categorical and classificatory method, [La Mettrie] adopts a fluid, restless, boundary-dissolving style of thinking aloud, trying out hypotheses, playing devil's advocate, putting forward contradictory claims, sowing doubts, all as strategies for unsettling the lines of demarcation between categories (body/soul, man/machine), and between physiological or philosophical schools (vitalism/mechanism, Lockean/Cartesian)" (67). Another key category that breaks down here is that of gender. Indeed, sexuality (often as expressed in acts of heterosexual desire) is presented by La Mettrie as a crucial instance of category blurring.

53. *L'École de la volupté*, in *De la volupté*, ed. Ann Thomson (Paris: Les Éditions Desjonquères, 1996), 136.
54. *L'École de la volupté*, 123.
55. *L'École de la volupté*, 125.
56. *L'École de la volupté*, 125.
57. La Mettrie, "Dédicace," in *L'Homme-machine, Œuvres philosophiques*, tome 1 (Paris: Librairie Arthème Fayard, 1987), 59.
58. *L'École de la volupté*, 132.
59. *L'Homme-machine*, 59.
60. *L'Homme-machine*, 83.
61. I vehemently reject La Mettrie's characterization of the person in this example as monstrous and I deplore the violence to which she was subjected; I have made the choice here to continue to use feminine pronouns in reference to her assigned gender identity, with which she apparently lived.
62. *Système d'Épicure*, in *De la volupté*, ed. Ann Thomson (Paris: Les Éditions Desjonquères, 1996), 161. La Mettrie also mentions this same image in the essay *L'Homme-plante* (1748), also attributed to him.
63. *Système d'Épicure*, 162.
64. *Système d'Épicure*, 162.
65. *Système d'Épicure*, 158. The text reads in French as follows: "Comment prendre la nature sur le fait? Elle ne s'y est jamais prise elle-même. Dénuée de connaissance et de sentiment, elle fait de la soie, comme le *Bourgeois gentilhomme* fait de la prose, sans le savoir." See Mary Terrall's *Catching Nature in the Act: Réaumur and the Practice of Natural History in the Eighteenth Century* (Chicago: University of Chicago Press, 2016) for an account of Gilles-Augustin Bazin's use of this same metaphor in his correspondence with René-Antoine Ferchault de Réaumur, his mentor and friend.
66. *Système d'Épicure*, 159.
67. *Système d'Épicure*, 160.
68. La Mettrie, *Histoire Naturelle de l'Ame* (Oxford: Aux dépens de l'auteur, 1747), 12.
69. La Mettrie, *Anti-Sénèque ou le souverain bien*, in *De la volupté*, ed. Ann Thomson (Paris: Les Éditions Desjonquères, 1996), 110–11.
70. Ann Thomson, "Émilie Du Châtelet and La Mettrie," in *Époque Émilienne*, ed. R. E. Hagengruber, *Women in the History of Philosophy and Sciences*, vol 11. (Cham, Switzerland: Springer, 2022), 377–89, 379, https://doi-org.libproxy1.usc.edu/10.1007/978-3-030-89921-9_17.
71. For a resonant reading of the resonance of "vulgivagus" in its connection to an ethic of "wandering," see Dufallo's analysis, in chapter four of his book *Disorienting Empire*, of "wandering" versus "erring" in the *DRN*. Dufallo concludes the chapter, "*De rerum natura* is a poem of profound sympathy for misguided humanity, but asks for bravery nonetheless: the courage, that is, to admit oneself a purposeful wanderer,

not *errans* but *vagus*, not Odyssean or even Aenean, but Venusian, Epicurean, Lucretian—and ultimately free within the boundaries of nature" (155).

72. Giovacchini, "Sexual Freedom and Feminine Pleasure in Lucretius," 118.

73. La Mettrie, *L'Homme-machine*, 85.

74. Helvétius, *Le Bonheur*, presented by Michel Onfray (Paris: Éditions Michalon, 2006), 13. The French text reads: "Dans ces lieux, de jouir tout s'occupe sans cesse./C'est ici que l'Amour, prolongeant son ivresse,/Découvre un nouvel art d'irriter les désirs,/Et d'y multiplier la forme des plaisirs."

75. Helvétius, *Le Bonheur*, 12. "Là du chant des oiseaux mon oreille est charmée;/Là d'arbustes fleuris la terre est parfumée./Leurs esprits odorants, leur ombre, leur fraîcheur,/Tout invite à l'amour et mes sens et mon cœur:/Dans ces lieux enchantés tout respire l'ivresse."

76. Helvétius, *Le Bonheur*, 62. "'Que je suis différent alors que je te vois!/Tout mon être se change en approchant de toi./Le ciel à mon amour lia mon existence;/C'est par toi que je sens, c'est par toi que je pense.'"

77. Helvétius, *Le Bonheur*, 73. "'J'éprouve en ce moment tous les maux de l'absence/Mais n'importe; je veux qu'en mon cœur agité/L'amour quelques instants cède à l'humanité.'"

78. Helvétius, *Le Bonheur*, 83–84. "Sexe charmant, c'est vous qui jadis sur la terre/Armiez pour les combats les enfants de la guerre:/Vous pouvez plus encore pour les fils d'Apollon;/Vous donnez des plaisirs: la gloire est un vain nom./Par de nouveaux bienfaits méritez nos hommages:/Vous fîtes les héros: faites encor les sages."

79. Helvétius, *Le Bonheur*, 43.

2. *Volupté* in a Ruined World: Puisieux's Libertine Images

1. Louis de Jaucourt, "Penchant, Inclination," in *Encyclopédie, ou Dictionnaire raisonné des sciences, des arts et des métiers*, vol. 8, ed. Denis Diderot et al. (Neufchastel: Samuel Faulche & Compagnie, 1765), 651. Consulted in *Encyclopédie, ou dictionnaire raisonné des sciences, des arts et des métiers, etc.*, ed. Denis Diderot and Jean le Rond d'Alembert. University of Chicago: ARTFL Encyclopédie Project (Autumn 2022 Edition), ed. Robert Morrissey and Glenn Roe, http://encyclopedie.uchicago.edu/.

2. Madeleine de Puisieux, *L'Éducation du marquis de ****, ou Mémoires de la comtesse de Zurlac (Berlin: Chez Bauche, 1753), II:2–3.

3. Madeleine de Puisieux, *Les Caractères. Par madame de P***** (Londres, 1750), 137. In French, this passage reads: "J'aime mieux une erreur qui fait mon bonheur qu'une évidence qui me désespère."

4. Madeleine de Puisieux, "Le Printems," in *Œuvres de Madame de P****, 1746–1747 [manuscript]. http://archivesetmanuscrits.bnf.fr/ark:/12148/cc45749f, 24. The lines read more smoothly in the French original: "L'hiver fuit et l'amour caressant la

Nature/De son souffle divin fit naître les Zephires/Créateurs à leur tour,/ils parent la Verdure/Pour élever bientôt des autels aux plaisirs."

5. Lucretius, *On the Nature of Things*, trans. W. H. D. Rouse, rev. Martin F. Smith, Loeb Classical Library 181 (Cambridge, MA: Harvard University Press, 1924), book 1, 3, lines 6–15. Lucrèce, *De la nature=De rerum natura*, trans. José Kany-Turpin (Paris: GF Flammarion, 1998), 53, lines 10–16: "Car sitôt dévoilé le visage printanier du jour,/Dès que reprend vigueur le fécondant zéphyr,/Dans les airs les oiseaux te signifient, Déesse,/Et ton avènement, frappés au cœur par ta puissance;/Les fauves, les troupeaux bondissent dans l'herbe épaisse,/Fendent les courants rapides, tant, captif de ta grâce,/Chacun brûle de te suivre où tu le mènes sans trêve."

6. Lucretius is currently in the midst of a(nother) revival, one that has stretched over at least the first two decades of the twenty-first century and shows no signs of slowing. Major recent studies on Lucretius include Thomas Nail's *Lucretius* I and II (Edinburgh: Edinburgh University Press, 2018; 2020) and Ryan Johnson's *The Deleuze-Lucretius Encounter* (Edinburgh: Edinburgh University Press, 2017). Nail dramatically revises the story of Lucretius's modernity (pace Greenblatt) but nonetheless positions Lucretius as a philosopher "for today."

7. Nadine Bérenguier, "Madeleine d'Arsant de Puisieux," in *Writers of the French Enlightenment II*, ed. Samia I. Spencer (Detroit, MI: Gale, 2005), *Dictionary of Literary Biography* 31. link.gale.com/apps/doc/H1200012625/LitRC?u=usocal_main&sid=bookmark-LitRC&xid=3b9854fd. Accessed September 14, 2021. Bérenguier also gives an excellent overview and analysis of reactions to Puisieux's work, especially the *Conseils à une amie* and the *Réflexions et avis sur les défauts et ridicules à la mode*, in her study, *Conduct Books for Girls in Enlightenment France* (London: Routledge, 2016), 135–42.

8. Recently, Lucretius's poem is beginning to be read for the potential it might hold for an understanding of women's pleasure, as well as for the ways in which it might have inspired individual women (including Margaret Cavendish and Lucy Hutchinson). See Jessie Hock's book on *The Erotics of Materialism* for a particularly fine example of this kind of analysis. Hock, *The Erotics of Materialism: Lucretius and Early Modern Poetics* (Philadelphia: University of Pennsylvania Press, 2021).

9. Gerard Passannante, *Catastrophizing: Materialism and the Making of Disaster* (Chicago: University of Chicago Press, 2019), 4.

10. Jonathan Israel, *Enlightenment Contested: Philosophy, Modernity, and the Emancipation of Man, 1670–1752* (New York: Oxford University Press, 2006), 817. As indicated in Chapter 1, the years 1747 and 1748 were particularly important for the development of materialist critique in both fictional and nonfictional forms, with the publication not just of *Les Bijoux*, but of La Mettrie's *L'Homme-machine* (1747), *Thérèse philosophe* (1748), and Benoît de Maillet's *Telliamed* (1748, a posthumously published dialogue on the origins of the earth), among other works.

11. In addition to the series of poems, none of them published, where "Le Printems" appears, Puisieux's body of work includes novels, two short stories, a

set of conduct books, a play, and the *Prospectus sur un ouvrage important* (1772), which outlines a plan for moral education of the poor and working classes. I am not including in this list the essay entitled *La Femme n'est pas inférieure à l'homme*, published anonymously in 1750 and then again in 1751, under the title *Le Triomphe des dames, traduit de l'Anglois de Miledi P****. The work, which has sometimes been ascribed to Puisieux's husband, Philippe-Florent de Puisieux, is attributed to Puisieux herself by Alice M. Laborde, who discusses the essay as an original work (and not a translation), given that Puisieux does not seem to have known English. However, in her very useful article on the attribution question, Camille Garnier makes what is to my mind a convincing argument that the essay is in fact a translation of an English pamphlet, *Woman Not Inferior to Man, or a Short and Modest Vindication of the Natural Right of the Fair-Sex to a Perfect Equality of Power, Dignity, and Esteem, with the Men*, published in London in 1739 under the pen name Sophia. Garnier suggests that the author may in fact be Lady Mary Wortley Montagu and the translator Puisieux's husband; in either case, the inclusion of the essay in Madeleine de Puisieux's corpus seems dubious. See "'La Femme n'est pas inférieure à l'homme' (1750): œuvre de Madeleine Darsant de Puisieux ou simple traduction française?" *Revue d'histoire littéraire de la France* 87, no. 4 (1987): 709–13.

12. For an excellent overview of critical reactions to Diderot's tendency to disavow coherence, see Andrew H. Clark's *Diderot's Part* (New York: Routledge, 2008). Clark builds a fascinating reading of Diderot's contradictions as participating in assemblages that "produce, dramatize, and foster multiplicity" (37). For a discussion of the intrinsic generativity of Diderot's fragmentary thought in the *Pensées*, see Blanca Missé's "Diderot's *Thoughts on the Interpretation of Nature*: A Materialist Aesthetics for Science," *The Eighteenth Century* 61, no. 4 (2020): 495–517. See also Marian Hobson on "Philosophy and Rococo style (2002)," in *Diderot and Rousseau: Networks of Enlightenment*, ed. Kate E. Tunstall and Caroline Warman (Oxford: Voltaire Foundation, 2011).

13. Puisieux, *Les Caractères*, 4.

14. Puisieux, *Réflexions*, 3.

15. As Julie Candler Hayes points out in *Women Moralists in Early Modern France*, this tension between general and particular is typical of the moralist genre, which is also heavily reliant on short and fragmented forms. Puisieux activates these formal and epistemological dynamics in the service of a materialist ethic, and thus obliquely (and sometimes directly) invokes a distinctly materialist tradition of thought and writing, one from which women were formally excluded.

16. Marie-France Silver, "Madame de Puisieux ou l'ambition d'être femme de lettres," in *Femmes savantes et femmes d'esprit: Women Intellectuals of the French Eighteenth Century*, ed. Roland Bonnel and Catherine Rubinger (New York: Peter Lang, 1994) 19, 183–201.

17. Puisieux, *Réflexions*, 72.

18. Puisieux, *Réflexions*, 124.

19. In the passage that raises La Mettrie's ire, she discusses Fontenelle's treatise *Du Bonheur* (1714) and Maupertuis's *Essai de philosophie morale*, published in 1749. She was obviously familiar with aspects of moral philosophy, both ancient and modern, although she did not herself write in this genre, choosing most often to adopt that of the maxim rather than the treatise. La Mettrie's caricature of her is specifically in response to her criticism of Maupertuis.

20. Puisieux, *Les Caractères*, 170–71.

21. Puisieux, *Les Caractères*, 172–73.

22. Puisieux, *Les Caractères*, 174.

23. Puisieux, *Réflexions*, 9.

24. I am reminded here of the second sentence of Peggy Kamuf's essay on "Accounterability," *Textual Practice* 21, no. 2 (2007): 251–66: "My uncertainty, even my confusion, is at least in part my own doing, and thus my undoing," (251). Puisieux similarly suggests that in exercising a certain agency in desire women create the conditions for this desire to come undone.

25. Lisa Robertson, *Nilling: Prose Essays on Noise, Pornography, the Codex, Melancholy, Lucretius, Folds, Cities and Related Aporias* (Toronto: Book*hug Press, 2020). In Puisieux's novels, short stories, and treatises, pleasure often seems to lie in the kind of divided will that Robertson identifies closely with her acts of reading Lucretius, Hannah Arendt, and Pauline Réage. Thus, where Robertson marks in her encounter with the Lucretian text a kind of meandering, another "undoing," Puisieux identifies something similar within her own writing: A rejection of order that allows her to write her books as she takes on her debts—without regard for proper beginnings, middles, and ends.

26. Puisieux, *Les Caractères*, 39.

27. In his book, *Seducing the Eighteenth-Century French Reader* (Aldershot: Ashgate Publishing, 2008), Paul J. Young attributes this entry to Diderot, but the ARTFL edition of the *Encyclopédie* leaves it without an attribution, even a hesitant one. In his review of Young's book, Philip Stewart suggests there is no evidence in favor of this attribution. The entry's emphasis on voluptuousness as an especially criminal form of pleasure does not particularly reflect Diderot's perspective as he expresses it elsewhere, in any case. For an enlightening analysis of *volupté* in the visual arts, particularly as expressed by the interaction between women and animals, see Jennifer Milam's article "Rococo Representations of Interspecies Sensuality and the Pursuit of *Volupté*," *Art Bulletin* 97, no. 2 (2015): 192–209.

28. "Volupté," in *Encyclopédie, ou Dictionnaire raisonné des sciences, des arts et des métiers*, vol. 17, ed. Denis Diderot et al. (Neufchastel: Samuel Faulche, 1765), 458. Consulted in *Encyclopédie, ou dictionnaire raisonné des sciences, des arts et des métiers, etc.*, ed. Denis Diderot and Jean le Rond d'Alembert. University of Chicago: ARTFL Encyclopédie Project (Autumn 2022 Edition), ed. Robert Morrissey and Glenn Roe, http://encyclopedie.uchicago.edu/.

29. Puisieux, *Les Caractères*, 39–40.

30. Lieselotte Steinbrügge, *The Moral Sex: Woman's Nature in the French Enlightenment* (New York: Oxford University Press, 1995), 37. See also Mary McAlpin's discussion of vitalism in *Female Sexuality and Cultural Degradation in Enlightenment France* (Farnham: Ashgate Publishing, 2012).

31. Desmahis (Joseph de Corsembleu), "Femme (Morale)," in *Encyclopédie, ou Dictionnaire raisonné des sciences, des arts et des métiers*, vol. 6, ed. Diderot et al. (Paris: Briasson, 1756), 472. Consulted in *Encyclopédie, ou dictionnaire raisonné des sciences, des arts et des métiers, etc.*, ed. Denis Diderot and Jean le Rond d'Alembert. University of Chicago: ARTFL Encyclopédie Project (Autumn 2022 Edition), ed. Robert Morrissey and Glenn Roe, http://encyclopedie.uchicago.edu/.

32. Denis Diderot, *Sur les femmes*, in *Œuvres*, ed. André Billy (Paris: Éditions Gallimard, 1951), 950.

33. Arguably, La Mettrie takes a similar approach to Puisieux considering the relationship of *volupté* to *délicatesse*, but with a different effect. In feminizing the figure of the philosopher, he extends femininity to men rather than inviting women into the field of philosophical inquiry.

34. Puisieux, *Les Caractères*, 40–41.

35. Puisieux, *Réflexions*, 74.

36. Puisieux, *Les Caractères*, 41.

37. Puisieux, *Les Caractères*, 40–42.

38. I am reminded here of the famous letter in *Les Liaisons dangereuses* in which the marquise de Merteuil reflects on her gradual and always clandestine acquisition of knowledge both sexual and philosophic. As other scholars have explored, women's adoption of empiricist methods of analysis—which seem to rely on "experience" in its most neutral form—also threatens to convey them too close to the fraught domain of sexual desire—wherein the permissible capacity to feel becomes the transgressive capacity to know—one that they cannot freely admit to possessing.

39. Puisieux, *Œuvres de Madame de P****, *Céphise, conte moral, et Poësies diverses*, undated, 32. I give the French original here: "Plaisirs, enfans divins, qu'êtes-vous devenus,/Autour de moi je ne vous trouve plus/Vous me quittez avec l'objet que j'aime/Vous me livrez à ma douleur extrême,/Et vainement je veux vous rappeller./Mes plus tendres désirs semblent vous éloigner./Au moins suivez les pas de l'amant que j'adore./Offrez-vous à ses yeux, qu'il vous caresse encore./Chassez loin de son cœur la peine, le tourment,/Faites qu'il soit heureux, mais jamais inconstant./Pour l'intéresser davantage,/Présentez-vous sous mon image,/Peignez-lui mon amour, cachez-lui mes regrets./Rapprochez vos transports, vos charmes, vos attraits./Et pour vous rendre enfin les maîtres de son ame,/Retracez-les avec des traits de flâme/Ces jours heureux, ces instants fortunés/Où dans vos bras et d'amour embrasés/N'existant plus que par notre tendresse,/Nous désirons tous deux mourir de votre ivresse./Eh! quoi . . . ce souvenir cause votre retour./Ah! fuyez-moi Plaisirs, laissez pleurer l'amour./Je ne veux vous revoir qu'offerts d'une main chere./Ramenez mon Amant, si vous voulez me plaire."

40. The heroid came back into fashion in eighteenth-century France, especially in the period between 1740 and 1770. See Renata Carocci, *Les Héroïdes dans la seconde moitié du dix-huitième siècle (1758–1788)* (Fasano: Nizet, 1988). Françoise de Graffigny also engages significantly with this genre, as I will discuss in Chapter 4. The construction of a feminine pleasure out of pain, a possibility that the heroid both permits and obscures, might be understood as a redeployment of the genre in the name of an illusive materialism.

41. For this reason, the marquis de Sade will later take the image of the virtuous woman as an icon to be destroyed on the way to a materialist utopia. From his vantage the problem is not masculine inconstancy but the weakness and vulnerability of women who, at best, are the prisoners of their own ideological commitments, always acting in bad faith.

42. Florence Lotterie, *Le Genre des Lumières: Femme et philosophe au XVIIIe siècle* (Paris: Classiques Garnier, 2013), 125.

43. In *Nilling*, Robertson writes of her own experience as a reader of Anne Desclos's [Pauline Réage] sadomasochistic novel *Histoire d'O* (1954): "My own readerly will was observably split. I obediently pursued a concept, I made my corresponding marks, I resisted, I was lazy, I looped back, I sometimes skipped forward without immediately noticing. Far from seeming problematic, this nilling split introduced a complicated duration into pleasure. . . . I felt that readerly desire achieves its lastingness, its pleasurable sense of suspended duration, in a complicitous nilling, a charged refusal. That is to say that in reading, I undo a text, as I resist my own autonomy. The undoing animates passivity, all that negates and resists rather than insists. It is a slightly unpleasant thought, and it pertains to the ambivalent discomfort of pornography" (28).

44. Nadine Bérenguier, "Madeleine d'Arsant de Puisieux," n.p. But in this instance, too, Puisieux's unusual contribution to the genre of libertine allegory is often deemed wanting—memorably dismissed by Vivienne Mylne and Janet Osborne as "flat and vapid." Mylne and Osborne, "Diderot's Early Fiction: 'Les Bijoux Indiscrets' and 'L'Oiseau Blanc,'" *Diderot Studies* 14 (1971): 164.

45. Alice M. Laborde discusses Puisieux's possible contributions to *L'Oiseau blanc* in *Diderot et Madame de Puisieux* (Saratoga, CA: ANMA Libri, 1984).

46. Madeleine de Puisieux, *Le Plaisir et la volupté* (A Paphos, 1752), n.p.

47. Puisieux, *Le Plaisir et la volupté*, n.p.

48. Puisieux, *Le Plaisir et la volupté*, n.p.

49. Crébillon fils, *Le Sylphe, ou Songe de Mme de R*** écrit par elle-même à Mme de S****, ed. Carmen Ramirez, in *Œuvres complètes*, vol. I, ed. Jean Sgard (Paris: Classiques Garnier, 1999 [online edition 2010]), 24.

50. Puisieux, *Le Plaisir et la volupté*, 9.

51. Puisieux, *Le Plaisir et la volupté*, 23.

52. Puisieux, *Le Plaisir et la volupté*, 54–55.

53. Puisieux, *Le Plaisir et la volupté*, 73.

54. Puisieux, *Le Plaisir et la volupté*, 95.
55. Puisieux, *Le Plaisir et la volupté*, 117–19.
56. See Joan Hinde Stewart's *Enlightenment of Age: Women, Letters, and Growing Old in Eighteenth-Century France* (Oxford: Voltaire Foundation, 2010) on the relationships between older women (including Françoise de Graffigny) and younger men during this period.
57. Puisieux, *L'Éducation*, I:1.
58. Puisieux, *L'Éducation*, I:2.
59. Puisieux, *L'Éducation*, I:2.
60. Puisieux, *L'Éducation*, I:9–10.
61. Puisieux, *L'Éducation*, I:148.
62. Puisieux, *L'Éducation*, I:174.
63. Puisieux, *L'Éducation*, I:182–83.
64. Puisieux, *L'Éducation*, I:185.
65. Puisieux, *L'Éducation*, II:166.
66. Puisieux, *L'Éducation*, II:189.
67. Puisieux, *L'Éducation*, II:169.
68. Puisieux, *Réflexions*, 261.
69. Puisieux, *Réflexions*, 126.
70. Puisieux, *Réflexions*, 300.

3. Illusions Without Error: Du Châtelet Loves Enough for Two

1. Gabrielle-Émilie Le Tonnelier de Breteuil Du Châtelet, *La Correspondance d'Émilie Du Châtelet*, 2 vols., ed. Ulla Kölving and Andrew Brown (Ferney-Voltaire: Centre international d'étude du XVIIIe siècle, 2018), II:1741–49, letter 599.
2. Eve Sedgwick, *A Dialogue on Love* (Boston: Beacon Press, 1999), 23.
3. See Ruth Hagengruber's article on Du Châtelet in *The Mathematical Intelligencer* 38, no. 4 (2016): 1–6.
4. Du Châtelet, *La Correspondance d'Émilie Du Châtelet* II:1741–49, letter 635.
5. Du Châtelet, *La Correspondance d'Émilie Du Châtelet*, I:1733–40, letter 286.
6. Feminist critics have nonetheless worked successfully to highlight the originality and significance of Du Châtelet's participation in what is sometimes referred to as a neo-Epicurean current of social thought. See Barbara Whitehead and Felicia Gottmann on Du Châtelet's innovative approach to Epicureanism in the *Discours sur le bonheur* and her translation of Mandeville.
7. For an excellent overview of the changing portrayals of Du Châtelet over time, with a special focus on the popular biographies by Nancy Mitford and Élisabeth Badinter, see Judith Zinsser's "Betrayals: An Eighteenth-Century Philosophe and her Biographers," *French Historical Studies* 39, no 1 (2016): 3–33.
8. See Anne-Lise Rey, "La Minerve vient de faire sa physique," *Philosophiques* 44, no. 2 (2017): 237. Rey proposes a new heuristic for understanding the

intellectual situation within which Du Châtelet and others are operating: "leibnizo-newtonianisme." Rey stresses that this category should not be understood as a school of thought or a tradition, but as the activation of a combination of influences in a particular context. Rey's focus here is particularly Du Châtelet's definition of substance as active and her reflections on liberty. In an excellent article on "the problem of bodies" in Du Châtelet, Katherine Brading argues that the tendency to approach eighteenth-century Newtonianism from a Kuhnian perspective—which treats open methodological questions as already closed—makes invisible the important contributions of Du Châtelet to debates around the status of bodies and the relationship between physical and metaphysical realms. See Brading, "Émilie Du Châtelet and the Problem of Bodies," in *Early Modern Women on Metaphysics*, ed. Emily Thomas (Cambridge: Cambridge University Press, 2018), 150–68.

9. Felicia Gottmann convincingly argues that, in her translation of Bernard Mandeville's *Fable of the Bees*, Du Châtelet opens a new avenue in neo-Epicureanism. As Gottmann writes, "Her so-called 'translation' provided the basis for the first secular defence of commercial society on an ethical level." Gottmann, "Du Châtelet, Voltaire, and the Transformation of Mandeville's Fable," *History of European Ideas* 38, no. 2 (2012): 227.

10. In a sign that Du Châtelet herself is aware of her entanglement with the literary image of the "jolie marquise," she writes to Algarotti asking if the marquise on his frontispiece is in fact an image of her.

11. Anne-Lise Rey's thoughtful article on "La littérarisation de la science newtonienne au XVIIIe siècle: une littérature pour les dames?" contends that Du Châtelet moves beyond a dynamic of "vulgarisation" or simplification in order to take seriously the possibility of a "physique fondée sur les images" and a metaphysics that operates in tandem with sensory perception. See Rey, "La littérarisation de la science newtonienne au XVIIIe siècle: une littérature pour les dames?," *Littératures classiques* 85, no. 3 (2014): 303–26.

12. In the second edition of the *Institutions*, published in 1742 with Du Châtelet's name attached, the author reveals her gender. See Mary Terrall, "Émilie Du Châtelet and the Gendering of Science," *History of Science* 33, no. 3 (1995): 283–310.

13. Terrall, "Gendering," 301.

14. Terrall, "Gendering," 303.

15. See Ann Thomson and Theo Verbeek on this borrowing. Ann Thomson's critique of the ascription of the prefatory letter to La Mettrie himself is persuasive, as I discuss in Chapter 1. Thomson also questions the attribution to Du Châtelet of the identity of the unnamed "Marquise" in *La Volupté*. Ursula Pia Jauch suggests that, in hinting that Du Châtelet had been his lover, La Mettrie aimed to upset Voltaire; see Jauch, *Jenseits des Maschine. Philosophie, Ironie, une Ästhetik bei Julien Offray de La Mettrie (1709–1751)* (Munich: Carl Hanser Verlag, 1998). For the argument that Du Châtelet played a "considerable role" in the life of La Mettrie (among others), see Ruth Hagengruber, "Émilie du Châtelet Between Leibniz and Newton: The Transformation of Metaphysics," in *Émilie du Châtelet Between Leibniz and*

Newton, ed. Ruth Hagengruber (Dordrecht: Springer, 2012), 52. Aram Vartanian also claims that Du Châtelet and La Mettrie were lovers.

16. Mme du Châtelet's Translation of the "Fable of the Bees," in *Studies on Voltaire, With Some Unpublished Papers of Mme. du Châtelet*, ed. Ira O. Wade (Princeton, NJ: Princeton University Press, 1947), 131–87, 131.

17. In the epistle to Bernard Le Bovier de Fontenelle with which he prefaces *Il Newtonianismo*, Algarotti will take up the same image deployed by Du Châtelet, with more stress on the stereotypically feminine aspects of the investment in the beauty of the body. He writes of his women readers that his work will not be in vain if he can make them enjoy cultivating their minds rather than curling their hair. Algarotti, *Il Newtonianismo per le dame, ovvero dialoghi sopra la luce e i colori* (Napoli [Venice]: n.p., 1737), n.p.

18. Du Châtelet, "Fable," 131. The French original reads: "Des réflexions si sensées, ne rendent pas à l'âme, cette flexibilité que le manque d'exercice lui ôte quand on a passé la première jeunesse. Les fackirs des Indes perdent l'usage des muscles de leurs bras, à force de les laisser dans la même posture, et de ne s'en point servir. Aussi perd-t-on ses idées quand on néglige de les cultiver. C'est un feu qui meurt, si on n'y jette pas continuellement le bois qui sert à l'entretenir. Voulant donc réparer, s'il est possible, une si grande faute, et tâcher de replier cet arbre déjà trop avancé, et de lui faire porter les fruits qu'on peut encore s'en promettre, j'ai cherché quelque genre d'occupation qui put en fixant mon esprit, lui donner cette consistance (si je puis m'exprimer ainsi) qu'on n'acquiert jamais, en ne se proposant pas un but dans ses études. Il faut s'y conduire comme dans la vie civile, bien savoir, ce qu'on veut être. L'irrésolution produisant dans l'une les fausses démarches, et dans l'autre les idées confuses."

19. Voltaire may have brought the text back from his stay in England and proposed it as a translation exercise for Du Châtelet, who was learning English at the time. The period of her work on the text coincides with Voltaire's stay at Cirey; they probably worked on the text collaboratively at least to a certain extent, as Felicia Gottmann discusses.

20. Du Châtelet, "Fable," 136.

21. See E. J. Hundert, "Bernard de Mandeville and the Enlightenment's Maxims of Modernity," *Journal of the History of Ideas* 56, no. 4 (1995): 577–93.

22. Elisabeth Wallmann is interested in the way in which Du Châtelet tempers Mandeville's vitalism by focusing on the exceptional quality of human life (as opposed to animal bodies). As part of this shift, Du Châtelet removes the poem with which Mandeville begins the treatise. See Wallmann, "The Human-Animal Debate and the Enlightenment Body Politics: Émilie Du Châtelet's Reading of Mandeville's *Fable of the Bees*," *Early Modern French Studies* 42, no. 1 (2020): 85–103. For a discussion of Du Châtelet's revision of Mandeville in the context of eighteenth-century women's political thought, which likens Du Châtelet's politics to those of Françoise de Graffigny, see Karen Green, *A History of Women's Political Thought in Europe, 1700–1800* (Cambridge: Cambridge University Press, 2014).

23. Du Châtelet, "Fable," 142–43.

24. As already mentioned, Gottmann explores how the appropriation of Epicureanism that Du Châtelet is operating in the translation will become a secular argument in defense of the ethics of commercial society, an argument later revisited and modified by Voltaire in his *Traité de métaphysique*. Gottman, "Du Châtelet, Voltaire, and the Transformation of Mandeville's Fable," 227–28.

25. Lucretius, *On the Nature of Things*, trans. W. H. D. Rouse, rev. Martin F. Smith, Loeb Classical Library 181 (Cambridge, MA: Harvard University Press, 1924), book 1, 5, lines 21–28.

26. Lucretius, *On the Nature of Things*, book 5, 453–57, lines 962–1014.

27. Du Châtelet, "Fable," 136.

28. Du Châtelet, "Fable," 136–37.

29. Du Châtelet, "Fable," 136.

30. Terrall, "Gendering," 301.

31. Du Châtelet, *Institutions de physique* (Paris: Chez Prault fils, 1740), 47.

32. Du Châtelet, *Institutions*, 47.

33. Du Châtelet, *Institutions*, 46.

34. Du Châtelet, "Fable," 133.

35. Du Châtelet, "Fable," 133.

36. Du Châtelet, *Institutions*, 12. Here she clearly comes down on the side of a "masculine" style, with an emphasis on the transparency and clarity of language, in opposition to a "feminine" one, which sees value in ornament. The distinction she makes is visible in the work of many of the most prominent Enlightenment *philosophes* and accords with her interest in the "male" way of thinking of the English (which appeals to her). See Elena Russo's excellent book on style in the Enlightenment for more discussion of the implications of this choice. Russo, *Styles of Enlightenment: Taste, Politics, and Authorship in Eighteenth-Century France* (Baltimore, MD: The Johns Hopkins University Press, 2006).

37. As Julie Candler Hayes points out in her wonderful chapter on figuration in Du Châtelet's physics, this dismissal of rhetorical ornamentation is itself rhetorically figured. Hayes contends that "The denial of the figurative in the *Avant-propos* is a necessary performance that is part of the identification of the writer as a philosopher; another part of that performance, initially, is identifying the writer as male, or at least effacing any overt suggestion to the contrary" (90). Du Châtelet's name appeared on the title page of the second edition of the work, but, as Hayes remarks, she revised the invocation of "pères et mères" in the initial framing of the *Avant-propos* to read "Hommes." Hayes argues that this revision effaces the "affectivity of all parental relationships," but I would suggest that this affect (or at least affection) returns in the suggestion that the creation of the work enables the child to take pleasure in the parents' pains. See Hayes, *Reading the French Enlightenment: System and Subversion* (Cambridge: Cambridge University Press, 1999), 86–110.

38. Du Châtelet, *Institutions*, 12.

39. Du Châtelet, *Institutions*, 2.

40. Du Châtelet, *Institutions*, 3.

41. Du Châtelet, *Institutions*, 4–5.

42. Du Châtelet, contra Newton, endorses hypothesis as a kind of scaffolding necessary for the construction of the house of knowledge, thereby emphasizing the creative or speculative dimensions of scientific reason.

43. Françoise de Graffigny, letter to Antoine Devaux, in *Correspondance de Mme de Graffigny*, volume 1, ed. J. A. Dainard and English Showalter et al. (Oxford: Voltaire Foundation, 1985), 224.

44. Du Châtelet, *Dissertation*, 48.

45. Du Châtelet, *Dissertation*, 1–2.

46. Du Châtelet, *Dissertation*, 14.

47. For an incisive and suggestive analysis of elasticity and its connection to the making of worlds in Du Châtelet, see Tracy Rutler's "Happiness and Disability: Émilie Du Châtelet's Adaptive Worldbuilding," *L'Esprit Créateur* 61, no. 4 (Winter 2021): 140–52.

48. Du Châtelet, *Dissertation*, 39.

49. Hayes, *Reading the French Enlightenment*, 98.

50. Du Châtelet, *Institutions*, 205–6.

51. In this passage, Du Châtelet also celebrates the capacity of scientific experimentation to lend plausibility to hypotheses concerning the material world, of which the existence of "particles of the first order" (homogenous, indivisible, monadic, elemental), and "particles of the second order" is one.

52. Du Châtelet, *Institutions*, 187.

53. Du Châtelet thus rejects the Epicurean contention that matter is infinite and infinitely diverse, although for Epicurus and for Lucretius bodies still follow certain patterns in the ways in which they combine.

54. Du Châtelet, *Dissertation*, 66.

55. Du Châtelet, *Dissertation*, 67. Du Châtelet's exploration of the motive force of fire recalls in certain important ways the work of Margaret Cavendish (1623–1673), whose poem "Of Fire and Flame" takes an atomist perspective on the question of fire's power and whose 1666 work of fiction, *The Blazing World*, foregrounds fire as a power that is both aesthetic and literal. In a forthcoming essay entitled "Blazing: Du Châtelet as Central to the First Paradigm in Newtonian Mechanics," Holly K. Anderson suggests that Du Châtelet would probably have been aware of Cavendish's novel. Du Châtelet herself privileges laboratory and philosophical craft in her investigation of matter's pleasures, while Cavendish's corpus cuts across the domains of science and fiction. See H. K. Anderson, "Blazing," in *The Bloomsbury Handbook of Du Châtelet*, ed. Fatima Amijee (forthcoming).

56. Du Châtelet, *Institutions*, 187–88.

57. Du Châtelet, *Institutions*, 191.

58. We might find an echo of the dynamic present here in the moment in her translation when she recalls the function of heterosexual love in the Lucretian

anthropology, where Venus acts to remake the violence of erotic desire into a more enduring set of attachments, thereby "softening" their power.

59. See Judith P. Zinsser's introduction to the *Discourse* in *Émilie Du Châtelet: Selected Philosophical and Scientific Writings*, ed. Judith P. Zinsser, trans. Isabelle Bour and Judith P. Zinsser (Chicago: University of Chicago Press, 2009), 345–46.

60. Robert Mauzi's classic book on happiness is the foundational critical text here. Vivasvan Soni has an important rewriting of this tradition from a Marxian perspective. See Mauzi, *L'Idée du bonheur dans la littérature et la pensée française au XVIIIe siècle* (Paris: Librairie Armand Colin, 1960) and Soni, *Mourning Happiness: Narrative and the Politics of Modernity* (Ithaca, NY: Cornell University Press, 2010).

61. See Barbara Whitehead's discussion of these influences in "The Singularity of Mme Du Châtelet: An Analysis of the *Discours sur le bonheur*," in *Émilie Du Châtelet: Rewriting Enlightenment Philosophy and Science*, ed. Judith P. Zinsser and Julie Candler Hayes (Oxford: Voltaire Foundation, 2006), 255–76.

62. Du Châtelet, *Discourse on Happiness*, in *Émilie Du Châtelet: Selected Philosophical and Scientific Writings*, ed. Judith P. Zinsser, trans. Isabelle Bour and Judith P. Zinsser (Chicago: University of Chicago Press, 2009), 349.

63. In a helpful and systematic article, Marcy P. Lascano illuminates the tensions running through Du Châtelet's seeming embrace of illusion in the *Discours sur le bonheur*. Lascano studies various categories of illusion in Du Châtelet, including illusions of the senses, illusions of the imagination, and illusions that may be said to be "of happiness" in the *Discours*. As Lascano points out, Du Châtelet does not wholeheartedly endorse an illusion without limits; instead, she sees reason and illusion as in relation to one another and self-determining. The key principle for Du Châtelet in the discussion of illusion in the *Discours* and elsewhere remains pleasure and, as Lascano puts it, "well-being." Reason can and should dispel certain illusions that we hold but others are profoundly linked to our happiness and need to be preserved as such. See Lascano, "Émilie Du Châtelet on Illusions," *Journal of the American Philosophical Association* 7, no. 1 (2021): 1–19.

64. Du Châtelet, *Discourse*, 349.

65. See Eric Schliesser's blog, "Digressions & Impressions," for his discussion of Du Châtelet's illusions: http://digressionsnimpressions.typepad.com/digressionsimpressions/2016/05/necessary-illusions-happy-on-du-ch%C3%A2telets-discourse.html.

66. Du Châtelet, *Discourse*, 349.
67. Du Châtelet, *Discourse*, 350.
68. Du Châtelet, *Discourse*, 350.
69. Du Châtelet, *Discourse*, 350.
70. Du Châtelet, *Discourse*, 354.
71. Du Châtelet, *Discourse*, 354–55.
72. Du Châtelet, *Discourse*, 355.
73. Du Châtelet, *Discourse*, 355.
74. Du Châtelet, *Discourse*, 357.

75. Du Châtelet, *Discourse*, 357.
76. Du Châtelet, *Discourse*, 357.
77. Du Châtelet, *Discourse*, 358.
78. Du Châtelet, *Discourse*, 358.
79. Du Châtelet, *Discourse*, 360.
80. Du Châtelet, *Discourse*, 360.
81. Du Châtelet, *Discourse*, 360. Judith P. Zinsser gives the source of this citation as Rochester's poem, "A Satire against Man," which appears to be a reference to his "Satyr against reason and mankind," probably written around 1674. But the lines that Du Châtelet cites do not feature in this work, which condemns rather than celebrates human nature.
82. Du Châtelet, *Discourse*, 361.
83. Du Châtelet, *Discourse*, 361.
84. Du Châtelet, *Discourse*, 362.
85. Du Châtelet, *Discourse*, 364.
86. Du Châtelet, *Discourse*, 363.
87. Du Châtelet, *Discourse*, 365.
88. Du Châtelet, *La Correspondance d'Émilie Du Châtelet*, 2 vols., ed. Ulla Kölving and Andrew Brown (Ferney-Voltaire, Centre international d'étude du XVIIIe siècle, 2018), II:1741–49, letter 553.
89. Du Châtelet, *La Correspondance*, II:1741–49, letter 652.
90. Du Châtelet, *Institutions de physique*, The Paris Ms, BnF Fr. 12265, in A Critical and Historical Online Edition (2021–2023), ed. Ruth E Hagengruber et al., chapter 10, version C, 180v/18: "pouroitil yavoir quelquun entieremt semblable amoi dans un autre monde?" Also ctd. in Hayes, *Reading the French Enlightenment*, 99.
91. Hayes, *Reading the French Enlightenment*, 99.

4. "I am, I live, I exist": Graffigny's Pleasure of Being

1. Madame de La Fayette as reported by Jean-Regnauld de Segrais: "C'est assez d'être."
2. Sara Ahmed, *Complaint!* (Durham, NC: Duke University Press, 2015), 25.
3. Chris Kraus, *Video Green: Los Angeles Art and The Triumph of Nothingness* (Cambridge, MA: The MIT Press, 2004), 62.
4. Gumport, "Female Trouble," N+1 13 (Winter 2012), https://www.nplusonemag.com/issue-13/reviews/female-trouble/. With the disappearance of *Lettres d'une Péruvienne* from bestseller lists by the end of the eighteenth century, Graffigny's novel once seemed to leave little philosophical imprint on its period, although assessments of the work's influence began to change with the reentry of the novel to the canon of French Enlightenment literature in the 1980s and 1990s, thanks in large part to the work of feminist critics and historians. For a critique of the long-standing tendency to view Graffigny's novel as "imitative" and "unoriginal," see Janet Altman's "Making Room for 'Peru': Graffigny's Novel Reconsidered," *Dilemmes du*

Roman: Essays in Honor of Georges May, ed. Catherine Lafarge et al. (Saratoga, CA: ANMA Libri, 1990), 33–46. Altman describes Graffigny's text as "a rigorous form of novelistic *Bildung*, anchored in the experiential and perceptual development of the heroine's body" (44). See also Altman's "A Woman's Place in the Enlightenment Sun: The Case of Françoise de Graffigny," *Romance Quarterly* 38, no. 3 (1991): 261–72. In this essay Altman argues for the need to make room—a "place"—for Graffigny in an Enlightenment canon from which her work had deliberately been excluded (a process starting after Graffigny's death in 1759 but culminating with the nineteenth century). Charlotte Daniels helpfully reopens the question of Graffigny's "modernity" in *Subverting the Family Romance: Women Writers, Kinship Structures, and the Early French Novel* (Lewisburg, PA: Bucknell University Press, 2000).

5. These are sets of knotted cords that were used by the Incans mainly for calculations and to record information. Graffigny takes obvious liberties with her description of the powers of the *quipus*, imbuing them with both sentimental and lyrical qualities.

6. Françoise de Graffigny, *Letters of a Peruvian Woman*, trans. Jonathan Mallinson (Oxford: Oxford University Press, 2009), 13.

7. Graffigny, *Letters*, 116.

8. Graffigny, *Letters*, 118.

9. Madeleine Dobie has a particularly incisive reading of the comparison that is often made between Graffigny's and Montesquieu's letters. Dobie emphasizes the open-endedness of Graffigny's language—and the relative determinacy of the novel's ending—as a way of countering readings that make of Graffigny a feminine response to Montesquieu's masculine point of origin. See Dobie's "'Langage inconnu': Montesquieu, Graffigny and the Writing of Exile," *Romanic Review* 87, no. 2 (March 1996): 209–24.

10. Still, it is important to note that Usbek and Rica leave Persia under a certain amount of duress, having made powerful enemies in the Persian court.

11. See Julia Simon on Zilia's transformation into property owner by the end of the novel. Simon affirms that Zilia both accepts Western systems of value and challenges them through the development of a "hybrid identity" that combines aspects of Peruvian and French culture. Simon, "On Collecting Culture in Graffigny: The Construction of an 'Authentic' 'Péruvienne,'" *The Eighteenth Century* 44, no. 1 (Spring 2003): 25–44.

12. Graffigny, *Letters*, 15.

13. Graffigny, *Letters*, 24.

14. See Heidi Bostic on Graffigny's deployment of images of light (and the sun, in particular) to signify women's pursuit of enlightenment through reason. See Bostic, "The Light of Reason in Graffigny's *Lettres d'une Péruvienne*," *Dalhousie French Studies* 63 (Summer 2003): 3–11. Aurora Wolfgang also discusses Graffigny's specific use of *antithèse* as a rhetorical figure associated with "moral order" in classical aesthetics (118). See Wolfgang, *Gender and Voice in the French Novel, 1730–1782* (London: Routledge, 2004).

15. Graffigny, *Letters*, 24.
16. Graffigny, *Letters*, 26.
17. See Dobie on this point,"Langage inconnu," 223. Dobie cites Gianni Nicoletti as a proponent of this view in his important critical edition.
18. Graffigny, *Letters*, 3.
19. In her chapter, "The Knot, the Letter, and the Book," from *Subject to Change*, Nancy K. Miller provides a magisterial reading of the "Avertissement" as performing a kind of displacement vis à vis both "glamorized 'feminine' suffering" and "the anti-conventional literature of the Enlightenment" (136). Miller reads the novel as "combining what in the century tended to remain separate, the *roman sentimental* and the *roman philosophique*, . . . and locating her subject of difference in writing and language—as opposed to in the seraglio—[Zilia] provides a figure of what female Enlightenment might mean" (136). See Miller, *Subject to Change: Reading Feminist Writing* (New York: Columbia University Press, 1988), 125–61.
20. This reliance resonates with Du Châtelet's effort to distinguish between illusion as a mode of perception and error as a form of falsehood.
21. In her article on *Lettres d'une Péruvienne*, Heidi Bostic carefully tracks Graffigny's (and Zilia's) attachment to reason as an instrument of social analysis that women may wield just as men do, while later on in her book *The Fiction of Enlightenment: Women of Reason in the French Eighteenth Century* (Newark: University of Delaware Press, 2010), Bostic convincingly follows Graffigny's commitment to the cultivation of enlightened rational inquiry through her other works, including her hugely successful play *Cénie* (originally staged in 1750 at the Comédie-Française) and the one-act *Phaza* (1753), which was never publicly produced. In her analysis of *Lettres*, Rachel Mesch highlights Graffigny's use of defamiliarization to render the values of *ancien régime* French society subject to criticism and revision. See Mesch, "Did Women Have an Enlightenment? Graffigny's Zilia as Female *Philosophe*," *Romanic Review* 89, no. 4 (November 1998): 523–37. As Mesch and Bostic both emphasize, reason consistently works for Zilia as a means of elucidating and analyzing the relation between the self and the social scene that this self inhabits and occupies, however ambivalently or hesitantly.
22. This oscillation is an important structural feature of the novel, one that Jonathan Mallinson expertly uncovers in the illustrations that accompanied the luxury 1752 edition overseen by Graffigny herself, who added two letters to the original—including the analysis of the French treatment of women in letter 34—and took a specific interest in the subjects to be illustrated. Mallinson gives a nuanced analysis of the contrast between two illustrations of the novel that appeared in this edition. Neither illustration, Mallinson argues, accurately anticipates the scenes that are still to come in the novel, thereby leaving both Zilia and the reader in a state of suspense—hesitating between contradictory interpretations of events. See Mallinson, "Re-présentant les *Lettres d'une Péruvienne* en 1752: illustration et illusion," *Eighteenth-Century Fiction* 15, no. 2 (January 2003): 227–39.

23. Robin Howells, *Regressive Fictions: Graffigny, Rousseau, Bernardin* (London: Routledge, 2007), 41.

24. *Lettres d'une Péruvienne* is regularly depicted as fusing together two seemingly antithetical genres, both coming into their own in the context of the Enlightenment: the *roman sentimental* and the *roman philosophique*. See Aurora Wolfgang on the formal and conceptual stakes of this opposition. Critics have also lingered productively on the uniqueness of the text, which is often presented as revealing the intellectual and critical potential that lies latent at the heart of a genre associated primarily with women. In her 2009 book on *Sensibility, Reading, and Illustration* (London: Routledge, 2009), Ann Lewis discusses how contemporary criticism has tended to shift focus away from the aspects of the novel that were considered most remarkable at the time of its publication—namely, Graffigny's "representation of feelings." Lewis notes, correctly to my mind, that modern critics are suspicious of the way in which the sentimental genre is too easily collapsed into a narrow treatment of love.

25. Dobie gives a very convincing critique of this approach to Graffigny, which she associates with the work of Altman and Duggan, in her article.

26. See English Showalter's *Françoise de Graffigny: Her Life and Works* (Oxford: Voltaire Foundation, 2004) for a rich and engaging biographical history, drawn in large part from Graffigny's extensive and wide-ranging correspondence. Showalter discusses Graffigny's participation in Mlle Quinault's salon in detail, along with her subsequent establishment of her own salon and her (successful) efforts to arrange Minette's marriage to Helvétius.

27. Graffigny, *Correspondance de Mme de Graffigny*, volume 5, ed. Judith Curtis (Oxford: Voltaire Foundation, 1997), 250.

28. Ctd. in English Showalter, *Françoise de Graffigny: Her Life and Works*, 323. The French original provides a better sense of the liveliness and verve of Graffigny's prose: "Je ne sais par quel hazard je m'avisai de nommer la metaphisique. Voila la corde qui fait danser tout le reste. Il parle, il ouvre son ame. Il me fait le resumé d'un livre qu'il va faire imprimer. Ah, quel livre! Lok n'est pas son decroteur. Le grand Lok, cet homme que jusqu'ici j'ai seul admiré, sera toujours grand, mais ce sera d'avoir indiqué ce que le Genie devoit dire. Son livre sera a portée de tout le monde par les details et l'adresse dont il est ecrit. Tout ce qu'il m'en a dit me le prouve comme si je l'avois lu."

29. John C. O'Neal has examined with nuance Graffigny's intervention in what he aptly names a sensationist aesthetics, with particular emphasis on her revisions of Condillac. O'Neal associates materialism with an emphasis on matter (rather than feeling or thought) as a determining cause of action, distinguishing between a sensationist commitment to "the sentient individual as the independent initiator of the movements entailed in the dynamic cognitive process" and a materialist insistence on matter itself as the origin of movement (200). I am interested throughout this book in the way in which femininity plays a specific role in animating matter and shaping feeling, thus cutting across the distinction that O'Neal so usefully sets out. Graffigny,

like Puisieux and Du Châtelet, takes up the question of pleasure from a position inflected by classical materialist (specifically Lucretian) ethics, without necessarily weighing in on the specific nature of matter itself. O'Neal also stresses the materialist critique of anthropocentrism, whereas sensationists, in his reading, remain humanists. O'Neal, *The Authority of Experience: Sensationist Theory in the French Enlightenment* (University Park: The University of Pennsylvania Press, 1996).

30. Graffigny, *Letters*, 117–18.

31. Jean-Jacques Rousseau, *Lettres morales*, in *Œuvres complètes*, Tome IV, ed. Bernard Gagnebin and Marcel Raymond (Paris: Gallimard, 1969), 1099.

32. Christophe Litwin, *Politiques de l'amour de soi: La Boétie, Montaigne et Pascal au démêlé* (Paris: Classiques Garnier, 2021), 174.

33. Graffigny, *Letters*, 102.

34. This more materialist (indeed, libertine) approach to the *sentiment de l'existence* is also not entirely absent from Rousseau, who was himself a close reader of Lucretius, but for him this feeling is more often positioned in relation to intellectual or psychological processes.

35. "Délicieux," in *Encyclopédie, ou Dictionnaire raisonné des sciences, des arts et des métiers*, vol. 4, ed. Denis Diderot et al. (Paris: Briasson, 1754), 784. Consulted in *Encyclopédie, ou dictionnaire raisonné des sciences, des arts et des métiers, etc.*, ed. Denis Diderot and Jean le Rond d'Alembert. University of Chicago: ARTFL Encyclopédie Project (Autumn 2022 Edition), ed. Robert Morrissey and Glenn Roe, http://encyclopedie.uchicago.edu/. For a close reading of this passage in the context of a larger presentation of the *sentiment de l'existence*, see Roland Mortier, "A propos du sentiment de l'existence chez Diderot et Rousseau : Notes sur un article de 'l'Encyclopédie,'" *Diderot Studies* 6 (1964): 184.

36. In his article on "Les avatars du 'sentiment de l'existence,' de Locke à Rousseau," J. S. Spink suggests a materialist genealogy for this feeling by including Cyrano de Bergerac in his account of the first two French authors to mention the *sentiment de l'existence* "comme concept et comme expression verbale," as Spink puts it (274). Bergerac writes of the capacity to "se sentir être" in *Les États et Empires de la Lune*. Could this narrative, one of the origins of science fiction, be an antecedent for Zilia's journey as well? See Spink, "Les avatars du 'sentiment de l'existence,' de Locke à Rousseau." *Dix-huitième siècle* 10 (1978): 269–98.

37. "Délicieux," 4:784.

38. Graffigny, *Letters*, 114.

39. Graffigny, *Letters*, 114.

40. Graffigny, *Letters*, 115.

41. Graffigny, *Letters*, 26.

42. Graffigny, *Letters*, 17.

43. Graffigny, *Letters*, 17.

44. Graffigny, *Letters*, 16–18.

45. Graffigny, *Letters*, 19–20.

46. Graffigny, *Letters*, 23.

47. Graffigny, *Letters*, 23.
48. Graffigny, *Letters*, 23.
49. Graffigny, *Letters*, 23.
50. Graffigny, *Letters*, 40.
51. Graffigny, *Letters*, 41.
52. Graffigny, *Letters*, 41.
53. Graffigny, *Letters*, 41. Rachel Mesch also discusses this moment in her article on Zilia as philosopher. For Mesch as well, the illusion of possession is a dangerous one. As Mesch writes, "Without access to the sociolect in which the mechanisms of power are couched within familiar and non-threatening terms, Zilia penetrates the psychological effects of the world view that authorizes and motivates the French voice. Although she temporarily delights in seeing from this position, Zilia cannot help but note its dangerous error. The sensation of omnipotence she experiences is countered by an implicit reminder that the French pleasures of possessing the universe are a threat to her Peruvian heritage" (530). I would add here that the pleasure of possession also plays a role in Zilia's negotiation of her relationship to Aza; it is not exclusively French. Still, it is as a Peruvian woman that Zilia practices a form of love and social connection in which her history of dispossession is recognized and the desire to consume and control finds a counter.
54. Graffigny, *Letters*, 41.
55. Graffigny, *Letters*, 42.
56. Graffigny, *Letters*, 42.
57. Graffigny, *Letters*, 38.
58. Graffigny, *Letters*, 39.
59. Graffigny, *Letters*, 33.
60. Lucretius, *On the Nature of Things*, trans. W. H. D. Rouse, rev. Martin F. Smith, Loeb Classical Library 181 (Cambridge, MA: Harvard University Press, 1924), book 4, 361–63, lines 1091–1104.
61. Lucretius, *On the Nature of Things*, book 4, 363, lines 1121–24.
62. Graffigny, *Letters*, 41.
63. Lucretius, *On the Nature of Things*, book 4, 371, lines 1207–8.
64. Graffigny, *Letters*, 42.
65. Graffigny, *Letters*, 99.
66. Graffigny, *Letters*, 98.
67. Graffigny, *Letters*, 98.
68. Graffigny, *Letters*, 102.
69. Graffigny, *Letters*, 102.
70. For a nuanced discussion of the fact that Incan culture does not recognize private property, and Zilia's ambivalent assumption of her role as a European property owner, see Simon, "On Collecting Culture in Graffigny."
71. Graffigny, *Letters*, 102.
72. Donatien Alphonse François de Sade, *La Philosophie dans le boudoir*, vol. 2 (Londres, 1795), 113.

73. Sade, *La Philosophie dans le boudoir*, vol. 2, 116.
74. Graffigny, *Letters*, 112.
75. Graffigny, *Letters*, 113.
76. Graffigny, *Letters*, 114–15.
77. Graffigny, *Letters*, 115–16.
78. Graffigny, *Letters*, 118.
79. For a brilliant examination of the relationship between sentimentalism writ large and empire, see Lynn Festa's *Sentimental Figures of Empire in Eighteenth-Century Britain and France* (Baltimore, MD: The Johns Hopkins University Press, 2006).

Postscriptum: Olympe de Gouges chez Ninon

1. Olympe de Gouges, *Molière chez Ninon, ou le Siècle des grands hommes, pièce épisodique, en prose et en cinq actes* (Paris: Chez l'auteur, rue & Place du Théâtre François, 1788).
2. *Journal encyclopédique ou universel*, Année 1788, Tome VI, Partie I (Bouillon: De l'Imprimerie du Journal, 1788), 68.
3. Gouges, *Molière chez Ninon*, 3.
4. The eighteenth century witnessed the development of the myth of Ninon de Lenclos (born in 1623 as Anne de Lenclos) as a figure of sexual and intellectual refinement and emancipation. Most of the accounts of her life from this period are marked by the inclusion of apocryphal anecdotes and inaccurate biographical details, including those concerning her parentage and birth. In writing this postscriptum, I have benefited not only from the work of established scholars including Gregory Brown, Roger Duchêne (whose biography of Ninon de Lenclos remains an important reference), and Sophie Houdard but from the master's thesis of Martine Hardy on Ninon de Lenclos and the online critical edition of *Molière chez Ninon* developed by Céline Grihard as part of a *Mémoire de master*.
5. Sophie Houdard, in an excellent article on Lenclos, explores the way in which Lenclos is represented as presiding over a society of libertine men, for whom she facilitates the transmission of a free-thinking philosophy (even though she does not herself generate this philosophy). As Houdard discusses, for both seventeenth- and eighteenth-century interlocutors Ninon's ability to participate in a male culture of erudite and witty critique was an index of her incipient masculinity. See Houdard's "Ninon de Lenclos, esprit fort dans la compagnie des hommes ou de la difficulté de concevoir *la* maître de philosophie," *Les Dossiers du Grihl* 4 (2010).
6. Gouges, *Molière chez Ninon*, 5.
7. Gouges, *Molière chez Ninon*, 5.
8. The epigram reads as follows: "On ne verra de cent lustres / Ce que de nostre temps nous a fait voir Ninon, / Qui s'est mise en dépit du con, / Au nombre des hommes illustres" (ctd. in Houdard, "Ninon de Lenclos").

9. Ninon was referred to as a "modern Leontion" in d'Alembert's *Encyclopédie* article "Courtisane" and her salon is a key point of reference for Diderot's description of Epicureanism—where her gathering place at the rue de Tournelles is described as "La plus ancienne & la premiere de ces écoles où l'on ait pratiqué & professé la morale d'*Epicure*." See Jean-Baptiste le Rond d'Alembert, "Courtisane," in *Encyclopédie, ou Dictionnaire raisonné des sciences, des arts et métiers*, ed. Denis Diderot et al., vol. 4 (Paris: Briasson, 1754), 401 and "Épicuréisme ou épicurisme," in *Encyclopédie, ou Dictionnaire raisonné des sciences, des arts et des métiers*, ed. Denis Diderot et al., vol. 5 (Paris: Briasson, 1755), 779–85. Consulted in *Encyclopédie, ou dictionnaire raisonné des sciences, des arts et des métiers, etc.*, ed. Denis Diderot and Jean le Rond d'Alembert. University of Chicago: ARTFL Encyclopédie Project (Autumn 2022 Edition), ed. Robert Morrissey and Glenn Roe, http://encyclopedie.uchicago.edu/.

10. For a fine discussion of Olympe de Gouges's use of print as a medium to craft a public (and private) self, see Gregory S. Brown's article, "The Self-Fashionings of Olympe de Gouges, 1784–1789," *Eighteenth-Century Studies* 34, no. 3 (Spring 2001): 383–401. Brown focuses in particular on Gouges's play originally entitled *Zamore et Mirza, ou l'Heureux naufrage* (1788) and later reprinted as *L'Esclavage des noirs, ou l'Heureux naufrage* (1792), which have contributed to the contemporary sense of Gouges as a champion of liberty specifically for enslaved Black people. Brown is interested in abolitionism as part of a public identity that Gouges deliberately takes on over time.

11. Gouges, *Molière chez Ninon*, 176.

12. Gouges, *Molière chez Ninon*, 176.

13. Gouges, *Molière chez Ninon*, 177.

14. Gouges, *Molière chez Ninon*, 177.

15. Gouges, *Molière chez Ninon*, 147.

16. For her part, Ninon suggests that Desyveteaux's madness needs to be respected as contributing to his happiness, and that it is in remaining faithful to himself precisely in his "folie" that his friends might eventually sweetly bring him close to reality.

17. In certain ways, Ninon's seventeenth-century Epicurean community as Gouges portrays it anticipates and echoes the "queer families" that Tracy Rutler has unearthed in eighteenth-century French literature.

18. Gouges, *Molière chez Ninon*, 192,

19. Gouges, *Molière chez Ninon*, 192.

20. Houdard, "Ninon de Lenclos," n.p.

21. Looking forward, this history might also include authors and activists like Frances Wright (1795–1852), a Scottish-born feminist and abolitionist whose *A Few Days in Athens, Being the Translation of a Greek Manuscript Discovered in Herculaneum* (1822) sympathetically explores Epicureanism.

Bibliography

Primary Sources

Alembert, Jean-Baptiste le Rond d'. "Courtisane." In *Encyclopédie, ou Dictionnaire raisonné des sciences, des arts et métiers.* Vol. 4. Edited by Denis Diderot et al. Paris: Briasson, 1754.

Algarotti, Francesco. *Il Newtonianismo per le dame, ovvero dialoghi sopra la luce e i colori.* Napoli [Venice]: n.p., 1737.

Batteux, Charles. *La Morale d'Épicure, tirée de ses propres écrits.* Paris: Desaint et Saillant, 1758.

Boyer d'Argens, Jean-Baptiste de. *Thérèse philosophe, ou mémoires pour servir à l'histoire du P. Dirrag et de mademoiselle Eradice.* In *Romanciers libertins du XVIIIe siècle.* Tome 1. Edited by Patrick Wald Lasowski with Alain Clerval, Marcel Hénaff, and Pierre Saint-Amand. Paris: Gallimard, 2000.

Cavendish, Margaret. "Of Fire and Flame." In *Poems, and Fancies Written by the Right Honourable, the Lady Margaret Newcastle.* London: Printed by T. R. for J. Martin, and J. Allestrye, 1653.

——. *The Blazing World and Other Writings.* Edited by Kate Lilley. New York: Penguin Books, 1994.

Choderlos de Laclos, Pierre Ambroise. *Les Liaisons dangereuses.* In *Œuvres complètes.* Edited by Laurent Versini. Paris: Gallimard, 1998.

Crébillon, Claude Prosper Jolyot de. *Les Égarements du cœur et de l'esprit.* In *Œuvres complètes*, Vol. II. Edited by Jean Sgard. Paris: Classiques Garnier, 2000 [online edition 2010].

——. *Le Sopha.* In *Œuvres complètes*, Vol. II. Edited by Jean Sgard. Paris: Classiques Garnier, 2000 [online edition 2010].

——. *Le Sylphe, ou Songe de Mme de R*** écrit par elle-même à Mme de S***.* Edited by Carmen Ramirez. In *Œuvres complètes*, Vol. I. Edited by Jean Sgard. Paris: Classiques Garnier, 1999 [online edition 2010].

——. *Tanzaï et Néadarné*, ou *L'Écumoire*. Edited by Jean Sgard. In *Œuvres complètes*, Vol. I. Edited by Jean Sgard. Paris: Classiques Garnier, 1999 [online edition 2010].

Cyrano de Bergerac, Savinien de. *L'Autre Monde: Les États et Empires de la Lune; Les États et Empires du Soleil*. Edited by Jacques Prévot. Paris: Folio, 2004.

Deleuze, Gilles, and Félix Guattari. *A Thousand Plateaus: Capitalism and Schizophrenia*. Translated by Brian Massumi. Minneapolis: University of Minnesota Press, 1987.

Desmahis, Joseph François Edouard de Corsembleu. "Femme (Morale)." In *Encyclopédie, ou Dictionnaire raisonné des sciences, des arts et des métiers*. Vol. 6. Edited by Diderot et al. Paris: Briasson, 1756.

Diderot, Denis. *Les Bijoux indiscrets*. In *Œuvres*. Edited by André Billy. Paris: Gallimard, 1951.

——. "Délicieux." In *Encyclopédie, ou Dictionnaire raisonné des sciences, des arts et métiers*, Vol. 4. Edited by Denis Diderot et al. Paris: Briasson, 1754.

——. *Éléments de physiologie*. In *Œuvres complètes*, Vol. 17. Edited by Jean Varloot with Michel Delon, Georges Dulac, and Jean Mayer. Paris: Hermann, 1987.

——. "Épicuréisme ou épicurisme." In *Encyclopédie, ou Dictionnaire raisonné des sciences, des arts et métiers*, Vol. 5. Edited by Denis Diderot et al. Paris: Briasson, 1755.

——. *Essai sur les règnes de Claude et de Néron*. Edited by Jean Deprun, Jean Ehrard, Annette Lorenceau, and Raymond Trousson. In *Œuvres complètes*, Vol. 25. Edited by Herbert Dieckmann, Jacques Proust, Jean Varloot et al. Paris: Hermann, 1986.

——. *Pensées sur l'interprétation de la nature*. Edited by Colas Duflo. Paris: Éditions Flammarion, 2005.

——. *La Religieuse*. In *Œuvres*. Edited by André Billy. Paris: Gallimard, 1951.

——. *Rêve de d'Alembert*. In *Œuvres*. Edited by André Billy. Paris: Gallimard, 1951.

——. *Sur les femmes*. In *Œuvres*. Edited by André Billy. Paris: Gallimard, 1951.

Du Châtelet, Gabrielle-Émilie Le Tonnelier de Breteuil. *La Correspondance d'Émilie du Châtelet*. 2 Vols. Edited by Ulla Kölving and Andrew Brown. Ferney-Voltaire: Centre international d'étude du XVIIIe siècle, 2018.

——. *Discours sur le bonheur*. In *L'art de vivre d'une femme au XVIIIe siècle*. Edited by Robert Mauzi. Paris: Les Éditions Desjonquères, 2008.

——. *Discourse on Happiness*. In *Émilie Du Châtelet: Selected Philosophical and Scientific Writings*. Edited by Judith P. Zinsser. Translated by Isabelle Bour and Judith P. Zinsser. Chicago: University of Chicago Press, 2009.

——. *Dissertation sur la nature et la propagation du feu*. Paris: Chez Prault fils, 1744.

——. *Institutions de physique*. The Paris Ms. BnF Fr. 12265. In *A Critical and Historical Online Edition (2021–2023)*. Edited by Ruth E Hagengruber, Hanns-Peter Neumann, Jil Muller, and Aaron Wells, chapter 10, version C. https://historyofwomenphilosophers.org/dcpm/documents

———. *Institutions de physique*. Paris: Chez Prault fils, 1740.

———. "Mme du Châtelet's Translation of the *Fable of the Bees*." In *Studies on Voltaire, With Some Unpublished Papers of Mme. du Châtelet*. Edited by Ira O. Wade. Princeton, NJ: Princeton University Press, 1947.

Encyclopédie, ou dictionnaire raisonné des sciences, des arts et des métiers, etc. Edited by Denis Diderot and Jean le Rond d'Alembert. University of Chicago: ARTFL Encyclopédie Project (Autumn 2022 Edition), ed. Robert Morrissey and Glenn Roe, http://encyclopedie.uchicago.edu/.

Fontenelle, Bernard Le Bovier de. *Du bonheur*. Edited by Isabelle Mullet. In <u>*Digression sur les Anciens et les Modernes*</u> *et autres textes philosophiques*. Edited by Sophie Audidière. Paris: Classiques Garnier, 2015.

"Génie." In *Encyclopédie, ou Dictionnaire raisonné des sciences, des arts et des métiers*. Vol. 7 Edited by Denis Diderot et al. Paris: Briasson, 1757.

Goncourt, Edmond, and Jules de. *La Femme au XVIIIe siècle*. Paris: Librairie Firmin Didot Frères, 1862.

Gouges, Olympe de. *Molière chez Ninon, ou le Siècle des grands hommes, pièce épisodique, en prose et en cinq actes*. Paris: Chez l'auteur, rue & Place du Théâtre François, 1788.

———. *Molière chez Ninon*. Édition critique établie par Céline Grihard dans le cadre d'un mémoire de master. Dir. Georges Forestier. 2013–2014.

Graffigny, Françoise de. *Cenie, pièce en cinq actes, représentée pour la première fois par les Comédiens François Ordinaires du Roi, le 25 Juin 1750*. Cailleau: Paris, 1751.

———. *Correspondance de Mme de Graffigny*. Vol. 1. Edited by J. A. Dainard, English Showalter et al. Oxford: Voltaire Foundation, 1985.

———. *Correspondance de Mme de Graffigny*. Vol. 5. Edited by Judith Curtis. Oxford: Voltaire Foundation, 1997.

———. *Lettres d'une Péruvienne*. Edited by Joan DeJean. New York: Modern Language Association of America, 1994.

———. *Letters of a Peruvian Woman*. Translated by Jonathan Mallinson. Oxford: Oxford University Press, 2009.

Helvétius, Claude-Adrien. *Le Bonheur*. Presented by Michel Onfray. Paris: Éditions Michalon, 2006.

Holbach, Paul Thiry d'. *Système de la nature*. 2 vols. Paris: Librairie Arthème Fayard, 1990–1991.

———. *Théologie portative ou dictionnaire abrégé de la religion chrétienne. Par M. L'Abbé Bernier. Liciencié en Théologie*. London [Amsterdam]: M. M. Rey, 1768 [1767].

Jaucourt, Louis de. "Penchant, Inclination." In *Encyclopédie, ou Dictionnaire raisonné des sciences, des arts et des métiers*. Vol. 8. Edited by Denis Diderot et al. Neufchastel: Samuel Faulche & Compagnie, 1765.

Journal encyclopédique ou universel. Année 1788. Tome VI. Partie I. Bouillon: De l'Imprimerie du Journal, 1788.

Laertius, Diogenes. *Lives of Eminent Philosophers*. Vol. 1: Books 1–5. Translated by Robert Drew Hicks. Loeb Classical Library 184. Cambridge, MA: Harvard University Press, 1925.

La Mettrie, Julien Offray de. *Anti-Sénèque ou le souverain bien*. In *De la volupté*. Edited by Ann Thomson. Paris: Les Éditions Desjonquères, 1996.

———. *L'École de la volupté*. In *De la volupté*. Edited by Ann Thomson. Paris: Les Éditions Desjonquères, 1996.

———. *L'Homme-machine*. In *Œuvres philosophiques*. Vol. 1. Edited by Francine Markovits. Paris: Librairie Arthème Fayard, 1987.

———. *Histoire Naturelle de l'Ame, traduit de l'Anglais de M. Charp*. Oxford: Aux dépens de l'auteur, 1747.

———. *L'Homme-plante*. In *Œuvres philosophiques*. Vol. 1. Edited by Francine Markovits. Paris: Librairie Arthème Fayard, 1987.

———. *Supplément à l'Ouvrage de Pénélope; ou Machiavel en Médecine*. Vol. 3. Berlin, 1750.

———. *Système d'Épicure*. In *De la volupté*. Edited by Ann Thomson. Paris: Les Éditions Desjonquères, 1996.

———. *La Volupté*. In *Œuvres philosophiques*. Vol. 2. Edited by Francine Markovits. Paris: Librairie Arthème Fayard, 1987.

La Mothe Le Vayer, François de. *De la vertu des payens*. Paris: Augustin Courbé, 1647.

Lucrèce. *De la nature=De rerum natura*. Translated by José Kany-Turpin. Paris: GF Flammarion, 1998.

Lucretius. *On the Nature of Things*. Translated by W. H. D. Rouse. Revised by Martin F. Smith. Loeb Classical Library 181. Cambridge, MA: Harvard University Press, 1924.

Maupertuis, Pierre Louis Moreau de. *Essai de philosophie morale*. Berlin, 1749.

Montaigne. "Que philosopher, c'est apprendre à mourir." In *Œuvres complètes*. Edited by Albert Thibaudet and Maurice Rat, Book I, chapter 20. Paris: Gallimard, 1962.

Montesquieu, Charles-Louis de Secondat de. *Lettres persanes*. Edited by Laurent Versini. Paris: Flammarion, 2019.

———. *Persian Letters*. Translated by Margaret Mauldon. New York: Oxford University Press, 2008.

———. *Le Temple de Gnide, nouvelle édition avec figures gravées par N. Le Mire*. Paris: Chez le Mire Graveur, 1772.

———. *Édition critique des Pensées de Montesquieu*. Edited by Carole Dornier. Caen: Presses universitaires de Caen, 2013. [Online], pensée 1062, http://www.unicaen.fr/services/puc/sources/Montesquieu/ [consulted on June 12, 2023].

Plutarch. *Moralia*. Vol. 14. *That Epicurus Actually Makes a Pleasant Life Impossible. Reply to Colotes in Defence of the Other Philosophers. Is "Live Unknown" a Wise Precept? On Music*. Translated by Benedict Einarson and Phillip H. De Lacy. Loeb Classical Library 428. Cambridge, MA: Harvard University Press, 1967.

Puisieux, Madeleine de. "Aux Plaisirs." In *Œuvres de Madame de P****. 1746–1747 [manuscript]. http://archivesetmanuscrits.bnf.fr/ark:/12148/cc45749f.

———. *Les Caractères. Par madame de Puisieux*. Londres, 1750.

———. *Céphise, conte moral*. In *Œuvres de Madame de P****. 1746–1747 [manuscript]. http://archivesetmanuscrits.bnf.fr/ark:/12148/cc45749f.
———. *L'Éducation du marquis de ***, ou Mémoires de la comtesse de Zurlac*. 2 vols. Berlin: Chez Bauche, 1753.
———. "L'Hiver," "Le Printems," and "Bouquet." In *Œuvres de Madame de P****. 1746–1747 [manuscript]. http://archivesetmanuscrits.bnf.fr/ark:/12148/cc45749f.
———. *Le Plaisir et la volupté, conte allégorique*. A Paphos, 1752.
———. *Prospectus sur un ouvrage important, par Mme de Puisieux*. Paris: Nicolas-François Valleyre jeune, 1772.
———. *Réflexions et avis sur les défauts et ridicules à la mode, pour servir de suite aux Conseils à une amie*. Paris: V. Brunet, 1761.
Robertson, Lisa. *Debbie: An Epic*. Vancouver: New Star Books, 1997.
Rousseau, Jean-Jacques. *Lettre à d'Alembert*. Edited by Marc Buffat. Paris: Flammarion, 2003.
———. *Letter to M. d'Alembert on the Theatre*. In *Politics and the Arts: Letter to M. d'Alembert on the Theatre*. Edited and translated by Allan Bloom. Ithaca, NY: Cornell University Press, 1968.
———. *Lettres morales*. In *Œuvres complètes*, Tome IV. Edited by Bernard Gagnebin and Marcel Raymond. Paris: Gallimard, 1969.
Sade, Donatien Alphonse François de. *La Philosophie dans le boudoir*. 2 vols. Londres, 1795.
Saint-Évrémond, Charles de Marquetel de. "Sur les opéra, à Monsieur le duc de Bouquinquant." In *Œuvres en prose*. Vol. 3. Edited by René Ternois. Paris: Librairie Marcel Didier, 1966.
Seneca. *Moral Essays*. Vol 2. *De Consolatione ad Marciam. De Vita Beata. De Otio. De Tranquillitate Animi. De Brevitate Vitae. De Consolatione ad Polybium. De Consolatione ad Helviam*. Translated by John W. Basore. Loeb Classical Library 254. Cambridge, MA: Harvard University Press, 1932.
Voltaire. *Alzire, ou les Américains, Tragédie de M. de Voltaire, représentée à Paris pour la première fois le 27 janvier 1736*. Paris: Jean-Baptiste-Claude Bauche, 1736.
———. *Élémens de la philosophie de Newton, mis à la portée de tout le monde par Mr de Voltaire*. Amsterdam: Etienne Ledet, 1738.
———. "Le Mondain." In *Mélanges*. Edited by Jacques van den Heuvel. Paris: Gallimard, 1961.
"Volupté." In *Encyclopédie, ou Dictionnaire raisonné des sciences, des arts et métiers*. Vol. 17. Edited by Denis Diderot et al. Neufchastel: Samuel Faulche, 1765.
Wright, Frances. *A Few Days in Athens, Being the Translation of a Greek Manuscript Discovered in Herculaneum*. New York: G. W. & A. J. Matsell, 1835.

Secondary Sources

Ahmed, Sara. *Complaint!* Durham, NC: Duke University Press, 2015.
Aleksić, Branko. "Casanova, à l'école buissonnière d'Épicure." In *Dix-huitième Siècle. L'épicurisme des Lumières* 35 (2003). Edited by Anne Deneys-Tunney and Pierre-François Moreau: 241–52.

Altman, Janet Gurkin. "A Woman's Place in the Enlightenment Sun: The Case of Françoise de Graffigny." *Romance Quarterly* 38, no. 3 (1991): 261–72.

———. "Making Room for 'Peru': Graffigny's Novel Reconsidered." In *Dilemmes du Roman: Essays in Honor of Georges May*. Edited by Catherine Lafarge et al. Saratoga, CA: ANMA Libri, 1990.

Anderson, Holly K. "Blazing: Du Châtelet as Central to the First Paradigm in Newtonian Mechanics." In *The Bloomsbury Handbook of Du Châtelet*. Edited by Fatima Amijee. London: Bloomsbury Academic, forthcoming.

Aravamudan, Srinivas. *Enlightenment Orientalism: Resisting the Rise of the Novel*. Chicago: University of Chicago Press, 2011.

Arenson, Kelly. "Ancient Women Epicureans and Their Anti-Hedonist Critics." In *Ancient Women Philosophers: Recovered Ideas and New Perspectives*. Edited by Katharine O'Reilly and Caterina Pellò. Cambridge: Cambridge University Press, 2023.

Barthes, Roland. *La Préparation du roman: Cours au Collège de France (1978–1979 et 1979–1980)*. Edited by Nathalie Léger and Éric Marty. Paris: Éditions du Seuil, 2015.

Benharrech, Sarah. "Botanical Palimpsests, or Erasure of Women in Science: The Case Study of Mme Dugage de Pommereul (1733–1782)." *Harvard Papers in Botany* 23, no. 1 (2018): 89–108.

Bérenguier, Nadine. *Conduct Books for Girls in Enlightenment France*. Farnham: Ashgate Publishing, 2011.

———. "Madeleine d'Arsant de Puisieux." In *Writers of the French Enlightenment II*. Edited by Samia I. Spencer. Dictionary of Literary Biography. Vol. 314. Detroit, MI: Gale, 2005. Gale Literature Resource Center (accessed September 14, 2021).

Bernier, Marc-André. *Libertinage et figures du savoir: Rhétorique et roman libertin dans la France des Lumières (1734–1751)*. Québec: Presses de l'Université Laval, 2001.

Black, Moishe. "Lucretius Tells Diderot: Here's the Plan." *Diderot Studies* 28 (2000): 39–58.

———. "Lucretius's Venus Meets Diderot." *Diderot Studies* 27 (1998): 29–44.

Blanc, Olivier. *Les libertines: Plaisir et liberté au temps des Lumières*. Paris: Librairie Académique Perrin, 1997.

Bostic, Heidi. *The Fiction of Enlightenment: Women of Reason in the French Eighteenth Century*. Newark: University of Delaware Press, 2010.

———. "The Light of Reason in Graffigny's *Lettres d'une Péruvienne*." *Dalhousie French Studies* 63 (Summer 2003): 3–11.

Brading, Katherine. "Émilie Du Châtelet and the Problem of Bodies." In *Early Modern Women on Metaphysics*. Edited by Emily Thomas. Cambridge: Cambridge University Press, 2018.

Brown, Gregory S. "The Self-Fashionings of Olympe de Gouges, 1784–1789." *Eighteenth-Century Studies* 34, no. 3 (spring 2001): 383–401.

Carocci, Renata. *Les Héroïdes dans la seconde moitié du dix-huitième siècle (1758–1788)*. Fasano: Nizet, 1988.
Casanova: The Seduction of Europe. Edited by Frederick Ilchman, Thomas Michie, C. D. Dickerson III, and Esther Bell. Boston: MFA Publications, Museum of Fine Arts, Boston, 2017.
Caviglia-Brunel, Susanna. *History, Painting, and the Seriousness of Pleasure in the Age of Louis XV*. Oxford: Liverpool University Press, 2020.
Cheek, Pamela. *Sexual Antipodes: Enlightenment Globalization and the Placing of Sex*. Stanford, CA: Stanford University Press, 2003.
Chu, Andrea Long. *Females*. London: Verso Books, 2019.
Clark, Andrew H. *Diderot's Part*. New York: Routledge, 2008.
Coats, Catherine Randall. "Writing Like a Woman: Gender Transformation in Montaigne's *Journal de Voyage*." *Montaigne Studies* 5 (1992): 207–18.
Cryle, Peter. *La Crise du plaisir, 1740–1830*. Lille: Septentrion, 2003.
Cusset, Catherine. *No Tomorrow: The Ethics of Pleasure in the French Enlightenment*. Charlottesville: University Press of Virginia, 1999.
Daniels, Charlotte. *Subverting the Family Romance: Women Writers, Kinship Structures, and the Early French Novel*. Lewisburg, PA: Bucknell University Press, 2000.
DeJean, Joan. *Ancients Against Moderns: Culture Wars and the Making of a Fin de Siècle*. Chicago: University of Chicago Press, 1997.
———. Review of *The Other Enlightenment: How French Women Became Modern*, by Carla Hesse. *The Journal of Modern History* 75, no. 4, (2003): 958–60.
———. *Tender Geographies: Women and the Origins of the Novel in France*. New York: Columbia University Press, 1991.
deLire, Luce. "Nature is a Transsexual Woman: Lucretian Metaphysics Reconsidered." *Classical Philology* 19, no. 2 (2024): 203–33.
Delon, Michel. *Le Principe de délicatesse: Libertinage et mélancolie au XVIIIe siècle*. Paris: Albin Michel, 2011.
Dobie, Madeleine. *Foreign Bodies: Gender, Language, and Culture in French Orientalism*. Stanford, CA: Stanford University Press, 2001.
———. "'Langage inconnu': Montesquieu, Graffigny and the Writing of Exile." *Romanic Review* 87, no. 2 (March 1996): 209–24.
Duchêne, Roger. *Ninon de Lenclos, la courtisane du Grand Siècle*. Paris: Fayard, 1984.
Dufallo, Basil. *Disorienting Empire: Republican Latin Poetry's Wanderers*. Oxford: Oxford University Press, 2021.
Dujour, Florence. *Le Fil de Marianne: Narrer au féminin, de Villedieu à Diderot*. Paris: Garnier, 2021.
Fauchery, Pierre. *La Destinée féminine dans le roman européen du dix-huitième siècle, essai de gynécomythie romanesque*. Paris: Armand Colin, 1972.
Femmes et libertinage au XVIIIème siècle ou les Caprices de Cythère. Edited by Anne Richardot. Rennes: Presses universitaires de Rennes, 2003.

Ferrand, Nathalie. "'C'est en habits d'homme qu'une femme peut philosopher': figures féminines du philosophe dans *Thérèse philosophe* et *La Filosofessa italiana*." In *La figure du philosophe dans les lettres anglaises et françaises* [online]. Edited by Alexis Tadié. Nanterre: Presses universitaires de Paris Nanterre, 2010, generated June 30, 2023.

Festa, Lynn. *Sentimental Figures of Empire in Eighteenth-Century Britain and France*. Baltimore, MD: The Johns Hopkins University Press, 2006.

Foucault, Michel. *The History of Sexuality*. Vol. 1. *An Introduction*. Translated by Robert Hurley. New York: Pantheon Books, 1978.

Garnier, Camille. "'La Femme n'est pas inférieure à l'homme' (1750): Œuvre de Madeleine Darsant de Puisieux ou simple traduction française?" *Revue d'histoire littéraire de la France* 87, no. 4 (1987): 709–13.

Garraway, Doris. *The Libertine Colony: Creolization in the Early French Caribbean*. Durham, NC: Duke University Press, 2005.

Gelbart, Nina Rattner. *Minerva's French Sisters: Women of Science in Enlightenment France*. New Haven, CT: Yale University Press, 2021.

Giovacchini, Julie. "Sexual Freedom and Feminine Pleasure in Lucretius." In *Women's Perspectives on Ancient and Medieval Philosophy*. Edited by Isabelle Chouinard, Zoe McConaughey, Aline Medeiros Ramos, and Roxane Noël. Berlin: Springer Verlag, 2021.

Girten, Kristin M. *Sensitive Witnesses: Feminist Materialism in the British Enlightenment*. Stanford, CA: Stanford University Press, 2024.

Galfelder, Hal. "Machines in Love: Bodies, Souls, and Sexes in the Age of La Mettrie." *Eighteenth-Century Fiction* 27, no. 1 (Fall 2014): 55–81.

Gargam, Adéline. *Les Femmes savantes, lettrées et cultivées dans la littérature française des Lumières ou la conquête d'une légitimité (1690–1804)*, 2 vols. Paris: Honoré Champion, 2013.

Goldstein, Amanda Jo. *Sweet Science: Romantic Materialism and the New Logics of Life*. Chicago: University of Chicago Press, 2017.

Gordon, Pamela. *The Invention and Gendering of Epicurus*. Ann Arbor: University of Michigan Press, 2012.

Gottmann, Felicia. "Du Châtelet, Voltaire, and the Transformation of Mandeville's Fable." *History of European Ideas* 38, no. 2 (2012): 218–32.

Green, Karen. *A History of Women's Political Thought in Europe, 1700–1800*. Cambridge: Cambridge University Press, 2014.

Greenblatt, Stephen. *The Swerve: How the World Became Modern*. New York: W. W. Norton, 2011.

Gumport, Elizabeth. "Female Trouble." *N+1* 13 (Winter 2012). https://www.nplusonemag.com/issue-13/reviews/female-trouble/.

Gutwirth, Madelyn. *Twilight of the Goddesses*. New Brunswick, NJ: Rutgers University Press, 1992.

Hagengruber, Ruth. "Émilie du Châtelet, 1706–1749: Transformer of Metaphysics and Scientist." *The Mathematical Intelligencer* 38, no. 4 (December 2016): 1–6.

---. "Émilie du Châtelet Between Leibniz and Newton: The Transformation of Metaphysics." In *Émilie du Châtelet Between Leibniz and Newton*. Edited by Ruth Hagengruber. Dordrecht: Springer, 2012.

Hardy, Martine. *Ninon de Lenclos (1623–1705), le parcours d'une libertine au XVIIe siècle*. Mémoire présenté à la Faculté des études supérieures et postdoctorales en vue de l'obtention du grade de maître ès art en histoire. Université de Montréal. August 2011.

Hayes, Julie Candler. *Women Moralists in Early Modern France*. New York: Oxford University Press, 2023.

---. *Reading the French Enlightenment: System and Subversion*. Cambridge: Cambridge University Press, 1999.

Hesse, Carla. *The Other Enlightenment: How French Women Became Modern*. Princeton, NJ: Princeton University Press, 2001.

Hobson, Marian. *The Object of Art: The Theory of Illusion in Eighteenth-Century France*. Cambridge: Cambridge University Press, 1982.

---. "Philosophy and Rococo style (2002)." In *Diderot and Rousseau: Networks of Enlightenment*. Edited by Kate E. Tunstall and Caroline Warman, 203–12. Oxford: Voltaire Foundation, 2011.

Hock, Jessie. *The Erotics of Materialism: Lucretius and Early Modern Poetics*. Philadelphia: University of Pennsylvania Press, 2021.

Hoffmann, Paul. *La Femme dans la pensée des Lumières*. Geneva: Éditions Slatkine, 1995.

Houdard, Sophie. "Ninon de Lenclos, esprit fort dans la compagnie des hommes ou de la difficulté de concevoir *la* maître de philosophie." *Les Dossiers du Grihl* 4 (2010).

Howells, Robin. *Regressive Fictions: Graffigny, Rousseau, Bernardin*. London: Routledge, 2007.

Hundert, E. J. "Bernard de Mandeville and the Enlightenment's Maxims of Modernity." *Journal of the History of Ideas* 56, no. 4 (1995): 577–93.

Israel, Jonathan. *Enlightenment Contested: Philosophy, Modernity, and the Emancipation of Man, 1670–1752*. New York: Oxford University Press, 2006.

---. *Radical Enlightenment: Philosophy and the Making of Modernity, 1650–1750*. New York: Oxford University Press, 2001.

Jacobs, Margaret C. *The Radical Enlightenment: Pantheists, Freemasons and Republicans*. London: George Allen and Unwin, 1981.

---. *The Secular Enlightenment*. Princeton, NJ: Princeton University Press, 2019.

Jauch, Ursula Pia. *Jenseits des Maschine. Philosophie, Ironie, und Ästhetik bei Julien Offray de La Mettrie (1709–1751)*. Munich: Carl Hanser Verlag, 1998.

Johnson, Ryan. *The Deleuze-Lucretius Encounter*. Edinburgh: Edinburgh University Press, 2017.

Judovitz, Dalia. *The Culture of the Body: Genealogies of Modernity*. Ann Arbor: University of Michigan Press, 2001.

Kamuf, Peggy. "Accounterablity." *Textual Practice* 21, no. 2 (2007): 251–66.

Kavanagh, Thomas. *Enlightened Pleasures: Eighteenth-Century France and the New Epicureanism*. New Haven, CT: Yale University Press, 2010.

Krier, Isabelle. "Montaigne, le plaisir et les femmes. Une perturbation sceptique de l'hédonisme épicurien ou un matérialisme inédit?" In *Les Matérialistes paradoxaux*. Edited by Patrice Bretaudière and Isabelle Krier. Paris: Classiques Garnier, 2023.

Laborde, Alice M. *Diderot et Madame de Puisieux*. Saratoga, CA: ANMA Libri, 1984.

Lacoue-Labarthe, Philippe. *Typographies*. Vol. 2. *L'Imitation des modernes*. Paris: Éditions Galilée, 1986.

Landes, Joan B. *Women and the Public Sphere in the Age of the French Revolution*. Ithaca, NY: Cornell University Press, 1988.

Laqueur, Thomas. *Making Sex: Body and Gender from the Greeks to Freud*, rev. ed. Cambridge, MA: Harvard University Press, 1992.

Lascano, Marcy P. "Émilie Du Châtelet on Illusions." *Journal of the American Philosophical Association* 7, no. 1 (2021): 1–19.

Lasowski, Patrick Wald. *Dictionnaire libertin: la langue du plaisir au siècle des Lumières*. Paris: Gallimard, 2011.

Lavery, Grace. *Pleasure and Efficacy: Of Pen Names, Cover Versions, and Other Trans Techniques*. Princeton, NJ: Princeton University Press, 2023.

La Vopa, Anthony J. *The Labor of the Mind: Intellect and Gender in Enlightenment Cultures*. Philadelphia: The University of Pennsylvania Press, 2017.

Le Ru, Véronique. *Émilie du Châtelet philosophe*. Paris: Classiques Garnier, 2019.

Lotterie, Florence. *Le Genre des Lumières: Femme et philosophe au XVIIIe siècle*. Paris: Classiques Garnier, 2013.

Lewis, Ann. *Sensibility, Reading, and Illustration*. London: Routledge, 2009.

Litwin, Christophe. *Politiques de l'amour de soi: La Boétie, Montaigne et Pascal au démêlé*. Paris: Classiques Garnier, 2021.

Mackenzie, Louisa. "La masculinité itinérante du *Journal de voyage* de Montaigne." In *Théories critiques et littérature de la Renaissance. Mélanges offerts à Lawrence Kritzman*. Edited by Todd Reeser and David LaGuardia. Paris: Classiques Garnier, 2020.

Mainil, Jean. *Dans les règles du plaisir. . .: Théorie de la différence dans le discours obscène, romanesque et médical de l'Ancien Régime*. Paris: Éditions Kimé, 1996.

Mallinson, Jonathan. "Re-présentant les *Lettres d'une Péruvienne* en 1752: illustration et illusion." *Eighteenth-Century Fiction* 15, no. 2 (January 2003): 227–39.

Martin, Christophe. *Espaces du féminin dans le roman français du dix-huitième siècle*. Oxford: Voltaire Foundation, 2004.

Martin, Jean-Clément. "L'érotisme au féminin ou la transgression discrète en temps de crise?" In *Genre Révolution Transgression: Études offertes à Martine Lapied*. Aix-en-Provence: Presses universitaires de Provence, 2015.

Mauzi, Robert. *L'Idée du bonheur dans la littérature et la pensée française au XVIIIe siècle*. Paris: Librairie Armand Colin, 1960.

McAlpin, Mary. *Female Sexuality and Cultural Degradation in Enlightenment France*. Farnham: Ashgate Publishing, 2012.

McDonald, Christie V. "Le dix-huitième siècle: 1715–1793." In *Femmes et littérature: Une histoire culturelle*. Vol. 1, *Moyen Âge-XVIIIe siècle*. Edited by Martine Reid. Paris: Gallimard, 2020.

———. "The Sophistry of Heuristics." *Modern Language Notes* 100, no. 4 (1985): 780–88.

Meeker, Natania. *Voluptuous Philosophy: Literary Materialism in the French Enlightenment*. New York: Fordham University Press, 2006.

Mesch, Rachel L. "Did Women Have an Enlightenment? Graffigny's Zilia as Female *Philosophe*." *Romanic Review* 89, no. 4 (November 1998): 523–37.

Milam, Jennifer. "Rococo Representations of Interspecies Sensuality and the Pursuit of *Volupté*." *Art Bulletin* 97, no. 2 (2015): 192–209.

Miller, Nancy K. *Subject to Change: Reading Feminist Writing*. New York: Columbia University Press, 1988.

Missé, Blanca. "Diderot's *Thoughts on the Interpretation of Nature*: A Materialist Aesthetics for Science." *The Eighteenth Century* 61, no. 4 (2020): 495–517.

Mortier, Roland. "À propos du sentiment de l'existence chez Diderot et Rousseau: Notes sur un article de 'l'*Encyclopédie*.'" *Diderot Studies* 6 (1964): 183–95.

Mortier, Roland, and Raymond Trousson. *Dictionnaire de Diderot*. Paris: Champion, 1999.

Mylne, Vivienne, and Janet Osborne. "Diderot's Early Fiction: 'Les Bijoux Indiscrets' and 'L'Oiseau Blanc.'" *Diderot Studies* 14 (1971): 143–66.

Nail, Thomas. *Lucretius I: An Ontology of Motion*. Edinburgh: Edinburgh University Press, 2018.

———. *Lucretius II: An Ethics of Motion*. Edinburgh: Edinburgh University Press, 2020.

Offen, Karen M. *European Feminisms, 1700–1950: A Political History*. Stanford, CA: Stanford University Press, 2000.

O'Neal, John C. *The Authority of Experience: Sensationist Theory in the French Enlightenment*. University Park: The University of Pennsylvania Press, 1996.

Passannante, Gerard. *Catastrophizing: Materialism and the Making of Disaster*. Chicago: University of Chicago Press, 2019.

Peakman, Julie. *Amatory Pleasures: Explorations in Eighteenth-Century Sexual Culture*. London: Bloomsbury Academic, 2016.

Pope, Michael. "Embryology, Female Semina and Male Vincibility in Lucretius, *De rervm matvra*." *The Classical Quarterly* 69, no. 1 (2019): 229–45.

Porter, Roy. "Enlightenment and Pleasure." In *Pleasure in the Eighteenth Century*. Edited by Roy Porter and Marie Mulvey Roberts. London: Palgrave, 1996.

Reill, Peter Hanns. *Vitalizing Nature in the Enlightenment*. Berkeley: University of California Press, 2005.

Rey, Anne-Lise. "La littérarisation de la science newtonienne au XVIIIe siècle: une littérature pour les dames?" *Littératures classiques* 85, no. 3 (2014): 303–26.

———. "La Minerve vient de faire sa physique." In *Philosophiques* 44, no. 2 (2017): 233–53.

Richardot, Anne, dir. *Femmes et libertinage au XVIIIe Siècle, ou les Caprices de Cythère*. Rennes: Presses universitaires de Rennes, 2003.

Robertson, Lisa. *Nilling: Prose Essays on Noise, Pornography, the Codex, Melancholy, Lucretius, Folds, Cities and Related Aporias*. Toronto: Book*hug Press, 2020.

Rubin, Gayle. "The Traffic in Women: Notes on the 'Political Economy' of Sex." In *Deviations: A Gayle S. Rubin Reader*. Durham, NC: Duke University Press, 2012.

Russo, Elena. *Styles of Enlightenment: Taste, Politics, and Authorship in Eighteenth-Century France*. Baltimore, MD: The Johns Hopkins University Press, 2006.

Rutler, Tracy. *Queering the Enlightenment: Kinship and Gender in Eighteenth-Century French Literature*. Oxford University Studies in the Enlightenment. Liverpool: Liverpool University Press, 2021.

———. "Happiness and Disability: Émilie Du Châtelet's Adaptive Worldbuilding." *L'Esprit Créateur* 61, no. 4 (Winter 2021): 140–52.

Salaün, Franck. *L'Ordre des mœurs: Essai sur la place du matérialisme dans la société française du XVIIIe siècle (1734–1784)*. Paris: Éditions Kimé, 1996.

Salem, Jean. "Réminiscences épicuriennes dans *Les Égarements du cœur et de l'esprit* de Crébillon." In *Dix-huitième Siècle. L'épicurisme des Lumières* 35 (2003). Edited by Anne Deneys-Tunney and Pierre-François Moreau: 187–210.

Schliesser, Eric. "Necessary Illusions in Love and the Great Machines of Happiness: On Emilie Du Châtelet's *Discourse*." *Digressions & Impressions* (blog). May 31, 2016. https://digressionsnimpressions.typepad.com/digressionsimpressions/2016/05/necessary-illusions-happy-on-du-ch%C3%A2telets-discourse.html.

Schor, Naomi. *Bad Objects: Essays Popular and Unpopular*. Durham, NC: Duke University Press, 1995.

Sedgwick, Eve. *A Dialogue on Love*. Boston: Beacon Press, 1999.

Showalter, English. *Françoise de Graffigny: Her Life and Works*. Oxford: Voltaire Foundation, 2004.

Simon, Julia. "On Collecting Culture in Graffigny: The Construction of an 'Authentic' 'Péruvienne.'" *The Eighteenth Century* 44, no. 1 (Spring 2003): 25–44.

Silver, Marie-France. "Madame de Puisieux ou l'ambition d'être femme de lettres." In *Femmes savantes et femmes d'esprit: Women Intellectuals of the French Eighteenth Century*. Edited by Roland Bonnel and Catherine Rubinger. New York: Peter Lang, 1994.

Soni, Vivasvan. *Mourning Happiness: Narrative and the Politics of Modernity*. Ithaca, NY: Cornell University Press, 2010.

Spink, J. S. "Les avatars du 'sentiment de l'existence,' de Locke à Rousseau." *Dix-huitième siècle* 10 (1978): 269–98.

Stalnaker, Joanna. "Diderot's Brain." In *Mind, Body, Motion, Matter: Eighteenth-Century British and French Literary Perspectives*. Edited by Mary Helen McMurran and Alison Conway. Toronto: University of Toronto Press, 2016.

Steinbrügge, Lieselotte. *The Moral Sex: Woman's Nature in the French Enlightenment*. New York: Oxford University Press, 1995.
Steintrager, James A. *The Autonomy of Pleasure: Libertines, License, and Sexual Revolution*. New York: Columbia University Press, 2016.
Stewart, Joan Hinde. *The Enlightenment of Age: Women, Letters and Growing Old in Eighteenth-Century France*. Oxford: Voltaire Foundation, 2010.
Stewart, Philip. *Engraven Desire: Eros, Image, and Text in the French Eighteenth Century*. Durham, NC: Duke University Press, 1992.
———. Review of *Seducing the Eighteenth-Century Reader: Reading, Writing, and the Question of Pleasure*, by Paul J. Young. *H-France Review* 9, no. 60 (May 2009): 235–37.
Terrall, Mary. *Catching Nature in the Act: Réaumur and the Practice of Natural History in the Eighteenth Century*. Chicago: University of Chicago Press, 2016.
———. "Émilie Du Châtelet and the Gendering of Science." *History of Science* 33, no. 3 (1995): 283–310.
Thomson, Ann. *Bodies of Thought: Science, Religion, and the Soul in the Early Enlightenment*. Oxford: Oxford University Press, 2008.
———. "Émilie Du Châtelet and La Mettrie." In *Époque Émilienne*. Vol. 11, Women in the History of Philosophy and Sciences. Edited by R. E. Hagengruber. Cham, Switzerland: Springer: 2022.
Tiffany, Daniel. *Toy Medium*. Los Angeles: University of California Press, 2000.
Tremblay, Isabelle. *Le Bonheur au féminin: Stratégies narratives des romancières des Lumières*. Montréal: Les Presses de l'Université de Montréal, 2012.
Vanoflen, Laurence. "Réécrire l'histoire de la femme: une fiction de Mme de Puisieux." In *Dix-huitième siècle. Femme des Lumières* 36 (2004): 223–36. Edited by Sylvain Menant.
Vanoflen, Laurence, ed. *Femmes et philosophie des Lumières: De l'imaginaire à la vie des idées*. Paris: Classiques Garnier, 2020.
Vartanian, Aram. *La Mettrie's L'Homme Machine*. Princeton, NJ: Princeton University Press, 2015.
Verbeek, Theo. *Le Traité de l'Ame de La Mettrie, texte, commentaire, et interprétation*. 2 vols. Utrecht: OMI-Grafisch Bedrijf, 1988.
Wallmann, Elisabeth. "The Human-Animal Debate and the Enlightenment Body Politics: Émilie Du Châtelet's reading of Mandeville's *Fable of the Bees*." *Early Modern French Studies* 42, no. 1 (2020): 85–103.
Warman, Caroline. *The Atheist's Bible: Diderot's "Éléments de Physiologie."* Cambridge: Open Book Publishers, 2020.
Whitehead, Barbara Mathews. "The Singularity of Mme Du Châtelet: An Analysis of the *Discours sur le bonheur*." In Émilie Du Châtelet: Rewriting Enlightenment Philosophy and Science. Edited by Judith P. Zinsser and Julie Candler Hayes. Oxford: Voltaire Foundation, 2006
Wolfe, Charles T. "'Cabinet d'Histoire Naturelle,' or: The Interplay of Nature and Artifice in Diderot's Naturalism." *Perspectives on Science* 17, no. 1 (2009): 58–77.

———. *Materialism: A Historico-Philosophical Introduction*. Cham, Switzerland: Springer, 2016.

Wolfgang, Aurora. *Gender and Voice in the French Novel, 1730–1782*. London: Routledge, 2004.

Young, Paul J. *Seducing the Eighteenth-Century French Reader*. Aldershot: Ashgate Publishing, 2008.

Zinsser, Judith. "Betrayals: An Eighteenth-Century Philosophe and her Biographers." *French Historical Studies* 39, no. 1 (2016): 3–33.

———. Introduction to *Émilie Du Châtelet: Selected Philosophical and Scientific Writings*. Edited by Judith P. Zinsser. Translated by Isabelle Bour and Judith P. Zinsser. Chicago: University of Chicago Press, 2009.

Index

Académie française, 62, 102
agency: nonhuman, 126; *papillotage* as oscillation of illusion and, 14, 101, 163, 194n20; of women, and desire, 76, 208n24; of women, patriarchal culture as ignoring and negating, 76. *See also* Du Châtelet, Émilie—metaphysics
Ahmed, Sara, 142
Alembert, Jean-Baptiste le Rond d': "Courtisane," 224n9. *See also Encyclopédie* (Diderot and d'Alembert)
Algarotti, *Il Newtonianismo per le dame*, 110, 212n10, 213n17
allegory: Helvétius's, of the poet and the feminine figure of Wisdom, 63–65; Puisieux's *Le Plaisir et la volupté* as libertine allegory, 68, 88, 89–90, 91–92, 95, 96–97, 210n44
Altman, Janet, 217–18n4
amour propre, 93, 100–101
Anderson, Holly K., 215n55
animism, 127
Arcesilaus, 36–37
Arenson, Kelly, 199–200n8, 201–2n32
Argenson, comte d', 90
Aristippus: Puisieux and, 71, 74–75; referenced in the *Encyclopédie*'s entry on *volupté*, 78
Aristotle, 49
artifice: Diderot's denial of distinction between nature and, 42; illusion as resource in a ruined world, 8, 13, 69, 76–77; *papillotage* as oscillation of agency and,

14, 101, 163, 194n20. *See also* artifice as pragmatics of pleasure and responsiveness to context; Du Châtelet, Émilie—illusion without error, pursuit of; Graffigny, Françoise de, *Lettres d'une Péruvienne*—illusion as resource in a ruined world; Puisieux, Madeleine d'Arsant de—artifice and craft of feminine pleasure
artifice as pragmatics of pleasure and responsiveness to context: cultivation of pleasure as goal sufficient unto itself, 5, 12–13, 69, 101, 128–29, 131, 186; deployment of artifice toward the ends of pleasure, 101, 124, 152; entwinement of nature and artifice, 89, 96–97, 101, 186; the feminine subject as iconic object of desire, 10; intersection between materialism and culture of feminine artifice, 11, 12, 28, 77, 88, 179; need for, as limiting delight's deployment as radical tool of social change, 14
the arts, eros diverted and sublimated into philosophy and, 63–65
ataraxia (Gr.), 74
Aubigné, Françoise d' (the future Madame de Maintenon), 180
Augustinian neo-Epicureanism, 118, 123
autonomy: of Du Châtelet, 107, 138, 140; Du Châtelet and cultivation of, 135, 137–38; Graffigny's pleasure in being and, 160, 166; right to, 116; science as zone of, 124
autonomy of pleasure (Steintrager), 4–5, 22

Barthes, Roland, 34, 199n7
Batteux, Charles, *La Morale d'Épicure, tirée de ses propres écrits*, 37, 43, 200nn15,17
Bazin, Gilles-Augustin, 204n65
becoming-woman. See devenir-femme
Benson, Jane, xi, 191n6
Bérenguier, Nadine, 71, 72, 90, 91
Bostic, Heidi, 218n14, 219n21
Boyer d'Argens, Jean-Baptiste de, *Thérèse philosophe*, 16, 25, 26, 206n10
Brading, Katherine, 211–12n8
Bret, Antoine: love relationship with Graffigny, 147; *Mémoires sur la vie de Mademoiselle de Lenclos* as source for Gouges's play, 179, 182, 183, 185
British Enlightenment, 4
Brown, Gregory S., 224n10
Brucker, Johann Jakob, *Historia critica philosophiae*, 43

Cartesianism: *cogito*, Rousseau's shift of valence of, 156; conjoined with neo-Epicureanism, 52; contrast with Newtonianism, 108–9, 211–12n8; the soul (*res cogitans*), 83. See also Descartes, René
Cavendish, Margaret, 4, 206n8; *The Blazing World*, 215n55; "Of Fire and Flame," 215n55
Caylus, comte de, 152
chaîne secrète, 34
Choiseul-Meuse, Félicité de, *Julie, ou j'ai sauvé ma rose*, 3, 192n4
Christina, queen of Sweden, 180; as character in Gouges's *Molière chez Ninon*, 180, 181, 184, 185
Chu, Andrea Long, 28
Clark, Andrew H., 207n12
classical materialisms. See Epicureanism (classical); Epicurus; Lucretius; Stoicism; Venus (in Lucretius's *De rerum natura*)
class. See elite privileges
Comédie-Française, 152, 179, 180, 219n21
commerce. See sociability with women (commerce; traffic in women)
commercial culture: and the age of pleasure, 15; Du Châtelet's neo-Epicurean defense of, 138, 212n9, 214n24; luxury economics, 15, 21, 27, 138, 171–72, 214n24, 222n70
community as materialist value: overview, 154, 177; Du Châtelet on intellectual work as mode of sociable interaction and collective social good, 117, 119–21, 122–24; Gouges's play describing cultivation of, by Ninon de Lenclos, 181–82, 183, 185–86, 224n17; Graffigny's *Lettres* and, 177; Graffigny's *plaisir d'être* and potential collective joy, 144, 154–55, 156; Helvétius's enlightened materialism and re-orientation toward collective happiness and reciprocity, 62, 63–65. See also Du Châtelet, Émilie—love and relationality; reciprocity
Condillac, Étienne Bonnot de, 220–21n29
consent: La Mettrie and, 54; Montaigne and, 23; *papillotage* and, 14, 194n20; Puisieux and, 194n20
constraint as enabling condition of pleasure: overview, 8–9, 12, 13, 14, 186; Du Châtelet and, 8–9, 109, 157, 175; Graffigny and, 8–9, 142, 146, 157, 174, 175; as libertine ideal committed to examining the material circumstances of pleasure's production, 8–9, 74; Puisieux and, viii–ix, 8–9, 74, 91, 101, 109, 157, 175; Puisieux's philosophical ethic of adaptation to constraint, 74–76. See also artifice; artifice as pragmatics of pleasure and responsiveness to context
constraints on women: and absence from libertine fiction and materialist philosophical argument, 2–5, 10, 11, 12, 192n5, 193nn6–7; Diderot on women as unable to practice philosophy due to, 50; Du Châtelet on the importance for women to cultivate pleasure due to, 124, 128–29, 130–31, 134–35, 137–38; empiricist methods of analysis closed to, 84, 209n38; Gouge's representation of persecution of Ninon as woman libertine, 181, 182–83, 184–85; Graffigny on, as enforcing women's social role as image-bearers, 170–71, 174–75; Latin and Greek education rarely permitted, 3, 84; pessimism about liberation from, 91, 101, 102; reputation, 82–83, 84; and women living as if they had no soul (Puisieux), 82; and writing about pleasure, 84, 209n38. See also Du Châtelet, Émilie—constraints experienced as woman of science; materialist philosophy as masculine purview—formal exclusion of women; misogyny; objectification of women; sociability with women (commerce; traffic in women)
courtesans and *hetaerae*: in the Epicurean Garden, 201–2n32; Lucretius's Venus among, 60–61

INDEX

Crébillon, Claude Prosper Jolyot de: feminine cultural authority as emasculating, 22–23, 24–25, 197n33; and Graffigny, friendship with, 152; Puisieux's *L'Éducation* as rewriting of *Les Égarements*, 69, 97, 110. Works: *Les Égarements du cœur et de l'esprit*, 22, 69, 97; *Le Sopha*, 90, 197n33; *Le Sylphe*, 90, 91–92

critique: allowing for recognition of vulnerability, not for hardening of an autonomous will, 175; as form of pleasure, 76–78

cultural differences: French literary efforts to grapple with, 142; resemblance and the reader's identification, 147–48. See also ethnic differences; racial differences

Cyrano de Bergerac, Savinien de, 52; *Les États et Empires de la Lune*, 23, 221n36

death, philosophy as apprenticeship for, 50–51, 203n48

Deleuze, Gilles, *devenir-femme*, 26–27, 52

délicatesse (illusive materialisms): overview, 202–3n44; as capacity more highly developed in women, 78–79; as limited by class and social status, 79; as networking sensation to heighten and diversify delight, 80–81; pain as heightened by, 102; vs. the sensualist norm of women's delicate constitutions as inferior, 79–80

deLire, Luce, xi

Delon, Michel, 15, 16

delusion: feminine pleasure as, 39; as "madness," Gouges's portrayal of Ninon de Lenclos's sympathy and compassion for, 183, 224nn16–17. See also Graffigny, Françoise de, *Lettres d'une Péruvienne*—delusion as error; possessive model of erotic passion, critiques of

Descartes, René: and Christina, queen of Sweden, 180; in frontispiece, 110, 111; metaphysics of Du Châtelet and, 11. See also Cartesianism

Desmahis (Joseph de Corsembleu), "Femme (Morale)," 79–80, 83

Devaux, Antoine, 124, 154

devenir-femme (becoming-woman) (Deleuze and Guattari), 26–27, 52

dialogue genre, 89

Diderot, Denis: as authority, ix; citing Batteux, 200nn15,17; condemnation and burning of work, 51, 59; critique as form of pleasure, 67–68; and the dialogue genre, 89; exclusion of women and feminine persons from the practice of philosophy, 46–50, 62, 80; and the feminine voice, 4, 52; as "good" materialist, 72, 207n12; and La Mettrie, distancing from, 51–52, 60; on Ninon de Lenclos, 224n9; and Lucretius, 39, 201n21, 203n51; on memory, vii–viii, 191n1; on the mind as book, viii; politics of reflexivity, x; and Puisieux, love relationship with, 11, 60, 71–72, 80, 198n48; Puisieux's *Les Caractères* said to have been the work of, 60; *repos délicieux* (libertine anticipation of *sentiment de l'existence*), 158–59, 160, 221n34; and Seneca, 43, 200n17; speculation and, 24, 73; and Stoicism, 43, 50, 51, 203n48; Tahiti as society existing both in its colonial despoliation and outside of it, 176

— NATURE AND SCIENCE: experimental science as uncovering nature's person, 39–42, 46; mathematical abstractions as detached from nature, 39, 40; the movement from darkness into light, 39–42; nature and artifice, denial of distinction between, 42; pro-constructivist naturalism of, 42

— NEO-EPICUREANISM: Epicureanism as condition of experience, 44, 45–46; Epicurus as a man in drag, 42–43, 50, 51, 200n17; Epicurus as genius, 44–45

— PLEASURE AND THE FEMININE: on contagion of femininity, 24, 26; delicacy of women's constitutions as inferior, 80; desire for pleasure as fundamental human need, 44; difference between love and hunger (fruitly feelings), 31–32, 33–34; feminine subjectivity as superficial self-consciousness, 46–50, 80; femininity as both object and subject of enlightened pleasure, 24–26; femininity as universal attribute of all bodies, 46–47, 49, 50, 62; gendered subjects as different by degrees, not in kind, 38, 41, 42, 46–47, 62; masculinist exception from the universal feminine, 49, 50, 62; nature as woman in disguise (*femme travestie*), 41, 42; orientalist tropes of the harem as symbol of male depletion, 197n33; seminal fluids emitted by women, 41–42, 203n51; sociability with women as positive mode of exchange, 43–44, 49–50, 52, 80; on suffering of women, 47, 48; women's bodies as twice concealed within them, 41–42

—WORKS: *Les Bijoux indiscrets*, 24, 26, 47, 72, 90, 197n33, 198nn47–48, 206n10; "Délicieux," 158; *Éléments de physiologie*, vii–viii, 31–32, 50–51; "Épicuréisme ou Épicurisme," 43–47, 50, 201–2n32, 224n9; *Essai sur les règnes de Claude et de Néron*, 43, 200n17; *Lettre sur les aveugles*, 72; *L'Oiseau blanc*, 90; *Pensées philosophiques*, 51–52, 59, 72; *Pensées sur l'interprétation de la nature*, 39–42, 46; *La Religieuse*, 47, 198n47; *Le Rêve de d'Alembert*, 10, 38; *Supplément au voyage de Bougainville*, 176; *Sur les femmes*, 47–50, 80. *See also Encyclopédie* (Diderot and d'Alembert)

disguise. *See travestissement* (disguise or drag)

Dobie, Madeleine, 142–43, 218n9, 220n25

drag. *See travestissement* (disguise or drag)

Du Châtelet, Émilie: overview, 1–2, 6, 11, 105–7, 138–40; and aristocratic femininity, 141; autonomy of, 107, 138, 140; on autonomy, cultivation of, 135, 137–38; on autonomy, right to, 116; death in childbirth, 11, 106–7, 139; elite status as Marquise, 105–6, 138, 140; enlightened philosophical *milieu* of, 1, 129, 150; exclusion from moralist writing canon, 192n5; feminine solidarity, absence of, 139; feminist scholars' recovery of work of, 11, 105–6, 108–9, 211–12nn6,8–9,11; future readership, imagined, 129, 135, 137, 139, 140; and Graffigny, relationship with, 11–12, 141, 150; Graffigny's politics likened to, 213n22; Greek and Latin education acquired by, 3; Helvétius, friendship with, 1; La Mettrie, putative relationship with, 59–60, 65, 113–14, 212–13n15; La Mettrie, significant engagement with the work of, 11; La Mettrie utilizing arguments from *Institutions*, 113–14; Lucretius as source, knitting together the anthropology and the invocation to Venus in unexpected way, 117–21, 123; and meaning as emerging not in the conclusion of life but in the making of it, 106–7; as no protofeminist, 109–10; racist and racialized assumptions in writing of, 115, 175–76; Jean-François de Saint-Lambert, love relationship with, 62, 106–7, 134, 138–39; theater and puppetry and, 2, 105, 133; Voltaire and her translation of Mandeville, 116, 213n19; Voltaire, love relationship with, 1, 110, 124, 134, 136–37, 212–13n15; Voltaire representing her as muse, 110, 112

—CONSTRAINTS EXPERIENCED AS WOMAN OF SCIENCE: ambivalences and contradictions inherent in her approach to gender, 109–10, 113, 214nn36–37; eroticization of the scene of knowledge (and revision of), 110, 111–12, 212n10; gender as limit of intellectual authority, 106; institutional prestige denied to, 106; La Mettrie's letter prefacing *Histoire naturelle* exciting critical assumptions about sexual connections to materialist men, 113–14; reliance on patronage networks and sexist expectations of her time, 109–10; whether to reveal gender when publishing, 110, 212n12, 214n37

—ETHIC OF PLEASURE: overview, 11, 12, 14–15; class and gender as factors in what it is possible to feel and whose passions are satisfied, 132, 134–35; constraint as enabling condition of pleasure, 8–9, 109, 157, 175; human intelligence loving perfection, 121; not easily fitting into libertinism or materialism, 108, 109, 113, 119, 150–51; pleasure as privilege, 9, 124, 128; virtue and pleasure, as universal good, 116–17

—ILLUSION WITHOUT ERROR, PURSUIT OF: overview, 1–2, 8, 124, 128–30; and autonomy, cultivation of, 135, 137–38; Barthes's "lures of subjectivity" and, 199n7; as consonant with avoidance of error or untruth, 2, 131; constancy, curing oneself of the illusion of, 137–38; convergence of reason and love and, 124, 131, 216n63; definition of happiness, 130; delight as found and sustained in the gap between illusion (the phenomenal) and reality (the noumenal), 107, 124, 128, 132–33, 150; and delight, maximizing, 124; and the future, 107; as genealogy for illusive materialism, 131; Graffigny's *Lettres* as navigating, 147, 149, 152, 154, 219n20; illusion as its own scene of struggle, 137–38; illusions as optical illusions, 131, 132; illusions as prosthetic for passions, 132; libertine ethics and, 136, 137–38, 217n81; love and study as entangled in the illusions that sustain them, 107,

124, 134–35, 136; love as dependence, 107, 136–38; love as the only pleasure that can "make us wish to live," 136; love is not there for the taking, 136; love of glory and, 135; love of study as greatest contributor to happiness for women, 135, 138; loving for two in the illusion of reciprocity, as speculative, 136–38, 149; multiplication of the self, wish for, 138, 139, 154; the passions as not available to everyone equally nor universally, 132, 135; the passions as of primary importance in life, 131–32; the passions do not come for the asking, 132; pleasure does not come for the taking, 124, 129, 130, 136; pleasure of the spectacle involves an oscillation between knowledge it is artifice (awareness) and the willed suspension of disbelief (enchantment), 133–34, 137; as practice focusing on what works to sustain pleasure, 1–2, 129–30; and prejudices, freedom from, 130, 131; receptivity to illusion, cultivation of, 130, 131, 133–34; and the second "other" nature, cultivation of, 134; speculation and, 107, 138, 139; turn to pleasure, 131; women's cultivation of pleasure, importance due to the constraints borne by, 124, 128–29, 130–31, 134–35, 137–38

—INTELLECTUAL WORK AND PLEASURE: and femininity as zone of imaginative possibility, 114; on the material conditions necessary for cultivation of the mind, 114–16, 120, 122–23; as mode of emulation, 120; as mode of sociable interaction and collective social good, 117, 119–21, 122–24; pleasure as inhabiting and animating the work, 113, 114; production of scholarship driven by pleasure, 113; as pure form of happiness, 107; as realigning the gendered associations of pleasure, 113; reason as universal (and dismissal of rhetoric), 121–22, 214nn36–37; as relational aspect of love, 114, 119. See also Du Châtelet—illusion without error, pursuit of

—LOVE AND RELATIONALITY: attachment to, human society combining the pursuit of pleasure with, 117–21; Graffigny's relationality without dependence and, 152; libertine focus on individual desire undercut by, 121; and love as key social relation, 117; multiple co-constitutive conceptions of love, 119, 120; of parents for children, 118–19, 123; as pure form of happiness, 107. See also Du Châtelet—illusion without error, pursuit of; Du Châtelet—intellectual work and pleasure

—METAPHYSICS: overview, 11, 105–6; freedom given to humans, 127; God as limiting the power of matter, 125, 126–28, 215n53; as illegible both as libertinism and traditional materialism, 109, 113; interpenetration of experiment and, commitment to, 108, 109, 211–12n8; and Kant, as progenitor of, 105–6; Leibnizian basis of, 11, 59, 109, 113, 121, 126, 128; "leibnizo-newtonianisme" as proposed heuristic for, 211–12n8; the pleasure God takes in his perfect creation, 121, 128; pleasure of humans guaranteed by creative power of God, 128; reason as guaranteed by God (principle of sufficient reason), 128; vitalism as tempered by, 127, 213n22

—AS NEO-EPICUREAN PHILOSOPHER: overview, 11; acknowledgment of mortality, 115; ascribed independent status for the originality and significance of her work, 108, 211–12nn6,8-9,11; attachment to pleasure, 114, 129, 138; on body cultivation and adornment, 114–16, 120, 122, 130–31; as combining the pursuit of pleasure with an attachment to love and relationality, 114–24; commercial culture, secular defense of, 138, 212n9, 214n24; education of women, defense of, 116, 120; Epicurean belief in matter and diversity as infinite, revision of, 127, 215n53; Epicurean condemnation of pursuit of glory, revision of, 135; expansion of pleasure to include intellectual work, 113; origins of human society combining pursuit of pleasure with attachment to love and relationality, 117–21; position of women and feminine persons in practice of philosophy as reworked by, 113; previously underestimated as translation or "vulgarization" of works of great men, 108, 212n11; revision of Mandeville's *Fable of the Bees* in her translation, 116–22, 212n9, 213n22, 214nn24,37, 215–16n58; and rhetorical ornamentation dismissed in favor of reason, 121–22, 214nn36–37; as working in the interstices of clashing paradigms, 108–9, 113, 211–12n8

—SCIENCE: atomism, 126, 127, 215n55; embrace of experimentalism that must be metaphysically justified, 108, 109, 211–12n8; fire, motive force of, 124–27, 215n55; hypothesis and, 125–26, 127, 215nn42,51; "leibnizo-newtonianisme" as proposed heuristic for, 211–12n8; Newton translation and commentary, frantic labor to complete, 106, 107; as pleasure source in itself, 121–24; as relational, 122–24; speculative/creative dimensions of scientific reason, 113, 123–24, 125–26, 215n42; as zone of human autonomy, 124

—WORKS: *Discours sur le bonheur*, 1, 108, 128–38, 139, 140, 216n63; *Dissertation sur la nature et la propagation du feu*, 124–28, 215n55; *Institutions de physique*, 110, 113–14, 115, 121, 122–24, 126–28, 139, 212n12, 214n36, 215nn42,51,53; letters to Saint-Lambert, 106–7, 138–39; Newton translation and commentary, 106, 107; translation of Bernard Mandeville's *Fable of the Bees*, 108, 114–22, 123, 130, 131, 212n9, 213nn19,22, 214nn24,37, 215–16n58

Duclos, Charles Pinot, 152
Dufallo, Basil, 60–61, 199–200n8, 204–5n71
Dujour, Florence, 201n20

education: constraints on women seeking, 3, 84; eroticization of the scene of knowledge (and revision of), 110, 111–12, 212n10; of women, Graffigny's promotion of, 148; women's right to, Du Châtelet's defense of, 116, 120
eighteenth century: as "age of pleasure," 15–17, 194–95n22; as "century of woman," 38, 201n20
elite privileges: pleasure as reconciling gender- and class-related divides, 16; women viewed as intrinsically connecting with materialist values, 7, 193n12

—AND THE ILLUSIVE MATERIALISTS: overview, 5, 9; *délicatesse* as dependent on, 79; Du Châtelet and, as Marquise, 105–6, 138, 140; Du Châtelet's "pursuit of illusion without error" and requirement of, 132, 134–35; Puisieux and, 75, 79, 101. *See also* constraints on women; ethnic differences; materialist philosophy as masculine purview—formal exclusion of women; racial differences

Encyclopédie (Diderot and d'Alembert): "Courtisane" (d'Alembert), 224n9; "Délicieux" (Diderot), 158; Du Châtelet present in, 105; "Épicuréisme ou Épicurisme" (Diderot), 43–47, 50, 201–2n32, 224n9; "Femme (Morale)" (Desmahis), 79–80, 83; "Génie" (Saint-Lambert), 44, 202n36; "Penchant, Inclination" (de Jaucourt), 67; "Volupté" (unattributed), 78, 208n27

ennui, 64
enslaved persons: illusive materialists as abolitionists, 224nn10,21; welcomed to the Epicurean Garden, 36
Epictetus, 75–76
Epicurean Garden: anti-Epicurean discourse condemning the inclusion of women in, 36, 43, 201–2n32; Diderot validating the participation of women in, 43–44, 47, 49–50, 201–2n32; Graffigny's pleasure of being and invitation to relationality without dependence as, 155–56, 175; Puisieux's transformation of theme of retreat into, 83; women and enslaved persons welcomed to, 36
Epicureanism (classical): castigated for a feminine attachment to pleasure, as emasculating, 35–37; cultivation of voluptuous satisfaction as goal of philosophical inquiry, 44, 45–46, 186; of Leontion, 3, 43; "Live unknown!" ("Lead a hidden life!"), 35, 36, 135; in materialist corpus, ix; matter as infinite and infinitely diverse, 215n53; Puisieux's rejection of both Stoicism and, as inflexible in principle, 74–75. *See also* artifice as pragmatics of pleasure and responsiveness to context; Epicurean Garden; Epicurus; Leontion; Lucretius; neo-Epicureanism; Venus (in Lucretius's *De rerum natura*)
Epicurus: boundless energy of, 44–45; commitment to writing and dissemination of insights, 45; the illusive materialists and references to, 13; matter as infinite and infinitely diverse, 215n53; sublimation of the passions into state of *ataraxia*, 74; withdrawal from public life recommended by, 78

—IN DRAG: Diderot's reworking of Seneca's image of, 42–43, 50, 51, 200n17; Ninon de Lenclos in drag as revision of, 181; Seneca's condemnation of the sect as, 36, 43, 200n17

Épinay, Louise d', 71
ethnic differences: the clandestine power of women as cutting across, 20; deployed by illusive materialists as status privilege, 9. *See also* Graffigny, Françoise de, *Lettres d'une Péruvienne*—ethnic identity

feminine subjectivity: as constituted in constraint, 77; Diderot on women as like children with superficial self-consciousness, 47–49; as iconic object of desire, 10
femininity as practice of pleasure (illusive materialisms): overview, 7–8, 12; diverse genres and forms as zones of, 8, 12; humanity as defined and guaranteed by, 8, 128; as ideally accessible to all, 8; no guarantee of pleasure, 8, 9, 75–76, 124, 128. *See also* constraint as enabling condition of pleasure; *délicatesse* (illusive materialisms); pleasure as pragmatics (illusive materialisms)
femininity as theory of experience: overview of neo-Epicurean embrace of, 37–39, 200n18, 201n20; as both object and subject of enlightened pleasure, 24–26; as contagious, 16–22, 26, 120, 197n40; gendered subjects as different by degrees, not in kind, 38, 41, 42, 46–47, 62; Helvétius's feminization of enlightenment itself, 62, 63–65; identification with, 33; luxury economics and the cultivation of aesthetic delight (Voltaire), 27–28, 214n24; the practice of philosophy as masculinist sociability extracted from, 18, 38–39, 49, 61–62; as universal necessary form all bodies take, 15–16, 23–24, 26, 34, 38–39, 46–47, 62; as vitality itself, 33. *See also* Diderot, Denis; La Mettrie, Julien Offray de—feminine epistemology elaborated by; materialist philosophy as masculine purview; *mollesse* (softness); neo-Epicureanism—bad materialisms; neo-Epicureanism—good materialisms; pleasure as materialist value
feminism: illusive materialists not protofeminist, 6, 9, 109–10, 161; socialist feminism, 3
feminist complaint, as genre, 142
feminist historians and literary critics recovering women's work: overview, 4, 193n7; Du Châtelet, 11, 105–6, 108–9, 211–12nn6,8–9,11; Graffigny, 11, 217–18n4; and inseparability of representation and lived experience of women and feminine persons, 4–5; and Puisieux's reception as influenced by her relationship with Diderot, 72; women's place in eighteenth-century culture as discursive field, 19, 196–97n30; women's writing as fundamental to the French Enlightenment, 6, 11, 105–6, 193n11. *See also* women's writing

femme manquée, 61
Fontenelle, Bernard Le Bovier de, 1, 129, 213n17; *Du Bonheur*, Puisieux's commentary on, 60, 74, 75, 85, 129, 208n19
Foucault, Michel, 198n46; on Diderot's *Les Bijoux indiscrets* and *scientia sexualis*, 24, 25–26
freedom: the countryside as site of sexual freedom, 91–92; Du Châtelet on divine agency and human capacity for, 127; Montaigne endorsing women's, 23; Sade on human right to refuse love as delusion of possession, 172
future readership, imagined: overview, 5, 13–14; Du Châtelet and, 129, 135, 137, 139, 140; Graffigny and, 147–48, 149, 176; Puisieux's exceptional feminine person, 13–14

Garnier, Camille, 206–7n11
Gassendi, Pierre, 37, 43
gender as constraint. *See* constraints on women
gendered subjects, as different from one another by degrees, not in kind, 38, 41, 42, 46–47, 62
genius: Diderot ascribing to Epicurus, 44–45; Diderot's ambivalence about women's, in argument against women as philosophers, 47, 49, 51; "Génie" (*Encyclopédie*), 44, 202n36; Graffigny ascribing to Helvétius, 154; La Mettrie ascribing to Diderot, 51
Geoffrin, Marie-Thérèse, 62
Giovacchini, Julie, 35–36, 61
Girten, Kristin M., 4
Gladfelder, Hal, 53, 203n52
Goncourt, Edmond and Jules de, 7, 193n12
Gordon, Pamela, 35

Gottmann, Felicia, 108, 116–18, 212n9, 213n19, 214n24

Gouges, Olympe de: as advocate for abolition of slavery, 224n10; extended quarrel with the Comédie-Française, 179; as illusive materialist, 186; and Louis-Sébastien Mercier, friendship with, 179–80; speculation and, 186; *Zamore et Mirza (L'Esclavage des noirs, ou l'Heureaux naufrage)*, 224n10

Gouges, Olympe de, *Molière chez Ninon ou le siècle des Grands Hommes*: on aging and the passage of time, 182–83, 184; among literary homages to eminent personages, 179–81; the author as character (Olimpe) in, and claims to authorship and authority, 181–82, 184, 185, 186, 224n10; Antoine Bret's *Mémoires sur la vie de Mademoiselle de Lenclos* as source for, 179, 182, 183, 185; community cultivated by Lenclos, 181–82, 183, 185–86, 224n17; feminine solidarity in, 182, 184, 185; and gender confusion implied by inclusion of women among the "grands hommes," 180–81; historical investments of, 179; and love, multiple co-constitutive conceptions of, 183–85, 224nn16–17; "madness," of a friend treated with kindness and respect, 183, 224n16; Ninon as emblem of *honnêteté*, 181, 182; Ninon as exemplary in loving and being loved, 183; Ninon as *femme de lettres* in, 182; Ninon as libertine, and inescapability of constraints due to her identity as a woman, 181, 182–83, 184–85; Ninon as "man in drag" and other masculine readings of, 181, 182, 223n5; Ninon's decision to retreat to a convent, 181, 184–85; Ninon's illegitimate son, 183, 184; reception of, 179, 180, 183; as speculative history of women, feminine persons, and materialist ethics, 186

governance, Helvétius's enlightened materialism and, 62, 63–65

Graffigny, Françoise de, 153; as aristocratic abused woman on her own, 141; and Antoine Bret, love relationship with, 147; community as ideal of, 177; and Du Châtelet, relationship with, 11–12, 141, 150; on Du Châtelet's *Dissertation*, 124; Du Châtelet's politics likened to, 213n22; education of women, promotion of, 148; and ethic of pleasure, 11–12, 14–15;

excluded from histories of materialism and libertinism, 12, 151; feminist scholars' recovery of work of, 11, 217–18n4; future readership imagined by, 147–48, 149, 176; and Helvétius, friendship with, 12, 62, 152, 154, 220n26; as illusive materialist, 150–51, 220n25; Lucretian ethics and, 220–21n29; materialist *milieu* of, 150, 152, 154; salon of, 12, 62, 152, 220n26; and salon of Mlle Quinault, 152, 220n26; and sensationism, 152, 154, 194n19, 220–21n29. Works: *Cénie*, 219n21; *Phaza*, 219n21. *See also* Graffigny, Françoise de, *Lettres d'une Péruvienne*

Graffigny, Françoise de, *Lettres d'une Péruvienne*: overview, 8, 12, 141–44, 175–77; antithèse and, 218n14; double positioning of Zilia, 143–44; as echoing in our contemporary world, 144, 176; errancy and, 145, 146; as fusion of sentimental and libertine fiction, 141–42, 150–52, 154, 219n19, 220n24; illustrations in, 219n22; images of light and shadow, 147, 218n14; introduction focusing on history of Peruvian culture in, 170, 176; as lamentation remade for sensualist ends, 142; "letter 34," 157, 170–72, 219n22; love as the only pleasure that can "make us wish to live," 136; luxe edition overseen by the author (1752), 141, 170, 219n22; making philosophy out of a feminine life, 142–44; materiality and materialism, pleasure as delusion of possession vs. zone of *volupté*, 167–68, 170; modern qualities of, 142–43; Montesquieu's *Lettres persanes* and, 142, 146, 218n9–10; open-endedness of signifying processes, 143, 218n9; plot summary, 145–52; preface, as placing the narrative under the sign of enlightenment, 147–48, 219n19; preface, intertexts named in, 142; Puisieux's *L'Éducation* and, 100; reception of, 12, 217–18n4; as speculative fiction, 151, 176, 221n36; Voltaire's play *Alzire* and, 142
— CRITIQUE OF FRENCH SOCIETY: overview, 12, 142; constraints on women as enforcing social role as image-bearers, 170, 174–75; copresence of error and, 173; critique as allowing for recognition of vulnerability, not for hardening of an autonomous will, 175; and cultural appropriation by Graffigny, 144; defamiliarization technique, 219n21; delusion of possession, 222n53; education of girls and

INDEX 247

women as prioritizing feminine ignorance, 170–71; ethnic identity as Peruvian allowing "alongside-ness" for, 151–52; hoarding of wealth and resources to the detriment of society as a whole, 171–72, 222n70; ideology of woman's nature operates as self-fulfilling prophecy, 174; and knowledge as arising from dispossession and undoing, 142; outsider ethnic identity as sharpening, 173; reason as instrument of, 151, 173, 219n21; superficiality and cruelty with which women are treated, 152, 157; vacuity of French culture setting women up to fail, 82, 171, 173; virtue, transcultural ideal of feminine, 12, 151, 170–71, 174–75; women's objectification and exploitation, 170
— DELUSION AS ERROR: cruelty as outgrowth of, 163–64; differentiation of delusions (to be countered) from illusions (to be cultivated and enjoyed), 172, 219n20; love as source of self-worth as, 171; and nature, experience of, 164–66, 167–68, 169, 222n53; omnipotent vision of the spectator as, 164–65, 167, 222n53; the possessive model of desire as, 163–69, 171–73, 176–77, 222n53; relational exchange of love as mutual enslavement as, 171–73; "sweet delusion" of fictive reciprocity as life-sustaining as, 147, 148, 161–63; Zilia in European rather than Indigenous dress, and failed reciprocity of Déterville's possessive interest, 166–67, 168, 169. *See also* Graffigny, *Lettres*—illusion as resource in a ruined world
— DISPOSSESSION AND DISAPPOINTMENT: abduction from Peru by Spanish and then French captors, 145–46, 149, 151, 157, 162–63; beloved, separation from, 145, 147, 161–62, 166, 171; betrayal and abandonment by the beloved, 142, 146, 149, 158–59, 172–73; constraint as enabling condition of pleasure, 8–9, 142, 146, 157, 174, 175; the delusion of possession and, 222n53; empire and, 143–44, 176–77, 222n53; genocide of the Inca, 146, 176; ignorance as deprivation, 146–47; knowledge as growing out of, 142; manor home ownership as partial recompense for, 155, 156, 157, 158; as prisoner and traveler, 145–46; *quipos/quipus/khipu*

(Quechua mode of writing), love letters to her beloved Aza, 145, 147, 161, 218n5; surviving, via the life-sustaining force of maintaining fictive reciprocity with the beloved, 147, 148, 161–63
— ETHNIC IDENTITY: overview, 8, 12; as "alongside-ness" allowing her to envision "pleasure in being" and "relationality without dependence," 151–52, 222n53; and ambivalence of Zilia's role as property owner, 222n70; attachment to the memory of Aza as preserving her attachment to, 160; as cipher for white, metropolitan women's fantasies of self-transformation, 8, 144, 176–77; and community (local but not global), 177; as distinct historical way of being, 176, 177; as hybrid subject, 142, 172–73, 177, 218n11; introduction to the text giving history of Peruvian culture, 170, 176; as outsider, 173, 175; and Peruvian Incan culture as lost and gone, 143–44, 176–77; and prejudice, struggle against, 147–48; racist logic of Déterville's sudden interest in Zilia wearing European dress, 167, 169; and social critique, 173; *va-et-vient* between disappointment and hope, 148, 219n22; Zilia's Peruvian subjectivity as static, 176–77
— ILLUSION AS RESOURCE IN A RUINED WORLD: overview, 8; as artifice carefully crafted, 150, 160, 163; criticized as regression to ignorance, 149–50; differentiation of delusions (to be countered) from illusions (to be cultivated and enjoyed), 172, 219n20; even as knowledge is withheld from her, 146–47; the indeterminate dream-state as passive opposite of, 162–65, 167; and the letters as animating fantasy, 147; life-sustaining force of maintaining fictive reciprocity with the beloved ("sweet delusion"), 147, 148, 161–63; as navigating Du Châtelet's pursuit of illusion without error, 147, 149, 152, 154, 219n20; and *papillotage*, 163; "pleasure in being" as enhanced and fortified via cultivation of Aza-as-illusion, 148–50, 151–52, 158–60, 169–70; realization of the capacity to use the power for herself primarily, 149, 159–60; reflection as necessity in, vs. susceptibility to reverie, 163–67, 169, 173. *See also* Graffigny, *Lettres*—delusion as error

—*PLAISIR D'ÊTRE* (PLEASURE IN BEING): overview, 8, 144, 149, 174–75; autonomy and, 160, 166; collective joy as potential of, 144, 154–55, 156; constraint and emancipation, oscillation between, 159; constraint as enabling condition of pleasure, 8–9, 142, 146, 157, 174, 175; corruption of, 156–57; cultivation of Aza-as-illusion as artifice enhancing and fortifying, 148–50, 151–52, 158–60, 169–70; cultivation of "second nature" allowing, 152, 159, 173–74; definition of, 144; Diderot's *repos délicieux* compared to, 158–59, 160, 221n34; as Epicurean Garden transmitting the management of pleasure, 155–56, 175; feminine solidarity in, 12; as "first feeling" nature inspired, 157, 159; "I am, I live, I exist" [*je suis, je vis, j'existe*], 155, 156, 157, 158; manor home ownership given as partial return of plundered Peruvian wealth, 146, 172, 175, 218n11, 222n70; the marriage plot as overcome and overwhelmed by, 8, 145, 148, 150, 156, 159–60, 174; mutuality, marriage as the end of, 150; and nature, study and observation of, 155, 157, 160; offering the happiness of simple friendship to Déterville, 146, 155, 156, 175; pleasure as voluptuous exchange (vs. delusion of possession), 164–66, 167–70, 222n53; realization of need to control the power of illusions for her own freedom, 149, 159–60; relational exchange of love as mutual enslavement, as delusion of possession, 171–73; as relationality without dependence, 144, 150–52, 158–61, 174–75; as relational/mutual, 149, 157, 160, 166, 169–70; Rousseau's *sentiment de l'existence* compared to, 149, 156–57
le Grand Condé. *See* Louis II de Bourbon, prince of Condé
Greenblatt, Stephen, 71
Green, Karen, 10, 213n22
Guattari, Félix, *devenir-femme*, 26–27, 52
Gumport, Elizabeth, 143

Hagengruber, Ruth, 108
Haller, Albrecht von, 54–55
happiness: definition of, 130; eros as diverted and sublimated into attachment to the collective, 63–65; love and study as purest forms of, 107; love of study as greatest contributor to happiness for women, 135, 138; treatises on, the 18th c. as known for, 1, 129. *See also* Du Châtelet, Émilie—illusion without error, pursuit of; Helvétius, Claude-Adrien—femininity and enlightened materialism
Hayes, Julie Candler, 123–24, 126, 139, 192n15, 207n15, 214n37
Helvétius, Claude-Adrien: condemnation and burning of work, 152; death of, 62; and Du Châtelet, friendship with, 1; genius ascribed by Graffigny to, 154; and Graffigny, friendship with, 12, 62, 152, 154, 220n26; immersion in salon culture, 62; wife of (Anne-Catherine de Ligniville), 152, 220n26
—FEMININITY AND ENLIGHTENED MATERIALISM: allegory of the poet and the feminine figure of Wisdom, 63–65; ambition rejected as source of suffering and unmet desires, 63–64, 65; femininity as the impetus of enlightenment, 62, 65; gendered subjects as different by degrees, not in kind, 38, 63–64; and re-orientation of society toward reciprocity and collective happiness, 62, 63–65
—WORKS: *Le Bonheur*, 62–65, 129, 154; *De L'espirit*, 62, 152, 154; *De l'homme*, 62
Heraclitus, "Nature likes to hide," 42
heroid genre, 86, 142, 143, 210n40
Hobson, Marian, 14, 194n20
Hock, Jessie, 4
Holbach, Paul Thiry d': *Système de la nature*, 191n6; *Théologie portative ou dictionnaire abrégé de la religion chrétienne*, ix
honnête homme and honnêteté, 27, 100, 181, 182
Houdard, Sophie, 185, 223n5
Howells, Robin, 149–50, 173
Hume, David, 11
Hutchinson, Lucy, 4, 206n8

idealism, Puisieux's works and, 82, 91, 93
illusion as resource in a ruined world, 8, 13, 69, 76–77. *See also* artifice; Du Châtelet, Émilie—illusion without error, pursuit of; Graffigny, Françoise de, *Lettres d'une Péruvienne*—illusion as resource in a ruined world; Puisieux, Madeleine d'Arsant de—artifice and craft of feminine pleasure
illusive materialists: overview, 30, 186; and clandestinity in women's writing, 7, 193–94n13; criteria for inclusion in this

INDEX

text, 9–11; definition of, 2; disagreement among ideas of, 7, 150; as "elusive," 2, 7; feminine solidarity as resisted by, 9, 75, 139; the heroid genre redeployed by, 86, 142, 143, 210n40; as interlocutors for important participants in materialist discussions, 1, 10, 11, 12, 71–72, 129, 150, 152, 154; as not identifying themselves directly as materialists, 2, 7, 10, 12–13, 84, 186, 224n21; as not protofeminist, 6, 9, 109–10, 161; and "second nature," cultivation of, 134, 152, 159, 173–74. *See also* artifice; artifice as pragmatics of pleasure and responsiveness to context; constraints on women; Du Châtelet, Émilie; elite privileges—and the illusive materialists; femininity as practice of pleasure (illusive materialisms); future readership, imagined; Gouges, Olympe de; Graffigny, Françoise de; illusion as resource in a ruined world; materialist philosophy as masculine purview—formal exclusion of women; pleasure as pragmatics (illusive materialisms); Puisieux, Madeleine d'Arsant de; *volupté* (Fr.)/*voluptas* (Lat.)/voluptuousness—and illusive materialisms

images: as conveying pleasurable sensation to the reader (Puisieux), 85, 89, 96–97, 98–100, 101, 130; as form of argument, x; of pleasure, as pleasure itself (La Mettrie), 33

Israel, Jonathan, 72, 193–94n13

Jacob, Margaret C., 193–94nn13–14
Jauch, Ursula Pia, 59, 212–13n15
Jaucourt, Louis de, "Penchant, Inclination," 67
Journal encyclopédique, 179, 180, 183
Judovitz, Dalia, 203n51

Kamuf, Peggy, 208n24
Kant, Immanuel: Du Châtelet as progenitor of, 105–6; progression toward critical maturity, 13, 101, 115; the sublime, 169; "What is Enlightenment?," 115
Kavanagh, Thomas, 15
Kraus, Chris: *I Love Dick*, 143; *Video Green*, 143
Kuhn, Thomas, 211–12n8

Laborde, Alice M., 72, 206–7n11
Laclos, Pierre Choderlos de, 10–11

La Fayette, Marie-Madeleine de: "It is enough to be," 141, 217n11; *La Princesse de Clèves*, 173
La Fontaine, Jean de, 84
Lambert, Anne-Thérèse de, 71
lamentation remade for sensualist ends, 86–87, 142, 143
La Mettrie, Julien Offray de: Cartesianism conjoined to Epicureanism, 52; condemnation and burning of work, 51, 59; critique as form of pleasure, 67–68; critique of final causes, 57–58; and Diderot, relationship with, 51–52, 60; and Du Châtelet, putative relationship with, 59–60, 65, 113–14, 212–13n15; Du Châtelet's *Institutions* as basis of some arguments of, 113–14; exclusion of women and feminine persons from the practice of philosophy, 58–59, 60, 61, 62, 65; gendered subjects as different by degrees, not in kind, 38, 53–54, 57, 62; the image of pleasure as pleasure itself, 33; and Lucretius, 52, 54, 57, 58, 60–61, 203n51; in the materialist corpus, 1, 2, and 10, 194n17; and Puisieux, misogynist attack on as *vulgivagous* (bad materialist), 59–60, 61, 65, 208n19
—FEMININE EPISTEMOLOGY ELABORATED BY: overview, 52; category blurring, 55, 203n52; and consent, 54; and feminine becoming, 52; femininity as condition of materiality, 58; fluidity and porosity as key attributes of (not all) bodies, 52–53, 58, 203nn51–52; gender no constraint on the male voluptuary, 38, 53–54, 57, 62; ideal voluptuous state (*demi-réveil*), 54; the impenetrable woman/feminine person whose body can engender neither children nor thoughts, and violence against, 55, 56–57, 58–59, 204n61–62,65; machine-man, 54, 58; the masculine philosopher invited to both contemplate and enjoy their femininity, 58, 61; the masculine philosopher's receptive intellect as space of conception, 55–56, 61, 62; as masculinist, 52–53, 203n51; *mollesse* (softness) of the male voluptuary, 53–54, 79, 209n33; nature portrayed as lacking conscious awareness and feeling, though generative, 57–58, 204n65; on nature's capacity for error, 56–57, 58; science and the sex act, analogy between, 54–55; seminal fluids emitted by women, 52, 203n51; seminal model of

— FEMININE EPISTEMOLOGY ELABORATED BY (*cont.*)
  reproduction, 57, 58; transphobia of, 56–57; uterine model of reproduction, 57–58; the voluptuous imagination as the art of self-deception, 53; voluptuousness as pleasure involved with art and conjugated in the mind or soul, 53–56, 78, 79, 81, 209n33; women's inversion of roles, 54; the writer as voluptuary, 53, 85
— WORKS: *Anti-Sénèque ou Discours sur le bonheur*, 60, 129; *L'École de la volupté*, 53–54, 55, 56; *Histoire naturelle de l'ârme* (prefaced by "Lettre critique. . ."), 51, 59, 113–14, 127, 212–13n15; *L'Homme-machine*, 54–56, 61–62, 203n51, 206n10; *L'Homme-plante*, 204n62; *Supplément à l'Ouvrage de Pénélope*, 51; *Système d'Épicure*, 56–59; *La Volupté*, 59, 78, 84, 86–87, 212–13n15

La Mothe Le Vayer, François de, *De la vertu des payens*, 37

Lascano, Marcy P., 131, 216n63

Latin: education in, rarely permitted to women, 3, 84; Puisieux as unable to admit to knowing how to read in, 84

Lavery, Grace, xi, 1–2

Leibniz, Gottfried Wilhelm, 11, 139; in frontispiece, 110, 111; metaphysics of, as basis of Du Châtelet's, 11, 59, 109, 113, 121, 126, 128

"leibnizo-newtonianisme" as proposed heuristic, 211–12n8

Lenclos, Ninon de: anti-Epicurean polemicists referencing, 37, 43; as emblem of *honnêteté*, 181, 182; as exception to the general absence of women in materialist philosophy, 3, 180, 224n9; as exponent of Epicureanism, 181, 223n5, 224n9; imprisonment in convent for "immoral conduct," 185; libertinism of, and inability to escape constraints due to her identity as a woman, 185; as "man in drag" and other masculine readings and self-stylings, 181, 182, 185, 223n5; as "modern Leontion," 3, 181, 224n9; myth of, 223n4; representation of, by Olympe de Gouges, 179–86; salon of, 179, 180, 224n9. *See also* Gouges, Olympe de, *Molière chez Ninon ou le siècle des Grands Hommes*

Leontion: anti-Epicurean polemicists referencing, 35, 37, 43, 201–2n32; Epicureanism of, 3, 43; Ninon de Lenclos as "modern Leontion," 3, 181, 224n9

Leprince de Beaumont, Marie, 71

Le Ru, Véronique, 108

Lespinasse, Julie Jeanne Éléonore de, 10, 11

Lewis, Ann, 150, 220n24

libertine ethics: and constraint as enabling condition of pleasure, 8–9, 74; Diderot's libertine anticipation (*repos délicieux*) of *sentiment de l'existence*, 158–59, 160, 221n34; fidelity as orthodoxy, 87, 210n41; Gouge's *Molière chez Ninon* describing persecution of Lenclos as woman embracing, 181, 182–83, 184–85; Graffigny's *Lettres d'une Péruvienne* as fusion of sentimental fiction and, 141–42, 150–52, 154, 219n19, 220n24; pleasure as emancipatory force, 8–9; pleasure as return or awakening to nature, 76, 77; satirizing the Augustinian model of desire, 123; shedding of attachments in, 76

libertine fiction: absence of women authors due to constraints on, 2–3; the countryside as site of sexual freedom, 91–92; and the eighteenth-century age of pleasure, 15, 16, 194–95n22; eroticization of the scene of knowledge (and Du Châtelet's revision of), 110, 111–12, 212n10; femininity ratified as the necessary form bodies take, 23–24; forms of violence inherent in seduction narratives, 69; Puisieux's *Le Plaisir et la volupté* as libertine allegory, 68, 88, 89–90, 91–92, 95, 96–97, 210n44; unveiling hypocrisy as delight of, 9; women authors published (early 19th century), 3

libertine materialist philosophy: absence of women authors due to constraints on, 2–5, 10, 11, 12, 193nn6–7; inflecting scientific inquiry, 41, 56; male authors subject to social sanctions for, 3–4; women authors persecuted for, 185. *See also* feminist historians and literary critics recovering women's work

Ligniville, Anne-Catherine de ("Minette"), 152, 220n20

Litwin, Christophe, 156

Locke, John, 11, 154

Lotterie, Florence, 3, 4, 89, 193n6

Louis II de Bourbon, prince of Condé, as character in Gouges's *Molière chez Ninon*, 180, 183

Louis XIV, 180

Louis XV, 24
Lucretius, *De rerum natura*: anthropology, Venus of, 118–19, 123, 215–16n58; anti-Epicurean polemicists' condemnation of, 35–36; as authority, 117; continued resonance of, 70–71; Diderot's epigraph based on, 39–40, 201n21; Du Châtelet and book four, 137; Du Châtelet knitting together the anthropology and the invocation in an unexpected way, 117–21, 123; generation as involving the mixing of masculine and feminine seeds, 203n51; the illusive materialists' approach to pleasure as inflected by, 13, 220–21n29; invocation of Venus as engine of voluptuous animation, 23, 54, 64, 70, 118, 206n5; La Mettrie and, 52, 54, 57, 58, 60–61, 203n51; materialism as therapeutics, 170; in materialist corpus, ix, 2, 23, 27, 37, 117; matter as infinite and infinitely diverse, 215n53; on mutual sensitivity, 169; on poetic works as source of delight, 119; possessive model of erotic passion, critique of (*errantes incerti*; wandering aimless), 168–69, 172, 174; promiscuity recommended as cure for unrequited desire, 60–61, 137; Puisieux's "Le Printems" compared to, 70–71, 206n8; and Puisieux's *volupté* commentary, as possible source for, 84; reemergence in fifteenth-century Europe, 23; revival in the twenty-first century, 206n6; Lisa Robertson's "complicitous nilling" in reading of, 208n25; Rousseau and, 221n34; understanding of women's pleasure in, 206n8; on vision, 39–40; *vulgivaga* as positive reference to an ethic of wandering, 60–61, 204–5n71. *See also* Venus (in Lucretius's *De rerum natura*)
luxe/luxury trade, 15, 21, 27, 138, 171–72, 214n24, 222n70

machines/mechanistics: constraints on women, and Puisieux's envy of women who resemble automata, 101–2; La Mettrie's machine-man, 54, 58; sociability with women and metaphors of women's power as, 19, 20, 21, 197n32
Maillet, Benoît de, *Telliamed*, 206n10
Mallinson, Jonathan, 219n22
Mandeville, Bernard, 2; condemnation, ritual burning, and banning of work, 116; *Fable of the Bees*, Du Châtelet's translation and revision of, 116–22, 212n9, 213n22, 214nn24,37, 215–16n58
Marivaux, Pierre de, 4
Martin, Christophe, 199n52
masculinity: denial of the forms of violence in seduction narratives, 69; as enfeebled and unappealing norm, 17; exclusivity of, 200n18; Helvétius's feminization of enlightenment and retrieval of a happier and more philosophical version of, 65; and the "two-sex" model of gender difference, 16–17. *See also* materialist philosophy as masculine purview
materialist philosophy: overview, vii; absence of women authors due to constraints on, 2–5, 10, 11, 12, 192n15, 193nn6–7; anthropomorphism, critique of, 220–21n29; authoritative pronouncements and orthodoxies, resistance to, ix–x, 33, 75; community as vision of, 154, 177; as ethical scandal, 51–52; *matérialiste* as pejorative term, 4, 10; *matérialiste* as term, La Mettrie and embrace of, 4, 10, 194n17; as reflexive habit or style of thought, x, 44, 45–46; turning point in history of, 9–10, 72, 206n10; vitalism, 10, 127, 213n22; willingness to productively disavow itself or to alter its form, ix–x. *See also* community as materialist value; Epicureanism (classical); feminist historians and literary critics recovering women's work; illusive materialists; libertine materialist philosophy; materialist philosophy as masculine purview; neo-Epicureanism; pleasure as materialist value; speculation as materialist nondogmatic tradition; Stoicism
materialist philosophy as masculine purview: as extraction from the feminine condition, 18, 38–39, 49, 61–62; Graffigny's *Lettres* as loosening, 151; the receptive intellect as space of conception, 55–56; the sphere of thought protected as realm of masculine sociability, 38–39. *See also* femininity as theory of experience; neo-Epicureanism — bad materialisms; neo-Epicureanism — good materialisms
— FORMAL EXCLUSION OF WOMEN: overview of, in context of neo-Epicureanism embracing prestige of feminine receptivity, 65–66; Diderot justifying, 46–50, 62, 80; and the illusive materialists not identifying themselves directly as materialists, 2, 7,

—FORMAL EXCLUSION OF WOMEN (cont.) 10, 12–13, 84, 186, 224n21; La Mettrie justifying, 58–59, 60, 61, 62, 65; Puisieux as profoundly critical of, 101–2; and the sensualist norm claiming women's intricate constitution produced inferior capacity of thought, 46–51, 79–80. See also constraints on women; Du Châtelet, Émilie—constraints experienced as woman of science; misogyny; salon culture; sociability with women (commerce; traffic in women)

mathematics: Diderot on preference for experimental science vs. abstractions of, 39, 40; pleasure as deriving from work of (Du Châtelet), 113, 123

Maupertuis, *Essai de philosophie morale*, Puisieux's commentary on, 60, 74, 75, 208n19

Maurepas, Jean Frédéric Phélypeaux, comte de, 181

Mauzi, Robert, 129

memory: Diderot on, vii–viii, 191n1; of pain vs. pleasure, 102. See also mind/brain

Mercier, Louis-Sébastien, *Maison de Molière*, 179–80

Merteuil, marquise de, 209n38

Mesch, Rachel, 219n21, 222n53

metaphysics. See Du Châtelet, Émilie—metaphysics

Miller, Nancy K., 219n19

mind/brain: the material conditions necessary to cultivate the mind, 114–16, 120, 213n17; material flexibility of, as source of both pleasures and vulnerability to harm, viii–ix. See also memory; perception

misogyny: anti-Epicurean discourse opposing *volupté* and *virtus*, 35–37, 38, 62, 199–200n8; and the fear of becoming (like) a woman, 23; La Mettrie's vitriolic labeling of Puisieux as "bad materialist," 59–60, 61, 65, 208n19; Puisieux's reception shaped by her relationship with Diderot, 72

modernity: and the absence of women authors from libertine and materialist critique, 4–5; and the age of pleasure, 15, 16; of Diderot's *Les Bijoux*, 24, 25–26; Du Châtelet's work as fitting uneasily into grand narratives of, 109; Lucretius's *DRN* as augur of, 71; Puisieux's work as fitting uneasily into grand narratives of, 109

Molière, 180; as character in Gouges's *Molière chez Ninon*, 180, 181, 183, 184; Mercier's *Maison de Molière* as homage to, 179–80

mollesse (softness): Diderot's *repos délicieux* and, 158; and Helvétius's allegory of the poet and feminine Wisdom, 63–64; the illusive materialists as avoiding or evading, 7–8; invocation of, as instrument of objectification, 79–80; of La Mettrie's voluptuous male reader, 53–54, 79, 209n33; and sensualist norm of women's delicate constitutions as inferior, 79–80. See also *délicatesse* (illusive materialisms)

Montagu, Mary Wortley, *Woman Not Inferior to Man* attributed to, 206–7n11

Montaigne, Michel de: endorsing women's freedom to desire and also to consent, 23; *Essais*, 203n48; in materialist corpus, ix, 27, 198n45; on philosophy as apprenticeship for death, 203n48

Montesquieu, Charles-Louis de Secondat, baron de: *chaîne secrète*, 34; and Graffigny's *Lettres d'une Péruvienne*, 142, 146, 218n9–10; "How can one be Persian?," 148–49; on political influence of women, 19–20, 21, 197n32; sociability with women as emasculating, 17–20, 21–23, 24–25, 26, 196nn28–29, 197n40. Works: *Céphise et l'amour*, 68; *Lettres persanes*, 17, 19–20, 24, 26, 142, 146, 148–49, 196n28, 218nn9–10; *Pensées*, 17–19, 20, 21–22, 26; "Que philosopher, c'est apprendre à mourir" (in the *Essais*), 203n48; *Le Temple de Gnide*, 68, 90

moralist writing: exclusion of women from, 192n5; tension between the general and the particular as typical of genre, 207n15

Morency, Suzanne Giroust de, *Illyrine, ou l'écueil de l'inexpérience*, 3

Mortier, Roland, 158

Mylne, Vivienne, 210n44

nature: and artifice, Diderot's denial of distinction between, 42; and artifice, entwinement with, 89, 96–97, 101, 186; capacity for error of, 56–57; delusion of possession in experience of, vs. zone of *volupté*, 164–66, 167–68, 169, 222n53; libertine conception of progression to pleasure as return to, 77; "Nature likes to hide" (Heraclitus), 42; passive theory of woman's nature, as operating to their detriment, 174; pleasures of, as intertwining with literary pleasures, 70; portrayed as lacking conscious awareness and feeling, though generative, 57–58, 204n65; Puisieux on women's pleasure as not natural, 76, 77, 89; as surpassing the capacity of the human mind to understand, 40; as woman in disguise (*femme travestie*), 41, 42

neo-Epicureanism: Augustinian, 118, 123; condemnation and burning of works, 51, 59, 152; condemned as turn to effeminacy from which the disciple can never return, 37, 200nn15,17; and the eighteenth-century "age of pleasure," 15, 194–95n22; as embracing the association with femininity, 37–39, 46–47, 65–66, 200n18, 201n20; gendered subjects as different by degrees, not in kind, 38, 41, 42, 46–47, 62; and human consciousness, 45, 46; as less a doctrine and more a condition of experience, 44, 45–46; proliferation of narratives about women (or written from a feminine point of view), 4, 38, 200n18, 201n20; self-interest as fundamental motivation for humans, Du Châtelet's revision of, 117–18, 119; Stoicism in dynamic relation to, 43; women and transmission of, 43. *See also* Du Châtelet, Émilie—neo-Epicurean philosopher; Epicureanism (classical); femininity as theory of experience; Lenclos, Ninon de; materialist philosophy as masculine purview; *mollesse* (softness); pleasure as materialist value; *volupté* (Fr.)/*voluptas* (Lat.)/voluptuousness

—BAD MATERIALISMS: definition of, 39; Diderot on La Mettrie as, 52; Du Châtelet's elite status and, 138; Graffigny and the specter of, 152; La Mettrie's misogynist attack on Puisieux as (*vulgivagous*), 59–60, 61, 65, 208n19; Puisieux's reception as, 72, 102–3

—GOOD MATERIALISMS: definition of, 39; Diderot as representative of, 72, 207n12; in light of Puisieux's designation as "bad" materialist, 102–3

new materialism, "sensitive witnessing" in women's writing as anticipating, 4

Newtonian vs. Cartesian paradigm shift, 108–9

Newton, Isaac: Du Châtelet's revisions of, 126; Du Châtelet's translation and commentary on, 106, 107; in frontispieces, 110, *111–12*

Ninon. *See* Lenclos, Ninon de

nonhuman agency, 126

nonhuman/human binary, critique of, 4

nonhuman/human relationality, 64–65, 119

novel as form, constraints on ability to address cultural differences, 147–48

objectification of women: and the age of pleasure, 15–16, 28; Graffigny's social critique of, 170–71; invocation of feminine delicacy as instrument of, 79–80; and sexy but insensible bodies as gendered, 32

O'Neal, John C., 194n19, 220–21n29

orientalist tropes of the harem as symbol of male depletion, 19, 20–21, 197n33

Osborne, Janet, 210n44

Ovid, 84

papillotage, 14, 101, 163, 194n20

Paris Academy of Science, 124–25

Passannante, Gerard, x, 71

penchants and inclinations: "Penchant, Inclination" (de Jaucourt), 67; pleasure as oscillation between (Puisieux), 76–77

perception: as living on within the body, vii–viii; material conditions of, as contingency, 39–40. *See also* memory

Persian culture, femininity and the harem, 19

Petronius, *Satyrica* 85–87, 53

philosophy: as apprenticeship for death, 50–51, 203n48; eros diverted and sublimated into the arts and, 63–65. *See also* materialist philosophy; sociability with women (commerce; traffic in women)

plaisir d'être. *See* Graffigny, Françoise de—*plaisir d'être* (pleasure of being); *sentiment de l'existence*

Plato, 49, 91; *Symposium*, 93

pleasure as materialist value: overview, 4–5; autonomy of pleasure, 4–5, 22; critique as mode of pleasure, 67–68; Du Châtelet's attachment to, 114, 129, 138; the eighteenth century as age of pleasure, 15–17, 194–95n22; and exclusion of women authors from libertine and materialist critique, pleasure as materialist value (*cont.*) 4–5; and femininity as "contagious," 24, 26; and femininity as privileged expression of materiality, 23–24; Puisieux's investment in, 69; as reconciling gender- and class-related divides, 16; as universal drive and fundamental human need, 44, 75–76, 77–78. *See also* femininity as theory of experience; *sentiment de l'existence*; *volupté* (Fr.)/*voluptas* (Lat.)/voluptuousness

pleasure as pragmatics (illusive materialisms): overview, 28, 29; and crafty cultivation of an ethic of pleasure, 14–15; definition of, 5; as instrument of getting by and making do, 14; women's experience of pleasure as not a natural condition, 76–77, 89. *See also* artifice; artifice as pragmatics of pleasure and responsiveness to context; constraint as enabling condition of pleasure; *délicatesse* (illusive materialisms); *volupté* (Fr.)/*voluptas* (Lat.)/voluptuousness—and illusive materialisms

pleasure of being. *See* Graffigny, Françoise de—*plaisir d'être* (pleasure of being); *sentiment de l'existence*

Plutarch, condemnation of the Epicureans, 35–37, 62

Pope, Alexander, 129

Pope, Michael, 203n51

pornographic literature, 15, 16, 25, 26, 89, 208n25, 210n43

Porter, Roy, 15, 194–95n22

positionality of the author: assessing privilege in Du Châtelet, 105–7; and critique as form of pleasure, 67–68; discovering Graffigny, 141–42, 144; feminine point of view of, 34, 106; previous book on plants, 33–34; reading Puisieux as libertine, 67–69. *See also* writing

possessive model of erotic passion, critiques of: Lucretius, 168–69, 172, 174; Sade, 172. *See also* Graffigny, Françoise de, *Lettres d'une Péruvienne*—delusion as error

préciosité, 89

prejudices: freedom from, Du Châtelet's illusion without error as dependent on, 130, 131; narratives running counter to, as resisted by readers, 147–48

promiscuity, 60–61, 137

prostitution. *See* courtesans and *hetaerae*; sexuality and sexual intercourse

Puisieux, Madeleine d'Arsant de: overview, 2, 6, 11, 67–69, 101–3; as Aristippean, 71, 74–75; and aristocratic femininity, 141; on the constraints imposed on her own life, 84, 90, 101–2; on the constraints on women, 68–69, 82–83, 84, 89, 91; conventional style and content of, 70, 71, 72, 109; corpus of, 72, 206–7n11; criticized as bad influence on Diderot, 72; criticized as "bad" materialist in reception of, 72, 102–3; criticized for cynicism, 71, 91; criticized for reluctance to embrace orthodox conceptions of feminine virtue, 72; and Diderot, love relationship with, 11, 60, 71–72, 80, 198n48; and elite privilege, 75, 79, 101; exclusion from moralist writing canon, 192n5; and feminine solidarity, dubiousness about, 75; and *La Femme n'est pas inférieure à l'homme*, attribution of, 206–7n11; future readership imagined by, 13–14; husband of, 206–7n11; lamentation remade for sensualist ends, 86–87, 142; La Mettrie's misogynist attack on, as *vulgivagous* (bad materialist), 59–60, 61, 65, 208n19; libertine ideal of, as committed to the material circumstances of pleasure's production, 74; Lucretius as possible source for, 84; and Lucretius's *De rerum natura*, comparison with, 70–71, 206n8; materialist *milieu* of, 71–72, 150; materialist tradition activated by, 73–74, 76–77, 102–3, 207n15; oscillation between the personal/concrete and generalizing/abstraction, 73, 207n15; pessimism about liberation from constraints on women, 91, 101, 102; racist and racialized assumptions in writing of, 100, 101, 175–76; reception of, 70–71, 72, 77, 102; as rejecting systematization and as unfaithful to precept, 72–73, 74–76, 77, 208n25; "sensualism" as criticism of, 74; and sensualist norm, revision of, 79–80; speculation and, 13–14, 71, 72, 73, 102; Stoicism and Epicureanism both rejected as inflexible in principle, 74–75

—ARTIFICE AND CRAFT OF FEMININE PLEASURE: agency in desire, 76, 208n24; allegorical counterparts with human couples as creating (lasting) *volupté* cultivated in the context of art, 87–88, 92–97; illusion as resource in a ruined world, 8,

69, 76–77; management of perception and sensation as necessary to avoid peril, 74, 76–77, 150; as materialist practice, 69, 76–77, 101, 150–51
— ETHIC OF PLEASURE AND: overview, 11, 12, 14–15; careful management and cultivation of the passions as goal, 74; and consent, 194n20; constraint as enabling condition of pleasure, viii–ix, 8–9, 74, 91, 101, 109, 157, 175; on contextual adaptation, importance of, 74–76; Graffigny's relationality without dependence and, 152, 171; men's pleasure as zone of ruin and devastation for women, 69, 76; pain and pleasure as the only real, viii, 74; perception as source of both pleasures and harms, viii–ix; pleasure as oscillation between sensual "penchants" and thoughtful "inclination," 76–77; the "state of woman" as specific interest and investment, 73; women's pleasure not a natural condition, 76, 77, 89
— VOLUPTÉ: allegorical counterparts with human couples as creating (lasting) pleasure cultivated in the context of art, 87–88, 92–97; allegorical personae as agents of pleasure (the arresting trope), 87, 88, 89, 154; allegorical personae as envoys of pleasure, 87, 88, 101; allegorical personae, mirroring and, 95–96; *amour propre* and, 93, 100–101; beauty/ugliness as material condition, 81–82, 83; constancy as lending substance to love, 97; constraints on the treatise she wished to write, 84, 90; constraints on women, renegotiation of, 91; *délicatesse* as bound to *volupté*, 78–79, 80–81, 83, 94, 95, 98; *délicatesse* as source of suffering, 102; distinguished from *plaisir*, 77–78, 81; equilibrium between virtue and desire, 68–69, 97–101; and *esprit* (soul, taste, spirit, wit), 82; femininity as allegory of embodiment, 89; free indirect discourse, 99–100; idealism and, 82, 91, 93; the image (poetic and visual) as conveying pleasurable sensation to the reader, 85, 89, 96–97, 98–100, 101, 130; inconstancy and abandonment of women as problem, 68, 87, 88, 90–91, 94, 96, 98, 210n40; *jouissance* distinguished from, 83; La Mettrie's essay on *volupté*, question of whether Puisieux knew of, 78,

84; libertine allegory and, 68, 88, 89–90, 91–92, 95, 96–97, 210n44; literary writing as allowing expression on, 84–85, 90; and materialism of experience, 85, 89, 90, 91; narrative structure used to convey, 98; *papillotage* in, 101; as pleasure conjugated in the soul (âme), 78–79, 81, 82–83, 93, 99, 102; as practical ideal, 89; relationships between mature women and young men, 69, 92–94, 95, 96–101, 110; reputation as material condition, 82, 84; and the sentimental genre, 87, 88; and the sight of the beloved, 81, 97–100; and taste, 78, 81–82, 98; virtuous action as, 83
— WORKS: "Aux Plaisirs" [*To Pleasures*], 85–89, 90, 92–93, 96, 98; "Bouquet," 70; *Les Caractères*, 60, 69, 71, 72–73, 74–76, 77–85, 88, 90, 208n19; *Céphise, conte moral*, 68, 87, 88, 90, 98; commentary on Fontenelle's *Du Bonheur*, 60, 74, 75, 85, 129, 208n19; commentary on Maupertuis's *Essai de philosophie morale*, 60, 74, 75, 208n19; *Conseils à une amie*, 73; *L'Éducation du marquis de ***, ou Mémoires de la comtesse de Zurlac* (rewriting of Crébillon fils's *Les Égarements*), 68–69, 93–94, 97–101, 110; "L'Hiver" [*Winter*], 70; *Le Plaisir et la volupté*, 68, 77–78, 85, 87, 88, 89–97, 98; "Le Printems" [*Spring*], 69–71; *Prospectus sur un ouvrage important*, 206–7n11; *Réflexions et avis sur les défauts et ridicules à la mode*, viii, 73, 74, 82, 93, 101–2

Puisieux, Philippe-Florent de (husband of Madeleine), and *La Femme n'est pas inférieure à l'homme*, attribution as translator of English pamphlet, 206–7n11

queer families, 224n17
Quinault, Mlle Jeanne, salon of, 152, 220n26
quipos/quipus/khipu (Quechua mode of writing), 145, 147, 161, 218n5

racial differences: deployed by illusive materialists as status privilege, 9; Du Châtelet's writing and racist and racialized assumptions, 115, 175–76; and fear of becoming (like) a woman, 23; Puisieux's writing and racist and racialized assumptions, 100, 101, 175–76; racial logic of Graffigny's

racial differences *(cont.)*
  Peruvian princess in European rather than Indigenous dress, 167, 169; women's embodiment described in terms of, 48–49. *See also* elite privileges; ethnic differences
Rath, Jessica, xi; *Early Girl (Burst Variant)*, 32; *Ripe Gambol*, 31, 32; *Ripe Still*, 31–32, 32
Réage, Pauline (Anne Desclos), 208n25, 210n43
reason: convergence of love and, in illusion without error, 124, 131, 216n63; Graffigny on reason as instrument of social critique, 151, 173, 219n21; speculative/creative dimensions of scientific reason, 113, 123–24, 125–26, 215n42; as universal (and dismissal of rhetoric), 121–22, 214nn36–37
reciprocity: Du Châtelet's loving for two in the illusion of, 136–38, 149; Graffigny's delusion of possession and failed reciprocity, 166–67, 168, 169; Graffigny's maintenance of fictive reciprocity as life-sustaining force, 147, 148, 161–63; Helvétius's enlightened materialism and re-orientation of society toward collective happiness and, 62, 63–65. *See also* community as materialist value
reflexivity, politics of, x
Reill, Peter, 9–10
reputation, 82–83, 84
Rey, Anne-Lise, 108–9, 211–12nn8,10
Riccoboni, Marie Jeanne, 10–11
Roberts, Marie Mulvey, 194–95n22
Robertson, Lisa, xi; *Debbie: An Epic*, 191n6; *Nilling*, 43, 77, 191n6, 208n25, 210n43
Rochester, Earl of, "A Satire against Man," 136, 137–38, 217n81
Rococo art and design, 4, 10, 15; ideal of *papillotage*, 14, 101, 163, 194n20
Rome, ancient: chastity as male civic virtue, 61; public life revolving around cultivation of masculine virtue, 35, 61
Rousseau, Jean-Jacques: and Lucretius, 221n34; on the salon as queer seraglio, 20–21, 197n35; *sentiment de l'existence* and *amour de soi*, 149, 156–57, 221n34; shifting the valence of the Cartesian *cogito*, 156; on sociability with women as emasculating, 20–23, 24–25, 26, 197n40; and women's voices, 4. Works: *Lettre à d'Alembert*, 20–22, 197n35; *Lettres morales*, 156
Roussel, Pierre, 79, 80
Rutler, Tracy, 197n35, 224n17

Sade, marquis de, 67, 210n41; *La Philosophie dans le boudoir*, 172
Saint-Évremond, Charles de: as character in Gouges's *Molière chez Ninon*, 185; "Sur les opéra," 194n20
Saint-Lambert, Jean-François de: love relationship with Du Châtelet, 62, 106–7, 134, 138–39; publisher of Helvétius's *Le Bonheur*, 62, 129
Salaün, Franck, 10
salon culture: Graffigny and Mlle Quinault's salon, 152, 220n26; Graffigny's salon, 12, 62, 152, 220n26; Helvétius and immersion in, 62; Rousseau's framing as resembling a queer seraglio, 20–21, 197n35. *See also* Lenclos, Ninon de
Scarron, Madame, 180
Scarron, Paul, as character in Gouges's *Molière chez Ninon*, 180, 183, 185
Schliesser, Eric, 131
Schor, Naomi, 34
science: Diderot's endorsement of experimental vs. mathematical approaches, 39–42; empirical/experimental, constraints on women's participation in, 84, 209n38; La Mettrie's analogy of the catalepsy of study with ecstasies of love, 54–56; libertine dimension of, 41, 56. *See also* headings under Du Châtelet, Émilie
seminal fluids emitted by women, 41–42, 52, 203n51
Seneca, *De vita beata*, on Epicurus in drag, 36, 43, 200n17
sensation: ceaseless movements of, viii, ix; as living within the body, vii–viii
the senses of the philosopher, as means by which ideas enter the body, 56
sentimental genre: Graffigny's *Lettres d'une Péruvienne* as fusion of libertine fiction and, 141–42, 150–52, 154, 156, 219n19, 220n24; Puisieux and, 87, 88
sentiment de l'existence: corruption of, 156–57; Cyrano de Bergerac and, 221n36; Diderot's libertine anticipation of (*repos délicieux*), 158–59, 160, 221n34; Graffigny's *plaisir d'être* differentiated

from, 156–59, 160, 221n34; of Rousseau (*amour de soi*), 156–57, 221n34. See also Graffigny, Françoise de, *Lettres d'une Péruvienne—plaisir d'être* (pleasure in/of being)

sexuality and sexual intercourse: the act of thinking as reproduction of the soul, 55–56; the catalepsy of study as analogous with ecstasies of, 54–56; as crucial instance of category blurring, 203n52; eros as diverted and sublimated into attachment to the collective, 63–65; multiple disparate conceptions of, as distinct "measured" dimensions, 60–61; pleasure experienced by both men and women in, 41; promiscuity, as insult to women, 60, 61; promiscuity, Lucretius recommending as cure for the wounds of love, 60–61, 137; seminal fluids emitted by women in, 41–42, 52, 203n51; and sociability with women viewed as emasculating, 21–22. See also *volupté* (Fr.)/*voluptas* (Lat.)/voluptuousness

sexual reproduction: seminal model of, 57, 58; uterine model of, 57–58

Showalter, English, 152, 154, 220n26

Silver, Marie-France, 74, 97

Simon, Julia, 218n11

sociability with women (commerce; traffic in women): overview, 21, 197n40; anti-Epicurean polemicists condemning inclusion of women in the Garden, 36, 43, 201–2n32; contagious effects of femininity, 16–22, 26, 120, 197n40; contagious effects of femininity, the materialists and, 24, 26, 33; Crébillon fils's portrayal of emasculation in, 22–23, 24–25, 197n33; Diderot on, as positive mode of exchange, 43–44, 49–50, 52, 80; Du Châtelet on women's education as source of inspiration and strength for others, 120; mechanist metaphors of women's power, 19, 20, 21, 197n32; Montesquieu's portrayal of emasculation in, 17–20, 21–23, 24–25, 26, 120, 196nn28–29, 197n40; orientalist tropes of the harem as symbol of male depletion, 19, 20–21, 197n33; the political influence of the feminine as emasculating, 19–20, 22–23, 24–25, 26, 197n33; Rousseau's portrayal of feminization and decadence, 20–23, 24–25, 26, 120, 197n40; and sexual pleasure, 21–22; and the turn toward pleasure, 22. See also salon culture

socialist feminism, 3

softness. See *mollesse* (softness)

the soul: Cartesian (*res cogitans*), 83; constraints on women, and living as if they had no soul, 82; female, the sensualist norm claiming superficiality of, 48–49, 79–80; *volupté* as pleasure conjugated in (âme) (Puisieux), 78–79, 81, 82–83, 93, 99, 102; *volupté* as pleasure conjugated in the mind or (La Mettrie), 55–56, 78–79, 81

speculation as materialist nondogmatic tradition: overview of the illusive materialists as reactivating, 6, 13–14, 28; Cyrano de Bergerac's speculative fiction, 23–24, 221n36; Diderot and, 24, 73; Du Châtelet on dimensions of, in scientific reasoning, 113, 123–24, 125–26, 215n42; Du Châtelet's illusion without error and, 107, 138, 139; Gouges's speculative history of feminine materialist ethics, 186; Graffigny's speculative fiction, 151, 176, 221n36; Lucretius and, 71, 73; Puisieux and, 13–14, 71, 72, 73, 102

Spink, J. S., 221n36

Spinoza, Baruch, 131, 163

Stalnaker, Joanna, 191n1

Steinbrügge, Lieselotte, 79, 202–3n44

Steintrager, James, 4–5, 22, 198n47

Stewart, Philip, 208

Stoicism: condemning Epicureans for feminine attachment to pleasure, 35–37, 43, 62; Diderot and, 43, 50, 51, 203n48; Du Châtelet's fire-as-world-soul and affinities with, 127; in dynamic relation to Epicureanism, 43, 50; on philosophy as apprenticeship for death, 43, 50, 51, 203n48; Puisieux's rejection of both Epicureanism and, as inflexible in principle, 74–75

subjectivity of the writer, 34, 199n7. See also positionality of the author; writing

suffering, ambition rejected as source of (Helvétius), 63–64, 65

suffering of women: Diderot on, 47, 48; and pleasure as not a natural condition (Puisieux), 76, 77; Puisieux's pessimism about liberation from, 102

Tahiti, 176
Tencin, Claudine de, 62
Terrall, Mary, 109–10, 113, 121
theater: Du Châtelet and, 2, 105, 133. See also Gouges, Olympe de, *Molière chez Ninon ou le siècle des Grands Hommes*
Thomas, Antoine-Léonard, *Essai sur le caractère, les mœurs et l'esprit des femmes des différents siècles*, 47, 49
Thomson, Ann, 51, 59–60, 194n14, 212–13n15
Tiffany, Daniel, 203n51
traffic in women. See sociability with women (commerce; traffic in women)
transphobia, 56–57
travestissement (disguise or drag): Ninon de Lenclos as man in drag, as revision of Epicurus as, 181; nature as woman in disguise, 41, 42; women's self-concealment as, 41. See also Epicurus—in drag

Vanoflen, Laurence, 72
Vartanian, Aram, 51, 59, 212–13n15
Venus (in Lucretius's *De rerum natura*): in the anthropology, 118–19, 123, 215–16n58; anti-Epicurean polemicists taxing the Epicurean attachment to, 36; invocation of, as engine of voluptuous animation, 23, 54, 64, 70, 118, 206n5; as *vulgivagous* (positive sexual valence in ethic of wandering), 60–61
violence: against the impenetrable woman/feminine person whose body can engender neither children nor thoughts, 55, 56–57, 58–59, 204n61–62, 65; denial of the forms of in seduction narratives, 69
virtue/*virtus* (Lat.): anti-Epicurean discourse condemning attachment to pleasure as immoral rejection of, 35–37, 38, 62, 199–200n8; chastity as male civic virtue, 61; Graffigny on feminine virtue, 12, 151, 170–71, 174–75; and pleasure, as universal good, 116–17; pleasure seen as the opposite of, 35; Puisieux on equilibrium between *volupté* and, 68–69, 97–101; Roman public life revolving around cultivation of masculine virtue, 35, 61; Rousseau on sociability with women as depleting men's capacity for, 21
vision: Lucretius on, 39–40; omnipotence as a spectator, as delusion of possession, 164–65, 167

vitalism, 10, 127, 213n22
Voltaire: defense of luxury economies and cultivation of aesthetic delight, 27–28, 214n24; Du Châtelet, love relationship with, 1, 110, 124, 134, 136–37, 212–13n15; Du Châtelet represented as muse by, 110, 112; Graffigny naming *Alzire* as intertext, 142; and La Mettrie's vitriol in *Anti-Sénèque*, 60, 212–13n15; on the nature and propagation of fire as subject, 124. Works: *Alzire*, 142, 144; *Discours sur l'homme*, 129; *Éléments de la philosophie de Newton*, 110, 112; "Le Mondain," 27–28, 199n52; *Traité de métaphysique*, 214n24
volupté (Fr.)/*voluptas* (Lat.)/voluptuousness: anti-Epicurean misogynist discourse opposing *virtus* to, 35–37, 38, 62, 199–200n8; *Encyclopédie* entry focusing on as illicit pleasure, 78; eros diverted and sublimated into an attachment to the collective, 63–65; as pleasure involved with art and conjugated in the mind or soul (La Mettrie), 53–56, 78–79, 81, 209n33; Sade on human right to refuse love as delusion of possession, 172; the sensualist norm claiming women's delicate constitutions produced impaired responsiveness to, 79–80. See also pleasure as materialist value; sexuality and sexual intercourse
—AND ILLUSIVE MATERIALISMS: as never guaranteed, 8, 9, 75–76, 124, 128; pleasure as zone of *volupté* (vs. delusion of possession), 164–66, 167–70, 222n53. See also pleasure as pragmatics (illusive materialisms); Puisieux, Madeleine d'Arsant de—*volupté*
vulgivagous: La Mettrie's misogynist labeling of Puisieux as "bad materialist," 59–60, 61, 65, 208n19; Lucretius's use of the term as positive connection to an ethic of wandering, 60–61, 204–5n71

Wade, Ira O., 108, 116
Wallman, Elisabeth, 116, 213n22
Warman, Caroline, 31, 32
Wolfe, Charles T., 10, 42, 194n14
Wolfgang, Aurora, 176, 218n14, 220n24
women's writing: contributions to *ancien régime* literary culture, 2–3, 192n3; female confession in repentant vs. philosophical modes, 143; historical turning point in, 10;

replacement of women authors by men, 201n20. *See also* constraints on women; feminist historians and literary critics recovering women's work

Wright, Frances, *A Few Days in Athens, Being the Translation of a Greek Manuscript Discovered in Herculaneum*, 224n21

writing: as mode of pleasure, 67–68, 102; nature's pleasures intertwining with pleasures of, 70; sensation as animated and reanimated by, viii; subjectivity of the writer, 34, 199n7. *See also* positionality of the author; women's writing

Yveteaux, Nicolas Vauquelin des, as character in Gouges's *Molière chez Ninon*, 180, 183, 224n16

Zeno, 49

Zinsser, Judith, 108, 217n81

NATANIA MEEKER is Associate Professor of French and Comparative Literature at the University of Southern California. She is the author of *Voluptuous Philosophy: Literary Materialism in the French Enlightenment* (2006), coauthor (with Antónia Szabari) of *Radical Botany: Plants and Speculative Fiction* (2020), and coeditor of *Women Imagine Change: A Global Anthology of Women's Resistance, 600 B.C.E. to the Present* (1997).